WHY ME?

WHY ME?

An Autobiography

ROBERT ANTHONY ADDIS

Order this book online at www.trafford.com
or email orders@trafford.com

Most Trafford titles are also available at major online book retailers.

Printed in the United States of America.

ISBN: 978-1-4669-2159-7 (sc)
ISBN: 978-1-4669-2160-3 (hc)
ISBN: 978-1-4669-2201-3 (e)

Library of Congress Control Number: 2012905394

Trafford rev. 03/21/2012

 www.trafford.com

North America & international
toll-free: 1 888 232 4444 (USA & Canada)
phone: 250 383 6864 ♦ fax: 812 355 4082

CONTENTS

Love & Luck

Bobby

EDITORS NOTE

I have to commend Bobby on writing his autobiography as he is dyslexic and finds writing difficult at the best of times. When he first approached me with his manuscript he felt that nothing could be done with it as it had no structure, was full of errors and was extremely difficult to read and comprehend. I didn't see it as a problem but more of a challenge. What he has in this autobiography is heartfelt, funny and serious. It has the makings of a great book.

Bobby didn't let his dyslexia bother him and worked at it, his end result, is a proud moment. Since then he has started writing science fiction and has the basis for another great book.

I have tried to keep to Bobby's style as much as possible but had had to edit parts, of which I believe enhance the manuscript. Below is an excerpt from Bobby's original to give you an idea of how it was in the beginning.

Frances Greves
Creative Writer

[From Chapter Eighteen, Dubai]

'I was having a shower late next morning after the night out with Akor and as I came out the bathroom bullock naked and walked to words the bed where one of Akor's girl's was still asleep with her head bared under the sheet I noticed that I had a mist call on my mobile, witch was on the side table next to the bed I sat down on the bed pushing the lifeless body over so that I had room I was just about to phone the number when it rang again, hallow I said not recognising the number and a girl with a broad American accent said hallow bobby then there was a pores and then she said is that Mr Addis I said yes OH! Good I've been trying to get you bobby and

then she said is it all right to call you bobby? Yes! Yes of course HI! I'm Jill Land Mark International OH yes right from the company that I had the interview with then she said yes that's right just to say that you have the job and to call in at the site office to pick up your work permit and sine a few papers then she went on to say in her very broad accent that she would texted me the address in Dubai and welcome to the company or something like that, I wasn't really listening to her after she had said that I had the job I was so glad that I got it, she went on to say did I know Dubai at all, and where the office was, and where the hotel they would put me up in while I was in Dubai was, I said no to everything she had asked me I said no I didn't know Dubai at all it was the first time in Dubai when I came for the interview and that was bad enough, she laughed a infectious laugh that made me smile on the other end of the phone, after she had finished laughing she said ill give you my extension number I interrupted her and said Oh good! she laughed again and said you will fit in very well here bobby and then said in a more sensible voice when you get into Dubai Air port phone me on ext and reeled off a number I waited until she had finished and said would you mind just texting me the number because I've got a hellish memory O.k. ill do that right know and when you get into Dubai phone me on that number then ill text you the address where the office is and all you will have to do is get yourself into a cab and get your but here! And gave a little giggle and once you get here ill give you all the info: you need bobby, I thanked her and I think she said something like "have a nice day" and hung up and then I phoned Akor to tell him the good news, but his phone said that it was switched off or out of coverage area so I shook the lifeless body that was still under the covers behind me and said come on get up I stood up and pulled the sheet that was covering her off to reveal this naked curled up body lying there, and all I got was a lot of abuse in Ghanaian as she sat up with her legs apart and her naked body in full view she pulled up the sheet to her waist again from the bottom of the bed leaving her small round breasts out in full view and said "what's wrong where are you going"? I stood there looking at her neat firm breasts and the out line of her feminine shape under the sheet that was pushed tight under her legs and said to her I was going to get some food for us she laughed and said "like that"! NO! And then she giggled and pulled one end of the sheet out from underneath her legs to reveal her naked body then she lay down on her back looking at me giggling and said "bobby from where I'm lying it doesn't look like it wants' to go any where but back in bed with me"!!

CHAPTER ONE

FINDING OUT

The year is January 11th 1957 and I'm at a very expensive public school. This is when I realised that I was different from the rest of my class. It was Monday morning, but this Monday would be so different to my usual Monday's. Mum told me that Dad would be taking my two older twin brothers and me to school today. They had received a letter from the school inviting them to see the head teacher that morning at 10am. One of my brothers wanted to know what the letter was about and all mum said was it was about Robert. She always called me Robert when she was in a mood or temper with me. Normally it would be "Bobby do this, Bobby do that." But today it was 'Robert.' I thought to myself what have I done at school to cause them to write to my parents. I was six years old and certainly not a model school boy.

The school was an old public school in Edinburgh. It was an old house that had been converted to a school. They did not believe in the cane or the belt for punishment but instead would stand you in the corner or put you outside the door. Another mad rule was that we had to change to soft indoor shoes when coming in from the outside. Education . . . well, I still have long heated arguments about it to this day with my brothers. I think it was bad education for all the money our parents were forking out for compared to a fee-paying school. I'm not saying all public schools are bad, just the one I was at . . . well, that's my opinion for what it's worth.

Well, ten o'clock came and we arrived at the front of the school. We walked through two large wooden doors into a long highly polished wooden floored corridor that echoed. As we walked along the corridor, there were four large doors; the one on the left was the one we wanted. It was the main office. There was another door next to that which was in use as a classroom and next to that was the cloakroom, where we hung our coats and changed our shoes. My father knocked on the door and it echoed along the corridor, a female voice told us to come in. My father opened the door and explained who he was and that we had an appointment with the head teacher.

"Yes Mr Addis, if you would like to make your way upstairs to the landing, there's a small office where Doctor Moffat is expecting you."

'Docky,' as we all called him (but not to his face) was an elderly man, balding and about six foot tall with a large grey moustache covering most of his top lip. It was stained with nicotine from the sixty or more cigarette that he smoked in a day. The ends of his moustache came down each side of his mouth to a point. He had a big round red face and looked a bit like a walrus.

We went upstairs as directed and knocked. Instantly Docky said, "Come in." He had a deep husky voice like a Sergeant Major on a parade ground. My father opened the door and we walked into a sparsely decorated room. Opposite the door sat Docky at his wooden desk with a red leather inlay and large red chair that matched the top of his desk, and his face.

"Come in and sit down" he said, pointing to three chairs opposite him. As we sat down, he said "Good morning Bobby" but before I could reply, he had held his hand out to my father and said, "Good morning Mr and Mrs Addis, I am glad you could make it this morning." He sat down again and picked up a brown folder, which he passed across to my parents to look at. As they opened it, Docky described my work to them as they looked at the contents. They discussed my work, their voices drifting away as my attention was drawn to the girls playing tennis over the wall in the neighbouring school. It was a school for girls only, in a large house very similar to the one we were in. I could hear the girls shouting orders to each other through the open window in Docky's office, as they hit the ball back and forth across the net. Even at six, my attention was very strong to the opposite sex. My friend and I used to watch the girls over the wall at break-time playing amongst them-selves. We would sit there and pick out the ones that we liked the best. In those days, there wasn't much to look at; they were all covered up in their navy blue pleated tennis uniforms. Not unlike today, where some of the girls at the school, near where I live, wear the shortest black skirts over black tights. I think if they wore skirts like that when I was at school . . . well! That's showing my age and I'm sounding like a dirty old man . . . maybe I am. Anyway, my attention was brought back suddenly when my name was mentioned and a long word. Docky said it again "Bobby's got dyslexia."

I looked at my parents, who looked at me in return and said "What do we do now?" Docky explained that they didn't have the resources for dealing with dyslexia, but he had an address of a Mrs Fraser which he wrote down on a pad with her name and address on and gave to my parents. Mum asked "What is dyslexia?" Docky then explained to my parents what it was. I tried to listen to what they were saying, but I couldn't understand. Hey, come on I was only six and more interested in the girls over the wall. Thinking back, what a crazy name dyslexia is for someone who can't read or write, even trying to spell it was bad enough. In the 1950's or earlier, nobody really knew what dyslexia was. They didn't talk about it and if they did, they assumed a child with dyslexia was a backward child, a dummy and very stupid. There were only a few teachers then who could spot it in a child, and even less that could fix it. I had a big problem; I couldn't read, write or store immediate information. It would not lodge in my brain. For example, if someone said to me 2+2=4 and then asked me twenty minutes later the same question, I would have forgotten the answer. Anyway enough of that, dyslexia was here to stay and little did I know how it would change my life.

The summer holidays were about to start. Little did I know that this would be the last time I would spend at my very proper speaking public school? Mum had phoned Mrs Fraser and found there wouldn't be a place in her school for another year. I was then sent to a fee paying school which happened to be just down the road. It was unlike the last school where we took the bus and my brothers were told to look after me. For the first time in my life, I was on my own in the jungle with no big brothers to look after me at school, or when I came home. Thinking back on it now, it must have been better for my parent's pockets as well when I left the good old public school.

CHAPTER TWO

NEW SCHOOL

My first day at the new school was a mixture of horror, dislike and loneliness. Right from the start I was classed as stupid. I didn't have a chance to tell the teacher of my problem and I didn't know if my parents had. I would have thought that the head teacher of the school would have received a letter from Docky, but it didn't get to the teachers, well I don't think so. It was too much of a problem for the teacher to be bothered about in a class of thirty or more. My classmates were on books and other things like reading and maths, far more advanced than myself. It was impossible to join in and keep up with them, so I ended up being left behind. I couldn't read ordinary books and it didn't take long for the other boys and girls to notice. They started to tease me and call me names. In the playground, I used to stand by myself while everyone else played. Sometimes a group of children would come over and shout dummy before running away laughing. I didn't fit in with the rest of them at all. I tried to join in but got told "go away dummy."

It was hard, and most days I would go home in tears feeling very sad and hoping that I wouldn't have to go to school the next day. It was so different from the last school; mind you my public school accent didn't help. Another name they called me was snobby and while I was trying so hard to fit in, my brothers were still going to the same school and having an almost stress free life and attending choir practice. Sometimes on Sundays I had to walk down the road with them in their long black gowns and white frilly neckerchiefs. I hoped that none of the boys or girls from my class would see me. How could I explain that to them? It was bad enough being a dummy and snob in their eyes, but to be caught walking down the road with two penguins, no way!

That brings me to an incident that happened. It was a weekend and my brothers had made a free-wheeling go-kart. It was roughly an old orange box that was fixed to long wide plank. It had four wheels that turned on a shaft, two on the back and two at the front. The two front wheels were attached to another long wooden plank that went underneath the main one and were connected by bolts. This plank moved allowing us to attach a rope which we used to steer. Or we used our feet, resting them either side of the wheels. Whilst they were trying it out, I was running alongside them shouting "give me a shot" as wee brothers do. All of a sudden, I ran straight into a lamp post and not your normal one at that. It was a steel lamp post with hundreds of points on it, and then wham. I still have the scar on my head to this day. A week or so later, I was wheeling my bike across the zebra crossing with one of my brothers, when a car didn't stop and knocked me over. You could say that I'm a bit unlucky. I have to manage this big bad concrete jungle all by myself; you will have your own opinion on that after reading this book.

A year had passed and eventually time was up at the school of 'hell'. It was time to meet Mrs Fraser, thank god. She was an elderly woman with grey hair tied back in a bun. What sticks in my mind even to this day is she had whiskers all over her chin which were also grey. She was alright; she had a kind face and didn't treat me as if I were a dummy. There were two other boys there, we didn't really talk other than the first days introductions, when Mrs Fraser said "this is Bobby, he will be with us for a year. Not like you two, who will be leaving in the summer." The first day was taken up talking to her and walking round her garden. It wasn't a school but her house and we sat at her dining room table. What a difference from my last school. It was like working and playing in your own home.

The second day came and I was handed a book to read. It was a thin book, red in colour and had on the front in big bold, gold letters 'Noddy and Big Ears.' On the first page was a picture of Noddy in his car and on the opposite page was bold black letters stating 'Noddy's in his car.' I had to read this one page with four words on it and then write it down. This was done over and over again, Noddy's in his fucking car. The first page took me about an hour or more. I was so sick of Noddy and his fucking car. Then, Mrs Fraser would ask me, "What is Noddy doing Bobby?"

"He's in his fucking car miss!" Well, that's what I would have liked to have said. I looked at Noddy in his car and even he was laughing at me with a big smile on his face. After it was well and truly stuck in my mind, we went outside into the back garden, walking and talking. In between talking Mrs Fraser would ask me what Noddy was doing and I would tell her. We came in from the outside and the other two boys were working at the table. I was told to sit on the floor and was given a tin. Inside were plastic bricks like Lego. I started to play with them as Mrs Fraser spent the rest of the morning with the other boys, until lunch time. Mrs Fraser made us sandwiches and a pot of tea, whilst we helped by taking it through into the front room and sat round the table. After lunch, I was told to sit at the table while the two boys went and did something else. Noddy was put in front of me again, but this time I was on the second page, fantastic. It's only taken all morning to read one fucking page with four words on it, oh well!! The second page was Noddy and Big Ears standing looking at a house and Noddy saying "this is my house." Well, again I had to read it again and again, and then write it down. Mrs Fraser would ask me questions, correct my mistakes and point out different things that I either read or spelt wrong. Then, it was time to go home at three in the afternoon. The day started at ten in the morning and ended at three in the afternoon. In between that, it was Noddy and his friend Big fucking Ears, day in and day out for a whole week.

They say that people with dyslexia are well above average intelligence for their age. Okay, I can't read or write or store immediate information, but I'm eight and a half and reading all about Noddy's fucking life. Either Noddy has to go or I will end up in an asylum screaming at the top of my voice "don't; don't let Noddy in for fuck's sake."

This went on for a year, yes a whole year. I got rid of Noddy. Well, one of us had to go and it was Noddy and his friend Big fucking Ears, who grinned at me all the time I was reading about his friend. I fixed them; I just shut the book on them, ha ha! See how you like it mate. But it was all in vain as I got another book the same thickness and colour. This time it was the black cat is on the mat. Oh no, not the fucking black cat's on the fucking black mat. Well, I thought, I'll just book myself into the asylum now as I've got this for a whole year.

Mind you, she was good, she was very good. Mrs Fraser did what she said. She had me reading and writing in a year. With that grey hair tied back in a bun and the grey whiskers, which I would have liked to have pulled out one by one. I came away from Mrs Fraser's reading and writing okay. I wasn't fast; in fact I was quite slow in reading, but . . . I could read. My spelling, well that's another thing. All I had been reading for the past two years was Noddy, the Black cat and other books like that. I was nine, maybe a bit more, but boys and girls of the same age were so much more advanced and confident with school work. She had done what she had set out to do and now it was time for me to meet the big bad world . . . but I don't know if the big bad world was ready for me!

CHAPTER THREE

BIG BAD WORLD

Whilst I was going to Mrs Fraser, we had moved house to another part of Edinburgh. My brothers were still going to the good old public school. The new house was much bigger and it had a lot of ground. It had a long driveway leading up to it. I can remember being scared at night of the long dark drive and the tall trees and shrubs that lined the drive. I used to run the full length of the drive, from the front gate and the streetlights, right to the front door without stopping to the porch light. I would get my breath back, before going in. It was next to another large house in its own grounds. They were identically built by two brothers. One house had an indoor swimming pool and the other, a large orchard and a conservatory, which had fallen down many years before we moved in. All that was left was the foundations where the boilers used to be. I used to hide down there and smoke dried leaves in my dad's pipe with a friend, mad or what? There was a pond in the field next to the house, where we had a home-made boat. It was a bit like a banana with a square front end that stuck up in the air. The bottom of the boat came down to a round hole that was patched, but let in water. The boat had no seats and thinking back it probably wasn't a boat at all, but we had good fun in it. I think we found it on the canal near our home. We dragged it to the pond where it sank several times.

This house was where I fell in love for the first time with the girl next door. Yes, the girl next door! I was seven and used to sit up in a tree, next to a stone wall that overlooked her garden. I used to wait there until I saw her, then my heart would start pounding . . . thinking back I never talked to her, I just sat in the tree to scared to say anything in case I got a knock back. I gave her presents out of my mother's old wooden jewellery box. I could have been giving the family treasures away for all that I knew, if we ever had any. I used to wrap them up and throw them down to her in the garden. She probably cashed them in and moved to the Riviera somewhere. Thanking that little boy that couldn't speak, but threw diamonds and other priceless stones to her from a tree. What was I like I ask you? And I didn't even get a kiss.

My brothers built a gang hut in another tree in the garden. We spent a lot of time playing in it. We even had silver candelabras hanging on the walls. No candles but I think we used to burn polythene or something in them to create some sort of light. The crazy things you do when you're small. That reminds me of when we were mucking about with a garden fork, seeing how far we could throw it. My brother said "let's see how close we can get it to each other without moving." So we did, taking it in turn to throw it at each other's feet. Then it happened . . . my brother threw it and it went straight into my foot. One of the prongs went into the ground next to my sandals, whilst another one went in between the skin of my big toe and index toe. The other two prongs went into the ground at the other side of my foot pinning it to the ground. My brother jumped up and down saying "I've got the nearest, I've won." As I started to cry, I remember my brother saying, "What's wrong it's not sore." He pulled it out and I hopped away into the house to tell mum.

Another thing I did was to play cowboys and Indians by myself whilst my brothers were at school or somewhere else like any normal kid. I don't think I was normal. As I said, there was a large field next to the house that joined on to a public park. I used to play by myself at cowboys and Indians and I was always an Indian. But this wasn't a normal game, oh no wait for it . . . I used to strip off everything apart from a thin belt that I wore around my waist. I used to hang from the belt two of my father's big white handkerchiefs, one in the front and one at the back. Now I was an Indian. I should have been locked up after Mrs Frasers and the key thrown away! Anyway I used to run around playing and hiding from people in the park. I was lying down on my back fixing the handkerchief over my little willy when I noticed a woman with a dog standing looking at me. I got up and ran in the direction of the big field next to the house. I don't know what she thought when she saw me; maybe she thought I had escaped from the loony home. She wasn't far wrong. I may not have escaped from one, but I think I was bordering on being locked up in one. I could well be a fucking loony and not known it. After I got back to the field and safety, I lay down on the grass to get my breath back in the sun and thought of that woman looking at me. It was enough to make my wee willy grow and make a slight bump in the soft white handkerchief. I was only eleven or younger, I took off the handkerchief to see this little thing sticking up for all its might, like a little flower bursting out of the soil for the first time and reaching up into the sky. So, as any normal boy would do (did I say normal), I took a firm grip with my thumb and my first two fingers and lay there in the grass on my back, in that summer's afternoon waiting to erupt. But at that age there's nothing to erupt, just a little tingle. That little tingle was enough to make me do it on other occasions, and I tell you it wasn't the first time I did it and it wouldn't be the last, just because I liked it so much.

Well enough of that madness. We didn't stay long at that house and were on the move again to another part of Edinburgh and another fee paying school. Lucky, for it was just around the corner from where the new house was in Corstorphine. It was a large inner city primary school, god what a revelation. There were kids there from all lifestyles. There wasn't your nice public school types here, oh no, I was put again into a class of about twenty or more pupils. No nice Mrs Fraser and working in her garden, no stopping to talk or sniff the roses. This new teacher was a mean son of a bitch, he wouldn't stand any nonsense and was mean through and through. He was middle aged, had black greasy hair and wore a white shirt with no tie and a crumpled grey suit that looked like it had been through a tumble dryer. Under his suit, resting on his left shoulder was a foot or more of a long leather strap, which he used regularly on us. I had it done to me on several occasions, but I remember the first time I had it done. I had never, never had the belt or anything like that before. I remember this particular time. I was told to come and stand in front of the class and hold my hand stretched out in front of me, one hand on top of the other. I remember he called it a double hander. He came down on me so hard it left red marks on my hand and wrist. He did it again to the shouting and cheering of the class. I was then told to go and sit down. It took a lot of willpower not to cry and I sat there with my hands between my legs as the pain was intense.

It was after the summer holidays when I joined this hellhole. I was put at the back of the class and the books handed out, they were given to the boy or girl at the front of the class and handed back. First the reading book, then spelling and so on until all the books were out. It was the same as the last school, the one before Mrs Fraser. They just didn't have the time for me. All the teacher said when I tried to explain anything was "Addis shut up" or "Addis come out for the belt." It was hopeless trying to explain anything, as he would not listen. So I shut up and just listened to what he was saying. Suddenly, horror struck, he said, "I want you all to read something out of the reading book in turn." It started at the left of the class and worked its way across to the right. Up and down each row until it came to me. I had to stand up and carry on from where the last pupil had finished. Well I was a wreck. I didn't know where the last pupil had finished until a boy in front turned round and showed me. Even then, I couldn't read the words or pronounce them. I was trying to pronounce each word before saying it. I was so slow, that two other boys started to take the piss out of me by stuttering. I was so embarrassed standing up in front of the whole class trying to read this fucking book. Okay, I could read but not aloud and in front of twenty or so boys and girls that were taking the piss out of me. I was a fumbling wreck until the teacher told me to give up and sit down. He told the other two boys that were taking the piss to shut up or come out for the belt. I sat there just staring at the book, hoping that it would swallow me up and make me disappear. When that had finished, the teacher said "you all have a poetry book in front of you; I want you to pick a poem out of it and learn it. Then I want you come out to the front and recite it." Terrifyingly I looked at the poetry book, fuck me it was Rabbi Burns, one of Scotland's well known poets. It was written in old Scottish dialect, I had no fucking chance. I looked at the book in horror, flicking through the pages hoping to find a small poem to read. Fuck, I couldn't even pronounce the guy's name let alone read one his fucking poems. Anyway, I had most of the term to learn it, or try.

I was at this school for roughly two years, where I made some friends and many enemies. My public school accent didn't help. They used to call me in their words "you fucking posh basara." I think they were trying to say you fucking posh bastard. I said this to some of them in my best public school accent. Their reply was a punch to the face, or they would repeat themselves up close and in my face "no you fucking posh basara." I thought to myself, I have to change and get tough like these guys, If I don't, I'm not going to survive in this jungle. It's not that I thought I was smarter than these guys, I wasn't. It's just they had a harder upbringing than me. They had to be hard to survive and if I'm going to make it in this jungle, I had to adapt and adapt quickly. God knows these guys could read, write and spell ten times better than myself. So I started to lie and got very good at it. I wasn't going to tell them about dyslexia because none of them would understand what it was, and, it would have made me an even bigger idiot than I was already. So, one lie led to another and before I knew it, it had turned into a big story. One of the stories was that my father was in the RAF based in Germany when I was born and that we had just moved here. That's why I can't read and write English. This was all right until one smart boy said, "okay then, speak some German." Shit, I had to think fast so my lie would stay a lie. So I came up with an idea and spoke in a made up language, just talking gibberish with an accent. It came out of my mouth as if it was real. Anyway, they wouldn't know German if they heard it. I thought to myself if one of them did, I could lie again and cover my tracks. Lying was easier than the truth, it got them off my back until the next time I had to lie, and there were plenty of those.

It didn't take long before the whole class was talking about me. In the eyes of the teachers, I was lazy and made up any excuse not to work. It wasn't that at all, I just couldn't keep up with the rest of them when it came to reading, maths or storing information. As not to distract the rest of the class, I was put outside the classroom door with my desk. I was given another book to read in my own time. No wonder the class thought I was a dummy. Every time it came to reading or maths, I was put outside. I wasn't getting anywhere in my education and the teachers would just ignore me. I would read the book the teacher gave me, starting at the beginning and reading one chapter. But it didn't make any sense. I would point my finger at the word as I read it, but

I tried too hard to read the word and not take in the story. It didn't matter how many times I read it, I couldn't make any sense of it, so fuck it. It was getting more a problem for the teachers and me, but other subjects I was okay at and there were no problems.

The term was nearly up, yes, time for the summer holidays. The thing I was dreading was looming up yes it was Rabbi Burns. I had taken the poem book home to get some moral support and pick out a poem, but I didn't get the support that I thought I would get. I was palmed off with "go and see your grandmother dear, I'm busy." My grandmother lived with us and looked after us whilst mum and dad went out to work. She was kind and had time for me, unlike the rest. I had time for her and god bless she tried to help me, but I think even my granny was stumped by Rabbi Burns. I think she said "you will have to get your father dear." Dad was busy with my brothers, so I spent a long time in my bedroom trying to pick out a poem and read it. It was hopeless, and it didn't matter how many times I came down to ask someone to help me, they were all too busy. I don't think they could pronounce the words either. I got no help and didn't learn a poem. When I returned to school, I was told to come out to the front of the class along with three boys and two girls and was given the belt for being lazy.

The new term wasn't any better than the first. The only difference was that I had made some friends. I was still put outside the class, but this time they put one of the brighter boys with me to help me read and help me with maths. All Tom wanted to do was play with his thing . . . yes, his dick. What is it about me that attract these people? I'm not telling a lie. He would sit beside me at my desk, show me what to read, or if it were maths show me what to do. He would then tell me to carry on, whilst he whipped out his dick and played with it. I ask you, how can you concentrate on something when right next to you there's a guy rubbing his thing and saying "Addis, Addis, do you want to touch it?" My reply was "get tae fuck." One of the few Scottish phrases I picked up at this school. It's not the sort of thing you would say in front of your mum or someone like that. Never the less, he was put out to help me get ready for the eleven plus exam, which was looming up.

Then it happened, we were sitting out on the landing. It was a short landing with stairs going up beside me to another landing. The landing where I was sitting with my desk was connected to another classroom at the other end. Besides that, stairs leading down to another two classrooms and so on. Anyway, I was to read a problem in my math book then work it out. But it wasn't making any sense as usual. I turned to Tom to ask him. He was doing his usual thing of playing with his fucking dick right next to me. Suddenly the other classroom door opened and two girls came out and caught him with it out. They couldn't help but see what he was doing, they stood watching him struggle to put it back in his trousers. They ran down the stairs laughing to themselves, and then shouted something back up, but I didn't catch what was said. It took a long time to live that down. It didn't matter what I said, nobody believed me. It was all over the school that we were playing with each other outside the classroom door on the landing, I ask you!

The three weeks leading up to the exam passed quite quickly, and then it was time for the exam to grade you for secondary school. The eleven plus was the exam in those days, it sorted you out into two different classes. If you were good at work, you were put into a class like 2-A-2, or 3-A-1, and so on. If you were not so clever, you were put into a lower class. Well, there was no hope for me. The day came for the exam, we were all put into the large hall and the papers handed out. The clock started and I looked at the paper. Shit, there's no way I'm going to do this. I looked again at the paper, it said to put your name, class, and date at the top of the paper. I did that and that's as far as I got. Nothing made any sense and that was it. The bell went, we were told to hand our paper in and that was my eleven plus exam . . . fuck me. You could say that I wasn't ready for the eleven plus. Two years were up and I was ready for secondary school. I don't know if secondary school was ready for me.

CHAPTER FOUR

GRAMMAR SCHOOL

It was the first day of secondary school, and if I thought that primary school was bad, this was ten times worse. There were hundreds of boys and girls from all walks of life again. The school itself was newly built. It was all glass and concrete, like everything at that time. It was the time when the architects and designers were building everything out of concrete. The modern look, ha . . . and it was massive. We all piled into the large assembly room to be told what class we were going into. I looked around to see if there was anyone that I recognized, but there wasn't, just a mass of boys and girls. It went on all morning until there were just a dozen boys and girls left and I was one of them. They were all the misfits, the ones that didn't want to work. If they'd had it their way they wouldn't have been there in the first place. Half of them were just out of approved school or they had just finished community service for breaking and entering. We were the dregs of the school and I was classed as one of them just because the education system let me down. They didn't recognize that I had dyslexia the day I started my schooling after Mrs Frasers. They classed me as a backward, a slow to learn pupil or a dummy. That's how I ended up with this rabble.

This was the start of my real education. The teachers who were sorting out the classes said they didn't have a class low enough to put us in to . . . yes! Once the teacher said this, there was a chorus of whistles and cheering from my class mates . . . well they were, I had to spend the rest of my school days with them. The teacher told us to shut up and continued to say they had no class low enough for us. They would have to make up a number for us and that was 3-B-3. I can remember telling my two good friends who lived just round from where I did in Corstorphine, about how I was left to the last dozen, the dregs of society, miss fits. They just burst out laughing. It was alright for them they were in a better class than me. Okay, they had studied for their eleven plus and got a better placing in the grammar school. Apart from that, we remained good friends. Even to this day, we still talk and laugh about me ending up in 3-B-3. The head master said as we were leaving they would be watching us as a class. To the applauses of whistles and shouting, we left the large hall to find our first class and the first victim teacher. They were a rabble. None of them were wearing any kind of uniform. It was just tee-shirts and jeans. The girls were not as bad; they would have on short skirts and white blouses, no tie just undone and sometimes a tee-shirt underneath. I was the only one with a uniform and I stood out like a sore thumb. I soon lost the uniform, blazer, tie and even the cap!! Can you believe it? Thinking back I must have looked like a proper geek, something else alongside the rest of them. But that didn't stop them from calling me names. I was singled out, no wonder and was left in my corner of the classroom while the rest of them were on the other side. I had my books and was trying to learn, but even then they would come over, pick on me and hit me. The teacher would then say something and they'd go back to their side. The teacher would normally just ignore them and let them do their own thing. Then the bell would go and we would go to find the next victim.

The first year at the grammar school was hell. If I wasn't beaten up I was picked upon. Towards the end of the first year I was getting harder but still not hard enough like the guys in the class. I stood up for myself but I still got beaten up and got told to "get back to your side of the classroom poshy." That's the name I was given and it stuck with me throughout my school years. The second year wasn't as bad as the first. Most of the class had accepted me, but there was still a bunch of them that were still a threat to me and I had to sort that lot out. I had been at the grammar school now for two years; well this was the start of the second year. I am now about thirteen and got on with one of the guys in the class. He said "I like you poshy." I used to hang around with him in the playground and even after school. He used to stick up for me when I got into difficulty. And there was always the school bully and his friends. At every break he and has compatriots would come looking for me to take the piss or give me a kicking for the fun of it.

They would then say "give us your lunch money Addis" and I would give it to them. They then started demanding more and that I should bring more tomorrow or else . . . and I did. I pinched money from mum and dad to save my skin. But I still got beaten up. I was a joke to them, a little posh kid, and a wimp. My friend was always there to pick me up afterwards. He was never involved but said to me "you will have to fight that fucker, you know that don't you Addis."

"How the fuck am I going to fight them, no way?" I replied after picking myself up from the ground once again.

"Not them, him!" he said. "You fight him and they won't do a thing to help him, believe me."

"How the fuck am I going to beat him? I'm not a fighter you can see that." I said.

"I'll help you."

And so we started. I wasn't learning much to do with education in the classes. All the time my books would be taken away, ripped up and thrown on the floor and the teachers did nothing in most of the classes we went to. That was something different from my public school days; we went from classroom to classroom to the different teachers, in public school the teachers would come to you. Like I said, I wasn't learning much, I had tried but every class I went to was the same. My books would be taken from me or I was picked on until I gave up on what I was doing. I was learning how to be streetwise and protect myself. Because in this school you were either with them or you were on your own. I had tried being on my own and trying to learn but it wasn't working. I think if you were in maybe in a higher class you wouldn't have all this bother. The higher classes seemed to stay away from the likes of my class. For some reason they kept away from the crowd that hung around me. I even asked my two friends, whom were in a higher class than myself if they knew Hairy Brown? Hairy Brown was the nickname of the school bully. They said "yes, but he doesn't bother us."

"Why me, why does he look for me and give me a kicking, is it because I'm useless? Or is it that I'm stuck in this class with this rabble and I'm easy pickings for him? I'll have to get hard and fight Hairy if I'm going to survive in this jungle." All this and more was whizzing around my mind as I lay in my bed at night. My friend made it defiantly clear to me, that there was no place for me if I was to remain a geek in the class or in the school. I had tried that . . . ! I tried to learn as the rest of the class, what they did best and that was fuck all.

It was on one of those occasions I got a split lip and a black eye. I tried to stand up for myself in the classroom but it didn't make much difference. All I got along with the black eye and split lip was another double-hander as the teacher, wielding a leather strap came down on my hands with all his might. I tried to say it wasn't my fault and was told to hold them out again to the cheering of the rest of the class. One of them shouted out "that's what you get poshy." They still took my books away and called me in their words "fuckin' snobby bastart" because of my accent. That night when I went home with my black eye and split lip my mother asked me what had happened.

"I was playing rugby mum" I said. Her reply was "you should be more careful dear." She didn't have any idea what I was going through at school. It's not as if they didn't care, I think I was a worry to them. After Mrs Frasers and several psychiatrists I think they thought I was bordering on being a loony, little did they know. How could they tell our relatives that they were locking me up and throwing away the key? I used to come home and go up to my room or I would go round to see my friend Duncan if I had a split lip or anything to hide. I can remember one of my brothers saying "but they don't play rugby at that school, its football." They knew the lies I was telling and tried to shit stir it sometimes. I don't think it mattered to my parents what game we played, all they would say is "it that right, okay, be careful." The first and second years were a nightmare. Every day I was in a fight or my lunch money was taken from me. I had to get hard, much harder than my last school, and telling lies wouldn't do. I had to get tough or get treated like shit for the rest of my school days and I wasn't going to let that happen. I had to prove to my class that I could stand up for myself. The best place to try it out first was with my good old class mates, the ones that bullied me. On saying that, the girls were just as bad, especially the twins. They would start something with me, then shit stir by saying something to one of the boys, He would come over and say "is that true poshy?" Before I could say anything he would hit me and the twins would bang the desk and laugh. Although I was getting harder, I could not bring myself to hit a girl. I would have to think of some other way to get my own back on them. I had to get respect and it would have to start in my class. Instead of being Mr Nice Guy and taking all the shit they would throw at me. I stopped trying to learn, there was no point in it. After school I would have a fight with one of my class mates. I would win some and lose some, but slowly bit by bit I wangled my way in with them and finally got their respect. Instead of sitting by myself on the other side of the classroom, I was gradually moving across until I reached the middle. Then after a few more weeks, I got across to their side. I was careful not to rock the boat if you know what I mean and be sent back to my side. It was a bit like a board game. I would throw a double six and start to cross, but if I did anything wrong I was sent back to start again. The girls were the worst, they would say "what the fuck do you want poshy?" There were two girls in particular that didn't let me away with anything, they were the twins. They went by the name 'the twins' and the whole school knew what you meant when you said the twins as everyone called them that.

As I said, with the help of one guy in the class I learnt how to street fight. Not your Queensbury rolls oh no, this was street fighting, where you punch to the stomach, the lower the better. As he bends over, you bring your knee up to meet his chin. Then with one hand holding his hair, you punch his face side on. As he falls to the ground you kick with your boot to his head or body until he stops moving or cries out in pain. Even then you would give him another two or three kicks for luck. Or you would punch him with both hands rapid, either side of him to the kidneys with your head down and in close. As he bends over, you bring your head up fast hitting him under the chin. That one was quite effective. Then there was the head butt that was good as well. You didn't talk, you hit first. You would bring the top part of your head down hard onto your opponents' nose, and then you would say "what did you say?" And most of the time you didn't wait for an answer. There was a lot more, some of it was really dirty fighting but it was effective. You had to fight like that, if you didn't you had no chance of winning. You had to fight dirty and even then, the dirtier the fight, the better chance you have of winning. So the day came that I had to fight Hairy. It was arranged that we would fight under the old railway bridge in the lunch break outside of school. It didn't take long before the whole school was talking about it and people were taking bets on who would win. I can tell you I was shitting myself. This guy was about the same height, but I was shit scared of him and what his friends would do at the fight.

It was well into the fight; adrenalin was pumping through my veins. It was hit for hit so far and my face was thumping from most of the hits that got through. I could feel blood running down over my eye from two good punches that Brown gave me. I didn't have time to think and my bottom lip felt like it was twice the size. My knuckles were red and sore with hitting Brown but I had to keep going. Every punch that made it through to his face made my knuckles hurt even more, but I didn't have much time to think before another punch landed on my face somewhere. I remembered what my friend had told and shown me and it was time to put it into practice. There was a ring of boys and girls shouting and cheering us on until Brown brought out a long silver object like a cork screw. Instead of being curly it was straight and about six inches long with a wooden handle which he gripped in his hand. The stiletto like spike sticking out between his fingers, the shouting stopped, there was a deadly hush. I backed away from Brown keeping my eye on this thing he had held in his hand. Wiping the blood away from my face with one hand I kept a constant eye on the weapon and kept backing away until someone pushed me back in. I tripped and stumbled forward as Brown thrust forwards in an upwards movement with the silver spike. I put my hand out to grab it but missed. It glanced off my arm up into my face just missing my eye by a fraction. It entered between the very corner of my eye and the top part of my nose. Blood gushed out and down my face, there was a deadly hush as people stood and looked on in horror. Brown took a step back still clutching the spike like thing with my blood on it, ready to thrust it forwards again. As he stepped back I took the opportunity and kicked him so hard between the legs that he bent over in pain. I gave another quick kick to his face with my boot, it glanced off his chin but it was enough to send him tumbling over backwards. As he fell down, one of his legs landed on a large stone that was sticking out of the ground. I jumped on it with both feet, snapping his leg just above the knee. He gave a loud scream and just to make certain he wasn't getting up, I gave his leg another hard kick at the part that was resting on the stone and looking a bit twisted. With one hand over my eye and blood running down my face, I was about to give him another kick when he shouted out "Addis! Addis! You've broken my fucking leg, fuck off." I gave it another kick anyway just for the hell of it. He tried to move out of the way but my boot hit smack bang on the twisted part that was still on the stone. He shouted out in pain and tried to crawl away. It was over; he wasn't getting up from that until a few of his friends helped him away.

The adrenalin was still pumping through my veins. I was still very much on a high and in shock. Blood was everywhere, all down my shirt and over my face. The pain was intense now that I was calming down. Someone handed me a jumper, I put it over my eye. At that point I didn't know if my eye had been hit, it felt damn close. I asked the guy who was helping me back if my eye was okay; all he said was that he couldn't see there was too much blood.

"God, you showed him Addis. Better go and get that seen to by the school doctor." He said.

To this day I don't know who gave me their jumper. I held it over my eye as several of my class mates helped me back to school. I was calming down and the pain was starting to take over. I said to them that we had better come up with an idea as to how this happened. There were several ideas but the best one was that I was freewheeling my bike to school and my bag caught up in the front wheel. The long aerial which held a flag went in my face as I went over the handlebars of the bike. Yes, we'll go for that.

I was sitting in the headmaster's office with my head back looking at the ceiling. The doctor was dabbing at my face with a wet cloth.

"It will need stitching." He said to the headmaster, then to me "you were very lucky. A few inches and you would have lost your eye."

The head interrupted, "are you certain that's what happened?"

"Yes sir, my bag slipped off my arm and got caught in the front wheel."

"What about the bruising to your face?"

I told him that I slid along the ground as I came off the bike and must have hit something.

"Okay, I'll call an ambulance and let your parents know."

The ambulance came and I was taken to hospital with my parents following behind in their car. I came back to the class on Monday to a victor's welcome. I was transformed from being the boy they picked on to their best mate. Even the girls said "you showed him Addis. Is your face sore?"

It was and it was black and blue with bruising. I had six very small stitches neatly done and I remember the female doctor saying to me whilst she was stitching "that she had better do a good job so I could keep my good looks."

At school everyone one was called by their surname or a nickname. Mine was either Addis or poshy. It soon got around the school "don't fuck with poshy." My life had changed in one day, all to do with that one fight. Hairy Brown was off school for a long time with his broken leg. His friends kept well away from me, even when Brown came back they just stayed away from me. No doubt they would find some other poor victim and start on him until he too stands up for himself. That's life in the jungle and no doubt it will go on like that long after I'm away.

My parents and brothers didn't have a clue what was going on. Maybe my brothers did but they never said anything to me. If they did know, I don't think that they knew how bad some of the things were that I had to put up with. After that fight, my life changed. I was a bit like Dr Jekyll and Mr Hyde the single person, in which two personalities alternate by the writer Stevenson. I had two lives, one I would spend with my family at home and the other I was spending with the gang. There were six of us, two girls and four guys including myself. They were hard and the girls were just as bad. The twins . . . yes I was accepted by them after that fight. These two girls both with identical long black hair and good looking, they used to come to school with very short skirts, white blouses and black bra, they dressed identically. They would have three or four buttons undone so that their breasts would stick out even more. They had great tits and they knew it. They used to tease and flaunt themselves all the time with their assets, to the male teachers. They were hoping that one of them would make a move, so they could shout out rape and all sorts of things Just to get the unsuspecting teacher into trouble. The twins were okay if you were with them but if you fucked them over in any way, they would lay into you with their belts. They had a small tack spaced out along the belt and sticking through and used to wear them all the time. I got on well with them after my fight; they accepted me as one of them and not the little posh boy that used to be bullied.

What I was learning with my classmates was education; well it wasn't the education my parents would have liked. I was learning how to break into houses on the scheme and told to look for money. They even told me where to look and not to waste time as I did at first. I even took rings and stuff like that. Then there was the cars and how to break into them with a long thin metal rod, and to look for the right car with valuables inside. What I didn't know about street crime I was learning very fast with the help of my fellow classmates. The other two guys in the gang, well they came to school wearing jeans and tee-shirts. They had all been told not to come to school dressed like that but they did it over and over again. None of the boys or girls came to school with the proper uniform, like I did at first. I soon left my blazer and cap at home; I even took my tie off and stuffed it in my pocket. I put it on to go home again. Their vocabulary wasn't any better than they way they dressed. It was "fuck this, fuck that and fuck-fuck." The girls were the same . . . and then there was Billy. He was called 'Long Billy'. I thought it was to do with his height because he was tall and built like a gorilla. But no, I soon found out why his nickname was 'Long Billy.' It was nothing to do with his height, more his manhood or cock. It was over twelve inches long. I'm not joking; it was like a big fucking snake. The twins used to tease him all the time to get it out and play with it at the back of the class. Billy did what they said most of the time, he was a bit thick. Well, we were all a bit thick in that class but Billy was thicker than the rest of us . . . if you can get any thicker? That's good coming from me, the pot calling the kettle black. At least he could read properly not like me. What I should say is, he's a bit slow, but well built.

There was this one time we were watching a film in the science class. You know when the film finishes and the projector is still running with the light shining on the screen and people put their hands up to project images? Well Billy, the twins, a couple of other guys and me were sitting in the front. Billy was sitting on the inside next to the light from the projector. He stood up, pulled out his cock and started to waggle it in front of the projector light. His enormous cock was projected onto the blank white screen to the whistles and laughter of the rest of the class and the teacher saying "Billy, put that fucking thing away," to more laughter. Most probably one of the twins put him up to it.

There was another occasion. The twins had bet the other girls in the class that Bill's cock was over a foot long when hard. So, one lunch-time the whole class stayed in. Nobody knew about this, just the class and four or five other girls that the twins had told. Not even the teachers knew or they would have told us to get out. The bet was on. We gathered around Bill at the back of the class as one of the girls said to him "come on Bill get it out." Billy unzipped his trousers and pulled out this sausage like thing and slapped it down on the desk. Several of the girls gave a scream. I don't know if it was in horror or wonder in how anyone could have such a long thing. And it wasn't even hard. Well, we all looked in awe at this prime Scotch beef sausage like thing of Bills. It started to grow with the help of one of the twins teasing it till it grew and grew. I sat squeezed together with two girls on either side of me, on the desk next to Bill's in amazement and envy. As did the rest of the boys watching this fucking monster grow. By this time it was about half way across the desk. The girl next to me gave out a gasp and said "shit." Bill's sausage had turned into a fucking raging monster with a very big, red looking head and covering most of the desk, I would say the whole of the desk lid and very hard looking. The other twin picked up a wooden twelve inch ruler and laid it along the side of Bill's hard-on. Right enough it was longer than the ruler and still growing. At the rate it was going it would reach the end of the school desk in no time. I tell you no lie; the girl next to me said "how the fuck are you meant to fuck a girl with that fucking long bustard of a thing? No way would I let you fucking near me with it."

Then another girl shouted out "Bill I'll give it a try." We all laughed and a guy shouted out "let's see you" to a roar of laughter and everyone shouting and egging her on. But like most of the guys in that class, we just looked on in awe. How any guy could have such a fucking long fat cock like that! In all my life I've never seen a thing like it. I've seen cocks on DVD's, but real life and next to me, no way. The bet was won. I don't know how much the twins made, they never told me. I think it was quite a bit because Bill told me how much he got for doing it. We cheered him but poor Bill couldn't get his monster back in his trousers, it was so long and hard. He had to take his trousers down, hold his foot long monster up against his stomach and pull his trousers up and over it with the help from the one of the twins. Even then it was sticking out well above the top of his trousers. We laughed again at him but I think Bill would have had the last laugh. He's probably making a film and loads of money with it . . . King Kong Billy!

There was another time with a small guy in the class. He was the smallest but tried to act hard. He was a joke, with very short hair that stuck up like a hedgehog. He had round white framed national health specs and a scout belt that he always too off to threaten you with, by swinging it at you. He wasn't even strong enough to hit you. All you had to do was grab it and pull; he would fall over or end up on the ground by your feet. Anyway this particular time, he was mucking about with the small hole that you have in the bottom of your wooden desk and got his finger stuck in it.

"Miss, Miss, ma fucking fingers stuck in the hole."

"Shut up." The teacher replied.

"Miss, Miss, honestly I have."

And that's when we gathered round the wee guy and someone said "he has Miss." The teacher came over and looked at this wee mans small finger sticking out, through the hole under the desk, all red and swollen. She was quite nice as a teacher. She would have been about thirty odd, with short blonde hair and not a bad figure.

"Get me some soap and water" she said and one of the girls went quickly to the cupboard, well it was more of a long narrow room where they stored the paint and other art things. This was the only class that I got on in and the rest of the class left me alone to get on with what I was doing. Miss Robertson was quite impressed with my work and used to help me a lot. I used to get most of her attention because the rest of them did their usual thing and that was sweet fuck all. The girl came back with a large square tub half full of water. Miss Robertson took it and sat it down on the floor beside her, slightly under the wee mans desk. Then she started to splash water over the wee mans finger then rubbed soap over it. She started to rub the wee mans finger as if she was masturbating it. I was kneeling down beside her looking at what she was doing, when she saw me looking at her. Realising then what she was doing, stopped, went bright red and gave me a nervous smile. I smiled back and nothing was said.

"Right, pull your finger out now" she said. It came out to the cheers and whistles from the class. She continued to say "don't put your finger in there again." She gave me a quick glance as she picked up the tub of water and the soap and smiled again. This time it wasn't a nervous smile like last time, it was more like a smile to say thanks for not saying anything. Because you could imagine what the rest of the class would have said and she wasn't a match for them.

We did a lot of petty crime together on Saturday and after school. There was one occasion where we broke into this house on the scheme and took a drum kit. We all took a piece of this set, with me ending up with the bass drum. I took it to one of the guys' home and put it in the shed at the back of his house. We said we would sell it and split the money. One of the twins said she knew of a guy that would sell it for her, so we left it there and went home. A couple of days later, three guys came round to my house and asked dad if the drum kit was still for sale. I don't know how or why they came to my house, but they did and my father said "we don't have a drum kit for sale." They said that I was selling one, so I was told to explain. Well I did by lying again, but first by finding out who sent them to me. All they said was that they'd heard I was selling one. I said it must be a mistake because I don't have one to sell and that got rid of them. Now it was my dad's turn, he said "what lies have you been saying now?" After a long explanation and lots of lying I was told to go to my room.

There was another time where we were kicking about the scheme again and came across a bike. It was virtually new and we all agreed we would knock it (steal it.) So we did and I was the one left holding it. It was suggested that I would take it back to my place because the rest of them stayed in or around the scheme and I lived in a better neighbourhood. The police wouldn't think about looking there. One of the twins said if I was going to ride it around the streets I had better paint it before taking it out. I took the bike home and on the way I had to think of a reason for having it. The bike was in mint condition. I reckon it was about two weeks old if that. I know my parents couldn't afford to buy me a bike like this, so where did I get it? Well I had to think fast because I was getting nearer and nearer to home, and my brothers would ask me questions as well. They wouldn't be so easy to fob off like mum and dad. Anyway I came up with a plan. I had bought it out of my holiday money because the bloke that had bought it from needed money fast for his mothers operation. He knew that he could get more for it if he advertised it, but he didn't have time. That's why he was selling off things outside the school. I said that I would bring the money straight to him tonight. I turned the last corner to my home. The lie was embedded in my mind ready for mum and dad and brothers, if they were there. To lie you have to be professional and I was. You just couldn't lie and then forget about it. You had to remember what you had said and not forget it or draw attention to yourself. Well, I kept to my lie and the whole plan went down well, I think. They weren't convinced, but my brothers were interested in the lie either, they just wanted a shot of the bike. It all blew over and I don't know if my parents believed me or not until one day I was riding it around the streets. I was near the house when this big bloke stopped me and said "where did I get that bike?" I had to keep to the original lies. "I bought it, why?"

"I don't fucking believe you and that's fucking why I'm coming tae ya home."

Okay, so off we went back home. In the way it was like the Spanish inquisition, he was asking me all sorts of questions. Fuck me, I knew I should have taken the twins advice and painted the bike. But I thought it would have brought more attention to the bike and my lies if I started to paint it straight away, especially when it was in good nick. We arrived at my house; the big greasy bloke said "I wanna see your faether, fucking now?" I called dad and the guy said the bike was his friends and was stolen about a month ago from outside his house in the scheme. My dad looked at me and said "did you know about this?"

"Who me, no dad."

So the police were called. The bloke stayed with the bike outside the house whilst my dad interrogated me inside about the bike saying "this is the last chance you have to tell the truth before the police come."

"Dad I did buy the bike?"

"Okay, that's it!"

The police arrived at the house. We all went into the front room and sat down. Then the questions started. They asked me where I got the bike. As I told them, one of the officers wrote it down in his notebook. He said "did I not think it was strange someone outside your school was selling things?"

"Not really" I replied.

The officer who had been writing everything down, but in and said "a bike in that nick, come on son . . . and for that price?"

I kept to the original story and said that he had wanted the money for this mothers operation and . . . the officer butt in again.

"What was the lad's name? What did he look like? How tall was he?" Both of them were firing questions at me one after the other fast, trying to catch me out and see if I was lying. The one with the notebook closed it and stood up followed by the other one. The greasy haired bloke had been checking out the room whilst the police were asking the questions. "You will be hearing from us Mr Addis. The bike fits the description we were given as it was stolen from a house on Sight Hill Housing Estate." As the police officer said that I got some funny look from my dad as if to say "you little bustard." But he never said anything. The officers and the big greasy haired bloke walked towards the door of the room and to the front door where they put their hat on. They said goodbye to my dad and wheeled the bike away down the path. I shouted after them "will I get my money back?" One of the officers turned round and said "treat this as a lesson son." They stood for a while at the bottom of the garden talking to the greasy haired guy, then got into their car and the guy took the bike away. I had time to think about everything that I was doing. It was the first time I'd had the law at my front door and I didn't like it. That night I made up my mind that the petty crime had to stop, and I would become respectable and stop going out with the group. It wasn't the first time I had brushed up against the law, but it was the first time as I said that they had come to the house and involved my family. I think it was my public school accent that for the first time in my life had helped with my situation. I was glad of the way I spoke and where I lived, the whole surroundings did a big part in getting me off. So I had a long, hard think to myself in bed that night and said 'what the fuck was I thinking about, no more Addis . . . go straight from now on.' Well that's if you can go straight, if straight is the right word. I think if the police hadn't come to my house on that particular wet September day my life might not have changed. In the sense that petty crime often leads to more serious crime and I would probably be sitting in a court room, waiting to be sentenced for a crime that I didn't do. Don't you know you're innocent even though you did the crime?

CHAPTER FIVE

THE ZOO

I was fifteen and about to leave school with no qualifications and no future prospects. My life looked dim to say the least. The whole of my education from Mrs Frasers up to fifteen was shit. Okay, I can't blame it all on the education department. Some of it was my fault. After a while I got lazy like the rest of the class. Knowing that the education department was not bothered with me or 3-b-3, we didn't fit into the system and the system sucks. "Not as if I hold any grudge or anything . . . ha. I often think if I didn't have dyslexia would I of had a better education or would I still have been lazy and fucked about at school. I can't blame everything on dyslexia as other people with it have got through their education and done well. I know there are different kinds of dyslexia but.? I had spent most of the summer at my uncle's farm in the borders. Mostly to do with my parents getting me out of Edinburgh for a bit and away from the people I was hanging around with. Not my two good friends, mostly the crowd from the scheme. The two twins they used to ask one of their male friends to call by the house and ask if I was in, as they hid around the corner. If I was home, I would go out with them and meet up with the gang again. Sometimes if we didn't meet the gang, the twins and I would nick sweets and drink. We'd end up in the park sitting in the wooden shelter, drinking the booze or eat things that we'd stolen from the shop near the park. The twins and I would try and start something between us. I think my mother would have called it "a bit of slap and tickle," I would have called it something different. The three of us would have some fun; we never had sex but came close to it. God, when I think back. I was so slow, if only! To have had two identical twins both with great bodies and reasonably looking, all to myself, life is so unfair? They must have thought I was a bit of a dickhead not to have tried anything with them. God knows I had plenty of opportunity with them in that shed. Thinking back I sometimes think that I should have had sex with them, what a chapter it would have made. Having sex with two identical twins, every man's dream, but it wasn't to be. I don't know what happened to them or the gang, they seemed to just drift away, and maybe it was a good thing. Where they went to I don't know. I did look for the twins when I came back from my uncle's farm but to no success, they had just vanished.

We were still living in the house in Corstorphine and I remember I was very sexually attracted to the opposite sex, I couldn't get enough. Saying that, I was still a virgin but it wasn't through the lack of trying. One night I decided to have a bath before going to bed. As I was running the bath, I had stripped ready to get in but as usual I'd put too much hot in and not enough cold. I decided to leave it for a while to cool down whilst I cleaned my teeth at the basin by the window. I couldn't see myself as all the steam from the bath had filled the small room. I decided to open the bottom part of the window, about eight or nine inches to let the steam out. It wasn't a frosty glass window like normal bathrooms; it had vinyl stuck on normal glass to give the appearance of looking frosty. It had been on there for a long time as it was black round the edges. It was peeling away in most of the corners but not enough for someone to look in, but you could look out if you wanted to. The bathroom was situated on the side of the house and looked onto another house with a stone wall separating the properties. As I wiped the mirror to look at myself cleaning my teeth as you do, I thought to myself "why am I looking at me cleaning my teeth?" But you do don't you? Anyway, I was standing there naked waiting for the bath to cool and admiring myself as I cleaned my teeth. I turned to look out through a narrow strip of vinyl that had come away. There was a light on in the house opposite, down in the kitchen. A girl was resting on her arms on the sink unit and looking straight up at me through the bottom part of the window that I had opened enough for her to get a good look at my nakedness.

At first my reaction was to shut the window, but the devil that was on my shoulder was saying "lets party." On my other shoulder was his counterpart dressed in white saying "close the window, be a good boy." So being me and a church going person, I did what was right and left the window open. The little devil in red jumping up and down with joy and the other in white just standing on my shoulder shaking his head, eventually disappearing with a pop and giving up on me. So, knowing that she couldn't see me looking at her through the space, I decided to stand there and show all. By the looks of her she was quite content to stay there, leaning on the sink unit with her arms supporting her head. I was a typical fourteen year old boy and feeling horny. I looked to see if she was still watching, she was. "Yes" I thought "let the party begin." I filled the sink with warm water and started to wash my wee man. Well it wasn't that small now; maybe it was all the attention it was getting. I tried to give it attention at least once a night in bed or in the bathroom. Anyway, it wasn't that small flower anymore that stretched out and up towards the sun, on that summer's day in the field playing Indians. No, it was more like an oak tree, solid and firm . . . well maybe not an oak tree, but I'll call it that anyway. Oak tree or not I pretended to wash it in full view of the girl, who was quite content to stay there looking up at this mad boy standing by the wash basin rubbing soap up and down his solid oak tree. It was like feeding it with fertilizer. The more soap I rubbed onto it, the longer it would grow. My horny devil and I loved all the attention. My dick and I had never had an audience before and it was playing the premiere so very well. Being upright and noticed, my heart was pumping blood around my body so fast I could feel it. I was even trembling with excitement knowing she was looking at me, this girl that I didn't even know. What a rush . . . more fertilizer, then a bit more . . . oh my god! But before I could finish getting to my goal and old man appeared on the scene. I could see the girl had turned to speak to him. I ducked down below the window ledge out of sight and peered over. I could see she was talking to him; she gave a quick glance up as she walked away with him. Then the light went off in the kitchen. I was so deflated, like someone had let the air out all in one go. I thought "fuck, I hadn't even made it to the finale." I had another look over the ledge before closing the window and going back to my bath, which was now warm and not as hot as I would have liked it, but beggars can't be choosers as they say. What a load of shit if that's what they say. I didn't see her again even though I locked myself in the bathroom on many occasions. Opening the window before putting the light on and peering over the edge to see if the light was on in the kitchen, but alas it wasn't to be. I had played my one night standing performance, if you know what I mean. The wee man played out many a role with me just looking on, practising for the main event.

I was fifteen and my very first job was at Edinburgh zoo, as a keeper looking after the animals. You didn't need any qualifications just some common sense. Well, I could do that. The zoo was split up into different sections. The lion section, the snake section and so on. I was in the lion section and given a uniform which consisted of a green hat, green jacket, a pair of riding breeches. Not the modern type but the old fashioned kind that were tight around the calf and then flaring out like two elephants ears round your thighs, black boots and gaiters. Never mind the uniform let's get on with looking after the animals. I had been at the zoo for about four months or more. I knew my way about and had made a lot of new friends. One in particular, his name was Tam and he was about the same age and height as me with long brown hair and a spotty face. We were both fifteen and had the same interests . . . girls! And not to mention we were both virgins, well I was, I don't know about him. Even if I had asked he probably would have said no. Believe it or not the zoo was a great place for meeting the opposite sex. We were like animals in heat. Well, I was and we were in the right place and it made sense. The animals had their partners so why not us. The only thing that was different was I just didn't want one! Every lunch time we went sniffing for the opposite sex. Girls from foreign countries visiting our beautiful Capital came to the zoo. Girls from colleges all over, doing research on one thing or another, there was always an abundance of females.

It was a hot summer's day; Tam and I were on our lunch break. We were on the hunt and came across twenty or more girls from a college. They were doing research on Alaskan brown bears. Well, that was right up our street as we feed them every day and what more do you have to know. We also looked the part in our green uniforms. Ha, little did they know that we were chatting them up. They thought we were being helpful, courteous and polite. If they even knew what was lurking within that green uniform was a monster we wouldn't have stood a chance. Well, I don't think so. It was on that particular's summer's day that Tam and I got talking to two of the girls. One thing led to another and I found myself on the grass banking at the top far end of the zoo where no one goes, with this girl. Fumbling awkwardly with the buttons on my breeches, "fuck" there were thousands of the fucking things and I only had twenty minutes left of my lunch break. "Fuck, fuck, come on" I thought to myself. Trying to be casual and talk absolute shit to the girl that was waiting patiently for this fumbling idiot. Eventually the girl offered to help me. I think she was getting tired of waiting. I said something stupid like "it's my first time." To which she replied "I can see that. She kindly helped undo my buttons as I stood in front of her, looking around to see if anyone was about. She had my breeches and pants down to my ankles in no time and playing with my dick. As she did, I had time to glance at my watch "fuck, ten minutes, and I haven't even got her pants down." So I knelt down in front of her, pushed her skirt up to find she had on these tight blue elastic panties. I tried to pull them down but my fingers got stuck in the elastic. It was so tight it as cutting of the circulation to my fingers. All I could think of was to get them out before they fell off. Again, she stopped what she was doing, pushed my hand away and pulled them down herself. Ah, so that's what it looks like? I had seen pictures and people saying different things about them. Such as they have teeth and if you put your dick in there it would get bitten off and other mental stud like that. But I still wasn't certain, well I wasn't stumped. But you never know and I was too young to get it bitten off . . . Well, fuck here it goes. But the time had run out, my lunch break was over. I bet your thinking, did I? Well, you're wrong. I left her lying on her back in the sun and went back to work, aye right. I was late back and severely reprimanded by the Head Keeper. I was told if it happened again (it probably will) he would have to tell the Overseer. But what the hell, it was great! There was nothing I could do wrong. Come on I had just lost my virginity, not my dick and becoming a man in fifteen minutes and so many seconds. Okay I needed help and was a fumbling egit. It had only lasted five minutes, maybe a bit less at the time, but.

I went with Pat; yes Pat was the girl on that hill and the girl I was going to marry. I went with Pat for some time. She taught me a lot to do with sex and I was a willing student. I remember one night going round to her house. We were going out somewhere and she asked if I would pick her up at her house. I figured that her parents would want to see me, that's why I thought she said come to the house. I thought I was a man of the world regarding the opposite sex. Ha, I was still very naive to say the least. Pat was the first girl that I'd ever had sex with and even then it was in, out and bang "how's your father." I arrived at her house, rang the bell and waited for a bit. Pat opened the door wearing just a towel.

"You're early, come in" She said and led me into the kitchen; "make some coffee if you want, I won't be long" she said and smiled.

She left me in the kitchen looking around for mugs and the coffee. As I was doing that, I could hear Pat splashing about it the bath. Well it sounded like that as I stood by the door of the kitchen listening and half expecting her parents to come out of one of the front rooms. I stood listening as I sipped away at my coffee. Then it all went quiet. Five or ten minutes later she appeared in tight jeans, white boots and a stripy coloured woolly jumper. It stopped just under her breasts leaving her tummy bare.

"What the hell happened to you then?" she asked.

"What do you mean?" I said with a blank look on my face as she pointed at my cup.

"I'll have one of those. I was waiting for you to come up so we could have a bath together, you numpty."

"What, where's your mum and dad?" Her next sentence hit me like a ton of coal.

"They're out you numpty."

Fuck me, talk about being naive, shit! How could I be so thick and miss an opportunity like that.

"I thought they were in the front room or something." I said as I handed her a mug of coffee.

"Come on, we'll be late for the film I want to see." She said making it quite clear that she wasn't going back upstairs. I went out with Pat for some time until I got caught with my arms around another girl, whom I was kissing during my lunch break at the zoo. Oh well, bye-bye Pat hallo Susan.

Two years had passed and there were lots of Pats and Susan's on the hill and a lot of instances over the five years that I was at the zoo. There was one where I was cleaning out the cage, thinking the animal was at the far end, but no it was just outside the cage making a desperate bid for freedom. I had forgotten to close the metal gate behind me. This animal looked like a huge porcupine with its body and tail covered in spikes, and it could run. Shit, it was off with me running after it. Each keeper has a whistle for this sort of occasion and mine was in my pocket. I was in a panic; I put my hand in my pocket, took out the whistle and blew on it as I ran after this fucking thing. My whistle didn't work it was full of sawdust, fuck. Luckily another keeper saw what was going on and managed to corner it, throw a large sack over it and we got it back into its cage saying "fuck you bastard, your days of freedom are over." It was about two or three weeks later when something else happened again. I was cleaning out the lion's cage when . . . no I didn't leave the gate open, I'd left a metal bucket full of sawdust in the cage after I'd come out and locked it. I pulled the sliding door connecting the two cages where the lion was waiting peacefully to come back in. I opened it and as I did the lion saw the bucket the same time as I but it was too late. The lion pounced on the bucket throwing it up in the air. It would knock it about in its paws and in seconds the bucket was shredded. It was like a kitten with a new toy. The Head Keeper saw everything and said "there's nothing we can do. We'll have to wait till it's finished playing with it and loses interest." We got the bucket out the next day, the lion was okay but there wasn't much left of the bucket. There was yet another instance where I was filling a metal water container for another big cat, this time a Jaguar. Hey, come on, I wasn't a complete walking disaster. All this happened over the five years I was at the zoo. I was outside the cage pouring water from a long nosed watering can into the metal container. I looked to see where the cat was. It's okay I thought, it's lying on top of the cage looking at me. The cage was a large open cage with grass and rocks and the odd tree. As I started to fill the container my girlfriend, well my current girlfriend that is, came into the enclosure where all the cats were. At that very moment I turned to talk to her and in a split second, the cat was down and biting the end of the watering can in one clean snap. Shit, it was scary to think that in a split second, the cat had come from the very back of the cage to the front without making any noise. Imagine if you were in the wild, you wouldn't have stood a chance.

It wasn't all bad at the zoo; there was a small brown bear that was donated to the zoo from Scottish Television. It was the bear from the Sugar Puffs advert. I don't know why they donated it to the zoo but it was so tame you could go into its cage. It would play and take food from me, which I had in my pocket. It would do lots of tricks as long as you fed it titbits. This went down great with the public. You weren't meant to play with it, but we did. I think the bear looked forward to us going in and mucking about with him. Then there was the Overseer's pet Cheetah that I used to walk around the zoo on a lead. Okay it was a pet but still a wild animal and you had to remember and respect that. It was quite a responsible job and the Overseer gave me books to read about Cheetahs, just in case someone asked me questions about it. Me . . . Read a book? Never the less I did it in my own time and people did ask me questions from time to time. It felt good to stand there and talk to them about it. I got on well with the boss man and his wife. They even asked me if I would be happy to give them a hand serving drinks, and bits and pieces at a function they were holding at their house. There would be a lot of important people there from the Zoological Society. It was after that party that the boss asked if I would like a job as a junior Game Warden in Nairobi. "There were people at the party who were quite impressed by you." I listened as he went on. "They said that if I was willing to go to night class to learn several languages and other things, they will take you on."

"I don't know" I replied.

"There's always a back door into things and I can help you there." The boss and his wife had taken a liking to me and my mannerisms. But I fucked it all up by letting my cock rule my head if you get my drift. Yes, I blew it.

There was myself, a new girl and four others, roughly all the same age. We had a chance to stay in this girl's house for a long weekend whilst her parents were away. But I was working at the zoo on Sunday and this was too good an opportunity to miss to spend the whole weekend with my girlfriend. So I had come up with a story, I said that my Gran who was quite elderly had fallen down the stairs. Yes you read it right; I said she had fallen down the stairs. I know I could have come up with a better lie than that. I said that I had to look after her because my father was away and my mother at work. This was okay, but what he did say was if he needed to phone me would it be okay? I said yes not thinking that they would. My girlfriend and I were away for a weekend of sex, drink and smoking bangers. That's the nickname they used for cannabis in a cigarette form, or a joint. It was the first time I had smoked a banger but it wouldn't be the last. I was kept down all the time at home. I had to have short hair when I wanted it long. I was made to dress like a . . . well; I'll give you a clue. White shirt, a checked sports jacket and flannel trousers, I ask you? I was fifteen not thirty five and looked like a geek. I wanted to rebel like everyone else was at my age. It was a good time; there was good music like 'The Stones', 'The Who' and even 'The Beatles.' It was time to rebel.

When I got my first wage I gave my mum some and went out to buy my own gear. Mum couldn't say too much because it was my own money. Okay she didn't approve of what I bought but what the hell. I bought loons; they were like skin tight pants, no pockets and flared at the bottom of the knee into a bell like shape. It took a long time to put them on they were so tight. I had to lie on the bed to fasten them, and then try to get off the bed without the button on the waist popping off or the zip splitting from the bottom. Once you were up it was okay, then there was my hipsters, they too were tight fitting but not as tight as the loons, these just sat on your hips. Then there were my brightly coloured paisley patterned shirts with a high collar, a bit like a Chinese style. My parents didn't approve and wouldn't let me go out dressed like riff-raff. I think that was the word they used. Just in case some of their friends saw me walking down the street. *What* would people say? So, most of the time I went out I took my other clothes with me and changed at my friends house before going out. Even when I said I was taking a girl to the pictures I had to put my white shirt on, tie, sports jacket and flannel trousers, fuck me! Most of my friends were wearing trendier clothes. Even the girls I was going out with at the time had on lace-up white PVC boots, a short dress and a transparent Mack, I ask you? Maybe they weren't the sort of girls you shouldn't take home to mummy.

Okay, back to the weekend. It was fab man! We all arranged to meet in a hotel called The Harp, just along the road from where I lived. The girl who I was dating lived further away near Haymarket in Edinburgh. The other two lived somewhere else but I won't bore you with that. Anyway, I was waiting in this hotel for this girl I had met a week ago. We were going away for the weekend, yes! I was sitting at the bar drinking a beer. Yes, I was underage at sixteen but I looked older and no one questioned my age. When my girlfriend walked in I nearly dropped my beer, so did the guy who was near me. She was wearing an extremely short white leather skirt, long white PVC boots that tied up the back, a black half-cup bra. I think that's what you call them. It fitted tight under her breasts pushing them up and out. Anyway, they were visible through the large knitted top she was wearing. Not the sort of girl mum would approve of. But what the hell, mum wasn't here. I felt a million dollars when she walked up to me and gave me a long, hard kiss and said "I'll have a drink please Bobby?" Five to six minutes later the other two girls came in. We stayed there for a bit drinking and then got the bus into Edinburgh itself, to this other girl's house. What a weekend that was until I came home and the shit hit the fan. The zoo had phoned to ask if I wouldn't mind working on Sunday because they were a man down. They said they were sorry to hear about my grandmother to my mum and that's when it all came out. I got such a row for telling a lie but luckily they never found out that I had stayed the weekend with a girl, had cannabis and a lot of booze. Not even my brothers heard a whisper about it.

The next day I was up in front of the zoological society committee to explain my conduct, it was tough. I couldn't say that I was away with my girlfriend for a weekend, drinking, smoking cannabis and having sex. How could I explain that? I don't think so. I just took what they threw at me. In the end I apologised for letting them down and lying to them. I was humble, shy and they gave me a week to finish up. Fuck, so much for being humble and shy. That was me out of a job with no future as a lion tamer in Nairobi. Well they say what's for you won't go by you, ha . . . that did. You could say that I fucked that up and you would be right. I would have to agree with you, but at the time. Have you not done anything that you looked back on and regretted? And said why did I do that? I bet you have and there's not one day that I don't think about what I did. If only I had stayed there and went on to night school, I could be who knows what in time.

CHAPTER SIX

TEA FACTORY

After the zoo I spent a lot of time at my uncle's farm again, my parents hoping that my uncle would take me under his wing if you know what I mean. Well he wasn't my real uncle he was my uncle by marriage. My mother's sisters daughter who married a royal navy Admiral's son, plenty money! Maybe my mum thought some of his manners would rub off on me. The farm was down in the borders, it was a large farm with a large house. My uncle didn't have to work the farm it was just a way of life that he liked. However, there wasn't any shortage of money; you could see that in the house and the dinner parties that he held there. That reminds me, my uncle did take me under his wing so to speak, he taught me a hell of a lot, especially how to ride a horse. We used to go out together in the morning after our horses were made ready for us by one of the farm hands. We would ride around the whole of the farm, taking in the three hills and a lot of flat ground. We would talk and he would tell me how he would like me to behave at dinner parties. We would then ride home again. I was becoming a good rider even if I did say so myself. I'd had lessons before, in Edinburgh at some riding school. My parents thought it would be a good thing, and it was. It helped me a lot. My uncle, his three daughters, and I used to go foxhunting together with the local proprietor. He lived on a very large estate in the borders who also entertained us with pheasant shooting. I wasn't very good at that but dinner parties I liked. Again, my uncle took me under his wing and was very strict about how I should behave. It was a while before he thought I was ready to be taken or be asked out to one. We used to have many dinner parties at his place, and every night before dinner, I would have to get changed. Then the cook would bring in the food and put it on the long polished table against one of the walls. His wife would then serve whatever it was we were having. Even his daughters had to get changed. I got on with the eldest one the best and can remember sitting down at one of his more formal parties opposite the eldest daughter. As I made polite conversation with the people at the table, I couldn't help but stare at my cousin. She was wearing a low cut evening dress that showed off her breasts considerably. I remember thinking "where did she get them from?" I had only seen her in baggy jumpers, jeans and wellies. But alas, time goes on and on and you lose contact. I heard that all his daughters married into money and sadly my uncle died. He was a great man and I had a lot of respect for him, but sadly, I never told him that. His wife survived him and she is still incredibly good looking and charming. I haven't been back to the farm even though I always said I would and time is running out.

Arriving back in Edinburgh I got another job in a factory in Leith, it was another part of Edinburgh where my brother was studying for his Second Mates ticket at Leith Nautical College. It was just down the road. My other brother was managing a farm in Argyll. Both of them were doing all right, I think. Anyway, I would meet with my brother and have lunch with him. We used to meet in this small restaurant and got well known by the lady who served us every day. I remember I used to order ice cream and fruit salad and she would say "you blinking pest" every time I ordered it. I don't know why she said it but I guess she just hated putting her hand in the freezer or something. It just stuck in my mind all these years for some reason. Anyway, I just thought I would tell you that useless piece of information. Okay, back to the tea factory where I was bagging tea and coffee. They import tea from other countries in large chests, and then transfer the tea into large stainless steel hoppers. They were large enough to hold about ten of these large tea chests. Down stairs is where I worked with ten other men and women, all bagging tea into small packets. The large hoppers were set in the ceiling above us. They were like massive funnels with a sliding trap door about an inch wide at the bottom. What we did all day was to hold the tea packet under the one inch slide and open and shut it. Once the tea packet was full you would pass it along to the next person. They would then seal it and pass it on to the next person who would put on a teaspoon or some other gimmick that was on offer at that particular time. If I recall at the time, Mum had an abundance of forks, knives and spoons. Upstairs was where they had their coffee roasting machines. They would buy in coffee beans from abroad in large sacks. They would then roast the beans on large, wide, circular gas burning plates with a foot high rim going all the way round. The longer they roasted the beans the darker they would get the stronger the coffee. The very dark beans were called continental and the lighter ones, regular and so on. Back to the tea on the ground floor and where I was working on the production line. Everything was going smoothly. I had made my way up the line to the front where you poured the tea into the empty packet and passed it along the line, no problem. The thin slide came right out in my hand and the tea kept coming out, more and more of it. I couldn't put the slide back in. The girl next to me tried and so did the next person but by this time the tea was everywhere and still pouring out. I couldn't do a thing until the hopper had emptied itself. It was everywhere, on everyone's clothes and we were all sneezing from the fine dust. It took us the rest of the day and the next morning to clean up the tea and it didn't go down well with the bosses. Production had stopped for two days with loss of money. I was taken off the production line and sent upstairs to where they were roasting coffee beans. I was told "perhaps you can do this simple job without causing too much damage and wasting time." I won't tell you what they did with the tea because you would probably never drink tea again!

This job was crap and I lasted about a fortnight. I was upstairs doing what I was told with the fucking beans. All of a sudden this guy started to punch fuck out of me for no reason, honestly. He was saying "you're no taking ma fuckin' job aff me ya posh bastar" . . . well really? I didn't want his 'fucking job' as he put it. You may think to yourself that I'm jinxed and you could be right. The scene upstairs in the coffee room was just like a movie set. There I was working away roasting beans, quite happy and minding my own business. When this guy jumped me from behind me and started to punch fuck out of me. I defended myself and we rolled over and over banging into bags of beans which tumbled down on top of us. He dived over them to get to me and I threw a bag knocking him down. There were coffee beans all over the place and torn bags. The place was a mess, it was mad. We were pulled apart and taken into the office to explain ourselves. But when the boss saw it was me that was it. After the tea incident, I was given a week's notice and the beans I was roasting, well they were burnt to fuck . . . I don't think they had a name for that batch . . . yes! I was looking for another job again and had a lot of time on my hands. It was round about August, my parents were going away on holiday, and I thought I would tag along with them. Luckily enough they were going to the south of France. I gave them some of my hard-earned savings to help with the cost and set off for sunny France. I was I think about seventeen maybe a bit more. That summer holiday was great. We got the ferry from Dover to Boulogne. Then my father drove through France stopping off at different campsites until we got to the south of France. The heat was great all through France, but as soon as we arrived in the south you could tell the difference. It was so hot that the GB sticker on the back of the car came unstuck. The weather was great and we got into a campsite right on the edge of the water in St Tropez, a mile from the harbour and the local market. Where we bought most of our food and talked to the locals in a mixture of French and English. Understanding what they were saying wasn't too bad, we struggled through. We would then go and look at the people on their yachts moored beside each other in the harbour. The people that owned them were just sitting at the back of them, drinking and generally having a good time. The campsite was good as well, right on the water's edge, as I said with all mod cons for washing or even cooking. I got quite friendly with some Germans they would be maybe twenty odd and were travelling through France. Then there was the French girl that I had met on the beach. I was sitting in one of those beach bars drinking ice chocolate. It was a drink out of a small bottle and was chocolate like I said, but I took a liking to it. Anyway, this girl came up to me and asked if I was English, I replied I was Scottish.

"Scottish, I like Scottish men."

Need I say that was the start of my real summer holiday? However, like most good things it had come to an end? We drove back up to the ferry and then started journeying home, stopping of at some friends of mum and dad's in England before continuing into Scotland and home. I wrote to Monique for a while with my gran's help but it faded away. When I came back I saw this ad in the paper, it said something like 'Fox Hall fruit farm requiring young men, good prospects in landscaping and two days off a week to attend college and a six month trial period. So off I go to work. After six months and the odd day off for college, I was told to go and see the boss man. He was blunt and to the point. He said the college report was crap but the practical side was excellent, (so what's new.) So, on the practical side he was willing to give me a three year course with college release . . . yes!

I had been at Fox Hall for about two years. In those two years there were a few disasters. Like always, my life wouldn't be the same without the odd disaster. Mario who was a fellow work mate and friend, we just seemed to hit it off straight away and became good friends, especially when he told me he had a sister and no it wasn't like that. Well he was Italian and his whole family were over here and could speak quite good English but if anything went wrong or he was asked to do something that he didn't like, he would pretend not to understand. They would ask me to explain to him or they would try themselves. Mario would stand there with a big smile on his face and I would have to go and do whatever it was he had been asked to do. It was on one of those occasions Mario and I were told to go and plough the far away field so they could plant fruit trees in it, after it had been ploughed and harrowed. So we went off on the tractor with the plough on the back, fighting to see who would drive the tractor. Pulling the wheel one way, then the other and nearly driving off the dirt track road into a fence. At that point, I gave up and he took over. We had done ploughing at the college, not much but we had an idea and they thought it would be good for us to get more experience. But . . . we ploughed the wrong field. Okay, it was just a slight mistake but who got the blame, yes me. All Mario did was to stand there with a big grin on his face whilst they shouted at us. He shrugged his shoulders as if he didn't know what was wrong. He would then laugh about it on our way home about the whole scene and I would say "you bustard" and that would start him off laughing again and I would join in.

There was another time where we were asked to take the tractor and trailer and tidy up the front part of the garden centre, as a Councillor was coming to visit. We had to rake the gravel, weed the flowerbeds and pick up bits and pieces and throw them in the trailer and dump them somewhere out of sight. Again we fought to see who would drive the tractor and every time we had to stop to pick up stuff or brush whatever it was, it was a mad dash to get to the tractor to see who would be the first there to drive it. This time I won . . . yes! Well, everything was going to plan and the place was looking quite tidy until I drove the tractor through this ornamental stone archway. It was advertising the different stones you could buy for building small walls and nice ornamental archways like the one I had just driven through on Mario's instructions. "Okay Mario" I said to his reply of "Si Si, carry on" but it wasn't okay. The only thing wrong was the trailer was too wide for the archway. And yes, the whole thing came down onto the back of the trailer. We came to a sudden stop with the coloured ornamental stone all around us, oops! Yes, I got the blame for it all. Mario would stand there shrugging his shoulders saying, "Don't understand." So I got the blame and was told to explain it to him. The mad thing about it was he knew all along what they were saying.

Mario said one Friday as we were going home, would I like to come out with him and his sister on Saturday night to a club that his sister like going to near the bridges in Edinburgh. I replied "okay thanks." Saturday night came and I met them in a pub called 'Paddies Bar' on Rose Street. That was the first time that I had set eyes on Mario's sister. She was stunning. She had long black curly hair down over her shoulders and a natural tanned complexion. She had deep brown eyes, big sensuous lips and a body that you would die for. After that night, I said to Mario if he could get his sister to come out with us again, and he did. After a few times going out with them both I asked her if she would like to go to the pictures with me. After that, we started to go out on a regular basis and got very close, if you know what I mean. She had a great personality, full of life and fun. I was nearly seventeen and Marana, Mario's sister was nineteen. We used to go to pubs, clubs, and parties together.

We were at this party in someone's flat in the middle of Edinburgh. Well, we were actually in a pub where we heard about it and thought, "Let's see what it's like?" The flat was dimly lit with red light bulbs replacing your normal white bulbs and ultraviolet tube lighting hanging from the ceiling. A very psychedelic way out sort of place and everybody was stoned. There were people smoking cannabis, dropping pills, snorting and plenty of drink. So what the hell, we joined in with everything that was being handed round. It didn't take us long before we were like the rest of them, well stoned. That's where we met this crowd of people all about the same age apart from one; he was an American lecturer and was heavily into astral projection. This fascinated the three of us, how you could will your spirit out of your body and go flying like Peter Pan? Maybe it was the chemicals that I had taken but I couldn't get my head round the fact that you could will your spirit out of your body. The way I was feeling with all the chemicals I had taken, I could have flown home without willing my spirit out of my body. I wanted no more about this and said, "Can we speak about this somewhere else." To his reply in a broad southern accent "Ya'll must drop by my place next Saturday, ya hear?" So we did, but before I tell you about this astral projection I must say that neither of my parents knew that I was taking cannabis or dropping a few pills here and there, neither did my brothers. They were on the straight and narrow but were alright, they used to take me out drinking with their friends. I never took cannabis or spoke about it when I was with them or Marana. I don't know why it just never came up. They looked on me as their baby brother and looked after me when I was out with them and their friends. It was good of them to be bothered; they didn't have to and were okay in that respect. I think that's how I grew up quite quick being around older people like my brother and friends and being accepted by them.

This astral projection is something else . . . The three of us were having a drink in a pub in the Grassmarket, a place in the old part of Edinburgh before going along to Bills' flat. It was just along the road from the pub. Bill was the name of the American that we met at the party. We walked along this old cobbled road looking up at all the stone buildings that had been houses at one time in the past. Now they were a mixture of shops, cafes, and restaurants but still had their old appearances. We walked and talked about different things and discussed the appearance of this old part of Edinburgh. We arrived at Bill's flat; it was one of these old stone buildings in between two shops. We stood outside an old oak door that must have been there for years. We looked down the nameplate for Bill's name. There were four on the list and Bill's was the last. It read "Bill's Place." We pressed the small button on the stainless steel intercom and Bill's voice answered. We told him who we were and he some "come up, it's the top flat." There was a quick buzzing noise and the latch of the big wooden door clicked, we pushed open the heavy door to see a circular stone stairway leading upwards. The steps were well worn in the middle from years and years of continual use. Bill wearing a tartan pair of shorts and a tee shirt greeted us with USA Georgia printed on the front. "Come—Come," he said and we were pushed into the front room where there were about three other people sitting on the floor on airbeds. Bill pointed to three empty airbeds and said, "Sit down" and we did. He put on some music with monks chanting through it. We were told to relax and listen to the music. As we were doing that, Bill offered us a cup of tea or coffee and apologised, as he had nothing stronger. We agreed to a coffee each and as he made his way to the kitchen, he introduced us to the three other people. One was an American girl, a student and Bill was her lecturer. She was studying philosophy or something like that. The other two guys were also students at the same university, very intellectual, way over my head but I tried to keep up with what they were discussing, I think. Bill came back with the coffee in three mugs and handed them out. He sat down next to the girl student and began to tell us about astral projection and explain what it was all about. I sipped away at the coffee and tried to take in what he was saying. Most of it was right over my head and I looked round at Mario and Marana. They just shrugged their shoulders and smiled back but we listened. The theory according to Bill is what should happen rather than what may in fact happen. You lie on your back and will your spirit to leave your body. You start at your feet and work all the way up your body. You say repeatedly to yourself that your feet are asleep, and then when they feel numb you start on your legs and so on until you get to your neck. By this time, if you have done it properly you should be experiencing a very strong rushing motion up through your body to your head. It should feel like everything in your body is being pulled up through your head and that your head feels like it's about to explode, very, very scary. We all lay down on the airbeds and did what Bill was preaching to us, saying over and over the things to ourselves. I backed out at the rushing part; I just got scared at the last moment. It's strange but it really actually works. It does feel very weird, like everything is being pulled up from your feet. Like your blood seems to be drawn up and up, and as it gets higher and higher the part that is left you can't feel. It's like someone is cutting of bits of your body and throwing them away and your only left with the bits that haven't been sucked up to your heard. It's a bit like a horror film where you wake up and find that someone has really cut off all the bits of your body and really throw them away. It makes you want to look up and down at your feet to see if they are still there and that nobody has cut the bits off. But the minute you do it all comes back to normal, thank fuck. I did it several times at home on my bed when everyone was out. I got past the rushing part after several attempts. You do find yourself standing outside your body, looking down at yourself on the bed. It's very way out, but your room might be different in the way that your bedroom door or window may be in the wrong place. What you have to do is picture in your mind what the bedroom really is like and where everything is and keep saying repeatedly to yourself in your mind until it sorts itself out, and it does believe me. The next stage is flying. You can laugh . . . and this was done without any chemicals in my system. Yes . . . you can actually fly like Peter Pan. I think whoever wrote Peter Pan must have experienced something similar. I won't go on about it because you are thinking that I am a complete fruitcake and writing this book from an asylum (maybe I am and I don't realise it!)

On our way to the pub after Bill's, I asked Mario and Marana if they had the same feelings. Mario said 'no not really' but Marana said she had the same feelings as I did but she chickened out at the last minute as well, she said she would try it at home. Marana and I got friendly with Bill and used to go round to his place, smoke a few cannabis bangers and a few beers and talk about astral projection. His theory is that when you die, your spirit goes to an astral plain (heaven). If it is heaven where your spirit lies, along with others and a baby is born and that spirit leaves heaven, or the astral plain. Which one I am not certain or if there is one at all, I don't know, then that spirit enters the new baby's body. When people get old the spirit in their body is getting ready to leave when they die, that's why old people need to be looked after because their mind is going, or the will to do things that they did when they were younger, or that it's harder to do things. It's the process of getting old, which makes the spirit younger in their old body ready to leave as they die and go on to the astral plain or heaven as a young spirit (baby). It will wait for another baby to be born and the whole cycle starts all over again. This was Bill's theory and I'm not saying that I believe it, but who knows?

About four or five months had passed since my first encounter with Bill and his friends. I was still working at Fox Hall and liking it. I was still going out with Marana and this was the longest I had been out with one girl at one time and not fucked it up. It was Wednesday and I was at work. Mario hadn't been in for the last couple of days and Marana hadn't answered the phone when I called. So after work I decided to walk along to where her parent's fish and chip shop was. Their house was next to it and I wanted to see what was what. Their fish shop was in a small village about five miles outside Edinburgh called Kirk Liston. It was a good hour's walk from where Mario and I worked. When I got there, it was closed and no one seemed to be about. I hung about for a bit just in case they came back. There wasn't even a light on in the house or shop and that was strange, it was well after 5pm and normally they would be open and selling chips and things. Mario and I used to walk there after work and I would get chips from his old man in the shop before getting the bus back to Edinburgh and home. I decided to get the bus home and that night I tried to phone again, but still no answer. Fuck, what's wrong, I thought. Thursday came and I got the bus to work as usual. As I was getting off the bus at the entrance to Fox Hall I saw Mario walking along the road towards me. I waited until he caught up and asked "where the fuck have you been?" he looked at me and walked right past. "Mario, Mario" I called as I walked after him. I grabbed him by the shoulder and he pulled away. I stood there as he kept on walking and thought, "Fuck this", ran after him and stopped him with force this time. I stood in front of him so that he couldn't walk away.

"What's wrong Mario?" I asked. He tried to get past but I stopped him. He said in his broad Italian accent.

"Bobby I don't want to talk."

"What the fuck have I done to you or Marana?" After I said this he broke down and cried. "What is it Mario?"

"Marana, its . . . it's Marana . . ." he took a deep breath and wiped his nose with his sleeve. By this time we were halfway down the long driveway at work, I was walking by Mario's side. "Bobby, Marana is . . . she's . . . she's dead."

"What!" I turned round to face him and said "no way, I was just out with her on Saturday night and had phoned her on Tuesday, she was laughing and her usual self, full of fun and laughing about what we were going to do this weekend. What happened?"

He began to tell me with tears in his eyes, stopping occasionally to sniff and wipe his nose and eyes. "She was found outside on the back patio. She had jumped from her upstairs bedroom window . . ."

"Fuck, was she high, pissed, how did it happen?"

"No, I don't know." He said trying to fight back the tears and sniffing again.

"Mario, what can I do?" He stopped and wiped his nose with his sleeve and took a deep breath.

"Come to the funeral on Monday, it's at 10am. Marana would like that."

"Yes my friend, I'll be there."

"My parents would like it too if you could come, they like you."

"Mario, Mario my good friend, of course I'll be there."

We continued to walk along the drive and didn't say another word to each other. I was gobsmacked; my mind was racing with what Marana had said to me. It wouldn't go away; it was racing round and round my brain, and wouldn't let up.

Monday soon came around and I was at the funeral in the small village of Kirk Liston. It was just a small funeral, just the family and a few of her closest friends. After the church, we went to the small cemetery then back to the parent's house in Kirk Liston. I remember saying to my parents that I was going to Marana's funeral and they said "okay dear, who?" I can't remember where my brothers were; I think one was on a farm in Argyll. The other was working with the merchant navy on a ship called The Fresno City, away on the high seas somewhere. I don't think they ever met Marana or Mario.

My father and mother had been looking for a hotel or some kind of business on and off for good year or so. They didn't have much money saved up and my father's dream was to have a hotel and all his family around him working it. It was soon to come true, my father retired and bought a hotel in the west coast of Scotland and we all moved there. My father had to see the boss of Fox Hall and explain why I had to leave before my three years were up. I only had one year to go and thinking back, Dad could have left me there to finish off my apprenticeship. But with everything that had happened, I wasn't thinking straight and I went with them. I lost contact with Mario and his family and after a phone call, the last time I spoke to Mario he said that he was going back to Italy. If only Marana was still alive, I would have liked to think that we would be married. Just because we got on so well together and had the same interests, I felt so relaxed with her. I remember Bill saying to me one night in the pub, if I wanted, he would contact her in the spirit world. I think I told him to fuck off. Maybe a bit strong but I wasn't in the mood for all that mumbo-jumbo stuff. Maybe he could have done it or maybe not. Either way I didn't take him up on it there was too much going on at home with the new hotel and everything.

CHAPTER SEVEN

THE HOTEL

The hotel was situated right opposite a nine mile fresh water loch. You couldn't ask for a better position. It was more of an old Scottish coaching inn than a hotel. It had nine bedrooms and a bathroom both upstairs and down. There was a reasonable size bar with a log fire and a hallway with another fireplace, larger than the one in the bar. Off that were two bathrooms, an office, a kitchen, a large lounge and dining room which had a large bay window overlooking the loch. The hotel was in need of a lot of work, it needed gutting. All the old beams replaced and the bedrooms re-decorated with new carpets. It would be a lot of painting, inside and out.

I remember it was round about June 1969 when my father got all of us together, sitting around the table in our old house in Edinburgh. That was when he started to say "I have retired as you know and bought this place. I don't have that much money so I am asking the three of you to help me out for one year of your lives and get this place up and running. Then, if you still want to leave, you can. I will help you in any way that I can, what do you think?" It was mainly directed at my brothers because dad had already been to see the owners of Fox Hall and asked him. It was now up to my brothers to say yes and they did. Three or more months later one of my brothers went with the old man and the old dear to the hotel, a little time after that I went up with my other brother and the work started on the place. It was still running as a hotel but didn't have much business. It was used mostly as a knocking shop for the enlisted men in the US Navy and their girlfriends. Well, I think they were their girlfriends if you know what I mean. It took a while to stop them bringing their girls up but mum was the dragon. What she says goes . . . She used to face them at the door of the hotel and tell them where to go, nicely.

It already had a barman working there from the previous owners. I think he was left to show my brothers and the old man how to run the bar. I remember there was always a fight between my brothers as to who was going to run it. I think it pissed off one of my brothers as to the fact that he and the old man went there first and then the other brother came in, and sort of muscled in on the action. I didn't fancy the bar myself I was more interested in the kitchen and dining room. Well, with my brothers fighting over the bar it meant that I had no rivals to compete with. After the territories were well established there was plenty of work to do on the hotel, day and night. Painting inside and out, stripping wallpaper and burning rubbish. Months and months went by and eventually the place was ready. The thought was going through all of our minds, well mostly mum and dad's and that was "will it be busy?"

There wasn't any fear of that it did get busy, very busy especially in the bar. The dining room was too, people were booking two to three days in advance to have dinner. Mind you, it had taken a good year to build up a good business and reputation in the bar and dining room. My brothers and old man took care of the bar. My mother did the cooking with the help of two local people in the kitchen. I did everything in the dining room from ordering the wine to waiting on tables and I even helped in the kitchen on the girls' day off. From cooking the vegetables to washing the big pots and everything else that was thrown at me from plates, cutlery and pots and pans. That was until we got a dishwasher which was so different. When it came to washing up, it was done during the night. But I still helped the girl to wash up all the big pots that were brought through at the end of the evening, in between waiting on the last of the patrons in the dining room.

The dining room was a long room with five tables that could seat four people comfortably down each side. At the bay window there was a larger table that took up the whole of the bay and could seat six. So in one sitting, you could seat at least forty six people if you wanted. But normally I had it laid for up to forty two. I got very good at waiting on tables and serving the correct wine with the food. It wasn't because I knew about wine, oh no, it was mostly patter at first. But a kind man who came to eat in the dining room regularly when he came up on holiday from England. On one occasion he brought a book with him and gave it to me because he was interested in the wine cellar we had in the hotel. The name of the book was 'The Beginners Guide to Wines" and it told you all about the correct wine to serve with the dishes you were producing. Do you know that book was so helpful; it told you about all the full bodied wines and what wine to serve with what. Oh, I could go on and on about it. What I will say was that it was an asset to me when I was serving wine in the dining room. That, along with the patter all went down a treat with the customers.

The old man got a kilt made and got well known as the proprietor of the hotel and he suited the part. He was the utmost host to the patrons that came into the hotel, being polite and courteous. He was good at acting the part. He did help in the kitchen too by making the starters for each order that came in. He did make a lot of us angry by taking his time and not hurrying at all even when the customers were waiting in the dining room. God he was slow. I think it was the only hotel that dried prawns individually before they were put in a glass to make up a prawn cocktail. They did look good afterwards. It was a bit like Fawlty Towers with John Cleese as the proprietor and me as Manuel. I used to come into the kitchen and tell the old man to "hurry up for fucks sake, the customers are waiting for their fucking starter." But that would just make him even slower if that was possible. I would then have to go back into the dining room and smile at the customer and tell them that "it won't be a minute sir!" even though they had been waiting for some time already.

As I was the only waiter the old man thought it would be a good idea if I wear a kilt. I got the whole works. I used to wear a shirt, tie my kilt with sporran, the socks and brogue shoes, the whole Scottish theme. I wore the kilt in the dining room and it went down a treat with the American's and their wives not to mention the local population. At that particular time Dunoon was full of American Navy Personnel and their wives and families. So the hotel got a lot of trade from them as did Dunoon itself. We got well known with the local people and the Americans and it was on one occasion I was asked out with my brother to a party. Our parents were away on holiday, a well earned break for them. The three of us were running the hotel with two or more staff.

There were six residents at this particular time and they wanted their breakfast early and that was okay. I would lay up the breakfast tables at night before the party and come back early in the morning. One of my brothers said he wasn't going and if we were going to the party to make certain that we were back in time for the breakfasts.

We came back in the morning with a massive hangover to find that the big wooden doors of the hotel were closed and we didn't know where our other brother was. To top it off, we didn't have a key. Oh dear, what do we do now? All the residents were inside and we were outside, oops. I came up with an idea to get in. If I went round the back and climbed onto the kitchen roof which was flat, I could climb through the bathroom window which didn't lock. It was an old sash cord window and the top part didn't lock at all. All I had to do was to lower the top part of the window, pull apart the small curtain, throw my leg over and climb in. The theory was okay. The bathroom window was a dormer type window. It jutted out from the main building like the rest of the windows. In the bathroom the basin was fitted tight into the rise of the window to give the bathroom more room. So I would have to be careful not to put my foot into the centre of the deep shaped basin. Anyway, I did this. I slid down the top part of the window, threw my leg over the top part of the window which was lowered right down. The net curtain hit my face as I swung my leg over and put my foot right in the basin which was full of water, splash. The next thing was that I felt two hands feeling my leg like a blind man would. I had put my foot into the middle of the basin where one of the residents was washing his face for the morning. "Oops, sorry" I said and quickly pulled my leg out of the water and giving it a quick shake. I came back out of the window back on to the roof and round to the front where my brother was. To my relief he had found the key that our other brother hid for us. He had told my brother where he had hidden it but at the time he couldn't remember . . . great. That morning I served the breakfasts thinking that someone would say something, but no one did.

Another incident was at night. The dining room was very busy. I was in my kilt waiting on the tables. There was a large man eating alone. He had a thick beard that covered his whole face. It hung down covering his collar and tie by about two inches. Well, there were different coloured glass globes that sat on thin black metal stands about four inches high on the middle of all the tables, with a small candle inside. The idea was that you light the candle and replace the coloured glass globe over the candle. It just made the table look nice, nothing else. I lit the candle on the table next to the gentleman for the next customer. As I did, the gentleman said "excuse me." I turned round to face him putting the used match back in the matchbox, not realising it was still alight. Whoosh, the whole box went up in flames inches from his beard. I took a step back as the gentleman jumped up clutching his beard and shouting obscene language. He grabbed his beard with both hands to check that it wasn't alight and the box of matches went up into the air like a rocket on Guy Fawkes and landed in the middle of the dining room floor. The whole room went quiet, you could have heard a pin drop let alone a box of burning matches. The gentleman calmed down when I apologised and gave him a complimentary bottle of wine. The dining room went back to normal, if it was ever normal when I was there.

The hotel was situated right on the loch-side; well a road ran between the hotel and the loch. At any opportunity I used to go water skiing and if I say so myself I got very good at it. There was one occasion on a hot summer's day where the loch was so still it looked like a mirror and was great for skiing. My brother's friends were over from Edinburgh and were out water skiing and having fun in the sunshine. I was waiting on tables and looking at them skiing past the dining room bay window, round the bay and back onto the beach. They did this in turn. The people having lunch there loved it, having their very own cabaret laid on for them. I had just to serve them tea and coffee and clear away the pudding things when one of my brothers friends caught my eye. He was standing at the dining room door and as I walked up to him he said "come and have a ski?"

"I can't, I'm serving lunches and haven't finished yet and I've still got my kilt on."

"Come the way you are, are you good enough to ski like that?"

"No I can't. I've got all these people here."

"Come on, do it for a laugh" He said.

I quickly went round the customers and asked if everything was okay for them, to the reply of yes, thank you. I followed him out of the hotel, across the road to the beach where the boat, my brothers and friends and ski's were waiting. I was okay at water skiing as I said. I could start off from the beach on one ski, past the dining room window, around the bay and back onto the beach without getting wet. So I took off my shoes and socks leaving my kilt, shirt and tie on. I put my one ski on and stood on the water's edge as the guy in the boat waited for my order to say "go." I checked that I was balanced okay and had sufficient slack rope beside me and said "GO." I went with my kilt blowing up round the top part of my knees. Luckily it didn't go any higher because being a true Scot it could have been very embarrassing. I skied out round the bay, passing the big dining room window where I had been waiting on tables just a moment ago to the surprise of the people who were sitting there, then back to the beach. I received an encore of clapping and whistling from my friends and spectators watching this mad man skiing in his kilt, shirt and tie. I felt like James Bond stepping from my ski and walking up the beach. I put my socks and shoes on and went back to the dining room to finish off waiting on the tables. I got astonishing looks from the customers who were in the bay window as they had just seen me ski past them a moment ago in my kilt.

Another incident was in the evening as I was waiting on a very attractive American lady. She was having dinner with her husband and was sitting opposite him. She was wearing a very short summery dress with a very low cut neckline that showed the top of her breasts off. She was about thirty odd and good looking. (And a nice pair of breasts they were too!" All through the evening as I waited on them between the other customers she would smile at me and push her breasts up and out if that was possible without them popping out of her dress. The neckline was pulled together by a bit of blue ribbon tied in a bow. BY the end of the meal I was standing close to the table to hand the coffee menu to her husband. As I looked straight down, the front of her thin flimsy summer dress to note that she wasn't wearing a bra and if she was I didn't see it. I got caught looking by her and she just smiled and looked straight at my kilt and said "is it true what they say about Scot's men?"

"What's that I said?"

"That they don't wear anything under their skirts?" She said smiling.

"But of course madam" I said, being the polite waiter that I was.

"Really" she replied in a very interested way and smiled again.

"They're called kilts madam, not skirts."

"What?" she said and I repeated myself to her once again and smiled myself before turning to her husband to take the coffee order.

"Two Irish coffee's" he said giving me the menu back oblivious to the conversation I'd just had with his wife.

"Thank you sir" I said and turned away to go get them. On my return to the table with the order that he had asked for in tall thin glass cups with cream on the top, on the tray, she looked straight at the front of my kilt as I put her coffee in front of her first. I took a quick glance down the front of her dress at her breasts that were well pushed up. She was concentrating on my kilt then looked up and caught me looking and smiled in a way that if possible she had seen through my kilt. She pushed her breasts out even more if that was possible and the other coffee slid off the tray spilling the contents of the tall glass all over the gentleman's suit. The glass ended up smashed on the floor, oops. I started to wipe the gentleman's suite with the towel I had over my arm and for some stupid reason I asked "is it hot?" to which he replied "of course it's hot." He wasn't very happy. I apologised and said quickly to the gentleman to calm down if that was possible. "Sir if you take your suit to the cleaners of your choice, the hotel will pay for it." I bent down beside the table to pick up the broken glass and wipe up the spilt coffee as best as I could without making a fool of myself. With my back to the gentleman's wife I felt her foot sliding up under the back of my kilt trying to lift it up and nearly putting me off balance. I turned to look at her; she just smiled raising her foot up even more and lifting my kilt higher. She turned her head to get a better look up my kilt. I glanced up at her husband; he was too busy wiping the excess coffee of the rest of his shirt to be bothered. I got up holding the broken glass and said "please accept another coffee from the hotel management sir." Grovel, grovel. I turned and smiled at this wife who was loving it and slid her foot back under the table. She knew that I was looking down her dress when the coffee slid off the tray. When they were leaving she said "what's your name?"

"Bobby" I said looking her straight in the eyes and trying to be professional. It was maybe a bit late for that but nevertheless I was trying and trying not to look down at her breasts as I was talking to her.

"Don't you worry about the suit . . ." she said as I interrupted "no, please I insist."

"Anyway" she said "we'll be back again. It was a lovely meal. I thanked her. "The entertainment was good as well" she said as they left the dining room.

There was yet another small incident where I was extremely busy and rushed off my feet. We had a sweet trolley with all sorts of cream gateau's and things on it. This particular time I was clearing another table and put what I thought was the cream jug back on the sweet trolley. As I did a woman from the table down from the one I was clearing said she would like some more cream. I picked up the jug from the trolley and very politely spooned it all over her pudding and turned to walk away when she gave out a scream. I had just poured mayonnaise over her gateau. Something else happened in the dining room. It wasn't all bad. This man was very particular about his wine. He would phone up the night before to ask if we could open the wine to let it breathe. Okay, I agree a good bottle of wine should be opened the night before but the wine he ordered was just an ordinary bottle. I think he just wanted to show off to his friends. Anyway the gentleman had arrived with his party and I had forgotten to take the wine out, fuck. The wine was cold and not even open, shit! What I did next was unbelievable even when I think back. I put the wine in the bottom oven to take the chill off it. Anyway I forgot about it then it was time to serve it, fuck. I took it out of the oven. Mmm I thought, its room temperature, ha. I took it to the gentleman's table and showed him the bottle. He turned to explain to his friends all about the wine that he'd ordered and mainly tell them a load of shit. Well, as I poured the wine I noticed a warm and very sweet smell coming from the bottle as soon as it hit the glass it steamed up with the heat, oops. I quickly lifted the glass away saying to the gentleman "its corked sir." Luckily he was deep in conversation with the other gentleman. I turned away to go back into the kitchen thinking what am I going to do? Again luck was on my side. My father had got another bottle out earlier knowing I would probably forget. Taking the new bottle of wine to the gentleman I explained to him that we had a bit of bad luck with some of the new wine that we had just got in. I told him that with him being a good customer we had another bottle just in case and that we needed to change wine merchants. He agreed with me as I poured a little wine for him to taste first. He approved of the wine and I put the bottle down, thanked him and turned away. I heard the gentleman say "bloody good service you get here." Little did he know that if he had tasted the first bottle he would have burnt his lips?

Another time there was five American women, high spirited and very noisy out celebrating something. They were sitting in the bay window on the long table that I had set. There were two women at the back by the window, one at each end and one sitting in the middle on the outside of the table with her back to the rest of the room. It was easier for me to serve them this way. Every time I came to serve them they would tease me and ask the usual things like "do you have anything under your kilt?" I would answer them saying something witty to a scream of laughter and giggles. Each one in turn would say something like "how is there no bulge in the front then?" The other laughing would say "because he's got that purse in the front to keep it down." They would all laugh again. It went on like that as I waited on their table. All sorts of questions and I would answer keeping the party happy so that they would enjoy themselves. I liked it too, getting the full attention of all five good looking women. It came to near the end of the meal and they all wanted fancy coffee's. I took their order and brought back five different ones. I put the coffee down giving the women at the ends theirs first. I then came round and stood next to the woman with her back to the rest of the room to lean over the table and give the women in the window theirs. The woman with her back to the rest put her hand right up between my legs and grabbed hold of my cock and balls in her hand, squeezed them and held on to them as I struggled to put the last coffee down in front of her without spilling it, professional to the end. She then shouted out "its true girls, they don't wear anything under their kilts and I have a handful to prove it." To the laughter of the rest of them at the table and the other remaining customers, who had their eyes fixed on this American woman with her hand up my kilt holding on to me quite tightly? It really was by my short and curlers! She wouldn't let go even to all the pleading I was giving her to do so. I was stuck there, bent over with the tray and my hands resting on the table looking at the two women in the window pleading to them. I was so embarrassed, really, when one of the women said in a broad American accent "Sam let the man's balls go." To another round of laughter and clapping from the customers at the six other tables, who were finishing off their meals and watching the cabaret at the top table.

There were many incidents in and outside of the dining room as well. It was the end of the night this time. I had finished in the dining room and we were all in the bar. We were relaxing as we did after everything was finished. My father was still in the kitchen counting the money or something. The bar in those days had to close at ten pm unless you had a supper licence that enabled the holder to serve alcohol for another hour and close the bar at eleven pm. Well, this night there was about twenty or more people (friends) drinking and having a good time well after eleven pm when someone looked out the window and said "there's the local bobby." He was getting out of his car and coming in to the hotel. There was a mad panic as my brother said to everyone "grab your drinks and go out the side door, go round the back of the hotel and go in the kitchen door." So off they trotted with their pints of beer, glasses of vodka and whisky in their hands. Normally the local bobby would come into the bar, check it was clear, have a chat then go on his way. This time he went into the kitchen to see my father who was still in there, drinking coffee. He offered the policeman a coffee who accepted and as they sat drinking coffee and chatting, the back door burst open and about twenty people laughing and shouting stumbled into the kitchen, drinks in hand. The first one stopped dead in his tracks when he saw the bobby and the rest fell in behind, spilling their drinks over the one in front as the bobby looked round in surprise and said "is there a party somewhere?"

That reminds me of another incident. Well, it was more what my mother said that stuck in my mind. We had two lesbian girls working for us. One in the bar and the other in the dining room with me, the one in the bar was so manly that she used to smoke cigars and drink pints of beer. The other one was so small and frail with blonde hair.

She was nice but if you said "boo" to her she would jump a mile. We all knew they were lesbians except for mum. I don't know if dad did, anyway they shared a room together. I don't know why mum didn't clock it, maybe she did. We were all in the kitchen getting something to eat before we went to work. The small blonde girl said to the other "I must wash my hair tonight." Before the other one could say anything my mother butted in "you must wash your hair too often because I hear that hairdryer on every afternoon?"

The butch girl said "it's not a hairdryer Mrs Addis." That's all she said and the other girl went bright red. We all laughed but my mother didn't get it, or if she did she didn't let on.

Another small incident was when we came back from shopping. We were taking the last items from the car when it started to slowly run back across the road, down the banking and ended up with the back of the car in the water, just as the traffic police drove past. They slowed down and said "just emptying the ashtray boys?" then drove off laughing. Well, I could go on but it is time for me to move on, out of the hotel and down to London where the streets are paved with gold. Just before I left I got talking to a friend that came to the bar quite often. He worked in the forestry on one of the big ploughs and was going down to London as well, giving up his job with the forestry. We decided to go together. Just before I left for London I met my future wife obviously I didn't know at the time that she would be my wife. She was about to work in the hotel doing office work and helping out in the dining room. What I can remember about her was that she wore brown boots up to her knees and a very short tartan mini kilt and matching green tartan waistcoat. I will tell you more about her later but for know I am off to London.

CHAPTER EIGHT

LONDON

London where the streets are paved with gold, ha! We arrived early morning by coach. I was knackered and so was Peter as we didn't get much sleep on the way down. Maybe it was the excitement or anticipation that we were going to make a fortune in London and have a good time well? We got our gear and made for the nearest café, it was about six am. We stopped at the newsstand and asked the chap behind the counter what's the best paper to get to rent a flat, mate?

"In London, around London or outside London?"

We both looked at each other and then back at the guy and said the cheapest."

"There's no where cheap down here" he said again. Sorting out the morning papers he went on to say "your best bet is to try outside London." He gave us a paper full of flats, houses, bed-sits and one room shared bathrooms. We sat down over our breakfast in a cafe just opposite the paper stand. Peter looked through the paper marking possible ones with a pen. I said "let's put our money together and see what we've got?" In total we had about £2,000 give or take a little. We spent all day in the cafe which, by luck had a public phone. Drinking coffee and phoning to the same old story "sorry it's too late, it's gone," or they wanted too much money. By this time we were both getting fed up and irritable. "Let's take a break" I said but Peter said no we must get a flat somewhere? I don't know what I thought it would be like; maybe I was a bit impatient. I thought that we would come down and get a flat straight away, I don't know? The day was getting on and we hadn't found a flat so the first night was spent back in the bus station on one of the benches. We talked for ages that night and both said that flats were too expensive. We would have to go for a bed-sit with shared bath. We got some sleep but the benches were hard and it was cold.

All I could think about was my lovely warm bed at home in Scotland. I lay there trying to get some sleep thinking what the fuck am I doing down here?

The next day wasn't any better and our money was dwindling away with breakfasts, coffees, something to eat at lunch time and more coffees and of course the phone. I was so sick of coffee! Peter had his full breakfast "like always." I had tea just for a difference. I gave the waitress a twenty pound note to pay for the stuff that we'd had and get some change for the first edition paper. We wanted to get an early start on the flat hunting. She just stood there looking at me and then down at the money that I gave her with a puzzled look on her face. I turned to Peter to help him look for flats and she left and came back with a smartly dressed man in a suit holding my twenty pound note? We both looked up as the man said "we can't accept this sir!"

"What' it's a twenty pound note" I said.

"We don't accept Scottish money."

"WHAT.! What do you mean you don't take Scottish money?" Peter butted in "what the fuck is this place like?" in a broad Scottish accent.

"Peter" I said "what's your problem?" When he loses the plot you can't understand him at all. He has a very broad Scottish accent and speaks very fast. To an Englishman he's like an alien from another planet. I could see that the guy couldn't understand what the hell Peter was saying, and by now everybody in the cafe was looking at us as if we were from another planet.

"Okay, okay!" I said "I'll go and get it changed." luckily there was a bank just round the corner but at that time in the morning it wasn't open but had a hole in the wall, not the bank that is! I put my card into the slot and pressed the right keys and out popped forty pounds in English notes, one twenty and two tenners. I looked at the slip of paper that had my balance, fuck there's not much in there I thought as I made my way back to the café. I paid the man and went back to Peter who was sitting at the table; he looked up and said I've got a bed-sit sharing bathroom in South Ealing."

"Great!" Then I thought, where the fucks South Ealing? At the exact same time as Peter said it to me. "I don't know" I said "but anywhere's better than the bus station!" We made our way to the underground and looked at the map of train routes on the wall. It was on the Ealing line so we made our way to South Ealing on the train and to the street that the house was on, it was number 12.

We crossed the road to the house. It was a semi-detected in a cul-de-sac. It looked alright. We walked up to it. I looked at the other gardens they were alright, well kept but number 12's had no garden gate and the garden itself was mess. The front door hadn't seen paint for years. It was a dull red with the numbers twelve on it in white letters, Peter knocked on it. As I looked round at the garden there were newspapers, beer and coke cans and crisp packets, what the wind had blown up against the hedge, if you could call it a hedge. The garden was a mess and as I said the grass was just a mud patch. My attention was brought back when the door opened and standing in the doorway was a tall skinny Indian gentleman with a suit that looked like it had been through a tumble dryer for weeks. He had on a white shirt opened down the front. We stood looking at him as if he was an alien.
"Well?" the man said.
Peter burst into conversation "we have come about the room."
"A—yes-yes come."

We were taken into the hallway. It had no carpets just bare boards with blobs of white paint splattered here and there. Shabby rugs that have seen their sell by date a long time ago. The doors inside were painted a bright yellow and the ceiling well . . . it was like the floor, a mess. We followed the Indian gentleman up the stairs and along the landing where there were more out of date rugs and more bright yellow doors. We walked over these rug type things. The Indian gentleman got out a bunch of keys from his pocket and opened one of the yellow doors saying "here you are boys." Well, the room was the same as the rest of the house, a mess! We walked in; there where two beds with two shitty brown mattresses on them and at each side of the beds were two small tables that didn't match. The varnish was peeling off them; well what little there was. In the middle of the room another larger table, like the two beside the beds with the varnish peeling of it and two odd chairs and more bare boards.
"Fuck me look at this place?" Peter said and before I could answer "let's get the fuck out of here" Peter said again in his broad Scottish

accent. I don't think the Indian gentleman under stood him. I pulled Peter aside and said "anything's better than the bus station, and it will give us time to look for somewhere else." The Indian gentleman turned and said "do you boys want this room?"

"Err-yes, yes okay we will take it." He then took a key off the bunch in his hand and gave it to Peter saying "that the same key, opens the front door" in his Indian accent. Peter gave him two weeks rent in advance grudgingly.

"Oh, where's the bathroom?" I said and the gentleman took me out of our room and pointed to a curtain covered doorway just along the corridor from where we were standing.

I walked down the corridor with him and as he pulled back the suspended cloth that he called a curtain I walked in. Turning to the Indian gentleman I said "is there no door privacy for when you have a shower, a bath, or even use the toilet?" He let go of the curtain. As it fell back down covering the entrance to the doorway he looked the curtain up and down. He then turned back to me with a strange look on his face as if it was a strange question to ask him and then said "No, no door. Your friend will have to stand outside to stop anyone coming in okay yes?"

"Okay yes" I replied. The words seem to come out of my mouth slowly as if I was a robot needing to be wound up.

"You are the only one's here apart from my wife okay yes?"

The bathroom . . . well I had to laugh. On the right there was the toilet and directly opposite the curtain where we were standing was the bath tight flat along the edge of the wall. In the middle of the bath was a shower nozzle sticking out of the wall, all rusty and hovering over the bath with two large taps on the wall just above the middle of the bath. There was no shower curtain just the round tubeless steel frame work that was hanging off the wall at one end, where the screws had long gone. By the look of the floor the excess water from the shower had missed the inner edge of the bath and had landed on the floor taking what paint there was on the floor off. You stood in the bath to have a shower with no curtain, if you wanted a shower at all. Looking at the bath, the shower would be the better option if it worked. The sink was opposite the toilet and was in the same condition as the rest of the bathroom it looked like shit! I stood there looking around the bathroom trying to take it all in. How anyone could show someone this as a bathroom. I noticed the paint was peeling of the ceiling where the steam from the shower had condensed back to water and left its mark. In the centre of the floor was another brightly coloured out of date rug. I was thinking that I better not tell Peter about this just yet!

It was like I was in a film. The Indian gentleman was the actor Peter Sellers playing the part of the Indian man. I just burst out laughing as we walked along the corridor back to my room half. I half expected Cato, the Chinese man you see acting alongside Peter Sellers to jump out of one of the yellow doors and start fighting with him. But no, he just disappeared behind the yellow door at the end of the corridor. In fact I walked back to Peter laughing to myself. I could hear the Indian gentleman talking to someone behind the door in his native language. I met Peter coming out of our room. He said to me in a grumpy sort of way "what are you so happy about?"

"Nothing." I wasn't going to tell him about the bathroom. I'll let him find out for himself later because that would have just finished him off, the mood he was in.

"Where are you going?" I said to him

"I'm off to get some pillows and blankets; I'm not sleeping on those mattresses they're filthy."

"Okay let's go and get some stuff and tidy it up a bit." I replied.

Luckily we had brought our sleeping bags down with us and by the look of the mattresses we would definitely be sleeping in the bags. As I said, I didn't even bother to tell him about the bathroom. He would find out for himself soon enough.

We stayed in that place for about six months. We tidied it up, getting posters for the walls and a better rug to replace the small one that was there. It wasn't difficult to find one that covered most of the entire floor. We slept in our sleeping bags on those mattress with new pillows that we bought from a market place we found along with the other bits and bobs that made it more homely, if that was possible. For all the time we stayed there, we never slept on the bed properly. We slept in our sleeping bags with blankets over the top of the mattresses and blankets over our sleeping bag. That night we talked well into the night about getting a job and what sort? Then I said that he could probably get a job in one of the building sites operating a digger. That would bring in good money and I could find something too and to get a paper tomorrow and start looking. "What do you think Pete . . . ? Peter?" He had fallen asleep and I was talking to myself. I lay there in my sleeping bag all warm and snug for the first time since I had arrived in London, on the mattress with my two new blankets and my two pillows that we had bought. I thought "it's not too bad here since we tidied it up; its warm and we don't have to pay for the heating. It will do until we get some money and a better place." Then I thought, "I wonder if Peter has seen the bathroom yet?" I then laughed to myself about the state of it. How anyone could rent out a place like this to anyone . . . Well, we're here!

Peter was about six foot and very well built and as I said talked with a very strong Scottish accent. Most people down here didn't understand him and that made him angry. It wasn't long before Peter got a job as I thought, on a building site as an operator on one of the machines. He was bringing in good money. I got a job selling central heating a couple of weeks later. It was a bit of a con.! What I had to do was the leg work. I would go to house after house, street after street. The streets where just like the soap's on the television, especially Coronation street if you have ever watched it. There where rows upon rows of them. I used to walk along each street knocking on each door and missing out the one's that had central heating by looking for the stainless steel vent that was normally on the front of the house. If they didn't have one I would knock on their door and ask them why they didn't have central heating? Most of the time they would say that they couldn't afford it or the door would just shut in your face. If and that's a big if, you got someone that would listen to you that's where I would came in with the punch line saying . . . . our company is in this area doing a promotion selling affordable central heating and you could be one of the lucky ones. Our marketing manager could be in this area and he could call on you and arrange to sell you one of the promotions much cheaper. If they said that I must talk to my husband first you would say "I'm not promising that he will call on you but you never know!" Little did they know that he was sitting in the car around the corner munching on a pie or something waiting for me to come back with my clipboard with all the possible sales ticked on it? We would go and come back to the houses that I had ticked later, so that the wife had time to talk to her man after he's had is meal and is relaxing. I said it was a con but the money was alright and I would get commission if the sale went through. Well we both had jobs and we started to go out to nightclubs, pubs and just enjoy ourselves.

I remember there was one incident in the flat. Well, it wouldn't be like me if something didn't always happen? Peter had come in from work, got changed and had gone out leaving a note saying that he would meet me in the club in Earls Court. It was Friday and I was going clubbing in London. I got my good gear out, put it on the bed, stripped down to my boxer shorts and went for a shower. Yes it did work, but I don't recommend the bath. I don't think there was a plug for it. Anyway I remember Pete ranting on about the bathroom when he saw it and I think he told me that he had to use the plug from the bath from the sink. The shower was bad enough with some of the water ending up on the wooden floor because of no shower curtain. I was taking a risk having a shower anyway with only a curtain for a door, "what the hell" I thought. I had to wash and the bath was a no-no. Trying to get the shower to the right temperature took a while. Playing with the hot them the cold then suddenly it would come together with the pipes shuddering and making weird noises . . . yes.

I stripped off and threw the towel and my jocks onto the toilet seat. I got under the shower and altered it so that all the water wasn't hitting the floor. I hoped that no one would come in as I started to wash, getting the shampoo for my hair and pouring it over my head. I had put a bit too much on; the shampoo was everywhere as it ran down my head, my eyes, face and body. I had my eyes closed standing under the shower rinsing the rest of the soap out of my hair with both hands when a woman's voice said "where are you from?"

Fuck. Rubbing the remaining soap out of my hair and eyes I tried opening them but there was still too much soap. I had to close them again because they were stinging. I reopened them again to see the landlord's wife sitting on my towel on the toilet seat. She was holding my jocks on her lap just a few feet away from where I was standing and looking street at my very naked body, I put one hand down to cover what I could but it didn't cover much, if anything. I wiped the remaining soap off my hair with one hand the best as I could. The landlady said *"you don't have to bother covering yourself; I have been looking at it for a while!* I thought "what the fuck, I'm stuck here absolutely stark-bollock naked and there's nothing I can do and she's sitting on my towel. I left my hand there anyway thinking it was better than nothing.

"Well, where are you from?" She said in an Indian accent and so calm about everything.

"My towel please and I will tell you" I said as I stood under the shower letting the spry hit my head and run down over the rest of my body.

"No tell me now and I will give you your towel" she said holding on to my towel even harder.

Well, I stood under the shower the complete full Monty and just a few feet away from my landlady in full Indian clobber right down to the red spot on her forehead. I reckon about forty odd and not bad looking. Well, what you could see of her. There she was discussing where I came from and having a conversation without taking her eyes off my dick . . . She would look up at me smile then look back down and carry on talking. "What! Am I mad?" I thought and said to her "please give me my towel or I won't be responsible for what might happen!" She laughed showing her perfect white teeth, a nice smile I thought.

"What, okay." She replied.

I was standing there naked but she did have a nice smile. She got up and held the towel in two hands outstretched across in front of her, beckoning me to come out of the shower and walk over to her like a bull fighter with his red cap teasing the bull.

"Give it to me?" I said trying to grab it with one hand and trying to keep my other hand covering my dick with no luck. I had to turn off the water and get out revealing all to her again.

Stepping out the shower I walked over to her as she walked backwards away from me. She said smiling "come and get it."

"Give it to me?" I said pleading to her and took another step forwards her as she came towards me and wrapped the towel around me. Her head was a few inches away from my face, she was that close I could smell her perfume. "Thank you" I said looking down and straight into her brown eyes. She finished wrapping the towel around me and tucked the end in my waist, and then sliding her hand down gave me a little tap. She then turned round and walked towards the doorway, pulling back the curtain. She stopped, and turned smiling then said "we must do this again?" before she disappeared through the doorway.

"What would you have done if someone had come in?" I replied.

She paused and looked back "like whom?" She said showing of her perfect white teeth again as she smiled.

"Your husband" I said grabbing my jocks that she threw at me underhand with her spare hand while her other hand held the curtain back.

"They're all out, I'm not stupid." She answered as the curtain fell back down and she was gone.

I followed her through the curtain on my way back to my room and watched her walk along the corridor. I thought that her bum had some wiggle in that Indian get up. She continued wiggling until she got to the yellow door at the end then she looked round smiled that MacLean's white teeth smile and moved her fingers in a gesture to wave bye-bye and disappeared. I dressed and thought about the landlady. Did she do that sort of thing to all the people that stayed here; I must ask Peter if she had done it to him when he was washing.

By the time I got to the pub it was mobbed. There was live music on and I squeezed my way through the people to Peter who was standing at the bar. I got up to the bar and him and he said "where the fuck have you been?" I started to tell him about the landlady but it was so busy and noisy. I just said "never mind I'll tell you later." It was a great night and I completely forgot to tell Peter about the landlady. We stayed at the club till the early hours then went home after grabbing something to eat at a takeaway that was still open. With all the drink and having a great time the landlady incident went right out my head.

We took turns standing outside the bathroom as each of us took it in turn to have a shower or a wash. Neither of us temped to have a bath. It was bad enough standing in it let alone lie in it. It was a start of another weekend and the incident with the landlady had completely gone from my thoughts. Considering it must have been a two or three months since it happened. I was late back this Friday and found a note again from Peter saying that he had stayed as long as he could

waiting for me but 'Time's money and money has to be spent?' that
was his best saying. The rest of the note went on to say that he would
see me in the club and it was my turn for the carry-out. Peter used to
finish work before I did most times and he liked to get out early on a
Friday night. It was about 9pm and I needed to have a shower. I was
hot and smelly with walking all day up and down the dirty streets. But
thinking what happed last time I decided to just wash myself before
going out this time. I stripped off down to my jeans and walked to the
bathroom carrying my toiletries and towel. I pulled back the curtain
and walked into the bathroom and over to the sink. Put my stuff down
on the chair and began to look for the plug for the sink. Fuck, where is
the fucking thing, I thought looking all over the bathroom for it, even
looking in the bath. In case Peter had used it in the bath, but I didn't
think he would somehow. Where he worked there was a place where
they could wash and change. Anyway he didn't get all that dirty sitting
in his warm cab in his boiler suit that he put on to keep clean. "Fuck
it." I couldn't find the plug so I decide to have a shower. I just couldn't
go out without a wash of some kind and with no plug the next thing
was the shower.

I would have to take my chance, I turned to the shower and leaned
over to turn on the water and try to mix it. As usual it took time to
get it right and the spray from the shower was wetting my jeans. So I
decided to take them off along with my boxer shorts and get the water
just right before getting under. God it felt good just letting the water
cascade down over my body. I stood there for a while just relaxing
under the warm water. Then I thought "fuck it" I had better get a move
on or I'll be late and Peter won't be happy and if I don't hurry up, you
know who will be along if she's in. But there wasn't any noise coming
from the room at the end of the landing or even down stairs because
I had listened before coming along. I washed myself and my hair and
put my head out of the way of the water to listen for any noise but it
was still quiet. I put my head back under again and rinsed off the excess
soap out of my hair with my eyes closed and decided to get out and
not chance my luck any further. Suddenly the landlady pulled back the
curtain and walked straight in and picked up my jeans and my boxer
shorts in one hand and the towel in the other. She walked to a few feet
from the shower, not to close so that she wouldn't get wet from the

spray and stood there with her hand folded still holding onto my stuff smiling. "Hallo again, it's been a long time since we had our little chat" she said smiling and then she carried on saying as I stood there under the shower, with the warm water bouncing of my head and running down my face, making it hard to keep my eyes open without holding my head out to one side of the shower.

"Where are you going tonight?" This time I turned off the shower and stepped out of it. She continued to talk moving backwards as I walked towards her.

"Mmm getting brave are we?" She said with a big grin on her face.

All I wanted was my jeans or my towel and kept walking towards her with the water dripping of me. As I did she constantly looked at my wet body as she walked backwards away from me and coming to a sudden stop as her heel hit the bottom of the edge of the wooden doorframe.

"Wait! Wait!" She said as she held out her hand in a gesture to stop me with the towel hanging down from her clenched fist her eyes examining the lower part of my body, as it started to grow uncontrollable. I stood there waiting to hear what she was going to say but not close enough to grab the towel.

Call me an exhibitionist but I was starting to like standing there letting her look at me and yes I was getting quite horny and she noticed the difference. She started to talk about different things, how she came to London and where have I been since I've been down here all without taking her eyes of my dick and smiling all the time. Well, sometimes looking up and then back down still talking away. It was weird I know, but I stood there letting her waffle on about things that I wasn't really interested in. But there I was, standing having a conversation with my landlady who I didn't even know about two months ago. I moved forward to take my jeans off her but she put her hand through the edge of the curtain and the doorframe holding them at arm's length out onto the landing. I stopped and said to her "are you going to give me my clothes because I'm going to be late." I heard them drop on to the landing floor outside. I stood there naked pleading with her to even give me my towel which she had clasped tightly in two hands now and holding it down in front of her.

I backed off not really wanting the towel and quite happy to stand there with my legs apart with my hands on my hips posing for her and playing along with her little game. I liked the careful concentration that she was giving my dick as it sprung into overdrive and was quite happy to be seen stretching out for the towel itself or something else? I started to really look at her standing there. She wasn't bad looking for her age as I said, about forty odd with long black hair and not a bad body. I noticed the way the light was shining on her thin pale blue Indian fabric from the bare bulb that was hanging down from the ceiling. It didn't look like she was wearing a bra. She had perfect round full firm looking breasts for a woman of forty odd. Well, I hadn't seen many forty year old women's breasts then, but they didn't sag! I looked again at the outline of her breasts quite visible now that my concentration was pinpointed on them. God, I thought "I'm getting to the point of no return" and that sent another message to my dick kicking it up another notch. I couldn't take my eyes off her breasts it was as if they had a magnetic pull on my eyes. She was still talking to me "well, what do you think?"

"About what?" I said breaking the magnet. "Sorry what did you say?" Taking my eyes off her breasts and looking back up at her face that was smiling. I couldn't help but smile back at her, apologise and say my thoughts where somewhere else. She laughed out loud a very infectious laugh.

"I can see that" she said.

I had forgotten about Peter and going out and was starting to get quite horny. It was showing very much by now. I was past the embarrassing stage and looking at her in a different way. 'Perving' at her to be precise. She was noticing the difference too as I stood there in front of her naked. She stood up straight and held the towel in her two hands and walked towards me, looking straight into my eyes with a big broad smile on her face. She stretched one of her arms around my waist as she started to wrap the towel around, holding one end of the towel in front against me and pushing my very erect penis up and pulling the other end of the towel tightly round with her other hand. Just before she closed the end of the towel over she held the two ends of the towel open and looked down as my dick sprung out hoping for more attention. Then with that big grin on her face she closed the two ends pushing my dick once again up tight against my tummy and tuck one of the ends tightly down between my tummy being careful not to touch my dick that was waiting to be set free and spring into action. When she did my nose was filled with the mixture of shampoo and perfume that wafted up from her head, it was so inviting. I just wanted to leave my head there, but she started to back away putting her hand in-between the towel and my stomach and started to pull me across the last bit of the bathroom floor and through the covered doorway pulling back the certain with one hand as she walked backwards out onto the landing. The curtain fell back down over my shoulders the minute she let it go of it. Once out on the landing I leant down to pick up my clothes. She stopped and looked down still holding onto the towel with her hand tightly tucked in my waist. she paused and then started pulling me again walking backwards slowly along the landing to the door at the end, turning occasionally round to see where she was going then back at me smiling and not saying a word. Once at the door, she stopped and turned round to open the door pushing it wide open with her other hand, still with her other hand still tightly tucked down between the towel and my tummy as if I would run back to my room the minute she let go. That thought was the last thing on my mind and my dick's, if it had a brain at all? She walked backwards still smiling into the room then said "shut the door?" I twisted round as she still had a firm grip of the towel and grabbed the edge of the door and gave it a hard push as it slammed shut, turning back to face her she pulled off my towel.

Her husband worked nights three weeks on and the one week off. I never asked her what her old-man did and she never really talked about him only to say that he was from Pakistan and the marriage was arranged by his parents. She had to fly to Pakistan to meet them and get married but she was born here in London. Her family were a very strict Indian family and moved her a while ago, she didn't believe in arranged marriages but to keep the families honour she got married and moved back here. Being she was brought up in London and going to school in London she has got used to a lot of the western ways that her husband couldn't quite get used to. Straight off, I thought of one he probably wouldn't get used to. It was always on the week he was off that he came looking for the rent and we always had it ready for him.

On the weeks that he was working she would catch me at night on the landing coming in from work or just coming from the bathroom on my way back to my room. She would stop me and say "Can I see you on Saturday night?" I can remember Peter getting angry with me on several occasions because I said to him that I was working late and I might not make it to the pub. He did say once "are you knocking off the landlady?"

"Why do you say that?" I said.

"Oh just the way you both talk to each other" he replied.

"Yes so! That doesn't mean that I'm knocking her off as you put it. She just stops me and we talk, I can't be rude and just ignore her" I said.

"You're both very meaty" Peter said and went on to say like a father giving me some good advise "don't get caught we don't want to be kicked out before we get another place."

Peter and I stayed at that flat for quite a while, but he was always looking for somewhere else and yes I saw the landlady regularly when her old-man was working. Think of me what you like . . . . it was good and I enjoyed spending the time with her. Okay, she was much older than me at the time and we knew it wouldn't last, but while it did it was superb. They say sometimes an older and more experienced woman is good for you! Maybe that's not quite the saying but it was good for me and I'll never forget the time I spent with her. God I wouldn't mind meeting her again now . . . . I never let on to Peter about the landlady but I think he probably thought that I was? Anyway, we moved to a better flat by Earls Court in London. We were in this pub one Saturday lunch time, it was one that we always frequented when these two guys that we were talking to said that they knew of a place by Earls Court. The only thing was it was a lot more money so we arranged to go and see it one Saturday. When we saw it we fell in love with it straight away. What a difference this place was, it was fully furnished and we had our own kitchen, two bedrooms and a toilet all to ourselves. Okay it was three times the rent that we were paying just now, but it was worth it. We were both still working and making good money but it was Peter's wage that would mostly pay for it because he was making three times more than me and it was regular. I would get paid regular as well but I would only get a bonus if a sale went through and that would be maybe every two weeks if I was lucky. On saying that we were settling down into the way of life down here and enjoying everything London had to throw at us. Peter had to go home and he left it up to me to move all the things that we had in the other place which wasn't much. I left most of the bits and bobs that we bought, apart from the posters, pillows and blankets. Everything else wasn't worth taking to the new place. He gave me enough money along with mine to pay for the deposit for the new place and left me to settle up with the Indian gentleman. Luckily he wasn't there and I saw his wife, gave her the money and said my goodbyes to her. After four or five hours later I left and as I was leaving she gave me her mobile number and said that I should phone her during the day so that if her old-man was in, he would most probably be catching up on sleep before going back to work so not to disturb him.

I spent the rest of the weekend sorting the new flat out, putting things away and putting the posters up on the walls that we had from the other place. When I was finished it looked great even if I say so myself. The only thing was it didn't have a landlady like the last one, but saying that I did have her number, I did phone her on many occasions and I would go round there when her old-man was working Peter was away well over two weeks and I didn't go out much while he was back at home. It made me think of home when I was just sitting in the flat. I got a bit home sick so, to take my mind of all that I decided to go out and check out the new neighbourhood. It was far more respectable than the last one we stayed in. There was this very exclusive club that was about a two hour walk from the flat, I didn't go in but I had a good look at it from the outside. It was all done out in red and gold and it looked like it had long red velvety curtains tied back over the long windows inside. I thought we must check that out when Peter gets back. I walked in to a continental looking cafe where there were round tables and chairs outside with people sitting having things to eat and drink. I plonked myself down on one of the round stainless steel chars to find that I had to go in to order. I returned with my Cappuccino to my table and sat down and relaxed and sipped away at my coffee looking at the world go by. It was quite hot and the sky was a pale blue with fluffy looking clouds drifting around. People where wearing their summer clothes especially the girls, great for perving! Some of them were wearing t-shirts and tight jeans and others were wearing short miniskirts. This one particular girl I spotted crossing over the street opposite me, well she was great looking and all she had on was a loose blouse that was tucked into a very short skirt that looked like a tennis skirt. It was straight in the front and had small pleats around the back. As she walked, what wind there was seemed to be concentrating on her and lifting and swirling her skirt about as she bounced along with a spring in her step. The way she was walking was in a happy go lucky manner made me study her even more closely. I sipped away at my coffee not taking my eyes off her, hoping that the wind would blow her small skirt up and I would catch a glimpse of her underwear. She had some walk.! As she disappeared round the corner onto another street and out of sight, I was a bit disappointed not to see a glimpse of underwear but there were many more as I sat there in the sun taking in the views. I finished my coffee, then walked leisurely back to the flat stopping at a fast food carry out shop on my way and got myself a Doner-Kebab to take home.

We got to know this crowd of people that went to this very expensive club called 'Chatters' the one that I saw when I was out walking when Peter was away. The first weekend Peter was back we went round to the club and tried to get in but the bouncer stopped us and said "sorry guys you're not allowed in with jeans on and you must have a tie."

Peter said in his broad Scottish accent "we just want to have a drink not fucking buy the place." The guy on the door replied "I don't make the rules mate." As we turned away the bouncer on the door shouted to us "what part of Scotland are you from mate?"

Peter turned round and said "Dunoon mate?"

"Ha, I'm fae Glasgow." We turned round and walked back to him as he said to us "how long have you been doon here?"

"About two months or so" Peter said.

He then pulled us aside to let other people in and said "come back with right clobber on and I'll let you in."

"Okay, thanks" we said and over the number of times we went there we got quite friendly with Bill the bouncer, mainly I think because we were from Scotland as well. Every time we went there he would let us in for free, all right it cost us a double of whatever he was drinking. The next time we went to the club we saw the queue. It was right round the corner so we both thought we would give it a miss. We walked by the people on the opposite side of the road and Bill spotted us and beckoned us to come over and made room for us at the door saying "VIP guests make way." He ushered us in saying "that's a drink you owe me guys"

"Okay" we said "that's no problem." We entered the club and immediately were standing on this red carpeted landing with red carpeted stairs leading off to either side and down to a large dance floor that was jammed full of people dancing and jumping up and down with their hands in the air. The music and the atmosphere just hit you and you just wanted to 'party.' It was, you could say fucking incredible. The bar was directly opposite you at the other end of the dance floor with a full length mirror covering the whole of the back bar wall. At each end of the bar were topless girls dancing in long metal cages suspended from the ceiling. On each side of them where similar red carpeted steps leading up again past the girls in the cages to another red covered carpeted balcony. There were large leather seats dotted all round the balcony in groups of two or three to a table with red shaded lighting on them. You could sit down in comfort and drink and look down on the people dancing and look at the topless waitresses all wearing red short pleated skirts matching the carpet with their white knee length socks. The place was amazing; it even had another level above us with larger leather seats and tables with the same lighting, same red carpet, but topless girl's pole dancing. You could even get a topless girl to sit with you but you had to pay for a bottle of Champagne.

We made our way down the steps and across the dance floor. Squeezing past people dancing to the bar, eventually getting our drink and nearly getting it knocked out of my hand by a girl dancing before I could get a drink out of it. She turned round and looked at me in a way to say sorry and kept on jumping up and down with her arm swinging around her head. It was madness trying to stand there and have a drink so Peter said "let's go up there" pointing to the landing. We squeezed past the rest of the people standing at the bar and made our way up one of the winding staircases leading up from the dance floor and past a blonde girl dancing in this cage in time with the music. I sipped at my drink on my way up the stairs, then stopped to take time to look at this girl that was now level with me with just a pair of very tight, small white pants on and her naked breasts bouncing about as she swung her arms about in time with the music. I stood memorized for a split second staring at this girl's breasts until Peters voice snapped me out of the trance that I was in. I continued to follow him up the remainder of the steps saying "did you see that girl's tit's Pete?"

"Yes" he said without turning round and made his way to a table with three big leather chairs around it. He sat down in one of them, putting what was left of his drink down on the smoked glass table top and looked down on the people on the dance floor, dancing and jumping up and down waving their hands in the air. I joined him, sinking down into this deep leather seat and like him, looked down on all the people. A waitress came up to us "can I take your order?" she said as we both looked round and up at the waitress. She was topless with perfect round firm looking breasts jutting out from her body. She laughed and said "my eyes are up here guy's, what would you like to drink?" I eventually closed my mouth to reopen it to give her our order without taking my eyes off her breasts. I then looked up into her smiling face as she turned away with our order. I couldn't take my eyes off her short pleated skirt and her long legs as she walked away down to the bar.

"She's gorgeous!" Peter said putting his tongue back into his mouth. There were more of them hanging around the bar collecting order. There must have been about a dozen all wearing the same very short red pleated skirt with perfect round breasts. I had never seen so many bare breasted girls and not one bad looking girl amongst them. I turned to Peter to say something but he still had his mouth open.

"What do you think Pete?"

"Bob its fucking great" he replied. The waitress returned with the drinks we paid her, leaving her a tip. "Thanks boys" she said and smiled then went to another table to clear the glasses off it and wipe the table. I couldn't help but see her blue knickers as she bent over.

"I like this place" Peter said. I turned back to answer him taking my eyes of the innocent young girls bottom.

As I said we met this crowd of people that frequented this club. They had so much money to spend it was unreal. They would order champagne like it was water, bottle after bottle with vodka chasers. They would do this all night in between dancing, and then they would go up on the level above us drink more champagne and get the topless girls to sit with them. There were about a dozen of them, girls and boys and always the same crowd. It was one weekend we were at the club and I was coming back from the toilet on the upper level. They had toilets on all the levels but I just wanted to have a look at the pole dancers. I bumped into one of the guy's and knocked his bottle of champagne out of his hand. It rolled across the floor out of control, oozing the liquid out of its long gold neck. "Oops sorry" I said turning round and going after the runaway bottle. I picked it up and handed what was left back to him. "I'm sorry; let me buy you another one?"

"No its ok, thanks" he said.

"No, I insist." I was a bit pissed or I wouldn't have insisted. The price of one of the bottles was nearly what I earned in a week. I got the attention of one of the topless waitress as I stood talking to this guy. "Could I get another one of these please?" I said pointing to the bottle that the guy was holding.

"What table sir and would you like some company?" she asked.

Before I could say anything, the guy I was talking to said "we are over there, the party of . . ."

Before he could finish, the waitress said "Oh it's for you Mr Johnston?"

"Ya ya for sure" he said. I think he was saying yes like you and I would say, but whereabouts in London was he from? ". . . and we are over there."

I gave her some money for it and she turned away in the direction of the bar. "Join us?" he said.

"No it's all right" I said "I'm with a mate."

"Bring him as well; we are over there, the nosy bunch!"

"Okay, thanks" I said and walked back down to where Peter was sitting. On the way back I thought to myself 'that guy had a lot of marbles in his throat . . . "Ya ya ya." When I got back to Peter I told him what had happened and said the bottle nearly cost me my fucking wages! "How much money have you got?" I asked him.

"Enough" he said. He got up and we walked up the red carpeted stars to the next level and to the crowd of very noisy people that were having fun. That's how we got to know this crowd.

After that we met them at the club when we were flush other times we just hid if they came in. It was on one flush night, we were all sitting up on the high level. I was looking at the topless waitresses and the half naked girls wrapping themselves round and sliding up and down the shiny stainless steel poles. One of the party members said "great place, great girls."

"Yes" I said.

"I haven't seen so many naked girls in one place before and all so very good looking. My names John and that there is my sister Jill" he said. He pointed to a girl wearing a yellow t-shirt with 'Fuck Me' printed across it in bold black letters. She saw her brother pointing and looked across the table and waved.

"I'm Bobby and that there is Peter" I said.

"Where are you from?" he said and went on to say "don't tell me is that a South African accent?"

I laughed and said "no I'm from Scotland."

"No way that's not a Scottish accent, your friend has one but I wouldn't say that yours was?"

"Well it is" I said.

"Look we're going to a party want to come?"

"Yes" I said. After more bottles of Champagne and vodka chasers and luckily before my round came, they decided to leave, thank God. There was about six of us all together as well as Peter. We all climbed into this taxi outside the club and off we went. On the way, john took a cannabis joint out all readymade. He lit it and took a long drag on it before passing it to me. I did the same and passed it to Jill who was sitting next to me. Then she did the same and passed it on and so on.

"Someone else light another" John said. "I knew that you smoked I could tell." He was getting on my tits a bit thinking that he knew everything about me from my accent and now he's saying that he knows that I smoke . . . what the fuck does he know? I must say I was a bit pissed. He then went on to say "you can tell if the person is a straight bod or not?"

I laughed and said "I know."

Peter butted in and said in my protection "he's not bent" and everyone in the taxi roared with laughter. "No, a straight bod is someone that doesn't smoke cannabis" this John guy said.

I looked at Peter and he looked at me as if to say 'fucking hell what a dick.' The taxi driver started to get uptight and told us to put that stuff out or he would get the police.

We arrived at this very plush Kensington area. The taxi drove through a sort of archway into a cobbled paved courtyard with large brightly coloured plant pots dotted about the courtyard. It was full of flowers and very fancy street lights with brightly collared hanging baskets full of flowers. It all looked very nice and well maintained. The thumping of the music hit us as we fell out of the taxi. It was coming from one of the flats, in the middle of what you could call a horse shoe shape of well kept two storey high apartments. I bent down to give Jill a hand up as I did she stood up, brushed herself down and sorted her hair.

"What is this place?" I said to her looking around at the plush area.

"Its Bills dad's town house" she replied.

"It's all right for some!" I said as Jill carried on as if she didn't hear me.

"His dads in international air freight, he . . ." she staggered and I went to help her by grabbing her arm. She swung round and put her two arms around me and looked up into my face with a glazed look. She smiled then continued saying "he's got his own airline or something like that, so if you want to go anywhere for free?" She stopped and turned round staggering. I put my hands out to stop her falling over again thanks "T-h-a-n-k-s" she said slurring the last thanks. As I helped her, she swung round and put both her arms around my neck, nearly knocking off my head and gave me a slobbery kiss partly missing my mouth. As she did my eyes were fixed on the people outside this place "this . . ." I thought "this guy's got loads of money." She still had her arm firmly fixed around my neck.

"He was at the same boarding school as my brother?"

"Who?" I said pulling her hands off my neck and back round to the front holding them tightly down between us. "Who is it Jill? Who are you talking about?"

"Bill, silly." She then struggled free and grabbed my arm and said "come on take my arm and I'll introduce you to them."

We walked on; Peter and the others had all ready disappeared into the house.

"Oh by the way, we call ourselves . . ." she stopped to fix her bag that was slipping of her shoulder. "We're the Slone Rangers."

"What?" I said.

She repeated herself and then said "you must have heard of us we're always in the papers." I wasn't listening to her I was thinking as we drew nearer to the flat, apartment, that whatever Bill's dad owned they must have lots of money. I took Jill's hand and walked towards maybe twenty or more people standing outside this amazing place. All were laughing and joking with a lot of 'ya ya,' 'rather' and 'for sure's' going on. They all had drinks in their hands and as we got close Jill said "hi gang." One of the guy's standing outside with a cravat, check shirt and flannel trousers on said in a deep very upper class English accent looking straight at Jill and ignoring me "hi darling who's the man?"

"Bobby Addis and he's one of the Addis's, you know the brush people?" She just said it for a laugh but it stuck. I smiled and just about to shake the guys hand when Jill pulled me past him and into the apartment to meet the rest of the crowd. Jill told everyone the same story and for a long time they were calling me Addis brush. They all thought that I was the son of the international brush company Addis. I didn't say I wasn't but I didn't say that I was. It was only when I met up with Peter once again in the party that he said "what's with the Addis brush thing?"

I said "don't ask, just let it slip Peter."

Then someone offered us a banger, another name for a cannabis joint. 'Why not I thought' then several pills where handed round. I left Jill with some guy at the front door as I caught sight of Peter and made a beeline for him, squeezing through the crowded room and saying to him as I got closer "what do you think of Hooray Henrys ya ya, rather, what." The way he looked at me was enough to say what he was thinking. I was about to make another rude comment about some of the people in the room when Peter stopped me by stepping on my foot.

"What!" I said then my eyes were covered by a pair of small hands. I recognised the perfume it was Jill, I put my hand up to pull them down onto my chest glancing at Peter as I held them there for a split second.

"Hey where did you go Bobby?"

Still holding her hands I turned round to face her, pushing her hands down and around behind her back. I held them there resting on her bum, looking down into her eyes and pulling her tightly into me. The three of us stood there chatting and getting pushed about in the crowded room. One of her 'ya ya' buddies squeezed his way through the room to where we were standing and said "there's some stuff on the table in the kitchen for you Jill, and if you too Bob if you're into it?"

"In to what?" I said cutting his conversion short. Before I could get answer I was led in the direction of the kitchen by Jill with Peter following. Fighting our way through the rabble as they ignored our constant attempt of being polite and excusing ourselves. We ended up just pushing them out of the way. We got to the kitchen where a small number of people were standing around a long wooden kitchen table. Girls and boys were taking their time, sitting down at the one end of the table where there were lines of coke or bombs and each boy or girl would sit down in turn and either snort a line of coke or take a bomb. They would then set a line up for the next person out of a small pile of coke that was on the table that the odd guy added to if he had any, and most of the guys did. Jill went first to a roar of laughter then it was my turn. Before I sat down I said to the bunch of guys and girls that I didn't have any to put down. The guy that was standing at the head of the table said that as I was a friend of Jill's they would oversee the matter this time, but next time I would have to bring some. I said thanks and sat down but instead of snorting a line, I opted out and went for a bomb. A bomb is just coke wrapped in a bit of tissue about the size of your small finger nail. All you do is just swallow it, to a cheer and stamping of feet. Then it was my turn to put a measured amount of coke into a tissue from the small spoon that was lying beside two plastic straws and a razor blade. They were lying next to the pile of coke on the table that people were still adding to. I thought while I sat there wrapping the drop of coke that I had measured into the tissue. Where do they get all this stuff from it's a class 'A' drug and by the look of it every third person has a bit?

I got up and walked over to where Jill was standing and pouring herself some champagne out into a tall thin glass and making a mess of it. The champagne was overflowing as it does if you pour it too fast.

"Here" I said. "Let me do it for you" as I took over the situation and poured myself one as well. In fact I took a full bottle and stood there in the kitchen topping our glasses up as we drank the chilled champagne; it was helping to fight the dryness in my mouth from the after affects of the coke. I looked at the rest of the people taking their turn along with Peter to another roar of cheering and the stamping of feet. There was an abundance of drink. Bottle after bottle of champagne, vodka and whisky, in fact there was everything you could imagine on the side dresser in the kitchen. By now I was feeling the effect of the coke along with the champagne. Jill and myself and half a dozen other people decided to leave the party in the early hours and go I don't know where. I just followed them like a little sheep following the flock. We walked and walked, I don't know where I walked even to this day but it was miles, or felt like it. We eventually arrived at a house belonging to one of the girls that was with us is in the flock and we all crashed out there.

I lay next to Jill in this bed along with another couple. I turned onto my back trying not to disturb the other three. I lay there trying to think about last night and whose house is this? I remember a blonde girl saying that we could crash out at her place because her mum and dad were away and that's about the lot. Maybe this is her place? There were too many blanks that had to be filled and the way I was feeling I couldn't be bothered thinking about it right now. Lying there next to Jill, I could feel her leg and her bum tight up against me as I lay there. Wait a minute . . . if I could feel her leg that meant that I . . .

Lifting the bedclothes just enough to peer under to see what state of dress I was in and the others, it wasn't as bad as I thought. I still had my boxers on. I looked at Jill's back and down at her bum as she lay there on her side next to the other girl that had her back to me as well. For a split second I looked at the two girls lying there and the guy at the other end, then back at Jill's perfect round bum that was covered with a pair of small blue knickers. Liking what I was looking at, I tried to look over at the front of her so that I could catch a glimpse of her breasts that where cradled firmly in a matching blue bra. I wanted a better look so I lifted the bedclothes a bit more and tried to peer over, but Jill caught me looking and said "having a good look are we." I let the covers drop back down embarrassed by getting caught. She turned right over onto her other side to look at me and cuddled up close, resting her hand on my tummy and playing with the waistband of my jocks. We talked quietly so not to disturb the others. On saying that, there were other bodies sprawled over the floor, all sleeping in the same state with half their clothes off or on with blankets thrown on top of them from last night. I imagine where they crashed out . . . . It was a mass of bodies. How we got the bed I don't know. I don't know what happened to Peter. I lost track of him somewhere between the party and going to this girl's house, no doubt I'll catch up with him back at the flat.

After that party Jill, Peter, John and I were always together and went to party's all the time, when there was any. It was at this other party that we nearly got caught at this large house just outside London. It belonged to lord so and so, he was an MP or something high in the houses of parliament. It was his son Philip that was throwing the party as daddy was away. Philip didn't like me, we just didn't hit it off you could say. He thought that Jill was too good for me. Maybe she was, but she was with me and he didn't like that. He tried all the time to separate us at the party and other times as well when our paths crossed. Which wasn't very often, but when they did he used to butt in and talk to Jill and ignore me, dickhead . . . enough bitching. We were at his party and there was a lot of Charlie going round, pill popping, snorting, and cases of the best champagne. That was made clear to me by dickhead, oh sorry Philip. Anyway it was Philip's brother that saved the day for Jill, Philip, Peter, me and two other people. There was a raid on the house and people panicked running everywhere with the police chasing them. We ran along this corridor towards a room that was leading off it, we were all laughing and joking. We got to the room, maybe it was all the chemicals that we had taken but the seriousness of the matter didn't hit us at all it was just a big joke. Maybe it was to them, they had the money and a card to get out of jail free, and I didn't! We were standing in this room that looked like a library with wall to wall books from the floor to the ceiling. Philip's brother went to the middle of the book case on one wall and a door appeared out of nowhere. "We were ushered into this small very dark room that didn't have any windows and smelt of dampness and he then shut the door behind him and it was pitch black. I could feel Jill's arms around my waist holding me tightly. I couldn't see her but I could smell her shampoo that she washed her hair with as I rested my face on the top of her head and listened for the police. We could hear them and other people shouting. Time drifted past as we stood huddled together in this small damp darkened room that was saving us from evil. When Philip's brother opened the door it took a second for my eyes to adjust to the light that was on in the library. We were told to be quiet as we walked back along to the kitchen where we fled from, but it was all quite and the police were away along with Philip. Yesss, oops sorry! It made the news that lord so and so's son was arrested in possession of illegal substances at a party at his country home outside London.

My time in London was nearly up and I decided to throw in the towel in and go home. London was great but you had to have money to survive like the Slone-Rangers. Well maybe not like the Slone-Rangers, that was taking it to the extreme but you do need money and a lot of it. Peter and I were lucky to have slipped in the back door of one of London's elite circle, if you know what I mean? If it wasn't for Jill and her brother and knocking that bottle of champagne onto the floor that night who knows? Fate perhaps, well yes maybe? Peter stayed in London and I flew home to bonny Scotland with no money. All my money went on the flight home to Glasgow and I didn't have enough to get me the rest of the way home. I had to phone my dad to come and pick me up at the airport in Glasgow. All I had from London was a hole in the sole of my boots, a pair of jeans, a t-shirt a jacket and a nine caret gold Dunhill lighter and great memories.

CHAPTER NINE

HOME AGAIN

It wasn't long before I was working back in the hotel in the dining room with my kilt back on. And I was with the girl that I briefly met before I left to go to London which was to be my future wife but I didn't know that at the time. It was winter and the hotel was quiet so I took a job at the local sawmill working during the day and then in the hotel at night with my wife to be. We got very friendly, as you do. We went to parties together, on holiday and then the obvious happened . . . yes, we got married and had the reception at the hotel. I was the first of the three brothers to get married, then a few years later my other brother got hitched and asked me if I would be his best man. I think my other brother; his twin didn't want to do it so I was asked. That reminds me of an incident at his wedding. It was just at the time where the best man reads out the telegrams. We were all sitting at the top table, I was sitting next to my brother and on the other side was the Minister. Anyway, I had to read out the telegrams and being dyslexic that was the only part I was dreading. I stood up and said what I had to say in the way of speeches and then . . . . the telegrams! I started to try and read the first two telegrams on the top of the pile and was making a balls of it. It was then that I had a brain wave, all I would have to do is read them out individually like I was doing but I would just make each one up as I read them out. No one would know. The Grooms side would think that I was talking about the Bride's side and vice-versa. It was going down a treat. I even got so confident that I would make up jokes about each side saying that Aunt Betty said something. Everyone would laugh then I would hand them to the Minister and he put them down in a tidy pile in front of him until he read one of the telegrams that I handed him. After I had the crowd in stitches about something I said about the groom, my brother. This time as I handed the Minister the telegram he looked at it, and with a puzzled look on his face he looked up at me as if to say "What are you doing?" He then looked up to the sky as if he was asking the Lord and then he looked back down to the pile of telegrams sitting in front of him as if he was praying for me. He never said a thing.

To get back to when I got married . . . We didn't have a house at that particular time. We were given a residential caravan for a wedding present . . . yes, a caravan! It was a second-hand one, off the caravan site that was next door to the hotel. When we were away on our honeymoon they sited it, and plumbed it in next to the hotel, well behind the hotel to the left on the ground belonging to the hotel. When we came back it was already for us to move into apart from bits and pieces to do. That leads me to a small incident. There were three small wooden steps leading up to the caravan and the second step was broken. My wife was always asking me to fix it, being a D-I-Y man. I decided to fix them after months of nagging. So I bought a plank of wood from the local do-it-yourself shop, some nails, a saw and bits and bobs as you do. I brought the things home and my wife said would I look after our daughter as she had to go to the hotel to work, plus she was pregnant with our other baby. I told her what I was going to do and it wouldn't be a bother. Our daughter was just coming up for a year old and she was all wrapped up warm in a baby bag! You know the thing you put the baby in, then you zip it up the front so they're all enclosed in this cloth bag with just their face showing. 'A grow bag!' as I called it.

Anyway I propped her up against this old piece of wood that was sticking out of the ground and talked to her and made stupid noises and started to fix the step. I got the plank of wood, got my tape out and measured the top step to get the right size. I then put the plank of wood on the top step to rest it so that I could cut it to size. I thought there's nothing to this D-I-Y-stuff. Just before I started to cut the piece of wood I looked round at my baby girl to see her rolling down the grass banking over and over . . . *shit!* I dropped everything and ran after her catching up with her in a clump of brambles, shit, shit! She was alright and smiling as if it was great fun. All she had was a very little scratch on her face. I picked her up in her grow bag, took her back up the slope talking to her all the way to where she was lying in the first place and put her down making her extra safe this time. I made more stupid noises to her as you do then continued on with my D-I-Y. Picking up the saw I started to cut the plank that was resting on the top step and found it was getting quite hard to cut for some reason. I stopped and had a look to see what the matter was and why the saw was getting stiff to push through. Oops, I had cut partly through the top step . . . fuck! I took the piece of wood off and looked at the step; it was all right I thought it's not right through. I carried on cutting the plank that was to be the second step on a tree stump that was sticking out of the ground, trying to balance it with my foot as I cut it and make stupid noises to my daughter that was looking at me. No doubt thinking 'god is that egit my dad! Anyway I finished the job, stood back and looked at my handy work and thought it's not too bad for me. I looked at the top step where I had cut it gave it a bit of a rub with my hand as if it would disappear but it didn't. I stood back to admire my handy work, thinking as I stood there that I'll get some brownie points for this! I started to clean up grabbing the saw, the rest of the nails and hammer before starting to walk up the steps to go into the caravan to put the tools away. I stood on the first step then onto the second feeling very proud of myself. I even turned to my daughter and said "see you were wrong daddy isn't an egit!" As I stepped on the top step it snapped with my weight and the hammer and saw went through the glass door of the caravan shattering it into little pieces . . . Oh fuck! Picking myself up, I looked round at my baby girl smiling away to herself properly thinking "you are a fucking egit." Cleaning up the mess I thought that I would leave D-I-Y—alone perhaps.

But before all this happened I had an accident at the mill. I was working one of the big saws when a large piece of wood hit me in the face, well the jaw and smashed it. I did about two somersaults and landed on my back, there was blood everywhere. I ended up in hospital going in and out of consciousness. They cleaned me up, gave me morphine to ease the pain, and sent me to a large dental hospital in Glasgow, where they took impressions and tried to piece together my jaw that was smashed in three parts. They eventually phoned my dentist for my dental records, I suppose to help them to work out what went where and to piece the jaw back to its original or near original way it was. They needed to rebuild it and luckily none of my teeth were broken, just the bottom part of the jaw was knocked right over to the left side of my mouth and in bits. I was there for two or three days then they sent me home with my jaw set and wired up so that I couldn't open it. I was okay but a bit black and blue with bruising. I had to attend the hospital twice a week so that they could check that it was healing correctly. I still worked in the dining room with my jaw wired together and it was one of the American officers that stopped me, he said as I was clearing his table "*Bobby* did they give you wire cutters to snip the wires?"

"No" I said the best as I could by just moving my lips then I said "why?"

"Just in case you're sick and choke on your vomit." Great, I was all right till then. I had never thought about it. Luckily it didn't happen, the wires were cut and I was back to normal if I was ever normal . . . apart from a scar on my chin.

Well, we lived in the caravan for quite a while and my wife gave birth to a baby boy. We were always looking for a place to live. Several places came up but they were always too much and then we found a place, a derelict cottage. It had no roof just four walls and a mud floor with bushes and small trees growing inside and on the walls. The cottage was a mess, but it had potential. What am I thinking about . . . look what I did to the steps of the caravan, and now I'm thinking of taking on building or renovating a whole house! It took a while to find out who owned it and if they wanted to sell. We eventually got it from the two sisters that owned it. Once they agreed to a price, then we got a mortgage and started work on clearing it out. We couldn't do much until we got plans drawn up and then submitted them to Argyll and Bute's Planning Department. Once we got them back after a long while, as you know that sort of thing takes a while, I had to look for someone to restore it back to its original state. I knew of an old man that came into the hotel pub. But, before that there was one thing that we were not allowed to buy and that was a very large story book that was in the grounds of the cottage. In fact it was the largest fairly tale book in the world! It stood about ten to eleven feet high maybe a bit more and it was about eight foot wide. Each page was an inch thick and made out of plywood I think. Each page was full of fairy stories all hand written in old Scottish words and fancy writing. It was the tallest story book in the world. Now it is fully restored and in the Edinburgh museum along with the smallest book, but when it was in the garden it was lying flat under some old canvases in a hell of a mess. The people that we bought the cottage from had it moved to a Nissan-hut on a caravan site down the road from the cottage. You could go and see the book, it was propped up inside this tin hut with branches from trees and bits of stuff out of the wood to make it look like an Elves house, and in fact it looked a mess. There was a piano which an old mad man used to play dressed up in Elves clothing and he used to bang away on this piano and shout out things. When I say bang away I mean bang away. He couldn't play it at all. He would shout out as he hit the lowest key on the piano several times and say "read the book the wind is coming?" I don't know what the wind had to do with it? But as I said he was really right out his trolley, completely mad. The book and the mad-man were there for some time until they came for him, the men in their little white coats and put him in a home, the best place for him. The book was then given to Edinburgh's museum to restore it and that's where it is to this day. Getting back to the cottage as I said, this old man was a retired builder, plumber come handy man. He could turn his hand to anything. Just the guy I needed I thought; I would do all the donkey work while he did all the professional work.

So one night we were in the pub, he was having a drink that I'd bought him. I said to him would he like to help me? We agreed to the price that suited both of us and work began. My wife and I with the help of the handy-man worked on that cottage as often as we could, but the hotel took up most of our time and always caused arguments when I said that I was going round to the cottage to work on it. I don't know why it caused a fuss, but it did with mum and dad but luckily the joiner or handy-man knew what to do. All we had to do at first was to supply all the materials for the job and tidy up after him. On saying that my wife and I had to dig out years and years of mud and rubbish out of the ground inside the cottage, then once we had cleared it we then had to dig down about four to five feet in order to concrete it and put in a damp course. The wooden joists were then put down, and then the wooden flooring across the full length of the cottage so the handy-man could start building uprights to separate each room. The cottage was a long low stone built type with five holes in the shape of windows along the front and a large hole where the door would eventually be. At the back of the cottage my wife and I took down part of the back wall with the help of the handy-man to fit French windows that we put in eventually, but for a long time there was just a large sheet of polythene draped over the hole where the wall used to be. We worked hard on that cottage as the kids played amongst the sand and the cement and all the dust, they got into some mess. All the labouring was done by my wife and I, she was excellent looking after two kids doing a lot of the manual work as well, plus working very long hours in the hotel.

We eventually got it liveable but nowhere near finished. It needed decorating, painted and carpets bought. We had to sort out the kitchen units and a whole lot of things but it looked great. There was a kitchen at one end with an Aga stove system and as you came out of the kitchen there was a bathroom on the left and a long corridor with a natural stone wall running along the whole of the right side of the cottage. It was split up by the five holes that where now proper sash corded old fashioned type windows and on the left side where the bedrooms would be, two of them. At the far end there was a large open-plan living room come dining room with a large stone built fireplace on the end wall. It was looking good! All our hard work and the handy-mans had paid off, we left the caravan and moved into the cottage, things where looking okay. I had a great wife, two great kids and two dogs. One was a Heinz 57 variety it was a mixture between a Scotty and something and the other was so different it was Irish setter pedigreed to the hilt, highly strung and completely bananas it was a bit like the lady and the tramp. Anyway we got the house finished and it was so good to live in a place with stone walls not wood and metal. We liked it so much it had character plus it was the first proper home we had as a family. We got it carpeted throughout, pictures on the wall and a lot of thing you buy to make the place a home. The next thing was to tackle the garden, it was still like a building site but I was still working in the hotel. I had to drive there now it wasn't just a walk up the back but it was worth it. But it was the time factor, working long hours at the hotel and then driving home it didn't leave much time to do much in the garden. That's if I wanted to do it on the only time I had off, what do you think?

CHAPTER TEN

DISASTER

It was six or seven months later maybe not as long as that, we were woken by dusty the Heinz 57 dog whimpering and the other dog barking. My wife turned round saying "didn't you let Dusty out last night?" I put on the light to see Dusty floating around in her plastic bed. I quickly jumped out of bed to find that the bedroom floor was about a foot deep in water. I opened the door of the bedroom to go and check on the kid's and the whole of the house was flooded. My wife got up and we made our way to the kid's room wading through about two foot of water. I could hear the kids giggling and on opening the door I could see why. Most of the toy's that where full of air where floating around their cot's and they where kneeling at the bottom of them pushing their bigger toys away and having a great time. It took us the rest of the day and most of the next to get the water out. We lifted the carpets and found where the water came from. We found that the river at the back of the house had burst its banks and as the house was a foot or more lower than the road and the old septic tank that was on the same level with the house. The flood water ran into the tank and back along the west pipe and up out the toilet and into the house. Luckily it was just muddy water nothing else. I can't remember if we were insured or not. I don't know if you've ever had your home flooded, the waters not that bad okay it's bad but it's what the water brings with it. Luckily as I said, the flood water had just run in and straight out the septic tank without getting mixed with you know what! But it had been in the tank and it was very muddy water and it left its mark. So as I said we had to lift all the carpets in all the rooms and redecorate the whole place again. It took most of all our money for paint and new wallpaper but we got there in the end, as you do. The place was looking good again and we loved our stone built cottage and the space it gave us, it was so different from the caravan.

After that incident our solicitor phoned us and suggested that we should up the insurance just in case something like that happens again, God forbid. It would mean you would have enough insurance this time to cover everything. We said we would do it BUT it slipped our minds. Well it didn't slip our minds we said that we would do it next week, as you do. We were out shopping at the weekend about a month after the call from our solicitor, with the kids getting the weeks shopping and an electric lawnmower so we could cut the grass. On our return home we were about the last corner from the house, we could see thick black smoke bellowing up into the sky and my wife said fuck the house is on fire! No no, it's not it's someone burning rubbish. As we turned the corner she was right, it was.! Fuck, fuck. We pulled up onto the grass verge about two or three yards away from the house. We couldn't get any closer because of all the people that were standing on the road looking at the house. One of the instructors from the outward bound School whom we knew very well came running up to me as I was standing a couple of yards from the car. I looked at the house in disbelief, completely bewildered.

"*Bobby I have phoned the fire brigade, they're on their way what can I do?*"

"*G*o and see my wife she's in the car with two kids!"

The house hadn't burst into flames it was just smouldering, with thick black smoke escaping where ever it could, getting blown up high into the sky. My wife came up and said "*the dogs, they're still inside!*" I ran round to the back of the cottage where the French doors were. They were black and I couldn't see in. I touched one of the small glass panels; there was about a dozen in each door. It was like burnt paper, disintegrating on touch.

I went to open the French windows and the rest of the blackened glass in the small panels just vanished and blew away in a current of hot air like it was paper. All that I was left with was a very black wooden door frame with a dozen small square panels where the glass used to be. And the heat well, it was just incredible. It was like pre-heating your oven to maximum then opening the door with your face in front of it.

The heat just hit me. I walked in, the smoke was hot and it burnt my face and throat as I tried to breathe. I had to go down on my knees and start to feel my way along the floor searching for the dogs. The smoke was thick, black and incredibly hot, I couldn't see a thing. Every time I tried to stare through the thick black choking smoke my eyes started to run. I could feel them burning in their sockets. I closed them but they still stung. My whole body told me to get out but I had to find the dogs! I started to fumble about insanely around the dining room come living room hopelessly searching. I had a picture in my mind were everything was and where I thought the dogs would lie, but they weren't there. I made my way along the long corridor but I could only make it just over half way. The hot choking smoke was too intense and the heat was just too much. I had to turn back crawling on all fours. The smoke was getting too much for me. I thought "my dogs, fuck where are they!" I even tried to shout and call their names but I choked on the thick black smoke. I tried to take a breath and choked again. I was desperately trying to catch a bit of clean air, any air. The hot smoke continued to burn my throat. I had to get back outside to the open and the fresh air. Turning round on my hands and knees my heart was pounding and heavy thinking about my dogs.! The tears from my eyes ran down over my hot checks as I desperately crawled back through the densely smoke filled corridor, choking on every breath, back to the doors and into the open air. As the first of the fresh air hit my lungs I started to cough, I was bent over with one hand on the side of the house and the other resting on my knee desperately trying to get my breath. I heard my wife's voice say *"well?"*

I had to say "no, I can't find them!" We walked round to the front of the house, both our hearts heavy thinking of the dogs and thinking we can always get another house, but we couldn't get another Heinz 57 Dusty dog or the mad Irish setter. By this time the house was a light at the far end. Maybe it was my fault by opening the doors that caused it to ignite, creating a through draught. The whole house was a time bomb just waiting. The flames were leaping out of the kitchen windows and up into the sky as we got back to the front of the house and to the screams of the onlookers standing along the roadside. There was a large bang and the flames emerged through the roof, getting blown about by the wind looking for something else on the house to devour in its path. We heard the sound of the fire engine, it appeared round the corner and the people that were looking on moved out the way to let them through and get to the house.

The tender blocked the whole of the road as the men rushed to get the hose out and start to pour water onto the house. There were hoses all over the road and water. As I talked to the man in charge he asked me if I had any gas cylinders or anything that might explode. I said "no I don't think so . . . yes, a calor gas fire." Just then there was a big bang inside, blowing out the front two windows onto the road? "That's the gas cylinder" I think I said just as the fireman put his hand out and said *"look out stand back!"* The flames leaped out of the windows. The other fireman on the end of the hose tried to keep the fire under control but there was only a limited amount of water in the tender. I heard over the noise of the tenders engine and the house crackling as the fire developed, more and more of the house sending thick black smoke and sparks spiralling up high into the sky that the pressure was falling. The fireman, who was just talking to me turned to another fireman and said *"connect up to the hydro . . ."* The main hydro was luckily just where we were standing; the metal cover had just been painted bright yellow and checked by the fire department a week ago. My wife and I stood looking in horror as the wind continued to whip up the flames into the sky right after the fireman had just got them under control. We moved out the way so that the other fireman could open the top of the bright yellow hydro cover so he could connect the hose giving a new batch of water. I thought "come on, come on!" I was in two minds of pushing him out the way and doing it myself. "GOD, I could do it much quicker myself!" Then as he connected the hose to the hydrant and turned it on we turned to look at the man holding the end of the hose, it was just like a carry on film! He was looking straight down at the end of the hose with water dripping out the end with a puzzled look on his face. He then would point it at the house and give it another shake. He then looked at the other fireman who was standing at the hydrant with his fire helmet and his brightly coloured jacket and trousers on and shouted to him "have you turned it on yet?"

Meanwhile the wind had whipped up the flames again and they where swirling around going *"munchety munchety"* devouring more and more of our house. I looked and thought that they might have saved it if they hadn't run out of water? My thoughts were interrupted by my wife shaking me and saying in a hysterical voice "do something for fuck sake!" There was panic in her voice and tears in her eyes. I looked at both the firemen, the one on the end of the hose and the other standing at the main hydrant and they both looked at me in disbelief. Just then the fireman in charge said to me *"the hydro appears to have no water?"*

"What! WHAT!" I said.

"Where's the nearest burn?"

"What, for fuck sake!" I said.

"No need for that sort of language" he shouted, up close and in my face.

What sort of language would you use if you were watching your house burn to the fucking ground? Then I got control of myself and said "there's a burn across that field, if you cut the fence and drive through. It will be all right I know the farmer and he won't mind.

He then turned to me and said to my amazement and disbelief "can't do that I might scratch or damage the tender."

"*WHAT!* Cut it, cut the fucking fence or I'll do it!"

"No" he said then grabbed the fireman who was standing at the hydrant next to my wife and our two kids who didn't know what was going on, with my wife standing in disbelief. *"Go and get the pump from the back of the tender and go across the field . . ."*

I stopped him and said "drive the fucking thing through, what the fuck's wrong with you?" He just ignored me and carried on saying *". . . to the burn and start pumping the water from it."*

I looked on in amazement as the two firemen walked across the field, yes, they walked. As they got to the burn I could see one of them running back to the tender and say to the other fireman that he had forgotten the filter for the end. By this time the house was well and truly away and there was nothing any one could do to save it. I looked at my wife holding the youngest of our kids in her arms with its dirty face and the other holding onto my wife's hand with a half empty yogurt carton in her other hand. Most of it was on her chin and down her front. No one was bothering to clean her there was just too much going on to be bothered with that! I looked at my wife and she looked at me in disbelief, tears in her eyes looking at our house burn away back to the four stone walls that it started out with. Looking on I couldn't help but think that the whole house was jinxed!

It took us a long time to find who owned the house. Then of course they couldn't make up their minds if they wanted to sell it or not. Then it flooded. And now it's burning to the ground taking everything we have and own along with it, leaving the four stone walls of the cottage standing, how we first found it. All the timbers burning away, everything we owned. Just the clothes we were wearing, no change of clothing for the kids. All they had were the clothes on their backs. A weeks shopping, an electric flymo, everything all gone up in smoke! We left the firemen to finish of putting out what was left of the cottage and tidy up as we walked back to the car. Through all the people still standing there, looking at what was left of the cottage all staring in disbelief. We didn't say anything, we just sat there looking at what was left of our burnt out cottage. I started the car and drove back to my parents' hotel not a word said between us. Everyone in the nearby village was so kind to us at that particular time. One family said if we wanted we could stay the night with them and bath the kids. Another couple, a lady doctor and her husband gave us nappies for the youngest one and lots of other things. They were so kind I don't know if we ever thanked them for their kindness. So if they ever read this book, both my wife and I thank you from the bottom of our hearts for your kindness that day. The fireman stopped at the hotel later that night and said to me that they had found the dogs, they were under the bed. I felt a heavy feeling in my heart as he told me. He said was that they would have died before the fire got to them from the smoke. He then told me that he had put them outside with a rug over them. "Thanks" I said.

Early next morning I went back to the cottage. I got there to see that there was nothing left, just a burnt out shell. Everything had either burnt or melted with the intense heat. I grabbed the spade and went to where the fireman had put the dogs. I dug a hole for both of them under a tree at the side of the cottage near the fence. I stood there for a while, looking down at the two small bumps in the ground saying a small prayer, trying to fight back the tears thinking that only yesterday they were running around here in the garden barking. I looked at what was left of the cottage "shit what the fuck am I going to do now? I felt so down there was no one to talk to and tell how I felt. I had lost everything. Picking up the spade I walked towards the cottage my eyes full, trying not to cry. I walked round the cottage looking at the burnt out shell and half burnt timbers and looking at the coal bunker that I'd built next to the cottage. It too had burnt away leaving the coal inside still burning. Walking on around and through the burnt out shell that was my dream cottage and all that hard work, thinking where the kids room was, the living room, the bathroom and then the kitchen. The Aga was still there, all the paint had burnt of it and it was covered with burnt out rubbish that had fallen on to it. Brushing of the bits and pieces I felt it, fuck it was still hot. I looked into the fire box it was still half full of coal and still alight. Standing there looking at the Aga thinking, "God what a good advert for Aga." For some reason a slogan popped into my mind:

Aga it's always there for you,
Warm on those long winter nights,
When you come in and put on the light's,
In rain and in sleet when you come in off the streets,
Even when your house burns to the ground,
It's there for you to cook on, reliable
It won't let you down.

Then I thought about the flymo that I had bought and smiled "Shit, I've nowhere to plug it into to cut the grass?" Thinking of these silly things made me feel a lot better, I even smiled to myself. Then I heard a sound of a car stopping. I turned round to see who it was; a BT van and a fat middle aged man with hardly any hair got out and walked over to where I was. "Mr. Addis, BT sir, I have come about the phone!"

"What" I said thinking that I didn't pick him up right.

"Did you manage to retrieve the phone?"

I cut him short waving the spade around my head saying "get the fuck away you stupid little man. Go on fuck off . . ." I let go the spade and it hit of the side of the van with a loud bang ending up on the road beside it.

"There's n*o need to be like that you know?*"

I cut him short and said again "go on fuck off!"

As he hurriedly got back into the van, I walked to get the spade as he drove off shouting out his window "the phone is the property of BT!"

"Go on fuck off!" He made a quick retreat down the road. I went to pick up the spade from where it bounced off the side of the van thinking "how could anyone in their right mind send someone all the way out here to see if I had saved their phone!

"Oh yes! I managed to unscrew your phone from the wall and give it a little clean while my house burnt down . . ." What a dickhead. Standing at the side of my car looking at the burnt out cottage I thought "oh well at least we're all safe. We can always find another house somewhere! Thinking back I could probably have taken the water board to court. They had turned off the water at the village about three miles down the road, so there was no water going up the glen whilst they cleaned and painted the hydro covers and inspected them. If I had taken a photo of the Aga and sent it in with what I'd said or something similar, I might have got money from them as well, who knows! But I didn't and there's no point looking back. Well we got our insurance for the cottage; it wasn't much. If only I'd done what I was told on that day! So don't put off tomorrow what you can do today! Great words from me . . . We got the money from the insurance and got a small four-berth caravan. We put it on the site (back to a caravan!) It was smaller than the one that we started out with. The council informed us that we had to knock the four remaining walls down because they were not safe to build on due to the heat from the fire. It had dried out the mortar in the stonewalls, so we were even worse off than before. All we were left with was a pile of rubble, burnt out timbers and a two-berth caravan after four year, fuck!

CHAPTER ELEVEN

HOPE

My wife did all the paperwork to apply for a two bedroom bungalow to be built on the site of the old cottage and more, plus look after two small kids and me in a very small caravan and another two year old Irish setter that we were told about. The woman that we got it from used to lock it up in a shed all the time because it kept running off. Well, that's just what we needed at this particular time another mad setter, but it was nice and it was so good to the kids. They used to pull its tail and ears and it just lay there taking it all until you let it out, then it would take off like a bat out of hell and the more you called it back the faster it would run away, but it would return when it was really knackered! Luckily, we didn't have any neighbours to worry about, well there were two but they didn't live near, it was just open fields and hills. We knew the farmer; I used to help him sometimes he was an elderly man in his seventies with bad arthritis, a great old guy. He used to travel all over the farm on a old grey petrol/diesel Massey Ferguson tractor that his father must of owned it was that old! He used to sit on the tractor and bang on the front of it with his shepherd's crook and his black and white border collie would do all the work. Like when he banged twice and shouted a command the dog would go right, if he wanted the dog to go left all he would do was bang once and shout another command and the dog would run off in another direction. To get him to lie down was just a long whistle. His dog knew every command. When he was rounding up the sheep or the cattle the old person didn't have to get off his tractor once, it was quite an amazing thing to watch him and his dog. If his dog got too tired, all it would do was just jump up on the tractor and sit on the back with the old person. He had lived on the farm all is life it was his father's farm and now it was his and he would leave it to his son. The only thing was that his son didn't want it, he had a son and a daughter and none of them wanted the farm, it was a shame in a way. The farm would be sold off after he and his elderly wife died, after all those years being in the one family.

We stayed in that caravan for quite a while. The winter was hellish you would put on the heater and the cooker to get warm and then the condensation would make everything damp. In the summer, the midges would get you if you opened the window and if you didn't, the condensation again would make everything damp. It wasn't the best of living arrangements but beggars can't be choosers as they say? My wife and I worked out that it would be cheaper to go for the old farm house at the top of the glen, which was coming up for sale, than to build a new bungalow from scratch and I mean from scratch. We would have to buy everything from knives, forks and spoons to, well everything you can think of from furnishings, painting the place and decorating everything again. You my say to yourself that a new house is better than an old stone built farmhouse but in all honesty, we didn't have the money to build and decorate a new house. It would be better to sell the ground with planning for a three-bedroom bungalow on an acre of ground and get a mortgage, buy the old farmhouse and get the hell out of here. So, when we had a row and I slammed the door so that I couldn't hear my wife going on at me I wasn't standing outside! We decided to go for it; my wife was already friendly with the young wife of the professor. He had bought the house for somewhere to stay in the country for his wife. They already had a house in England where he lectured in a university but it was too quiet for her so they agreed to sell the house to us for a bit more than they paid for it. When they bought the farmhouse it was a mess, he was getting it restored back to what it was like but it was still in a mess. All he had done was three rooms and that was a kitchen, one bedroom and a bathroom. He just had the three rooms watertight so when they came to stay they had some comfort, but not much! There were no wooden frames for the glass to fit in the windows all they had was corrugated sheeting over them to stop the rain from coming in. Apart from the rooms they lived in, the rest of the house was just as it was when they bought it, part of the roof was leaking and the rain ran down the walls and stained them. Over the years, it rotted the floorboards. But it was better than the shitty caravan! The transaction went through and we had an old eight-roomed stone built farmhouse that needed a hell of a lot of work, but it was heaven compared with the caravan and we started all over again. You may think that we were mad going for the farmhouse in the state it was in, but it had a homely atmosphere and it didn't have any neighbours apart from the old farmer who had all the ground around the farmhouse. He had bought the ground off whoever owned it before the professor. Therefore, the farmhouse did not come with any land only the ground it was sitting on and that wasn't bad. It had a long drive way and a biggish garden, outhouses with a large long stone built barn/garage. At the back looking over the fields to the hills, was another long wooden shed for storing hay or something like that? It was a great outlook over fields and hills and was a great place to bring up our kids. It was only two or three miles up the country road from where the other cottage was, but it was amazing. Okay, so it had to have a lot of work done to it, but we already had a bedroom and a bathroom done and a kitchen, it was ten times better than the caravan was. I phoned up my trusty old friend the do-it-yourself handy man that helped me build the cottage and he was more than happy to help me with my new project to restore the old farmhouse.

It has been a year since the three of us started to restore the house. Once we got the upstairs finished, the place was looking amazing. My wife had applied for a grant to help us with the roof. The roof itself was structurally okay but needed new roof slates. They were mostly fucked to put it mildly and most of them were missing. We patched it the best we could to stop the rain from coming in, we took slates from an old building across the field from the house, which was falling down, and the farmer said that we could use them to patch our roof luckily they were the same. Then we got the grant it was a 90% grant so that meant that we could get the roof redone in the old traditional slates so it would match the old farmhouse. As well as the roof, we got new double glazing windows, front and back doors in the same old tradition. The company that was doing all this for us did a few other things as well for us as they were there. By the time they left, the old farmhouse was looking good. I found out who had the house before the professor. It belonged to a family who had it for years and years. There were two brothers, a sister and a father; I don't know what happened to the mother. Anyway, it was two cousins that got married and their kids weren't all there, if you know what I mean? The father brought them up by himself. They were left the house and whatever money he had, but as I said they weren't all there and when the money ran out they all stayed in the house together. To keep warm when the wood and coal ran out they started to burn the furniture and then the wooden window frames and anything wooden that they could find in the house or outside. However, as time went on the chimney got blocked and the smoke just came down into the house and out the windows or where the windows used to be. They had already burnt them by knocking out the glass and ripping the wood apart. It wasn't long before they were taken into care and the house was sold and the money was spent on looking after them. Over the years they lived there the smoke had left its toll on the woodwork it was thick with soot all through the house. We had to clean most of it off but every time you added water and whatever we used to clean it off, it would just smear and spread further. The room with the fire in it was the worst, we eventually gave up and covered up the walls with plasterboard and the ceiling and persevered with the wooden doorframes and the skirting's.

We lived there for about twenty years or so. The kids had a great time growing up there they had a pony each and my wife had her own horse. The kids went to the local school in the village and they and my wife got onto Scottish television on the news protesting against the closure of the local school. The STV news film crew came and filmed my two kids going to school and coming back, but the local people in the village and us lost and they closed the school and the kids eventually went to the grammar school in Dunoon. We still had a lot to do to the farmhouse but we did it bit by bit. When we got extra money, I left the hotel and worked for a Forestry company as part of a ten-man squad. I did this for about two years learning everything to do with forestry. I then had a break from forestry only to go back to it after four years. I bought a small cafe called Papa-Sam's, we sold pizzas and Mexican food mostly to the Americans that were staying in Dunoon at that time and other local food like fish and chips. Most of the trade was with the Americans. We got a good name for making pizzas and the Mexican food so at the end of each month when the Americans were paid it was mobbed. We even did a pizza delivery and then I went into renting out videos in the same place. We used to say, *"Rent a video* *and get your six and a half inch pizza free!" I*t was good but when the Americans knew they would be leaving Dunoon I thought it was time to sell and get out before they left.

Just before I sold the Pizza place, I took time out and went with my son and some of his friends' paintballing. Well the real reason why my son asked me was, one of his friends couldn't make it and I took his place to make up the numbers. It was great fun firing paint balls at the other team until I jumped down onto a wooden bridge, slipped and broke my leg in three different places. The game had to be stopped for the paramedics to come and take me to hospital, to the embarrassment of my son when he found it was me that broke my leg? I got to the hospital with bones sticking out my leg, I was told it was the tibia, the fibula and my ankle was even broken and had gone round the wrong way instead of pointing up it was just dangling and flapping down the wrong way. I was given morphine and a while later the doctor and the nurse came back and started to push the bones back into my leg one by one. They then straightened up my foot with me looking on as if it was someone else's leg, I didn't feel a thing. They put a plaster on my leg, kept me in for a night then sent me home with a plaster the full length from round my foot all the way up to the top of my thigh. After a while I went back to get it cut off and shortened down to just below my knee.

I sold Papa-Sams and went back to the forestry contracting the same work as before, but I was self-employed instead of being employed. Working for myself a lot of people say is better than working for someone. I don't know, I did both and there's a lot to be said for a monthly wage coming in regularly than struggling to make ends meet all the time and getting things on tick! I got into felling trees as well as planting, weeding and fertilizing them. Everything I had learnt with the forestry even deer dragging which I will tell you about in a while. It took me a long time to get the swing of cutting the trees down. I didn't make much money at first because I was totally inexperienced and like any visceral work there's an easy way and a hard way and until someone shows you the easy way, you can struggle for ages the hard way trying to make money with no success. At the end of the day you are completely fucked, or you haven't been quick enough to put your lifting bar in the gap that you've cut in order to lever the tree over. It comes back on your saw jamming it! Eventually when you have managed to get the tree over, after spending a good half hour or more you find that you have bent your saw bar and you don't have a spare one. By the time you have done all that, the days fucked and you are the same! As an example, you have to cut a hundred trees down to make some money. If you don't cut them down you don't make enough money it's as simple as that . . . and not forgetting you have to get some petrol, oil, and a new bar for your saw before the next day and money to take home to live on? It's a hard, hard life in the wood and very dangerous not just cutting the ones that are standing, that's no problem when you get into it. The wind blow is the big problem it's so dangerous. Wind blow is where all or most of your trees are blown over by the wind and some of them are broken off half way up or they are trapped under another tree that has fallen over and landed on top of the other, bending it over and holding it down. There could be eight or more trees like this all in a big heap. The tension on these trees to cut is scary to say the least. One wrong move or wrong cut and you are either snapped in half by the one that was being held down by the one you cut by mistake, or your head is ripped off your body with the tree that was under the one you just cut when it springs up like a catapult and as fast as one. You don't have time to think so when your cutting wind blow you've got to have your wits about you and know what tree to cut first and where to cut it, so you don't get hit by the one underneath.

Apart from the difficulties of working in the wood, more downs than ups, I met this other contractor his name was Robby, he was from Oban. His father owned a fishing boat but Robby was taking time out from fishing and cutting trees down, or so he said? I got on all right with him but at first, he didn't talk much. He kept himself to himself and it was only when I went to him for help. I had a tree hung up; well more than one, in fact there were about six. A tree when it is hung up it means that when you've cut it it's fallen onto another tree that is standing and you can't get it down. You can sometimes, if it's small, put your shoulder underneath it, lift it up and run with it in the opposite direction so it comes down. These trees were big fuckers and the only way to get them down was to cut another tree onto it and hope that that tree will knock it down. You can cut the bottom of the tree so it shortens it and by doing that it might slip off the one it is resting on, but you don't want to do that because you are losing money. Anyway, I got Robby to help me and he laughed at me and said "what a fucking mess Addis." That's when he started to talk to me and show me how to cut properly. I got on well with him after that. My wife and I even went to stay with him and his wife in Oban. His father and mother and the rest of his family lived on Mull, an Island off the west coast of Scotland. We even went to stay with his family on Mull on several occasions for weekends. We got very friendly with the whole family; his old man even said if I wanted a job on the boat, he would give me one. I laughed and said, "I might take you up on that if I don't make in the cutting scene."

Robby said, "You might as well start now with my old-man because you're no good at cutting?" At that, they all started to laugh.

I left that contract and Robby and started one of my own. However, I always asked Robby for advice and kept in touch with him and his family. I even got a job on his old man's boat. Well it was a fourteen-day trial but I'll tell you about that later. I met this other contractor several weeks after on another job. We got talking as you do and both said instead of fighting for contracts between each other we should join forces and make up a company and call it Add-ski! We came up with the name I think, sitting on the hillside one afternoon having a break from cutting. I think he suggested Add-ski. It was the start of my name and his nickname and we put them together and came up with Add-ski. Well we started to work together, he lived in a small flat about twenty miles away from the farm house and I used to go and pick him up every day until my wife said why doesn't he come and stay in the spare room here it will save you going to pick him up all the time. So he did. We did all sorts of work from landscaping people's gardens, to grass cutting, and that reminds me of an incident. We were landscaping a garden, I was driving a quad bike across this garden on a slope when it tipped over and landed on top of me trapping my arm in-between the bars of the bike and a rock that was sticking out of the ground and snapped my arm! Yes, you could say that I'm unlucky! I went to casualty where I was told that there wasn't a doctor on duty so I was given a couple of pain killers and told to wait for the doctor and sent to the day room where there were two other patients sitting in their dressing gowns watching TV. That's no lie. I was there for an hour with my arm swollen up like a balloon waiting for the doctor. Once again, I got a plaster on my arm for so many months. However, we even dragged Deer off the hills that people had shot. The forestry got many foreign people coming over here to Scotland for Deer stalking and to shoot Stags. They would take the head of the Stag with the antlers on, home as a trophy. The Forester would tell where they had shot the stag and it was our job to go and find it and drag the headless body down off the hill. It was very hard work dragging them off the hills. Once we even climbed the wrong hill! You would have to walk up the hill and then along to find where they had shot the stag. Normally the Forester would tape of the area around the stag so we could see where it was when we got close to it. Trying to find a stags body lying down in the bracken and heather on a hill the same colour was a nightmare sometimes. When we had walked for miles, we would come across it, then tie ropes round its legs, and drag the 280lb stag sometimes bigger, along and down the hill to the road. It's not as easy as it sounds. It used to hit every little bump on the hill then we had to stop, lift it up or round it and then carry on dragging it. It then would come to another bump and stop us again in our tracks. Sometimes we would have to bring them down through the wood, fighting with the stag and the low branches of the trees it was a nightmare. Even then, we would get lost in the wood. I can hear you say, "Why didn't we use some motorised transport?" Mainly the hills that we climbed were too steep for any bike and the woodlands were too thick with the trees being planted so close together.

Anyway, Addski grew and grew and we employed about twenty or more people, got large machinery, two skyline winches, harvesters and forwarders to go in to the forest cut the trees down, and pull them out of the wood down onto the forestry road where we worked. They say that one harvester is the equivalent to about twenty men cutting by hand! But they are very fast; to see one in full swing is incredible plus we had a mobile sawmill that would cut whole trees into planks or fencing posts. It was quite a good set up but the big machines where very expensive to maintain plus the lease hire. Overall, there was a lot of money going out and not so much coming in. We also did a chemical spraying contract with the forestry commission, but even with all that going on with wages and repairs, just the running cost of the whole operation was a lot. The final crunch came when one day I was coming home with four men in a pickup after a day chemical spraying. It was a very hot summer's day and we were all knackered. I was driven across this field on our way home and drove into a deep ditch at speed, the two men travelling in the back where thrown out over the front of the pickup and landed on the other side of the ditch. The pickup was a right off. The other two men and I were all right or so I thought. One of the men said after the weekend that he was suffering from a back injury after landing on the grass on the other side of the ditch and took Addski to court. Well with all the lawyers' fees, Addski went down. The fees where draining Addski. We couldn't prove that the man's back injury wasn't caused by the crash so Addski went into bankruptcy so that we wouldn't have to pay out thousands to this man and court fees. However, Addski wasn't a limited company, we owed money to people, and the running costs of Addski, the lease hire of the harvester, the forwarder, two skyline winches and men to pay off. We didn't really think it through properly. Well I didn't think so but that's just me. I don't know about my wife and my business partner if they thought it through or not but by this time I wasn't talking to them and left it all to them. I didn't want to go into bankruptcy but we didn't have a choice, it was either pay out a great sum of money to this person or . . . ? Either way we had a great sum of money to find. Addski was in debt and the debt had to be paid! With my business partner not having any money, it all landed on me and my wife who was my business partner. The house had to go and the money that my mum had left me when she died! Moreover, that was the last nail in the coffin for my wife. She'd had just enough of me. Our nice farmhouse had to go to pay off some of the debt that Addski had built up while working. It would have been all right if I hadn't driven into the ditch and the guy hadn't tried to take Addski to court. Addski could probably have kept going I don't know?

In addition, at that particular time in my life my marriage wasn't going all that well! It was mostly my fault while I worked at Papa-Sam's. I used to come home late. I would have a drink before going home, one drink would lead to another one and by this time, I was either drunk or so late that my wife was in bed. At first, she would stay up but as I was drunk and couldn't have a conversation she gave up after hitting me with the coal scuttle several times or whatever she could get her hands on at the time. It didn't make much difference because when I woke up the next morning and said to her that "I must have fallen over last night because I have a big lump on my leg" or wherever she hit me; I just got the silent treatment. When she wanted to go shopping and asked me where the car is, well I couldn't remember and when I did remember it was in a ditch up the road with the front end caved in, *oops!* As time went on, it got worse. I hear you say how could it get any worse. I was a bastard to her, the woman that stood beside me through thick and thin who had brought up our kids mostly by herself, No, all by herself while I worked at the hotel. She would bath them, feed them and put them in their beds with no help from my parents. She didn't get on with my parents all that well. It wasn't all her fault, they didn't even ask if they could help by babysitting to let us get a night off and go out together somewhere. It must have been very difficult for her sometimes. Her parents were dead before we got married. Apart from her step mum and her two very young stepbrothers, she coped very, very, well. Now my kids are grown up and doing their own thing in life, they are an inspiration to her.

In addition, to top all that I go and have an affair with another woman! That final thing finished our marriage I think. I had to do that to her . . . Bastard! Yes I am I must agree with you. I don't know why I did it right on her door step so to speak and not away somewhere else so that nobody knew us! It really doesn't matter where I did it, I shouldn't have done it in the first place and I don't know why I did . . . maybe it was lack of sex? Nevertheless, who in their right mind would have sex with a husband that came home late and drunk, I know I wouldn't. Well thinking back if the affair wasn't enough for her to divorce me when the business went, well what I can say . . . Dickhead or something stronger! We divorced amicably even though there wasn't anything left to share. The funny thing is we stayed in the house of hell the three of us all in our own rooms until it was sold. Well I stayed in my room. It's not as if I'm saying anything? The kids were all away at university and the atmosphere in the house was bad. It was only when my son came home from university one long weekend that he said to me, quote "Dad get a life" unquote. Therefore, that prompted me to move. Addski was finished and so was my marriage so what the fuck was I staying here for? Maybe I was too set in my ways to look for another place. Anyway, I had to move soon, they were coming to repossess the farmhouse. Therefore, I left and rented my brothers cottage but I'll tell you about that later and the other two. After putting up with sitting in my bedroom night in night out while, the other two had the run of my house. I would come down for meals, which I would eat alone in one room while the other two would eat together, I would then go back to my room and watch TV like a lodger and that went on until the house was sold nearly a year later. It took all that time to wind up everything, the bankruptcy and the divorce on top of everything else. My wife and my business partner they moved out as well and moved into a cottage together, but as I said I'll get to all that soon. I need a holiday and I saw this advert in a magazine while sitting in my room in the house of hell an all-*inclusive* holiday to Jamaica. Three weeks in the sun away from here, fuck it four week's that's for me! It was a lot of money, well the flight was but when I get there I wouldn't have to pay for anything. I thought I might as well spend some more of my mother's money that she had left me than leave it to the creditors, so off I went to sunny Jamaica leaving them behind in the rain, wind, sleet and snow . . . yes!

CHAPTER TWELVE

JAMAICA

I arrived in Jamaica not knowing what to expect. The plane doors opened and I waited for my turn to step out and walk down the steps on to the tarmac. On my way to customs the hot Jamaican air hit me 'yes, this is fucking great I thought.' I walked along the tarmac runway following the row of other people making their way to the tinted doors of the waiting room in customs. I didn't think that I would be so glad to feel the cool air from the air-conditioning wafting around as I waited for my turn in the long queue of people. With my passport in my hand and kicking my bag along the smooth tiled floor, we inched our way to the two men stamping passports and asking questions in front of me. Then finally, it was my turn. I smiled and gave the man my passport he looked at it fingering through the pages then looked at me and said, "You are from Scotland?"

"Yes" I said.

"How long are you staying in Jamaica?" he said without taking his eyes of my passport.

"About four weeks" I replied.

"Where are you staying?" I told him and then he looked up at me stamped my passport and said "we don't get many Scottish people coming to Jamaica have a nice stay." I picked up my passport thanked him and bent down to pick up my bag. As I heard him say next, I made my way to the automatic tinted doors that opened then closed behind me.

I was back in the bright baking hot sunshine to be greeted by thirty or more Jamaicans all shouting "taxi! Ya wanna taxi mun, you wanna taxi" Most of them were small mini buses seating about six to eight people in them. My bags were taken out of my hands by a tall black guy wearing a blue t-shirt and a pair of faded jeans; he had long black tight curly hair pushed under a knitted bonnet that had all the colours of the Jamaican flag knitted around it. On his feet, he wore a pair of well-worn shabby brown sandals. He greeted me and said in a Jamaican accent "ya mun welcome to Jamaica where do you wanna go mun?" I told him the name of the hotel. As I got into the front of the mini bus, I appeared to be the only one going with him. He put my bag on one of the seats behind me, closing the sliding door and climbed in the driver's side. He turned to me "ya mun a very nice place it is. It is very popular man with you whites," he said in broad Jamaican accent.

"How long will it take us to get there?"

"It's about an hour's drive mun is that okay?" We set off out of the main town and into the country leaving the tarmac road behind. We continued along a dusty track with big potholes that he drove off the road to avoid and then back on again slowing down for people on bikes or just walking. I had the window open, as there wasn't any air-conditioning in the bus and put up with the clouds of red dust from the other traffic that was being whipped up as they past us by. We drove on through small villages with wooden and corrugated sheeting shacks made up as shops with vegetables outside or hand carved wooden objects, occasionally slowing down and even stopping for the people that were crowding the narrow winding dust track road carrying large bundles of sticks on their heads or dragging large wooden barrows full of different things. We drove through yet another village on our way and the driver turned to me and said, "Would you like some mun?" Then he would wipe his nose and repeat himself to me "You know mun?" Then he would wipe is nose again and look at me waiting for an answer "You know what I'm talking about mun would you like some?"

At first, I thought he had a cold and I couldn't understand what he was talking about. I smiled politely then he repeated himself again "mun you know what I mean mun?"

The penny dropped "Oh yes what have you got?" He then pulled out this tray from under the dash just below the radio and on it well, there was coke, heroin and charley (hash) all individually wrapped up in Clingfilm. Then there were the pills, all sorts and some stuff that I didn't even know.

"There you are mun take your choice" he said.

I looked at the large selection "how much for the charley?" he then reeled off a price. I took the charley opened it and smelt it "how much for the charley man?" I said again. He told me a price "no way!" I said, "I could get it cheaper at the hotel?"

"Possibly but you're not there yet mun?" he said laughing.

"Okay, okay" I said agreeing with the price. He pulled over and started to roll a joint, when he had finished he handed it to me with a lighter and I lit it.

"Ya mun try tat mun?" he said as I took a long hard draw on it, filling my lungs then letting it all out. "Ya mun good no! Its home grown mun, my cousin he grow it in our village on the hill."

"Yes, yes!" I replied trying to get my breath back and then taking another long draw. "What about the police, don't they stop you growing it?" I said.

"No mun they don't bother us mun as long as everyone's happy you know what I mean?" He started up the bus to continue our journey. I offered him some Jamaican money for the charley (hash) "No, no mun take it. If you took anything else I would take the money because I have to pay for them but the hash is home grown ya know," he said as I sat back and started to enjoy getting an instant buzz. I shared the joint and rolled another one with the papers that he gave me as we drove along the dusty road on our way to the hotel. We smoked about four joints before getting to the hotel; I was liking Jamaica more and more and getting well on the way to getting stoned,

We arrived at this spectacular large white horse-shoe shaped hotel with flags flying from all different nations on long white poles. They started from one end of the hotel going right round the front ending up at the other side in the same shape. I looked for a Scottish one but there wasn't one, on saying that there was a Union Jack there. It was immaculate and so were the grounds leading up to it. There were palm trees and in between them there were bushes with brightly coloured tropical flowers all over them, each one covered with different colours leading up to the front of the hotel. There were Jamaicans in light blue jackets and dark trousers waiting to take your luggage. Well, the first appearances were great. We stopped and a very smart Jamaican man in one of the blue jackets opened the door of the taxi.

"Good evening sir can I take your bags?"

Before I could say yes, the driver had got them and put them down at the other Jamaicans feet. He took them into the foyer of the hotel and all I had to do was to pay the driver and thank him. "Ya mun you have a nice time hear?" I smiled, got my money out, and paid him with a tip. "If you want to go anywhere mun just call mun?" he said and pushed a card into my hand. I gave him the money then turned and walked into the hotel across the red stone tiled floor passing a large extravagant looking water fountain on my way to the reception where my bags were along with two good-looking Jamaican girl receptionists. I stood for a minute or two looking around at the hotel foyer.

"Yes can I help you?" a girl's voice said.

"Hi, I have a reservation in the name of Addis?"

She looked at me and then down at the booking ledger. I checked her out whilst she was looking down the ledger for my name. She was very nice; she was dark in colour with an olive type complexion, short tight curly hair, and large round red earrings that matched her very sensuous red lipstick lips. She wore a see through white blouse and a tight light blue skirt that matched the colour of the men's jackets. She looked up and said, "Can I have your passport please?" I reached into my pocket, pulled out my passport, and gave it to her. Thanking me, she took it and fingered through it until she came to the bit where my photo was. She looked at it and then wrote something down in the register, giving me another chance to study her white lacy bra with decorative patterned holes on it through her blouse, hoping to get a glimpse of one of her olive coloured nipples. She looked up, caught me looking, and smiled a big smile showing her white teeth. We looked straight in each other's eyes, hers where a deep brown. I was mesmerised by her and a bit embarrassed by getting caught looking at her breasts.

"Number 14?" She asked.

"Sorry?" I said not catching what she said.

"Your chalet, number 14 Mr Addis" she replied with a smile and summoned one of the men standing about in their blue jackets. He came over to where I was standing and lifted my bags.

"Take Mr Addis to number 14," she ordered.

"Thanks" I said, turned, and followed my bags across the red tiled floor and towards a very large glass door before leaving the hotel foyer. I looked back at the girl behind the desk she was already looking at me and smiling. I smiled back, turned round to follow the man in the blue jacket and my bags, and nearly knocked into someone. "Sorry, sorry!" I said picking up what I'd knocked out of her hands and giving it back to her. We left the hotel foyer through a series of large wooden archways supporting glass windows from the ceiling to the floor in the same shape and full length of the hotel wall, then down several steps into the dining area with blue carpet and tables situated in a half circle round a large wooden dance floor. In front of all that, the stage and to the left at the far end of the room was the very spectacular large round all glass and mirror effect bar with three or more barmen in red jackets serving a crowd of people. We walked past the dining area with the stage through some more glass and wooden archways, down some more large steps, and out into the very hot sun and on to a concrete patio with different brightly coloured tables and chairs. Above our heads, was a wooden trellis with exotic different coloured flowers wrapping them-selves round the wooden trellis and hanging down.

Off the patio on to another open patio with red and blue concert coloured slabs was the pool with more tables and sun loungers with umbrellas. It was a large pool in two levels, in the middle of the far end was another type of bar with people standing in the water beside it. Continuing on our way to the chalets, we walked through what you could say was a Garden of Eden along a gravelled path winding its way through the well-kept grass and different coloured tropical shrubs all in full bloom, and trees dotted across the grass with again different collared blossom, and well kept flowerbeds, with hundreds of flowers. The whole place was very well kept and amazing, all this leading us to the twenty or so chalets dotted around this fabulous Garden of Eden. Some of the chalets had verandas and some didn't. Mine didn't, and beyond the chalets passing through a high hedge was the long beach with its white coloured sand and palm trees dotted about with hammocks slung underneath them with sun loungers in rows with red and blue umbrellas shading them. All sorts of water sports you could think of, they even had a large trampoline with a high metal framework with a platform on each end and two trapezes slung between them. A round bar built under four palm trees and at the far end of the long beach was an large sign in black and white saying nude bathing beyond this point. My chalet was great it had everything you could want. I started to check it out, the bathroom first. It had everything and very clean. The guy brought my luggage in, I gave him a tip. "Tank's mun" he said and left shutting the door behind him. I took a good look around inside the chalet; there was a large mirror above the long desk type table that had a large light on it with an even bigger cream coloured lampshade on it. A phone and small leather chair so you could sit and write a letter if you wanted, and all sorts of writing materiel in a red leather folder with the name of the hotel on it. In the three drawers on each side were pamphlets telling you what was on and where to go while you were staying here. Yes, my holiday is about to begin. I started to unpack and look around the rest of the chalet. When I say unpack I meant that I just threw the cases in the bottom of the wardrobe and closed the door with all my clothes still in them. I started to inspect the chalet, sitting on the very large bed looking about. There was a small fridge with at least eight bottles of beer and half a dozen miniatures, nuts, and other bit and bobs. I closed the fridge door, sat back down on the bed again, and noticed there were small tables on each side of the bed. They had lights with long coloured lampshades the same colour as the one on the desk. A radio was fitted into the wall on one side of the bed and the long window that started about four foot off the floor. It went up nearly to the ceiling and had no glass in it, just slatted wooden chutes. You could quite easily fall out closing the chutes if you weren't careful. It was the same for the chalet opposite, which wasn't that far away. In fact, if they had their chutes open as well you could see each other quite easily. Then there were the mirrors? There was a long one above the desk on the wall opposite the bottom of the bed. Another on the wall at the top of the headboard and wait for it, a very large mirror on the ceiling covering the whole of the bed, "is this kinky or what!" I thought to myself, "I'm going to like this." I stretched out on the bed on my back and looked at myself in all three mirrors. It didn't matter what one you looked in, they all reflected your image on the bed at different angles. Then I remembered what the girl in the travel agency said to me when I phoned up to book the holiday, she said over the phone "would I like to stay in the chalets or the hotel?" I thought the chalet would be better and then she said "The chalets . . . well beware of the mirrors?"

I didn't know what she meant at the time so I said "what?"

She then just said, "Beware of them?" That's all she said. I wondered if they have a hidden secret, but no, Boo-hoo.

I got off the bed grabbed the keys where I had thrown them and left the chalet to go and check out the beach through one of the openings in the tall hedge. It was late evening, the beach was deserted, the sun hadn't quite set, and was a big round red ball floating on the horizon. I continued to walk along the beach past the bar that was closed for the night. It was built under three large palm trees. I looked about at all the signboards advertising all sorts of water sports skiing, paddle boats, wind surfing, and lots more. It was still very warm with hardly any wind. I walked out along the wooden jetty where some of the boats were tied up. I looked out at the setting sun then down at the crystal clear water, it looked very inviting. I turned round and walked back off the jetty and continued along the beach. I had walked the full length of the beach and ended up in the nude bathing part. There was no one about so I kept walking and checked it out. It was the same as the rest of the beach except it didn't have water skiing but had all the rest of the water sports. It even had its own bar in a middle of a big heart shaped pool with water all around it. Away from the water's edge and several feet away from the pool going back along the beach, was a long wooden shack with a corrugated iron roof and low long window with a wooden blackboard with large white letters. It was advertising full body massages with tropical sensual oils and the price was in dollars, everything was in dollars. I made my way up to the main hotel through the Garden of Eden. There was the sound of insects along with the strong smell of perfume from the flowering shrubs and the blossom off the trees. As I walked away from the beach, I was thinking to myself "I must try out the nude bathing and the massage place before going home." The sound of the insects got louder as I walked further away from the beach. I went up to the big glass and mirror bar that was full of people drinking and listening to the cabaret. As I got closer to the bar, the insects were drowned out by the noise of the eight or so Jamaican girls in very short grass skirts and very skimpy tops. They didn't really cover anything apart from their very essences and even then when they jumped up and down some of them were having difficulty keeping their breasts covered up to the cheers and laughter from the audience.

I sat down on one of the tall stainless steel chairs swivelled the top part round to look at the girls dancing on the wooden floor in front of the stage. A full brass band played 'Reggae' for them; I turned back to the bar to catch the eye of one of the barmen so that I could get a drink. One of the barmen saw me from round the other side of the bar and came towards me in his red jacket and black trousers. "Hi" I said.

"Yes mun what can I get you?"

"Double Vodka and something?" I was hesitating on a Vodka cocktail! He reeled of several names. "Yes the one with the crushed ice and cream, put two Vodkas in it please," I said. What, I'm on holiday come on! I got my drink and thanked him before sipping away at my long cool drink and looking about the place. There were a lot of Americans, Philipinos, Chinese, even a few Arabs, and not very many Brits, which is a good thing in a way. You don't want to be talking to a lot of British people when your abroad well I don't! I don't think there were any Scots. I ordered another long creamy drink and swivelled the top part of my chair round to look at the Jamaican girls dancing. There wasn't one bad looking one there; they were all great lookers with fabulous bodies. The drinks where going down fast and furious. I turned back to the bar to get another drink but not the same, the cream was a bit sickly after the second one, so I asked if he could suggest something else with a double shot of Vodka in it. Again, he reeled off several more cocktails.

I interrupted him and said, "Give me a double Vodka in a tall class with tonic and fill it up with ice please?" He turned round and picked up a tall thin glass that was on the counter in front of him and started to fill it with ice, I watched him. He then picked up a couple of slices of lime on the end of the knife that he just cut from a whole lime that was among other fruit on a thick wooden board beside him. He turned to me before putting the Vodka in and said "You know-mun, you should ask for Smirnoff Vodka?"

"Okay, then Smirnoff it is?" He walked along to the other end of the bar, picked up a large bottle with a blue label saying Smirnoff in big silver letters, and brought it back to where he had left the tall glass with the ice and lime in. To my surprise, he didn't even measure the amount of Vodka that he poured into the glass he just kept going until it was full. I was about to say you've forgotten the tonic when he opened the class door of the fridge and picked up a small can of tonic off the shelf that was full of different soft drinks and cartons of cream and put them down in front of me. I thanked him but thought to myself how the fuck am I going to pour the tonic in? He smiled then leant over to me, "leave it mun a while so tat the ice melts then pour da tonic in mun." I smiled as he continued "so tat you get the effect of the good Vodka mun." He then bent down picking up a glass from the draining board underneath the counter, along with a dishcloth. He leant over to speak to me again, close so that no one would hear. Whilst wiping the glass he said, "I will give you the good stuff not the cheap stuff mun." I wondered to myself, why he was telling me this, I've only had about four or so vodkas.

"Ya mun, they sell the cheap vodka to people so they can make some money for themselves." I smiled again leaning down to take a sip out of the glass without touching it as it sat on the counter. Still looking up at him and nearly choking with the amount of Vodka in it. I didn't complain as he kept on talking. "I can see you like vodka so . . ." he paused as he put the glass down next to the rest of clean one's on the counter next to him and put the dishcloth over his shoulder and leant over to me. "You're not American mun?"

"No, Scottish" I answered.

He smiled, "we don't get many Scottish here mostly Americans, loud ones," he whispered. "I'm Bob, after Bob Marley our greatest singer mun, you know Bob Marley mun?"

"Yes" I said. We talked away, in between him serving. I was about to ask for another drink when he said, "Here try this mun?" He gave me a drink; it was in a long glass again with a lot of ice. I could taste the Vodka this time, it had some other things in it as well, but I don't know what. It went right to the spot and I thought "fuck" I won't need many of these. He came back after serving someone and said "how's tat Scotty-mun good no!"

Before I could say yes he was away again serving someone else in between talking to Bob 'Well' more drinking than talking? I think I had maybe eight or more of those drinks on top of the ones that I already had I was getting a bit pissed . . . Like you do on your first night on holiday, don't you. Before I made a complete fucking fool of myself I decided to have an early night but on saying that! I don't know what time I left the bar. I remember Bob Marley or whatever his name was saying, "I'll be in the beach bar tomorrow mun"

As I stumbled and half ran through the Garden of Eden, trying to keep on the path and not ending up face down in the perfect kept flowerbeds or in one of the shrubs sniffing the scent from very close. I staggered on, I mean walked on to my chalet. The next morning I awoke with the sun shining through my long window, face down bollock naked on the top of the bed feeling like shit. I had managed to take off the bedspread and had thrown it on the chair along with my clothes. Lying there, I thought if there was a hidden camera, they must have had a good laugh at me last night. I rolled over onto my back and looked at my not very brown body for a while thinking 'I've got to get a tan.' I lay there staring at myself in all the mirrors individually. 'Did I see a red light flicker in the top right corner of the mirror on the wall opposite at the foot of the bed . . . ? No!'

I looked again to see if I could see it again. No, I must have imagined it. Getting of the bed, I forgot about the long window with the long wooden shutters that were still open. I was greeted by a smiling young lady who just happened to be standing in her long window a couple of yards away in her chalet next to mine. She was looking straight at me; she hesitated then gave me a short quick wave. I smiled and turned my back and walked to the wardrobe at the other side of the room to get my raggy-ended very faded denim shorts, my trunks, and a t-shirt out of the tidy bundles of clothes that I put away in here. Ha, they were still in the bag and would probably stay there for the four weeks. I took them into the bathroom and got under the shower, not with my clothes. I didn't stay long in the shower and didn't bother drying myself off either. I just flung my clobber on and slipped into my worn brown sandals. Grabbing the chalets large towel, I headed off to the beach and the sun.

I don't know what time it was but it must have been quite early, there was nobody about apart from two Jamaican boys raking the beach and putting out the sun loungers and umbrellas in straight rows. Several men were putting cases of things outside the bar not that far from me that was not yet open. I didn't want to go and annoy the boys raking and tidying the beach so I picked one of the hammocks that was slung between two poles in the sun, putting my towel on the hammock I started to get on? 'Well' I tried three times to get on that fucking thing and every time I ended up face down eating the sand under the hammock. I picked myself up yet again and looking around to see if there was anyone looking at this fucking nutter trying to get on a simple rope hammock. Well they say persevere, so I did and I finally got on. I swung around like a chimpanzee in a cage on its tyre, suspended by a rope from the top of the cage. The only thing different was that I was too scared to move in case I fell out again. I soon relaxed in the hot sun thinking 'that the sun was hot now, what would it will be like later.'

I must have dozed off and was wakened by a Jamaican girl in a police uniform; she was prodding me with her baton. "Hey mun is you ok?

It took a second or two to come too, out of my deep sleep and gather my senses. "Yes, yes I'm okay." I answered, looking up into her face.

"What room are you in mun?" she said in a demanding voice.

"I'm staying in one of the chalets" I said sitting up now wide awake with my two legs either side of the hammock trying to steady myself so I didn't flip over while talking to the guard. I wiped the sweat off my face with the edge of the towel that was between my legs and looking up into her face again.

"Hotel security, are you all right mun"? She said without a smile on her face.

"Yeah fine thanks."

She looked down at me "the two barmen asked me to check on you they were concerned" she said in a sexy broad Jamaican accent.

"I'm fine, I'm ok thanks."

"O.k. mun just checking" she said without even smiling. She turned round and walked away towards the bar. I sat there for a second and looked at her walk away in her tight blue skirt looking at her round bum wiggle as she tried to walk through the sand in her shoes. She got to the bar and stopped and said something to the two barmen them carried on wiggling. What a wiggle, what a bum! The sun was hot and I wiped the sweat that was lying in the crinkles of my stomach and off my forehead again and looked about the beach. It was full. There were lots of people now, in the water on all sorts of things floating and most or all the sun beds were full or they had towels on them with items belonging to the people that were either in the water or at the bar. I got off the hammock with a stumble and made my way to the bar. The sand was hot under my feet. I had left my sandals at the hammock and I wasn't going back for them. I was glad to get off the hot sand and sit down in the shade of the bar at the counter. "Hi, can I have a long cool drink with two vodkas in it please?" The barman went round to the other side of the bar and talked to the other barman who had his back to me and was talking to some other people at the bar. They were looking at four people swinging on the trapezes. I looked straight through the bar and out the other side and looked up to see two people swinging upside down with their legs wrapped round the wooden bar, catching the other two as they sailed through the air turning to catch their opposite partners on the trapezes to an audience of on lookers clapping and cheering.

The other barman came round clutching a long drink full of ice it was the barman from last night "Hi mun how are you today mun"? He said with a big smile on his face.

"Hey Bob I'm Okay thanks I think?

We laughed, "Did *you* make it back last night-mun?"

"I reckon so. I woke up this morning naked on top of my bed unless someone put me there!"

We laughed again "hay-mun I would have heard if they had-mun." he said and I interrupted

"Hey, the security guard woke me up."

"Yea-mun I told her to go and check on you" he said smiling as I sipped away at the long cool drink that was hitting all the right places and listening to what he was saying.

"Yeah-mun I was concerned."

Putting what was left of my drink back down onto the wooden counter I interrupted him "Bob give me another one of those please?"

"Mun that went down okay?" He took my glass away and retuned with a new one. Then carried on saying "When you didn't move mun I sent her."

"You did, did you?"

"I thought you might have had too much of the ganger-mun and all that drink last night-mun."

I put my hand up and to stop him "thanks but I'm all right" I said.

"We say here if your all right, 'irie-man' it means okay every tings fine you know-mun."

"Okay" I said. "I'm irie-man."

"That's it mun. You no-mun if you ever stuck for substance you know what I mean-mun? You can get any ting from the small boats tat come in to the bay here mun."

"Okay thanks I'll give it a try." I said passing my glass over to him. "Give me another of those drinks Bob please with Smirnoff."

"Yea-mun I know" he said and went round to the other side of the bar. He came back holding the thin tall glass and put it down in front of me.

"I'll take it back to the hammock with me," I said.

He then butted in and said, "no-mun I'll bring it over."

"Thanks" I said stepping out of the shade of the bar and onto the hot sand again and running back to the hammock, getting on first time, yes. Just as Bob brought my drink, "you made it first time mun?" He said I didn't hear him as I was fixing the towel underneath me and swinging my legs up and onto the hammock. He repeated what he was saying "getting on to the hammock mun . . ."

"You saw me, this morning," I said.

"Yeah-mun we both had a good laugh-mun this morning."

"You bastards" I said joking. I took the drink from him and tried not to spill it as the hammock swung from side to side. Trying to get my balance again, he laughed then said "hay-mun it was very entertaining."

We laughed and then he said, "if you like I will show you the real Jamaica?"

"Okay that would be great thanks," I said.

"Not this mun this is not the real Jamaica mun I'll take you on Wednesday next, on my day off okay. I will introduce you to my family and my sister mun" he then turned and went back to the bar.

I lay there taking in the views the beach had to offer and sipped away at my long cool drink trying not to spill it as the hammock rocked gently from side to side in the very hot sun. I was looking at the topless girls lying on the sun loungers and splashing about in the sea. My eyes rested quite pleasantly on two girls both standing just a few yards away from me rubbing sun oil over there incredibly tanned sexy bodies in turn. I lay gently rocking from side to side just looking at their perfect round full breasts with no white bikini marks just a deep golden tan all over right down to the very skimpy triangles of fabric. They were held in place with what you could say a bit of string that disappeared between their round farm cheeks of a bum. I thought that the triangle of fabric must have been the smallest thong that I had ever seen it just covered the sensual part keeping them decent. Then I saw Bob walking over to the hammock out of the corner of my eye. "Hey mun you have an eye for beautiful tings no?" he said laughing.

"Yeah mun!" I said smiling back. I was getting the local lingo if you known what I mean. He put a half-empty bottle of Smirnoff down in a bucket of ice.

"I'm off mun there's someting there for you to sip on mun a present from us you no," he said putting it down in the shade of the hammock.

"Thanks" I said.

"No problem mun" he replied then turned away to walk up to the main hotel. He turned back "don't forget the boats mun check them out mun?"

"Okay thanks," I shouted back. I lay there the rest of the day, soaking up the rays, and sipping away at the vodka using the ice in the bucket that hadn't melted to dilute the vodka. I looked at the long narrow boats with outboards on them weaving their way through the people swimming and wind surfing. I watched them just lying on their airbeds floating about on the surface of the water coming and going and the men on them whistling to get their attention. Some of the people waded out to the side of the boats and bought what they wanted from the guys it was so open the security guards didn't seem to bother with them at all?

As the day rolled in I was getting quite red and thought to myself 'better not over do it on the first day hell, I'm here for four weeks.' I got up off the hammock, took the empty bottle and the bucket back to the bar, and thanked the guy.

"No problem mun" he said taking it from me. I then started to make my way up to my chalet. The effect of the vodka that I had just being sipping away at hit me. I wasn't drunk but I knew that I had been drinking and that's when I thought I haven't eaten anything all day. You could get food all day and all night long up in the main hotel, I just hadn't bothered to leave my hammock to go and get some? I got to the chalet it had been cleaned and the clothes that I had left about had been put tidily away, the bed had been made and clean towels put out. That's when I remembered about the towel I had left on the hammock! Fuck it I'm not going back for it! I stripped off and looked at myself in the mirror where my denim shorts had been. It was white where I thought it was reasonably brown compared with the rest of my body that was very red. I looked down at myself in the mirror and thought I got to go to the nudist part of the resort and get an even suntan all over! Bugger the white parts. Still looking down at myself, I thought of those two girls on the beach with there all over even tan, yes! I want to look like them, well you know what I mean, to have a dark even tan with no white bits, however, that meant I would need to go starkers? Could I do this, walk about starker's revealing all to everyone? I looked again at myself. Turning round and looking this time in the mirror at the top of the headboard of the bed so that I could see my back view in the other mirror. 'Fuck it go for it Addis' I thought as I turned to go for a shower. The water was sharp like a needle effect. It stung my red shoulders and other parts of my naked sunburned body as it cascaded down over me and bounced off the floor then disappearing down the drain. It was like torture until I got used to the sharp like effect. Leaving the torture room, I went to lie down on top of the bed for a bit still wet from the shower. The room was hot from the days' sun even with the window fully open. I stood at the window looking out at the other three chalets and the Garden of Eden for a second. Then I thought about the woman this morning standing in her chalet. I looked to see if her window was open but it was closed. I got onto the bed and lay looking at myself in the mirror on the ceiling. You may think 'this guy is always looking at himself?' I can assure you its very hard not to look at yourself when all the mirrors show off your body at different angles all at the same time when lying on the bed. Fuck me; was that a red light flickering in the right top corner of the mirror on the wall above the dressing table? I looked again trying to pin point it, no. I looked again, no. I dozed off and awoke with the loud noise of the insects outside the window. Getting off the bed, I went over to the window to look out. The sun had gone and the strong smell of perfume from the tropical shrubs and trees filled my nostrils. I stood listening to the insects; they were so loud in the still night. Liking the feel of the cool night air wafting over my sunburned body I suddenly realised that the other chalets chutes were open as well. The woman in the chalet next to mine was standing with her back to me in a long flowery dress. I stood there looking at her for a split second then turned and walked past the mirror. I stopped and looked to see if there was anything in there but all I could see was my reflection. I grabbed a clean shirt, boxers from my bag in the closet, sorry wardrobe, slipped them on and my trusty denim shorts, sandals, and off to the hotel for food and more drink. I wasn't one for dressing up at night unless I had to and I didn't have to. I looked like Robinson Crusoe with bright red skin.

It was Wednesday and Bob said to meet him on the beach about seven in the morning. He would pick me up in his boat because he wasn't allowed to meet me at the front of the hotel for security reasons. I was a bit early so I walked along the beach looking at the two Jamaican lads raking the beach and fixing the sun beds into straight lines again after people had pulled them about and turned them round. Following the sun the day before as it drifted across the sky, I had on the usual gear not like me to over dress. As I walked along the beach going in the opposite way to the guys raking so not to disturb them towards the nude bathing, I thought again about going there and that made me look at my red legs which weren't red any more they had gone a light brown. Good I thought, they look a lot better not like a lobster like they did three days ago. The nude bathing popped into my brain again and how I could get there. Then it came to me I could walk down the path leading away from my chalet in the direction of the nude bathing instead of going the other way with a towel wrapped round me no one would suspect that I wouldn't have anything underneath. Moreover, I could go early so that the beach was quiet. My thoughts were interrupted by a noise of an outboard engine I turned round to see Bob Marley coming round the point. By the time I got back, Bob's boat was about near the beach with him waving. I waded out to meet him, grabbing the front of the boat, and stopping it from coming any further and nearly knocking me backwards into the water. Then I walked round to the side of the boat and climbed in.

"Hey mun?" he said as I climbed into the boat and sat down on one of the seats opposite him. I bent down to fix my sandal that was coming off then I looked up.

"Hey everything okay Bob?"

"Ya mun irie, you know" he answered as he put the boat into reverse. We were off on my 'magic mystery tour' of Jamaica. That is if I don't get my throat cut on the way. I had taken some money but left the bulk of it in the safe along with my gold chains in the chalet in the wardrobe. All the chalets had their own little safe and a small key so if you didn't want to take your valuables onto the beach you could lock them up in your very own safe. He rolled a joint, lit it and handed it over to me after taking a long hard suck on it himself and we headed off in the direction that he came from "good-mun yes, its home grown" he said as I took a long hard drag on the joint.

We must have shared between us about four joints before getting to the other bay where the car was. My tolerance was quite good with smoking hash, most of my life on and off and having buckets and other means of smoking it with my business partner at night at home. But this home grown stuff, well it was good. I helped Bob pull the boat up onto the beach and we walked to the car. We stood outside the pickup and had another joint as we talked.

"hey mun you know you don't look like the usual holiday maker tat comes here, in fact you look like the white men tat work on the fishing boats here mun, tats for certain" he said smiling as he put things into the back of the pickup that he brought out of the boat.

"Thanks" I said as I looked at myself.

"It's true mun?" he said putting the last of the boxes into the pick-up. It was an old rusty Chevy pick-up like most of the cars or pick-ups in Jamaica they were all American imports like in the main town. The main influence was definitely American with signs advertising hamburgers' instead of beef burgers, gas for petrol, and a lot's more things. Even by the look of the place, you could think you where in some desert location in the good old US of A. If it wasn't for the corrugated steel and wooden shacks that were thrown up with wood not even overlapping the other. In fact there was big gaps in the sides about two to three inches where there wasn't enough wood to finish it off or the wood tapered to a point at one end and the other end it was to match up with what was straight. All the produce that they were selling was outside, on wooden boards supported on trestles; we pulled in for gas, sorry petrol. I stuffed some money into Bob's hand "No-mun no need for tat."

"Take it" I said and put it in his breast pocket.

"Thanks mun" he said as he shuffled his way over to the glass window to pay. He then got back in and started up the pick-up and we were off on my magical mystery tour. Hopefully not to end up with my throat cut and dumped in a ditch somewhere.

We left the main street and headed up into the hills off the tarmac and onto dirt track roads with more of these roughly thrown together corrugated and wooden shacks, some selling woodcarvings, fruit or just old men sitting together outside. We continued to climb the winding dusty red track road full of women carrying large bundle of sticks on their heads.

"Hey mun do you fancy some beer"? Bob said as we stopped.

"Yeah okay" I said.

We pulled up alongside of one of these shacks with a long wooden shutter the full length of the shack with three large hinges at the top and sounded the horn. The flap opened up to reveal a large room with a long deep freeze some wooden shelves with some bottles of their local beer and more of these wood carvings of tall wooden men with large cocks. Well I think they were men and posters of young Jamaican girls advertising different things. We got out the pick-up and walked up to the opening

"Two beers mun" Bob said and the guy reached into the freezer and pulled out two bottles of beer opened them and put them on the wooden counter.

"Tanks mun" he said and turned to me and gave me a beer. I sipped at it and looked at the small boys and girls standing looking at me from the opposite side of the dirt track road and laughing. I smiled back at them and continued to look around at all the people walking past as Bob spoke away to the guy in the shack. Then Bob tapped me on the shoulder and handed me a banger saying, "here try this-mun" and handed me a lighter as well. He turned back to the guy and said "hay-mun tis is my friend from Scotland" as he introduced me to the guy in the shack.

"Hi" I said nearly choking on the banger that Bob had just given me.

"Hey mun how are you?" the guy behind the counter said.

"Hey I'm irie mun thanks" I replied and both of them laughed. The guy behind the counter smiled and said "tats good-mun."

We got back in the car and set off again with the people that were walking in the middle of the road moving to the side to get out the way. I sat back smoking my banger and looked at a crowed of nice looking girls moving to one side and looking in at us as we drove past them. "Mmm nice girl's man!" I was getting stoned but I thought to myself, keep it together Addis . . . ! We drove on up the hill passing more people just standing talking and more girls with short white pleated skirts and red tops on and not a bad looking one amongst them. "Where are they going?" I asked Bob.

"There on their way to work in the hotels mun" he said trying to avoid them as they split up and went round both sides of the pick-up shouting at him. We got to another village with more old men sitting about and more people selling more of the wooden carvings. I think the wooden carvings are the main thing they sell to tourists. Every village we go to, they seem to sell them. All shapes and sizes. In this village, they were selling loads of different fruit at the side of the dusty track. We stopped and the red dust blew up around the pick-up and then settled down again. We got out for more beer. This time there were two men sitting opposite each other at a table outside the shack type bar at the side of the road chopping up some white powder and mixing it with cannabis? Bob said something to them and one of the men looked up 'irie Bob mun no problem mun' he said. Then he looked at me, smiled then, and continued chopping at the white powder on the table in front of him. He carried on talking to the other man. I stood looking for a while when I heard a girls voice say, "Did you say two beers Bob?" I looked up from the two men that were sitting at the table and to a girl this time instead of a man serving. She was nice looking. I studied her as she opened the two beers and placed them on the counter she had on a very skimpy blouse that was unbuttoned right down the front then tied in a double knot holding it together just under her bust. Revealing her large cleavage and well formed breasts. I had to get closer so that I could have a better look at her so I joined Bob at the counter. "Thanks Bob" I said taking the beer that he just bought and looked closer at the girl and at her waist and her pierced tummy button, plus her thin tight white short shorts that clung tight to her shape revealing more of her olive coloured skin this time her round cheeks' of her bum. Every time she walked or bent over to get the beer out of the freezer, nice I thought studying her trying not to be too obvious when Bob said, "hey mun this is my cousin mun."

"Hi" I said looking straight at her breasts not caring if she saw me or not.

"Hi, I'm Roxana" she replied" putting her hand out.

"Hi Roxana" I said taking my eyes of her breasts and pulled her hand towards me and kissed it.

"Hey mun tats my cousin," Bob said.

"You didn't tell me that you had such a lovely cousin?" I answered him back without taking my eyes of her. She pulled her hand away, smiled then bent over the freezer to get the beers out and gave me a quick look round to see if I was still looking and smiled. She knew that I was looking at her bum and she seemed to take her time getting the beer out as well! Maybe it was just me. I was in a trance with my eyes fixed on her bum. "Are all the girls great lookers like her Bob?" I said so that she could hear.

"Ya mun most of the girls here are fuckable!"

Well that's not the way I would have said it but it was true I haven't seen a bad looking one yet. One of the men sitting in front of the bar handed Bob a banger and they said something. I didn't hear I was too busy looking at Roxana bending over the freezer again getting more beer out for some other people. It wasn't just beer she sold either, there was fruit and tinned stuff as well, and more of those weird wooden carvings of men with very long cocks. They seemed to be obsessed Showing off weird wooden carvings of men all shapes and sizes with very long cocks?

"Hey mun try this mun, we call it Moochee its coke, and cannabis mixed together mun," Bob said handing me the banger after taking a draw on it himself. I said no at first but Bob insisted on it sucking on it nervously, but trying not to show it. We passed the banger back and forth between us until it was done I didn't feel any different I don't think. I was a bit stoned but I was stoned when I arrived at the bar.

An elderly woman came up to the bar and said to Roxana could she buy the bunch of bananas that were on the counter, well. Unexpectedly I turned round and said, "Leave those fucking bananas they're mine!"

They weren't I don't even know why I said it. Roxana quickly said "it's Ok Martha he don't mean what he saying you no." The poor old woman was taken aback and looked at me and then at Bob. I had lost it completely for a second or more but then regained my composure and got it together again. I said that I was sorry to the old woman and handed Roxana some money saying that I would buy the bananas for her. Roxana shoved it back at me.

The old woman said "It don't matter young mun but you be careful tat's Moochee you've just had and its very strong it takes people in different ways you know you did good to get it together so quickly you no." She gave a little chuckle and looked at the rest of them who were already laughing. I started to laugh too. I couldn't stop smiling. I had a fixed grin on my face. I was stoned, well and truly stoned!

"We go to my brother's plantation," Bob said. I put the money that Roxana had shoved back at me onto the counter and said to the little old woman "I insist. Let me buy those for you please?"

"Okay young mun tanks." Roxana picked up the money and smiled. I then turned to Bob and asked him the time for some reason? Time was irrelevant. The whole day was irrelevant. In fact, time didn't matter at all. I was finding it hard to keep it together I was losing it. Bob and Roxana were talking. I had a fixed stare, with my eyes wide open looking at Roxana's round breasts just held together with her blouse that was tied together with a large knot. It sat just underneath the bottom part of her breasts. Their voices would drift away then come back. I was mesmerised by Roxana's breasts studying them inch by inch all over and noticing her nipples' sticking through the material. Roxana was observing me but she didn't say or do anything to stop me from looking she just carried on talking to Bob. I couldn't help myself and I knew I was being so obvious and I would try to listen to the conversation and try to make sense of it. However, my eyes would home in again on Roxana's breasts. Then onto her nipples' that were getting bigger or was I imagining it. My mouth was dry I had no saliva and my beer was empty. I knew that I had a stupid grin on my face and the more I tried to concentrate on not looking at Roxana's breasts I would get paranoid about it. I had to get it together and quickly. On the other hand, is this where I get my throat cut?

I was getting so paranoid about things, fuck Addis get it together. Bob put his bottle down on the counter, turned, and said something to the two men sitting at the table. He then started to walk to the pick-up. I turned to follow Bob when Roxana leaned over the counter and grabbed hold of my t-shirt and pulled me towards her and then gave me a kiss on the side of my face that took me very much by surprise. She let go and smiled at me as I smiled back at her. I stumbled down the two steps leading back down onto the road. Bob shouted from the pick-up "come on mun we go to my brothers."

"Hold on I need another beer my mouth is so dry I said"

"Okay mun get me one too," Bob shouted back from the driver's side where he was standing waiting for me.

"Two beers please Roxana?" I said and added "you know I just used that for an excuse to see you bend over that freezer again, mmm you've got a nice bum Roxana" I said as she bent over the freezer once again then I suddenly thought what On earth, did I say that for? She looked round as she was bending over getting the beer out showing her tight white shorts that had slipped up even further between her dark olive coloured cheeks of her round bum. If that was possible and said, laughing "thanks mun." She got the two beers opened them and gave them to me smiling. I gave her the money and as I was leaving, she shouted, "I'll see you at the club Scotty bye."

"What club?" I said and then shouted over to Bob who was standing at the pick-up "what club?" He just waved to Roxana as he got into the pick-up. I said again "Bob what club?"

"Never mind mun get in," he said. I did handing one of the beers to him. We set off nearly spilling the beer over my legs. I relaxed back in the seat and just stared at all the people drifting past, sipping away at my beer letting the hot sunlight flicker over my face, as it managed to fight its way through in the gaps of the shacks. As we were leaving the village, I looked round. "Do the police not bother you Bob?" I asked. We must have had well over the limit in drugs and alcohol to be driving. "No mun there no problem here you know, as long as their happy you know what I mean"?

We drove up into the hills and the dusty road ended up as a dusty single track winding its way up. We had left all the shacks and people behind and now I could see for miles and miles over the tops of the hills. There wasn't a cloud in the sky; the hot sun beat down on me through the front windscreen of the pick-up. "Fuck its hot!" I said as Bob interrupted, "Ya mun it's good no, we're here mun." We got out and I was still clutching the half-empty bottle of warm beer that I was still sipping away at. We walked along the hill then down a small path to a long wooden shack with bundles and bundles of cannabis hanging up outside, I presume drying out. Bob's brother came out of the shed and greeted us "hey mun how are you?"

"Fine irie mun thanks," I said. He then turned to Bob and said something. I couldn't hear my mind was still fucked up with taking moochee and I was still a bit paranoid. I couldn't help thinking is this where they cut my throat after seeing the cannabis and dump me over the hillside?

"This is where I grow all my cannabis mun" he said pointing to the hillside that was covered in sugar-cane plants. I couldn't see any cannabis at all only the large bunches that where drying in the hot sun. He must of seen the strange look on my face as I tried to look for the plants and said, "come I'll show you mun come here mun look?"

I followed him down to the rows where the sugar cane where growing. There were rows upon rows of sugar cane growing in lines along the hillside as far as you could see. It was just like a vineyard. He said, "Come mun look?"

We walked across the hill and in between the rows of sugar cane where the cannabis plants sitting in between the sugar-cane plants. There was one sugar-cane plant and one cannabis plant. "Millions mun, these are nearly ready for harvesting mun." He picked a bud of a plant, sniffed it, and gave it to me, it was sticky, and it smelt very strong. "What kind is this?" I was trying to pretend that I knew what I was talking about.

"It's skunk mun? I grow skunk here mun and on tat hill over there is someone else's plantation. They grow another type of cannabis come I'll show you what I do with them mun? We walked back along in between another row on our way back to the hut. Bob's brother explained to me in detail how he dried the plants and what he did with the buds. Then how he took the cannabis to town and sold it and how many people like him sold a lot of it in bulk.

"To whom? I said but all he said was "tat don't matter mun" he wasn't going to tell me so I didn't push it. I thought to myself 'I already have enough information for him to cut my throat and leave me in a ditch somewhere'. We got back to the hut where Bob was sitting on upturned wooden crate in the shade of the shack out of the sun drinking a beer. "Sit mun I'll get some beer?" Bobs brother said as he disappeared into the shed. I sat down on the wooden crate next to Bob; his brother pulled over another and sat down outside the hut in the shade of the very hot sun. We talked about Scotland and my home and did I smoke and take other drugs. "Yeah man bits and bobs but it was illegal to do so," I said.

"Ya mun it's the same here but maybe not so bad here you know mun." Bob said. We sat there in the hot afternoon sunshine drinking beer and smoking cannabis in a homemade wooden pipe talking about everything. This was until Bob said, "come on Scotty I've got more people to take you too plus our family and my two sisters." We got up and started to walk back up the hill "hay mun have you had a black girl since you been here mun?" Bobs brother shouted. Turning round I shouted back "no."

"Hey I will fix tat mun" he answered, and then shouted to Bob to fix it that I get a black girl tonight.

For all the beer I had drank I wasn't all that pissed. Maybe the paranoia that kept sweeping over me about different things was keeping the booze at bay. I don't know. I was quite happily stoned apart from the odd paranoia thought that flashed through my mind now and then. Nevertheless, I was enjoying the buzz from all the chemicals and I could still carry on a conversation. Okay, saying that I haven't spoken to a straight person for a while, so Bob must be in the same shape as myself I thought. We set off back down the hill to meet a Rasta mun as Bob put it, a friend of his in the second village. On our way back I remember asking Bobs' brother what time it was at the hut, I think he said it was six or was it seven. I don't know. At the time, it went right over my head. I was a bit paranoid about something or other I don't know what. I was probably thinking that he was going to cut my throat. I was trying to make conversation and trying to be sensible for some reason, again I don't know why. It seemed a good thing to do at the time. We stopped the pick-up and walked across the dusty road towards this guy who was getting up from one of three large patterned fabric recliners. They were similar to the ones you would have in your sitting room. He had them on a wooden porch outside this long shack where he had a boogie box betting out Jamaican music.

He must have been about six foot tall maybe more. We met him as he was coming down the three wooden steps that ran the full length of the porch in front of his shack. He stood on the bottom one that made him even taller. He had long brown dreadlocks that were right down his back and down the side of his face. A knitted beret was on the back of his head, it was holding in the rest of this hair, and had all the Jamaican colours. The beret was the same kind the taxi man had on when I first arrived in Jamaica. Putting out his hand to shake mine he said, "Welcome to Jamaica mun?"

We walked back up onto the wooden porch. He seemed to slither across the wooden porch, his whole body moving in time with each movement of his legs, all in time with the music. I think that's the best way to describe his walk. He pulled over two other chairs and shouted out a girl's name to bring two beers. "You drink beer?"

"Yes, yes, I have been drinking beer all day with Bob" I said.

"No doubt been smoking some ting too mun, If I know this mun here?" He said putting his arms around Bob and embracing him. He laughed then said something to him, which I didn't quite make out what. Bob agreed with him put his hand in his pocket and brought out some money and gave it to him. Bob's friend then turned to me and said, "How are you mun?"

"I'm Okay man irie thanks" I replied. He made a gesture with his hand for us to sit down. He sat in one; I was in the one opposite and Bob in the one next to me. We sat down in these large chairs on this wooden porch at a round wooden table. Bob's friend then said to me, "I see you have picked up some of our language tat's good mun" and smiled. We talked about his parish. He told us how people came to him if they wanted advice, legal advice or to talk about God or any problems that they have. I could see why! Not just because he was a Rasta-man, he had a kind looking face, a face you could talk to. The beer arrived and a young girl put them down on the table in between us. She turned away and went back into the shack. "Not bad, nice bum" I thought to myself. "You know, I haven't seen a bad looking girl yet; they have all got good looking bodies and nice round bums!" I said.

"You tink so mun, tats good but wait till you see Bobs sister mun you tink these are good?" he said and smiled. I have seen your cousin Roxana haven't I Bob. She was good looking." I said turning to Bob but he was busy leaning round talking to someone else. I turned back to carry on talking when he said, "Where are you staying mun?" I told him and took another sip of my beer straight from the bottle. We talked about different things about Scotland and about what I did there. Bob joined us again, gave his apologies, and said he had better get me back to the hotel before they send out a search party for me.

"Ya mun we can't have tat can we?" the Raster-man said. I never knew his name; it was just raster-man. We got up, made our thanks, started to walk back to the pick-up, and got in, before turning and waving.

"There's one more mun I want you to see before I take you back, oh and we got to get you laid mun" he said and laughed. We turned off further down the road onto an even smaller track and drove along it very slowly. We spent half an hour or more trying to avoid the big holes. Sometimes we had to drive off the track altogether with people running out of the way. We pulled off the track alongside half a dozen shacks to the sound of more reggae blasting out of the nearest one. Bob sounded his horn. We were already out and talking between ourselves when a tall, well built very black Jamaican came out. Bob put out his hand to shake this guy's hand, but it wasn't your ordinary handshake. They sort of shook hands then slid their fingers along each other's palm right to the ends of their fingers then snapped their fingers and clenched their hands in a fist and hit the top of each other's fist. After all that, Bob introduced to this very dark Jamaican man. "Hey mun how are you?" he said and again I said, "Fine irie mun thanks" and shook his hand.

"Come in mun and share a banger with me mun?" We followed him into his home. There were about six other people in this room; four of them were girls, all good looking especially the one that caught my eye. She had long black curly hair that came to a fringe in the front and then fell down around her head and over her shoulders, resting on the outline of each of her breasts. Her face, well it was heaven. She had the usual olive skin, big luscious lips, green eyes and long black eye lashes, a great body. Which wasn't concealed very well with what she had on and what I could see of it as she lay back in one of the big leather chairs? The two guys, they had long curly hair with dreadlocks but not has long as the last guy. I was introduced to them and joined them round this table.

The place was amazing inside, but from the outside, you would have thought it was a shack. Well it was but what I mean is it had holes in the sides where the wood didn't meet along the front. If you went close enough you could look straight through into the room inside, like the rest of the shacks about the place. It had a tin roof, but inside you had all the mod cons of a normal house? On saying that, I'm not saying his house wasn't normal it was. It wasn't what I thought it would be like. It had a leather suite a smoked glass wall unit that ran the full length of one of the walls with a huge stereo and two major speakers' that were blasting out reggae again. I think that's all they play here? A big tropical fish tank sat in the middle of the smoked glass unit with some of these wooden men with very big cocks and other ornaments dotted about on it. There was a big framed poster of Bob Marley playing in some concert and on the round smoked glass table was all sorts of chemicals, pills, bottles of beer, some white spirit like Vodka in small straight glasses. They were drinking these in one go before they sipped at their beer. There were lines of coke or speed I'm not sure. One of the guys had his head down and was snorting a line as we sat down. He looked up in fright at me, wiped his nose and was going to say something but was interrupted.

"Hey it's okay mun its cool he's a friend mun" Bob said as he sat down beside me at the table. Instantly I was offered a line from one of the girls that was chopping and sorting out another line for the next person.

"Yes thanks," I said. Well, when in Rome do as they do or something like that. However, I was in Jamaica so whom the fuck cares. I was handed a banger that was going round the table and the big black guy gave Bob and myself a bottle of beer each. He asked if we wanted what they were drinking in the thin glasses. We both said yes and he went away, came back with two small thin glasses, and put them down in front of us. He filled them up with some white spirit like Vodka; I can't remember what they called it.

"Hey mun Scotty never refuses any ting mun," Bob said to an encore of laughter and stamping of feet. The good-looking girl leaned forward out of her deep chair pushing her left breast back in the side of her baggy t-shirt and said to me "Where are you from?"

"Scotland" I answered. She looked at me with a puzzled look on her face and said "don't know" before slumping back in her chair and fixing her breast that had slid out the side of her t-shirt again and smiling at me.

This time there were three bangers going round and a steady flow of the white spirit and coke or speed. I was asked if I wanted to try some crack.

"No man, it's okay no thanks" I said.

"Ya mun it's good" Bob said.

"Okay then" I said. I was a bit scared mainly because of what I have heard about it, that it's very addictive. I watched as the big guy got this crystal and started to scrape some of it into a long straight pipe with a round bowl on the end. He sealed it with the end of his banger, and then gave it to me with a lighter. I put my head back so not spill it and took a suck on the pipe nervously. He said "no mun suck it in deep long and slow." I did, sucking then sucking repeatedly, filling my lungs with crack and finishing what was in the pipe before handing it back to him. I let out what was left of the smoke "thanks man" I said and watched as he passed it to someone else. Then I waited to see what was going to happen and how I would react? Looking at the others, they were doing the same. We just carried on talking between ourselves sipping at the beer and handing bangers round the table.

"You okay mun?" The big man said.

"Yeah man" I replied waiting for the same reaction like when I took moochee. Then Bob told the rest of them about the incident at Roxana's place and they all fell about laughing. I felt great. It made me feel like I could do anything. I don't know if it was the crack or just the mixture of everything I had taken, or just the company. Everybody was just having fun. I can remember staring at the girl in the big leather chair; her breast was hanging out the side of her t-shirt again. I looked up at her face and smiled, and then Bob asked me something. I turned round to answer him then back round at the girls breasts once more as she pushed it back under and sorted her t-shirt. I looked up at her face again to her smile. God she was nice! Then the girl opposite said, "Would you like a line?"

"What is it?" I asked.

"Speed" She replied.

"No thanks, I'll pass," I said and cracked a joke. I said something like "I think I'm talking enough crap just now without the help of speed" to reeks of laughter. The guy next to me said that he would take it. He got up, leaned over the table and picked up the straw that was cut in half. He began to snort the line and another one next to it before sitting down again. I sipped away at my beer and talked about God knows what. The crack was O.k. it made me feel great as if I could do anything like I was superman, but mainly it put you in a good mood. I can only talk about my experience with most drugs and touch wood I've never had a bad trip yet. However, that's me. I don't know about other people they may be different.

That was it more or less. We left after a while I don't know how long we were there but it was getting dark and I was well stoned and a bit pissed. But overall, I was feeling great and thinking what a great day it's been. On my way out I turned to the guy who's house it was and asked him if I could use his bathroom. He put his arm around me and led me out the back. There was a tall shed with a slanting corrugated roof, a wooden door that didn't quite meet the end of the roof. There was a gap in the framework of the door at the top about two feet wide then the roof. There was eight or nine other shack like houses like the one I was just in. I said thanks and made my way across this courtyard of shacks. I passed what looked like a shower I stopped, looked, and found it was a shower. It was of wooden construction, round in shape with long wooden planks about waist high all around. They were nailed side by side. Some of them not connecting to the one next to it sometimes leaving a wide gap that you could see through. Supporting the flat corrugated roof was a large round metal drum that I suppose holds the water for the shower. There were six large round wooden posts and leading down from the drum was a stainless steel pipe that connected to a large round stainless steel shower. What I thought was strange, was that there was no top part to the construction. If you were to have a shower, the top part of your body was in full view. The bottom part was hidden behind the planks, well some of them.

The whole thing was very heath Robertson, if you get my meaning. Anyway, I made my way to the toilet. It was like all the other ones, just a large hole in the ground that you stood over and peed into. If you wanted to do the other like I did, you had to squat over the hole and do your thing. As I was squatting over this deep smelly hole, I heard two girls' voices talking. I looked through the crack in the door to see these two Jamaican girls taking their clothes off. There dark bodies silhouetted against the evening sky. They got into the shower and pulled a cord that was hanging down from the top of the shower. Water started to flow and cascade down over these two naked girls to screams of laughter. Their naked bodies relished in the fitted water jet. I finished what I was doing and made my way back to the house passing the two girls, their naked bodies quite visible to me as they washed each other's body. They weren't concerned with my presence at all they just smiled. I hesitated on passing to look at them and then carried on round to the front of the house. I could see Bob and the guy talking and as I made my way towards them Bob turned towards me and walked with me to the pick-up.

What I did feel after a while or heard in my head was a loud snapping sound and I told Bob. At the time, all he said was "that it was the effects of coming down off the crack that's why it's good to smoke cannabis. Therefore, when you come down off the crack you come down on to the cannabis buzz. It's not as hard as coming straight down off crack alone. I can see why people take it. You feel great and so far as I've said I've not had a bad trip yet. What I can say is, sitting in the pick-up going back down the hill on our way to meet Bob's family; I was feeling a bit down. Maybe that's the effect of coming off a crack buzz I don't know. Bob interrupted my thoughts by saying, "we will stop just down here mun, and we will get you laid before you go back to the hotel mun."

I said "no man don't bother its okay." But we stopped outside yet another shack. We got out of the pick-up and really, I didn't need this. I was stoned, pissed, sweaty, and hot. What he had on his mind was the last thing on my mine, but as Bob put it, quote "to fuck a black girl" unquote. So I followed him into this shack to meet this other guy. We shook hands and he asked if I wanted a beer. Bob answered for me saying, "Yes two beers mun and my friend wants to fuck mun." That's one thing about Bob he doesn't mince his words he gets right to the point. We got our beer and the guy disappeared. I turned to Bob and said "Bob I don't need this man lets go." Before he could answer, the guy came back, stood at the door, and beckoned to me to come. I put my beer down beside Bob and gave him a passing glance of disapproval with this idea, but it was too late.

I was ushered into a room. There was a wooden bed with a mattress on it and that's all. Like all the other shacks, the walls were made of wood and not good wood at that. Again, there were gaps in the wood that you could see out or in fact, people could look in. I sat down on the hard mattress and waited with the sweat running of me. It was hot; there were no windows just the gaps in the wooden walls to let the cool air in. But there wasn't any cool air. It was hot outside as it was inside or was it just me being a bit nervous. Either way I was hot and very uncomfortable. Suddenly the door opened and a young girl came into the room. She had very short curly hair and thick red lipstick. She walked over to me and stood beside me looking down at me sitting on the bed. She must have been about fifteen not much more. She was dressed in a short white wrap around fabric sort of dress that was held in tight at the waist with a belt made out off the same fabric. It made her breasts stick out and her nipples show through the thin fabric. I looked up into her face to her smile; she said, "We fuck yes?" Before I could answer, she had undone her dress and it was on the floor lying in a heap by her feet. She was completely naked.

I stood up and started to take my clothes off with the help of the young naked girl. I didn't say a word. By this time, I was hot with perspiration pouring of my forehead and feeling uncomfortable. She lay down on the bed and waited for me to do my thing? I got on top of her but I couldn't get an erection. I lay with my back arched and my hand there trying to get it hard enough to enter this young. She was waiting patiently and kept saying, "You fuck me yes. What you doing?" She put her hand down between my legs and pushed my hand out of the way grabbing my cock and said, "Soft cock no fucking good." This didn't help matters at all. She then pushed me off. I stood up naked with this flopping thing between my legs beside the bed with a roar of clapping and cheering coming from outside. I think the whole neighbourhood were looking through the cracks in the wall cheering which didn't help.

It was dark when we got back to the bay where we'd left the boat. We drove down onto the beach, stopped, and rolled another banger and shared it; talking away standing outside the pick-up and looking at the big red round sun start to set in the sky. That is when Bob said, "come on mun help me push the boat out?" I waded out into the warm water pushing the boat until it was off the sand. Bob jumped in and with a couple of pulls of the cord, the outboard engine rocked into life. He put it into reverse; I gave another big push and jumped in. We headed back along the beach; the hotel was just around the next bay. It was so quiet apart from the boats outboard pushing us through the very clear blue sea. I looked up from the water to see another big hotel with its lights all on and lights all along its private beach. Then I caught sight of my hotel and the bay and as we got closer, I could see the lights on in the big glass bar and the coloured lights that were dotted all the way down from the main hotel, shining light on to the paths that weaved their way through the shrubs and the trees to each chalet. The engine came to a shudder and stopped as the boat drifted in the last bit of water until it came to a stop on the sandy bottom. I jumped out into the shallow water and thanked Bob. I then waded out waist deep pushing the front of the boat backwards and out into deeper water. I stood there looking at Bob pulling away at the cord of the engine as the boat drifted further out, then I heard it spring into life and Bob push the control of the outboard away from him to steer the boat out and back the way he came giving me a wave as he went. He had said before I got out that he would take me to see his family on his next day off if that was okay. I said it would be. I turned, waded to the shore, and walked along the beach then up to the chalet. It was quiet apart from the insects making their usual racket and a distant noise from the bar. I was knackered but I was quite pleased with myself I hadn't let the Scottish side down. I had coped well with all the chemicals and beer that I had taken all day and not made a fool of myself apart from when I told the old lady to go and fuck off. Overall I coped quite well I think and the bonus was I didn't get my throat cut. Now I just wanted to go to sleep! When I got back, I was stopped by the security guard who asked me who I was and what was

I doing here. I told her that I was staying here on holiday and this is my chalet. She didn't believe me and asked me to accompany her to reception if I didn't mind. Maybe the way I was dressed made her stop me. I wasn't your ordinary holiday maker with a clean shirt and neat white shorts and nice white ankle socks, oh no. All I had on was a black t-shirt with some faded out logo on it, my short faded denim shorts, and worn out sandals. I was a bit pissed and well stoned and not to mention unshaven. Not your usual holiday type I suppose. We arrived at reception and was told to stand while the guard went to speak to the receptionist. I watched them talk as the guard pointed to me and the girl behind the desk smiled. The guard came back over and apologised. "No problem" I said smiling. I looked at the girl behind the desk and held my hand up to say thanks and she acknowledged me with a smile. I thought while I was up in the main hotel that I would go and get a big steak and salad in the restaurant. I had eaten a pastry thing earlier that Bob got for me I didn't know what I was but it was okay. I had a bad attack of the munchies and have to tell you that they cook a mean steak here. While they cooked my chosen steak, I went to check out the salads. There was such a variety of different tropical stuff to choose. The food was good and they had a large menu but I just wanted a big fat juicy steak! I sat down with my steak in the restaurant and started to tuck in. God it was good! As I sat there looking about the place, I wondered what the time was as I was the only one here apart from the staff. I could hear laughter and music coming from people in the bar. I thought that I might give it a miss tonight, go back to my chalet, and crash out in the room of mirrors.

The rest of the week was spent just lying in the sun, water-skiing and wind surfing? I didn't really master it at all. Scuba diving, that was amazing. They taught you in the hotel pool first on how to use the aqualungs. You had to pay extra for that. After so many hours in the pool with the instructor, you received your official certificate. It was well worth it. Then they took us out in a boat to another bay. There were about eight of us all together, once we got to where we were going they dropped the anchor. We were advised to put our aqualungs on and then the instructor came round and checked every one in turn to make sure they were okay. Our instructions were to sit on the side of the boat with our backs to the water and check our breathing. Once everyone was ready, we held our masks and fell backwards into the water. The instructor dived with us it was amazing down there. Just seeing all the small fish and other marine life that the instructor showed us as we swam around was fantastic. After a short while, we had to go back up to the boat. One by one, we got in and took our stuff off before talking between ourselves about how amazing it was, as they took us back to the bay where the hotel was. It was afternoon and the sun was so hot that I thought that I would go for a swim before going up to the hotel for some food. After I had eaten, I found my hammock and settled down for the rest of the day just soaking up the rays and Bob brought me my half-full bottle of vodka in the ice bucket with ice every day to sip away at, life was great. Oh and of course, I must not forget perving at all the good-looking girls on the beach.

It was on one of those lazy days that I thought that I would go and try out the nude bathing and get rid of the white marks for the last time. The rest of my body was a deep dark brown but every time I stripped off there was this white patch where my trunks had been. Early the next morning I got up, and had a shower. I stepped out, wrapped the large towel around myself slipped my sandals on leaving my trunks and my faded denim shorts in the chalet and set off in the other direction to the nude bathing. I walked along the path passing the other chalet where the woman was, the shutters where fully open but I couldn't see her as I looked through the long window as I passed. I could hear music coming from inside. I continued on to the beach, my heart was racing as if I were a small boy doing something naughty for the first time. Well in a sense I was, not a small boy but doing something naughty. I was finding it hard to keep myself under control if you know what I mean. There were a few people putting their towels on their sun loungers and positioning them in the sun when I got there. I did the same without taking my towel off. I took my sun lounger down to a few feet away from the water's edge so that the rest of the sun loungers were behind me and lay down with the towel still round me. I was trembling and my heart was thumping with mixed feelings. Should I go back to the chalet or take off the towel? Fuck it. Lying on the sun lounger I undid the towel and let the two ends flop over the sides I was naked. I could feel the sun's rays doing its thing on my white parts and on the rest of my body, lying there with my eyes closed trying to relax. Eventually I did only to be interrupted by an elderly couple fixing their sun loungers beside me, well not right beside me but close enough. They were German and we acknowledged each other by a smile. I turned and looked around me the place was filling up and on the other side were a couple cuddling each other very close. I looked out at the naked people playing in the water and thought 'they don't seem to care at all if their seen.' My eyes were drawn towards this naked couple in their mid twenties wading towards me. The man was pulling the blonde girl, who was laying on her front on an airbed,

They got to the edge of the water; it was too late to cover myself and would only draw attention. so I just lay there frozen revealing all to this good looking blonde that had got up of the air bed and was now standing at the foot of my sun lounger with nothing on. She was looking at me while her partner lifted the airbed out of the water. I smiled a nervous smile and tried not to stare. "Hey I'm Trish and that's Wayne," she said.

"Hi I'm Bobby."

"Oh my God you're English" she replied.

"Not quite, I'm Scottish" I said.

"I love the way you talk" she said fixing her hair up on top of her head with a clip of some kind and standing with her leg apart revealing her large round tanned breasts and her trimmed pubic area with no white bits. Not like me, I was brown all over apart from where my shorts had been and it looked mad, typical Brit.

"Thanks" I said "you don't look bad yourself. I mean talk. I like the way you talk, can I start again?" she laughed and stood there looking right at me inches from my very white patch. She turned round to talk to the guy that she was with and I lowered my eyes to study her even more.

"Darling" she said "this is Bobby he's from Scotland?"

"Hey" he said in a very broad American accent and then went on to say "were going for a drink want to join us Bob?"

"N-n no thanks" I replied nervously.

"Come on" she said.

"Okay then" I said grabbing either end of my towel to wrap around myself before getting up. Trish said, "You don't need that, were just going up here?" Wayne went on in front carrying the airbed while Trish stood and looked at me getting up from the sun lounger and leaving the towel draped over it. "That wasn't too bad was it Bob? Now all you have to do is walk with me past all these people that are going to look at your ding-a-ling!" She laughed again as I stopped in my tracks. "Come on I'm teasing you," She said smiling.

"How did you know it was my first time on this beach?" I asked trying hard to have a casual conversation with Trish when she surprised me by saying, "When I stood staring at your ding-a-ling and that white patch that you Brits' seem to be reluctant to let the sun get to" she said smiling.

"You did that on purpose?" I said.

"Yep" She said and laughed aloud again and then said, "You were quiet" she laughed again and put her hand up to fix the clip that was holding her long blonde hair up but the wind caught it. She just threw her head back letting the wind catch it all and blow it about all over the place and then said "anyway you had a good look at me when I turned to talk to Wayne didn't you?" She turned to face me and looked me in the eyes.

"Well, yes I did and what I saw and what I see now is great."

"Thanks Bobby" she answered.

We met up with her partner who was standing waist high in the water in the pool at the bar ordering drinks. "Bob what do you want to drink? He asked.

"A long cool drink with Smirnoff please." I replied.

"Darling what about you?" she had her usual. I was so glad to get into the pool just so that I could stand waist high and cover myself. There were many people in and around the pool all naked. The bar itself came right out into the pool. You could swim up to it or stand at it like we were doing. I got my drink and talked away to them both, slyly perving at Trish without making a fool of myself. What a body! We stayed there drinking round for round. All they did when you ordered your drink was to take your chalet or room number, write it on a special pad then you signed the bottom of it. We carried on talking and I found out that they were from Washington D.C. We swapped stories and had more drinks. I was becoming more relaxed the more I drank and talked to them both. We arranged to meet up in the main bar that night for dinner. I asked Wayne where he got the airbed. "Take that one," he said. He went on to tell me where you get them.

"Thanks" I said getting out of the water and catching Trish's eye, as she looked straight at my ding-a-ling, then up at my face, and smiled. Whilst Wayne was in deep conversion with another couple and the barman, she said, "don't forget to put some sun block on your ding-a-ling it's getting red."

I'll see you tonight," I said and chuckled to her and smiled back at her, screwing my face up in a way to say shut up. This time it wasn't that bad when I left the pool, the drink had given me Dutch courage and I had the airbed to hide behind. I went back to my sun lounger put the airbed down beside me and fixed the towel and lay back down on it thinking its not to bad this nudism I'll come back tomorrow. It's amazing what a few drinks can do to boost your confidence. I lay there and looked down at my ding-a-ling as Trish called it to see if it was red. No, it's not that bad I think she was taking the piss. I lay there for some time letting the hot sun beat down on my body. I looked around trying to get Dutch courage to take the airbed out onto the water, as I was getting rather hot lying in the sun and the water looked so inviting. I decided to go for it. Getting up, I grabbed the airbed and walked into the sea. The water was great. It was just right, warm and so very clear. I waded out so far so that I was decent and jumped on. The whole thing flipped over and I was under the water in seconds. I stood up, tried it again and the same thing happened. I walked back in to shallower water, my ding-a-ling in full view of the whole beach not to mention the people floating about on their airbeds. I tried again and the same thing happened. I immediately thought I'm drawing attention to myself and my nakedness. People are going to be looking at this naked idiot trying to get on an airbed. The only thing about being naked was it made me more self-conscious. I tried to do it another way by pushing the airbed between my legs. Standing there with my legs apart and my ding-a-ling bobbing about on the surface of the water I tried to push one end of the bed through my legs, "fuck me" how could something so easy be so difficult. It was getting just like the fucking hammock. By this time, I was sure people would be looking at my nakedness and me and thinking *what* is he trying to do.

I spread my legs wide apart, bent over, and stuffed the front end through my legs from behind. God knows what I looked like from the shore, bent over with my white bum sticking up in the air. I got it through, up, and out the other side so that I was standing in the middle, with the front and the back of the airbed out of the water. I lifted one leg slowly out of the water and laid it on the airbed then the same with the next one. Yes that's it I was on but my ding-a-ling was all squashed up underneath. I started to paddle with my hands and got a bit further out before sorting myself out and getting comfortable and letting the sun beat down on my bum. It was great. I just lay there drifting and bobbing about on the water. Looking over the front of the airbed and down through the crystal blue clear water and looking at the small fish swimming below me. I could feel the sunshine beating down on me so I splashed the cool water over my back and my bum thinking how can I turn over without falling off. I decided not to bother and let the sun do its thing on my back. My back was all right because it was brown and could cope with the sun but I had my doubts about my bum being white.

I ended up using the nudist beach and the airbed off and on through the holiday to get that even suntan that I wanted so much. My bum did cope with the sun that first day on the airbed. But there was one incident that embarrassed me and I don't know how to tell it to you. I suppose the only way is to tell it how it happened. Well, I was down on the nudist beach and decided to go back to the chalet. I wrapped the towel round myself and laid the airbed on the sun lounger as advised. I started to walk along the beach back to the chalet when I came to the shack that advertised full body massages with tropical oils, the one I told you about earlier. It was situated right in the middle of the nudist beach. I was reading the large white letters on the board when a young Jamaican girl came out in a white short skirt and matching jacket and said, "You like me to massage you and make you feel good?"

"No thanks it's okay." However, she kept on at me "come in lie on table" she grabbed my arm.

"No, no, no money sorry." I said but she insisted. Pulling at my arm and smiling at me, "doesn't matter give me your room number or chalet number? Come lie down please," she said. She was a true native with a very strong Jamaican accent.

"Oh, okay." She was very persuasive. Like all Jamaican girls, she looked good in her short tight white uniform and being a sucker I gave in to her pleading and being me, I'll try anything once. The shack was just a large room with a low long table with a large towel covering all of it. A long low open window with the shutter propped up looked out onto the beach. There wasn't any privacy. If you where lying on the table, anybody passing by could see all of you, if you know what I mean. On saying that, everybody had seen everything earlier. I was on a nudist beach come on. However on the shelves inside the shack were plastic bottles with white labels stuck on them saying 'authentic oils.' There were many folded towels all neatly stacked each side of the green bottles. Next to them, on the walls were posters advertising authentic oils. In bold blue lettering across them in Jamaican was where they came from. I was told to lie face down on top of the towel on the table with my legs apart and relax. She undid my towel, pulled it out from underneath me and laid it loosely over my bum with the two ends hanging over each side of the table. I could feel her massaging my foot squeezing and rubbing each one with her oily hands. She asked me where I came from and we struck up a conversation between us. Asking each other things as she moved up one of my legs slippery squeezing, rubbing and chopping away at the top part of my leg then squeezing the inner part then on up to the bottom of the towel, then back down and start on the other doing the same.

She stopped and I could see her go and get another new bottle of the thick green oil, open it and come back. She pulled the towel off my bum leaving me naked on the table in full view of passersby. Luckily there wasn't any. She proceeded to pour oil over my bottom and rub it in using both her hand on each cheek. Squeezing, and pushing them up and out as far as they would go. Separating them then pushing them together again, slipping her hand down between my legs. Sometimes she would touch the back of my testicles. Then back up, running her fingers up tightly between the cheeks of my bum and making me tense and then relax it again as the last of her fingers slipped through between my cheeks. I felt more oil getting poured over the back of my testicles and slide around them. The feeling was a bit strange. I felt the oil slide round and over them and slip slowly down between them and the inner part of my legs. I could feel her fingers rubbing the oil in and over my testicles and start to massage them, pulling them down, and squeezing them around. Massaging them with all of her fingers then sliding her finger up between my cheeks making me tense my bum again. She did this for a while pouring more oil on my bottom. Then she moved on up my back to my shoulders. Squeezing, massaging her way up with more oil. I couldn't help but think while laying there that I was glad that she had stopped when she did because I felt it a bit erotic and aroused. The minute that thought entered my head I started to get an erection, I couldn't stop it. I tried thinking of other things so it would subside, anything even my ex-wife. But no it just got harder and harder. 'Fuck' what I'm I going to do when she asks me to turn over, Shit? I could feel her massaging her way slowly down my back talking to me as she did. Down, down onto my bottom then she put her hand between my legs, oh God. Back to my balls again slipping her fingers around them she squeezed gently pulling them down and separating them. She rubbed them for a second or so but it was enough to put me over the edge. She brought her fingers up through between my cheeks again slowly then with both hands on each cheek, she pulled them up and pushed them apart as she massaged and squeezed them hard.

That was it. I was so sexually aroused by now and there wasn't a damn thing I could do. I just hoped she would continue on my back to give me time. I turned my head to see where she had put the towel. I couldn't see it, shit. I was in a bit of a panic. I don't know if she could hear it in my voice as we made small conversation but she went on talking and asking questions about all sorts of things. All I could think about was my fucking hard-on that I was lying on and up to know was able to conceal it. Then it happened. Yes, she asked me to turn over. I pretended not to hear and turned my head to look at her for the first time since I had lain down on my front. She was smiling showing off her white teeth.

"What did you say?" I asked.

"Turn over please" she said smiling. Shit, there was nothing for it I had to turn. As I did, my erection sprang into action wondering why it had been suppressed for so long. I could see her looking at my erection as it sprang up to say hello to her. I couldn't hide it. I lay there, on my back on the table in full view of her and any passersby that might walk by. It just stuck up like a centre pole in a tent. However, there wasn't any tent. Very erect and very, very clear to her, she stood looking down at it smiling not saying a word. Pouring more oil on her hands, she looked at my embarrassed face. Smiling she said to me "you like massage no?"

Nervously I said, "Yes, it's okay."

"More than Okay I tink" She said and laughed. She walked round to the side of the table so that I was in full view of anyone walking past the window and started to massage my leg. She worked her way up with both hands right up to the top part of my thigh, pulling, pushing, and squeezing with my erection moving in time with her hands. She was being very professional and very careful not to touch me there. I looked at her only to see the side of her face right over my erection obviously looking straight down at it. Fascinated, I think by the way it moved every time she massaged my inner thigh. She looked round with a big smile on her face "you like massage very much yes" she said. I looked at her not saying a thing and gave a nervous smile before looking back up at the roof hoping it would subside, but no. "I get more oil for other leg," she said as she walked past me smiling looking straight into my eyes

Going to a shelf behind me, she left me lying there naked hoping that nobody would pass the window and look in and see me there like this. Then I heard voices close by Shit. Yes, right enough a couple walked past and looked in. They paused for a bit then went on giggling between themselves. I started to get up but she stop me saying "not finished." She came back with a full bottle and walked round to the other side of the table, opened the bottle and started to do the same on the other leg again working her way up to the very top of my thigh. This time I could see her face clearly. I looked into her eyes and watched her as she massaged my thigh. I could see that she was pulling my inner thigh back with both hands in a turning motion and as she did, she looked at my erection move. She did this for a while pushing and turning my thigh with her oily hand. Turning her head, she looked at me smiling. I pretended not to look at her. I was a bit embarrassed about the whole thing and without a word of a lie she turned back and looked at my erection once again. She then moved on up onto my tummy still with a smile on her face. What the hell, I thought lying there looking at her as she poured more oil onto my tummy and rubbed it in as she massaged. Sometimes looking back down at my erection then up into my eyes she moved up and away from my erection, thank fuck. She moved on up my body massaging and then walked round the back of my head and started to massage my shoulders for a while. She walked round and stood by the side of the table looking at me lying there on my back. She turned round picked a towel of the shelf and started to wipe her hands and then turned back round to me smiling not saying a word. She just stood there wiping her hands and looking at my naked body lying on the table and at my still hard erection. I was about to say something when she said, "finished. You like my massage yes?" Before I could say anything, she said again, "you come back yes?" and handed me a folded towel. I wrapped it round myself as I got off the table. I stood at the side of the table still very embarrassed and thanked her.

"I do massage in room or chalet as well if you like?" She said.

"Yes maybe" I replied and thanked her again for such a good massage. She walked me to the door, opened it, and then said, "I come to chalet you ask for me at reception?"

"Okay" I said leaving the wooden shack and continuing my way back across the hot sand back to the chalet.

"I come to chalet before you go to Scotland for even better one?" I waved and shouted back okay.

I got to my chalet and just threw myself down on the bed. I lay there thinking of the massage lady and myself. Lying there with a hard-on, on that table in front of her as her hands massaged away inches from my dick. I must go to reception and find out how to book her to come to the chalet here and do it again. It would be so kinky in front of all these mirrors. I must find out what the extras are. I lay there quite relaxed thinking about the extras and listening to the loud sound of the insects outside my chalet the bullfrogs doing their bit. The room was hot and the only thing that was keeping it cool was a large fan circling around above me. All that oil that the massage lady put on me made my body sticky in the heat of the room so I decided to take a shower. I went into the bathroom stripped off and stood under the shower with my two hands stretched out in front, resting on the tiled wall. I let the water bounce of my head and run down over my shoulders and back. I held my head down and looked at the water twisting and turning as it disappeared down the drain. I felt so relaxed standing there that I thought of the masseuse. She was all right. She had made me feel so very relaxed well not completely; there was one part of my body that just did not want to relax. I looked down at it dangling down between my legs with the water dripping of it and thought why the fuck didn't you do that half hour ago you fucking thing. I washed and got out of the shower. Drying myself off roughly I walked back into the room, stood in front of the mirror, and used the hairdryer to dry my hair. While I stood in front of the mirror, I thought that I might have a lie down for an hour or so. I was due to meet Bob in the main bar so that we could arrange a time and place to meet is family before his day off tomorrow.

I put the hairdryer back down on the dressing table and finished off combing my hair. I turned to go lie on the bed when I saw the woman from the next chalet standing in her open window in her long white evening dress. She was looking at me. It was too late to hide or cover myself up so I just gave her a wave as I walked to the bed. I don't know why I waved maybe it was the embarrassment of being caught with no clothes on again that made me do it. I don't know. Anyway, I don't know how long she had been standing there. She could have been standing there for the full time I came out the shower and stood in front of the mirror drying my hair. I just forgot about that long fucking window that all the chalets have. On saying that, I did close it when I left the chalet so it must be the people that clean the chalet that opened them. With her chalet, being so close to mine you cannot help but notice people standing in the next chalet, it's the way they are built close with an odd shrub or a tree separating them. Anyway she had a good eye full and the way she applauded by putting her hands together in a clapping motion she must of approved of what she had seen. I lay down on the bed and thought that I would have a sleep before going up to the hotel. I must have dozed off and woke again as there was the noise of people laughing outside my chalet; I lay there listening to them as they walked along the path in front of my chalet, Americans by the sounds of it. A red dot flickered in the top right corner of the mirror. This time I didn't move I just lay there naked on the bed and tried to pin point the red light. Yes, there it is again. There is definitely something behind that mirror. Or even all the mirrors, I don't know. What could I do? I suppose I could smash it and see what's behind it. But what if I was mistaken? Thinking back, I had seen bits of mirror outside other chalets. Maybe someone else had seen the light and broken the mirror. I wasn't that bothered about it and I could be mistaken. I thought that I'd better get dressed and go to see Bob. Getting off the bed, I had another look. Right enough there was another flicker. Fuck me I thought what's it all about? Do they make their own porn and sell it or what? I must ask Bob.

I sat down at the bar and ordered my usual drink. I asked the barman who served me if he could get Bob to come round after he had finished serving a customer. He said he would. I swivelled round on the chair to look at some of the people that were staying in the hotel. Some of them were on the stage in fancy dress being hypnotised. They were doing crazy things not knowing they were doing to the applause and laughter of the audience especially when they did something funny. As I sat there, I was getting more and more engrossed in the people on the stage. I hadn't noticed this woman standing ordering drinks next to me at the bar until she said in American accent, "hey I didn't recognize you with your clothes on."

"What, sorry what did you say?" She was about to repeat herself when I recognised her. Getting up of my seat to say hi properly she put her hand out for me to shake it. I turned it over, kissed it, and said, "Hi I'm Bobby."

"Hi I'm Tiffany and what I said was, was that I didn't recognize you . . ." she stopped herself, "it sounds corny the second time round."

We laughed and I said, "You're the lady in the next chalet to mine?"

"Well done Bobby," she replied. I was about to say that I was sorry about the incident but she stopped me short by putting the point of her fingers softly over my mouth and smiled, "are you with anyone here in the hotel?"

"No I'm by myself," I said.

"Oh, I haven't seen you on the beach or around the hotel?"

"Well I've been here. Maybe we just keep missing each other. Are you with anyone?"

"Yes I'm here with my . . . I waited for her to say my husband but no. "I'm here with my sister and her husband."

"Oh" I said thinking 'mmm.'

"We're taking a vacation together. I'm just getting over a relationship." We talked and drank together at the bar. She wasn't in any hurry to go anywhere. Then Bob came round, "hey mun how are you mun?"

"I'm okay thanks Bob." I said and introduced him to Tiffany. As they talked, I took the opportunity to study Tiffany. She was about the same height as me with short-cropped brown hair, with big brown earrings that matched her hair. A pinkie kind of lipstick and similar eye shadow, she wasn't bad looking, about thirty and quite a nice curvy figure. She was standing there in that tight fitting long white evening dress that I had seen her standing in the chalet in. It had a low-neck line that went into a V, showing off her round firm breasts. From where I was standing it was quite visible that she wasn't wearing a bra. Bob left to go and serve someone. She turned back to me and we talked. We seemed to get on all right as we sat at the bar drinking. I asked her if her chalet was the same as mine did it have all the mirrors. She said 'yes it did and so did her sisters chalet.' "It's a bit kinky isn't it?"

I laughed and said, "Yes, I can't help looking at myself when I lie down on the bed." She laughed and said that she did the same.

"Do you think there's a hidden camera behind it taking photos?"

"Why do you say that?"

"Oh no reason, I just think it's kinky as well, having all those mirrors, it doesn't matter which way you lie on the bed. You can see every part of your body in them and I mean every part," I said. She smiled and said "yes I know." She told me that her brother-in-law said that he saw a red light flash as they both were lying on their bed one afternoon doing you know what. She blushed a little.

"Funny you should say that. I was drying my hair in front of the mirror after coming out the shower before . . ."

She interrupted me and said, "I know. I was watching you from my chalet" and gave a big smile.

"Oh, that's right you did. I'm sorry I didn't realise that the window was open," I said. She just smiled as she turned to order another drink from the other barman that walked past. "Anyway" I said "after being inconspicuous to you I thought that I would lie down on my bed, after a while I thought that I saw a flicker of a light in the top hand corner of the mirror." She leaned over to say something so that no one would hear what she was going to say about the mirrors and the light.

As she did, the front of her dress opened a bit. It was enough for me to see her full left breast and nipple just hanging there without any support. Instantly she put her hand down to pull the fabric together after noticing me staring at her breast. "Sorry Bobby sorry."

Looking back up at her face, I smiled. "You do have great looking tits I-mean breasts. I couldn't help but notice them as your dress opened, sorry."

"Ta for the complement. I suppose I can't complain after seeing you posing for me bollock naked."

Just then, the barman came back with her drink and put it down in front of her. "Could I have another one as well please?" I asked then turned to Tiffany as she sipped away at her drink. "I wasn't posing. I didn't know . . ."

She interrupted "Oh yes you did? I enjoyed every minute of it."

"How long were you there for?"

"Right from when you came out the shower."

"Fuck me! You were there all that time." she nodded as she took another drink. I jokingly said we must do it again and we both laughed. "Have you eaten yet? Would you like to join me or are you waiting for your sister?" She finished taking a drink out of her long glass fighting to keep the ice from spilling out as she caught one in her mouth and crunched it with her teeth. She put her hand up to wipe away the excess water from the melted ice that dribbled out of her mouth and smiled.

"Yes, no . . . I mean yes I would like that and no they are away into town."

"Okay great. Come on then let's get a table and sit down." We got up and I waited for Tiffany to pick her drink up. I told her to go first not because I was a gentleman but because I wanted to check her out. What a wiggle she had in that tight long dress and not a bad bum. As we moved across the room weaving in and out of the table and chairs that were dotted all around. In front of the large wooden stage that were full of people enjoying the hypnotist still working is magic. We went through the glass door at the end of the room into the dining room and waited for a waiter to find a table for us even though plenty were empty. A waiter came over and ushered us to a table for two. It was in the corner, under a wooden archway filled full of different coloured flowers. We sat down, picked up a menu each, and looked at it.

After the meal and several bottles of wine, we sat there talking. The conversation turned back to the mirrors and did I think that there was a camera behind them

"I don't know. However, I did see a red light flicker as I lay on my bed. Your brother-in-law said that he saw one as well. Therefore, there must be something there. "Do you not think so?" She agreed and asked if I would have a look at hers on our way home. I said I would but didn't know what I would see. As when I looked at mine, all I saw was my reflection, but I would have a look. She thanked me then said, "Do you fancy another bottle?"

"Yes go on," I said. "It's not as if we were paying for it." Everything was inclusive. The evening went well and I did end up going back to her chalet and checked out the mirrors. Well, that's one way of putting it.

Well before I end this chapter about Jamaica if you're still reading, Bob the barman took me to see his family and his great looking sister who I treated to dinner. Well, that's a lie. I didn't have to pay for anything because I took her to the hotel that I was staying in, cheapskate. After that night, we spent the rest of the holiday together. She would stay with me in the chalet. Her brother would drop her off by boat and we would go and eat. Then we would go back to the chalet or her brother would come for me. I would go out with her and her brothers and their friends. We went to the local clubs in the main town and would snort, smoke bangers, pop a few pills then we would come back to the chalet together. The main thing I tried was crack. It was amazing. I can see why people get addicted to it. It just made you feel so great. The massage lady, well I went to reception and booked her to come to my chalet one afternoon. I found out if I paid her a bit more she would do other things in front of all the mirrors. All in all the holiday was great. I found out later there was a camera in the room all the chalets had them. As for the massage lady, she was part of the set up too. Oh well, I hoped they enjoyed looking as much as I did doing.

CHAPTER THIRTEEN

HOME TO A NEW LIFE

The aeroplane landed at Glasgow's International Airport. I made my way back to the farmhouse of hell in heavy rain only to find that the house was being sold in a week. I didn't even unpack. I got what was left of my things and moved into my mother's cottage in the village. My business partner and my ex-wife moved into another cottage together and still are there to this day I think. The house sold and the money paid off most of our creditors. When my mother died, she left the cottage to my brother, so I arranged to rent it from him as he spent most of his time in Edinburgh. The cottage was split up into three and he let out the one on the end full time. The one in the middle was a holiday let and the one on the other end is where I started to live. It's not what I thought it would be like to be quite honest. I thought being single again would mean partying with young girls but oh no. It was more like being bored, lonely, and having no one to talk to. The worst thing was being alone at night. The first night was the worst. My mind would not switch off. It was like a computer downloading stuff all the time to my brain, what the fuck I am going to do now. You know night-time is the worst time. Everything looks bleak, as you are lying there alone. It wasn't long before I got the cottage like I wanted it. I could do most things like cook, keep the place clean, thanks to the training from the hotel. It was furnished with my brothers things but beggars can't be choosers and I was grateful there was stuff there. Else, it would have been bare boards and a mattress on the floor. I still had my mobile mill. I had asked a friend if he wouldn't mind hiding it for me so *you know who* wouldn't find it and sell it along with all the other things to pay off our creditors.

Through this friend, I got a job working on a private estate and set up the mill there to cut trees down and make wooden planks, fencing posts, and other things for the estate. Everything was okay. I was working and had somewhere to sleep. The owner wanted me to cut and supply wood for the joiner to rebuild cottages on the estate using freshly cut timber from the estate. It didn't matter how many times we said to the owner "you can't use the timber straight away. It would have to be kiln dried then stress treated before you can use it for building." But he couldn't understand? He would say, "I've got all these trees here on my estate and I can't use them to rebuild my cottages, balls! It didn't matter how many times we would explain it to him all he would say was "work with the joiner and be sure to have the wood ready by the time he came back up from London." I cut the wood as he wanted, but it all warped. I pinned it and would turn it over but it wasn't any good. Therefore, the joiner bought timber from the local timber yard to use on the cottages and explained to the owner when he came back up that the wood off the estate wasn't any good. Eventually the proprietor bought a large run-down sawmill with eight blokes all ready working there. I was sent up there to work between the mill that he bought and with the wood on the estate, but he still didn't have an idea about wood. I don't know why he bought a sawmill because he didn't listen. Saying that, he listened to the wrong people instead of listening to the people that were working there and that knew the machinery. But no, he brought people up from London to advise him how to run it. What do I know? I didn't care a damn because he never listened. It didn't matter how many times you told him anything. But he didn't make his money by being stupid. I think it was a way to make him money by using some of the 'great money' to invest into some other business, but I didn't say that.

Anyway, I stayed there for about three years or so. I settled into a routine making okay money and spending it as fast as I was making it. One night I got a phone call from a friend saying why don't I come up to Glasgow and have a night out in the pubs with his girlfriend and her mates. So I did and nearly every weekend after that they would ring up and say was I coming up? I would go up and meet them in their flat. I would buy food, drink, and hash and take it with me just to say thanks, as you do, well I did. It was on one of those weekends when his girlfriend suggested that we go to the club that she and her friends go to?" I instantly thought that I was too old for clubbing and said that to them. They booed me and said don't be daft. They were all about mid twenties-thirties, but my friend was about thirty-four and stayed in a large three bedroom top floor flat. He worked offshore on an oilrig. He had so many weeks on, and so many weeks off. His girlfriend worked in a hotel somewhere in Glasgow as a hotel receptionist and not bad looking. She was a bit younger than he was. I would say about twenty-four or five and they seemed to get on okay together. They all decided to go this Saturday. We had a few drinks in the flat and roughly two chillums each. A chillum is a long narrow glass like object for smoking hashish. You can get them in all kinds of shapes and sizes, similar to a Hookah Pipe. This one sat on the floor and was about four foot high, with a glass like bowl at the bottom of which you put water in, or in this case Vodka. We passed it around each of us, and then it was time to hit the pubs and clubs and whatever else was available. Ginger's girl turned round to me and said, "Don't worry grandpa well take good care of you."

"Thanks" I said as she grabbed my arm and led me out of the flat. We went and quite honestly, I thought that I would be the oldest swinger there. Nevertheless, there were a few not many, mostly the average age was eighteen to thirty, I think.

It was at this club that I met an old friend that I hadn't seen for years. It was his night off and he said that he always came here on his night off. I interrupted him and asked him what he was doing here. He continued to ask what am I doing here. I explained that I was with Ginger and I had been coming up to Glasgow on a regular basis since my divorce. I had been coming here with Ginger and his girlfriend Pat and their mates. The friend that I was talking to in this club was managing another club in Glasgow for this young tycoon. I think that's the best way to describe him. He had loads of money and this friend at the club that he worked in introduced me to him. It was the weekend again and we all decided to go to this other club where my friend worked as the manager. We all thought we might get in for nothing since I knew the main man, well not the main man but the man. Off we went and right enough we did get in for nothing. We were introduced to the main man, not just my 'man' but the main man. In my mind the owner of the club was very cocky and a self-assured kind of guy in his mid thirties. He was in to everything if you take my meaning. His penthouse flat was just out of this world to an ordinary guy like me. The pile on the white carpet in his lounge was so deep if you lay down on it you would disappear. The whole place was amazing with no money spared. It must have cost a small fortune to get it like that. Even the big bathroom with its sunken bath and his way-out shower and Jacuzzi, God I could go on about it. It was the sort of place I would love for myself, maybe that was it. I could see myself in his shoes, ha. The girls that hung around him they were incredibly good looking and not just one, the whole fucking lot. The lifestyle of this guy was amazing. I don't know which impressed me more, his lifestyle the penthouse, or his fast cars. I think it was the whole set up. I was just gob-smacked for a young guy to have so much. It reminded me of the Hoorah Henrys in London, the Slone Rangers but somehow you expect London to have all those sort of things, not my hometown. Okay he didn't speak like them but I think he probably had about the same amount of money the way he flashed it about. My mother would have said, "He's new money." New money, old money . . . money is money in my mind. It doesn't matter who's got it if you get my drift. Anyway, as long as I was getting invites to his parties through his manager I didn't care if he was new money. At least he had money.

One weekend we were asked to another one of his parties in his penthouse. We were very privileged. There's only a selected few that are asked up to his penthouse. We wangled it through my friend the manager. After that first party, our names kept on coming up on his personal list, yes! As always, there was an abundance of pill popping, smoking, snorting, drinking Champagne and other drink if you wanted it and loads of food. The smoked glass table at the door always had a young attractive girl behind it, organising lines of speed for everyone to snort as they came in. You had the choice of two lines or just one but you had to have one before you were allowed in. I was standing in the middle of the room with the four of my friends as they talked amongst themselves. I stood there with them, perving as usual. My eye caught sight of these three young girls standing across the room talking amongst themselves and only wearing a slip. I think that's what you call it, an underskirt the thing that your wife would wear under her evening dress. But these girls didn't have an evening dress on, all they were wearing was the small underskirt that ended well above their knees and so very clearly visible, no bra's. Pat, Gingers girlfriend caught me looking and pinched my bum "put that tongue back in your mouth old-yin." I turned to her rubbing my bum where she had pinched me and saw her smiling at me. As I smiled back, I said "was it that obvious?"

"Yes grandpa" she replied and laughed. I carried on talking to her, glancing over to the three young girls looking at their breasts that were so visible through the thin material. My eyes caught a Kenyan lady that was standing talking to a crowd of people by the window. Our conversation stopped and Pat turned round to see what had made it stop.

"Bobby, this is . . ." and she told me her name.

"God, can you get me to meet her, she's fantastic?"

"I'll try" she said and continued to explain to me what she had in mind. "If you go to the toilet, I'll go over to her and start talking to them."

I interrupted her "yes, and then what?"

"You come over and I'll introduce you" she finished.

"Okay." I replied. It worked. I walked over to Pat who introduced me. She was great looking, black obviously. With long hair, red lipstick revealing two full sensual lips, a great figure and sprayed on white pants showing of her round African bum. We talked, talked more, and arranged to meet in the club next weekend, great. Unfortunately, I didn't make it. I tried to let her know but couldn't. I even phoned Pat hoping that she might see her in the club or outside because she knew who she was. I even asked her to find out where she worked and lived. What it is to have good friends? I even phoned up Carol. She would know. She knew everyone and everything that went on in Glasgow. She grow up in the slums of Glasgow, a great looking girl, but the minute she opened her mouth she had that high squeaky voice and her vocabulary, well she didn't have one. Every word ended in fuck that, fuck this and fuck you, fucking bastard. She always reminded me of my old school mates the twins.

I met Carol when she was eighteen. At the time, I was doing a favour for someone that I had met through someone in Sandbank, not to mention any names. Sandbank is a small village just outside Dunoon where I had the pizza place. I was in this close, an entrance to a block of flats in Pollack Road in Glasgow. It's not a very good area to be in after dark if you get my drift. I was on the fourth flight of stairs on my way down when I heard this man and girl's voices screaming, swearing, and shouting at each other from the next level. I came down to see this drunken man beating and slapping this young girl around outside this doorway of this flat. There was a baby in its carrycot in the doorway. I stopped him "what's the problem mate?" I said trying to be tough.

"Fuck off or you'll get the same." He said and went to slap the girl across the face again when I pushed him out the way. He was so drunk that he slipped and fell down against the wall. I grabbed my opportunity, grabbed him by the throat, and knocked his head against the wall. "I'm making it my problem mate." My former school education kicked in, oops. It sounds very heroic but he was drunk and slipped. Maybe I should have kept on walking past them but I didn't. Maybe if he wasn't so drunk I wouldn't have been so brave, all these maybes. I was there and did what I did. The drunk was her husband. He used to do this all the time to her. I got a mouth full from Carol for helping her at the time as well. Anyway, that's how I got to know Carol. I said to her at the time "if you have any problems just call me." She did. Her sister phoned me and asked me to come and help. Carol's husband had beaten her up and thrown her out of her flat. She was scared for her little girl. They didn't want to call the police for certain reasons. I didn't ask why. "What can I do? You must have friends up there that can help. Her sister said "yes" they did but she didn't want to involve them for some reason. It sounded very dodgy. She went on to say, "Carol's husband is scared of you because of what you did!" I laughed and said, "If he wasn't so drunk I would have just walked past."

"No you wouldn't you're a nice guy." Call me soft or just a fucking nutter. I arranged to meet her in a pub called the 'Counting House' in George Square. We all used to meet there from time to time before going off to different clubs. After I saved the night like a knight in shining armour, well not quite like that but I did sort it out. I had two girls pushing me on all the time from behind and a small baseball bat that one of them gave me. After that, she phoned quite often at the pizza shop and I would go up the next night or whenever we arranged to meet. It was mostly to do with her husband; he was a dick to say the least. As I said, he used to beat her every time he got drunk and I mean really beat her, like giving her black eyes and so many bruises over her body. Just being there in her flat was enough to stop her husband. After that first time, he didn't know what to make of me, lucky for me. Her mother, sister, and I helped her to leave him eventually with the help of the court. She moved to another block of flats with her baby girl and we became very, very good friends, no sex, just a very good bond between us. She helped me out with a problem that I had ongoing that's why I was up there in the first place. She knew the right people and they helped me to sort out my problem. Thinking back I have asked her why me? Why me on that night when she had all these much heavier guys up there? But I'll never get the truth out of her, but that's just Carol. Lucky for me everything on that night went all right but it could have gone all wrong. It's funny how things happen? If I hadn't been in that gang and helped to stand up for myself at school and put into practice what I'd learned, I probably wouldn't have been at that place and Carol wouldn't have told me about this guy that she new and how he could help me with the problem I had at that particular time. I probably wouldn't have had to help her in the first place. It's a crazy world.

I met some of Carol's girl friends months later when I was visiting her in her new flat just to see how things were going. What a difference in her. She was more relaxed and happier. She even had her friends there when I knocked on the door. I said that I would call back but she insisted and said "no, no come in." I followed Carol into the room; there were four of her friends sitting around this wooden coffee table in the living room. They were having a loud discussion about something; I don't know what but was soon to find out. I was told to sit down by Carol then she told her friends my name and that I helped her to get this flat. One of them called Brenda asked me if I ever been to a massage parlour. "No I haven't" I replied. Brenda was quite slim looking; it was quite hard to see what her figure was like because she was sitting down. She had long black hair that came down to her shoulders with a fringe, blue eyes and a nice smile. She had on a light blue v-neck jumper revealing her deep cleavage and her well-formed breasts that stuck out as she lent forwards to pick up her mug of coffee that was sitting on the table, and a pair of faded jeans. Carol butted in and said, "We were discussing different massage parlours, Brenda and Jill both work in one and she's a pole dancer." She pointed to a very curvy busty blonde sitting well back in a chair. She smiled but didn't say anything. They were all good looking girls I thought as Carol introduced me to them all one by one. Brenda said "We never use our real names. I use Patricia!"

"Oh right" I said "why?"

"Why what?" she said and the blonde-haired person that was sitting in the chair sat forwards and interrupted the other girl.

"Why do they use different names?"

"Yes" I said. She told me all about it, and how all the girls had to go regularly to the doctor for check up's. Jill said putting her mug down on her lap and holding it there. "We're the cleanest girls in Glasgow?" She lifted her mug back up to take another drink, looking at me as she did it.

I asked them different things about it.

"Why don't you go along? Its ten pounds to get in then you strip off. You get a locker to put all your clothes in and a towel to wrap around yourself," Brenda said. The blonde girl, called Sam, cracked a joke. I didn't hear what she had said but they all laughed. There was another girl; she was smaller than the rest with short blonde hair and again good looking. She wore a tracksuit so I couldn't see what her figure looked like. She leaned forwards out of another deep chair and said, "You can decide what girl you want as well, just like now." They all laughed.

"So which one would you like?" Jill said smiling, they all laughed again.

"Oh yeah, how much will it cost? I said smiling, looking at each one of them in turn.

"You haven't got enough for us all." Sam said "and you couldn't cope with the four of us." They all roared with laughter.

I looked at Brenda and Jill in turn, "where is this place?"

Brenda told me where it was and I said that the next time I'm in Glasgow I'll come along.

Jill interrupted "no you fucking wont, you're too fucking scared?" in her Glaswegian accent.

"I will," I said "next time I'm here I'll come along." I then cracked a joke saying "it would be worth it to see you both naked." Looking straight at Jill, she just smiled and sank back into her chair. I didn't want them to think that they were any less of a person because they were working girls, in fact, I didn't, and they weren't. They were all great looking girls and great company to be with, as Carol was. They were all good looking as I said and had great bodies and nice breasts. Thinking about it, I wouldn't mind seeing them naked and trying to cope with the lot at once. Even if I couldn't, it would be great to try. What a chapter it would make in this book?

They weren't going to take no for an answer about me coming and having a massage. They even arranged a night out afterwards in one of the clubs were Sam would be working. So I arranged to meet Carol at her flat and she would then tell me how to get to the place where Brenda and Jill were working. The night came and I made my way to Glasgow and to Carol's flat, where she gave me a drink and offered me something to smoke. "You know you don't have to go if you don't want to?" She said.

"No, I said I would go. I don't want them to think that I'm scared of going."

"Okay" she said, refilling the bowl at the top of the long glass bong with more hash and lighting it. Taking a long suck on it, she then handed it over to me, still holding her breath with her mouth full of smoke. Letting it out, she told me how to get there "just leave you car here and take a taxi; It would be a lot easier." She said. After a few more buckets and a mug of tea, I got a taxi outside Carol's flat. I asked the driver to drop me of just around the corner from the place. I didn't want him thinking that I was going in there.

I walked round the corner and right enough there it was. I walked up to the doorway. My heart was thumping. I rang the bell, the electronic lock buzzed as the catch opened the door. I walked in and along this corridor to where a neon light sticking out from the wall said in blue and red letters "Tiffanies." I stood outside still trembling with excitement or fear I don't know which. I composed myself and rang the bell. Again there was a buzz and the door opened. I walked in, the door automatically closed behind me making a click as it made contact with the lock. I was left in this hall. In front of me was a girl behind a desk. She smiled as I walked up to her. "Hallo, what's your name?" she asked. I told her and she wrote it down in a large red book that was open in front of her. She said smiling, "that will be ten pounds for your entrance fee." I gave it to her and she turned round and picked a towel off a pile of all neatly folded, and with that a key. "Is it your first time?"

"Yes" I replied.

She started to tell me that it was ten pounds entrance fee and then the prices varied on what I wanted from the girl of my choice. Then it was time to pick. "The rooms are up the stairs and along . . ." She leaned over the counter and pointed round behind her where the changing rooms, showers, and toilets were. "In the room over there . . ." she turned back and pointed to a door just opposite us. "Is where the girls are, okay" she said and smiled.

I thanked her and picked up the towel and key with a black bag fastened to it. It had number five in large white letters on it. I walked in the direction of the locker room still shaking with excitement or anticipation for what was to come.

The locker room wasn't what I thought it would look like. Well I didn't know what to expect really. It had a red carpet, in fact the whole place was done out in it. Apart from the four showers and the toilets, they had red and white tiles on the floor and up the walls in each shower compartment that were behind me. The place was very clean and tidy. Along one wall were the lockers with numbers that matched the number on your black bag. I sat down on a long wooden bench. Opposite me was a large mirror covering most of the other wall with a shelf. It had hairbrushes and hair dryers dotted along it. I sat there and started to take my clothes off. Starting by pulling my jumper and shirt off in one go, then my shoes and socks. I stood up and took off my jeans and underwear in one go and quickly wrapped the towel around myself before someone came in. Once the towel was securely wrapped around me I bunged everything into the locker with my number on it. I kept out the money to pay the girl, which I put into the black bag and zipped up. Then off to the room where the girls were, passing the girl behind the counter. She smiled at me as I past by and went into the room.

The room was all done out in Victorian style with large red velvet curtains tied back and pelmets in the same material, with large red chairs. I sat down in one of the chairs feeling extremely self-conscious and on edge. At once one of the girls who were sitting down looking at a large TV said to me "would I like some tea or coffee or a soft drink?" I went for tea. She brought it over and said her name was Mandy. She introduced me to the other six girls that were there. They were scantily dressed. I said hi to them and sipped on my tea looking at each of the girls in turn. There was no Brenda or Jill. I thought what should I do. I can't just sit here. I was about to catch the eye of one of the girls that were sitting down when the door of the room opened and Brenda walked. She was wearing red and black tight bodice that fitted tight into her waist, stockings, and high heel. She looked so different from when I last saw her in the flat. She saw me sitting and smiled. She walked over to me and sat down beside me. "I didn't think you would come?"

I smiled "I nearly didn't. I was shitting myself sitting in the taxi coming here and worse when I got here." She smiled and took my hand "come on virgin boy!" She got up, I followed her out of the room, and up the stairs where there were about ten or more rooms leading of the landing, some open and some shut. She led me into a dimly light room with a round bed with mirrors on all the walls apart from one where there was a round bath with gold taps. She told me to lie on the bed and turned round locking the door. Turning back, she had her hands on her hips, "what would virgin boy like?"

I don't know if it helped because I met her at Brenda's that night and we smoked and had drinks together and got to know each other I think it did. Anyway, I started to relax and talk to her as she sat on the bed next to me as if we were in Carol's flat. She then asked me to turn over onto my front and as I did, she took the towel off then asked if I would like oil or talc for the massage. I went for oil. My head was resting on a soft pillow and I looked up into the mirror that was just above me to see Brenda kneeling in between my legs. As she rubbed oil onto me, she asked me what I would like her to do to me. She then reeled off what she would do and prices.

Afterwards as I sat on the edge of the bed with the towel resting on my lap I looked at Brenda getting dressed and thinking what a great body she had and those round breasts I really enjoyed that. I said to her "what time do you finish and I'll take you for a drink after if you like"

"It's better if I meet you at Carol's and we can all go out for a drink and go and see Sam dancing," she said.

"Okay, I'll see you there." I left her in the room went down stairs to get changed and as I passed the girl behind the desk at the door on my way out I said bye and left. I decided to walk along the busy street just because the sun was out and it was warm. It was roughly an hour's walk back to Carol's place. As I walked through the crowded street I thought to myself "that wasn't too bad at all." I got back to the flat and started to tell Carol all about it. She listened and smiled as I ranted on and on about it, not in too much detail but she knew anyway what it was like. I was like a small boy telling his mother a story for the first time. As I said, she listened to me and smiled as a good friend would do and then I said to her "before I forget Brenda and Jill are coming here then we're going somewhere that Sam's dancing?" Carol then said once I stopped ranting, "Oh right are they? I know the place. We'd better eat, you'll be hungry after all that exercise" and laughed a cheeky laugh. "I'll go and get some fish and chips from the shop along the street. We both laughed again and I said "was I that bad?"

"Yes" she said and laughed again.

"I'm sorry" I said, "I'll get the chips. I know where the place is I passed it on my way here."

The three of us went to the club where Sam was dancing. What a night that was. I did that on a regular basis. You may think it strange paying for sex, well it is, but it was different somehow. Maybe because I knew them and I wanted to see what it was like and knowing Brenda made it a lot easier for me to go to that sort of place. She couldn't have been nicer to me. Nevertheless, that was her job and being nice to the punters was all part of a day's work. I respected her for it. If she were busy, I would go upstairs with Jill. Anyway it was fun and was the only way I was going to see them both naked. All right, it cost me, but what the hell. They both had bodies to die for and the sex was okay. We would meet back at Carol's place, then go and see the blonde bombshell dancing.

I still see Carol and Sam, the other two just drifted away once I stopped going to the massage parlour. Sam has a flat in Greenock, which she shares with another girl who works in Glasgow Airport. Sam still pole dances. Perhaps should I say exotic dancing to give it its correct name? Sam corrected me on this. You should see her dancing it is fantastic. She slithers up and down a stainless steel pole wrapping her legs around the top of it. She then slides down slowly onto the floor. All this is done with a very tiny g-string on. No bra, but as I said she has a very shapely figure and silicon breasts that just seem to stick out in front of her without moving much. She is something else to watch. I've had her do one of her lap dances for me and I can tell you it is very, very arousing the way she dances in front of you. She is good at what she does. She has a sun-bed of which she said I can use. I do from time to time, as I want to keep my Jamaican suntan topped up.

I go along to Sam's, strip off, and get under the sun-bed. About twenty minutes later, Sam brings me a mug of tea, lifts the canopy, and sits down. We talk as I lie there. Okay I had to admit I've had sex with Sam. It just happened one afternoon as I was finishing of under the sun bed. Normally she just leaves me to get on with it. Afterwards I go through and we have a mug of tea and talk. One afternoon as I was finishing off my tan under the bed, Sam came into the room while I was still underneath. She lifted the canopy, as I'm lying there naked, leaned on the top, looked down at me and said, "Would I like some tea or a fuck?" I'm telling you no lie, that's how she said it and that's how we got round to having sex. However, on most occasions I go up to Glasgow with her to see Carol while she goes to work. Then we all meet up later in a club or where Sam's dancing. She said to Carol one night in her flat that she was just using me for sex, nothing else. It's been like that ever since right up to the present day. There have been nights where she has had other men. If I was coming to see her on that particular night she would say Bobby I have company. I would take the hint and wait for her to phone or I would phone her another time. She seems not to want a long-term commitment with anyone. I think with the sort of work that she does it suits her, and me! Anyway, going back to the beginning when I met the Kenyan woman, Carol found out where she worked, her phone number and where she hung out at the weekends. However, all that had to go on hold. I was going on another holiday this time with my kids who were now adults and their partners to America. I was treating them with the rest of the money that my mum had left.

It was one weekend when they were visiting me. I asked them would they like to go to Florida for a week. I would treat them and their partners with what money I had left from my mother. They said like any normal kids would say, "no you keep it you might need it?" So once they had discussed it with their partners and arranged a suitable time I made all the arrangements and we were off to Florida U.S.A. I booked a three-apartment bungalow with a car and its very own heated swimming pool for two weeks. The place was amazing. There was my daughter, her boyfriend, my son and his girlfriend and myself with Sam but at the last minute, she couldn't make it. She had over booked her dancing. As I said she's a pole dancer but she does it freelance so she can pick and choose when and where she wants' to work. She had forgotten about a booking or something. Maybe she was a bit embarrassed to go on holiday with me and my kids I don't know. Anyway, I had booked the flight with the tickets and it was too late to cancel so instead of wasting the ticket, I asked my sister-in-law if she knew someone who would like to come and she did! She was a friend of hers that had just split up with her husband. So being the guy that I am I said, "Come along, no strings attached. You can do your own thing or join in with us if you want. All you will need is some spending money for yourself, everything else is paid for." So she came along with the five of us, wouldn't you?

Florida was great. We went to Disney World, spent all day there, and didn't even see all of it. We went to other places and had meals out. The food was amazing. The driving well, that was okay until I decided to go up the wrong side of a five-lane motorway to the screams of horror from everyone in the car. It was okay I fixed it. I had to behave myself no smoking cannabis or anything like that. Well I was with my kids and their partners. My kids knew that I dabbled a bit, but their partners didn't know and for the girl that came with us, she was a police officer.

After Florida, we all went back doing our own thing. My kids still come to see me when they have time. The girl that came on holiday with us, well she went back to her job as a police officer and I didn't see her again for ages until I was staying with my brother and his wife. They had a bed and breakfast and a livery business with about six horses in this large country house outside Edinburgh. I remember staying there, one new Year all dressed up in my kilt so that I could go to the street party that was on in Edinburgh. She had people staying there for the New Year festivities specially this couple. She was okay but he was well . . . ?

I started to chat her up as you do after a few drinks and one thing lead to another. I could see that she wasn't bothered with her partner or whatever he was.

"Do you fancy splitting and go to a few pubs where there's dancing?" I asked.

"Yes that would be great!" She replied smiling. So I arranged for a taxi to come and pick us up while she went to tell her partner, although I don't know what! He was busy in the other room talking to my sister-in-law and other people that were staying there. Whilst I stayed talking to a girl that I had known for years, she was there at the party, as well as many friends that I hadn't seen for a long time. Anyway, this friend clocked what I was up to and said, "You're not doing what I think Bobby?"

Luckily, before I committed myself the other girl came back and stood in the doorway of the room where we were talking and made a gesture for me to come. So I did, saying my goodbyes to the friend that I was talking to and leaving everyone at the party, naughty, naughty. I don't know what she told her partner. What could she say really?

I had just gone off with the girl that he had come to stay with for the New Year. I was only borrowing her for the night; he could have her back the next day, broken in. On my way out of the room where I left my good friend the girl, she shouted my name. I turned round just as she threw me a bunch of keys. I grabbed them as they sailed through the air towards me. I looked at her with a strange look on my face looking down at the bunch of keys that she had just thrown at me, then back up at her, and smiled.

"Just in case you don't make it back, there are the keys to my house."

Clenching them tight in my fist, I said, "Thanks Sheila" and turned to follow the girl that already had left the room. Just before leaving the house, Sheila came to the front door to shout to me as I was getting into the taxi. "That's why you're leaving. It's with her isn't it?"

I just gave a quick wave to her as I got into the taxi. As it pulled out of the drive and onto the road, I thought *it's good to have good friends.'* I don't think her boyfriend would agree with me on the same matter if he knew what I was intending or where I was taking her. It is great to have good friends; they are very hard to come by. Well she was right, we didn't make it back, one thing lead to another and the keys came in very handy!

We arrived back the next day about lunchtime. I avoided her partner the best I could but I got hell from my sister-in-law for leaving her to explain things. I apologised and she was all right about it in the end. I was invited back on several other New Years if I behaved myself, yes!

I met this girl a couple of times after that night and she came to stay with me for a weekend and I took her out to dinner. We had drinks before dinner and two or three bottles of wine with dinner and more drinks afterwards. You guessed it . . . we were a bit pissed! When we left there, I drove home. I know I shouldn't have done it. Anyway, on the way home I thought it would be a good idea to stop in at my brother's hotel. It was late but he would be there locking up or just tidying up for the morning. Anyway, we arrived and banged on the front door as I thought my brother was still doing things. He came to open the door and I said, "Hey can we have a drink?" To his reply, "Do you know what time it is?"

Luckily, he was the only one there and was in one of his Guinness drinking moods. After all the formalities were over, we got down to some drinking. It was fast and furious. I was on double vodka and cider, yes, cider! I was using the cider as a mixer for my vodka . . . potent. The girl I was with was on double baileys with extra brandy in it. After a while, we were rat-arsed, right out our tree, so we stayed the night. I was more than half way up the spiral stairs on my way to bed when my brother said something. I turned round to answer him when I fell from nearly the top of the stairs and landed onto the hearth of a concrete fireplace knocking myself out. I lay there for some time unconscious with my brother kicking me and pouring water over me, saying "Get up you stupid bastard get up" or so he told me later.

I woke next morning in bed, the girl next to me she was still asleep. I got out of bed, went to the mirror, and looked at myself with a massive hangover. My face was black and blue with a black eye. I couldn't think what had happened. I didn't remember a thing about last night. I had a stinking hangover; I felt like hell and looked like it as well. I walked back to the bed, the girl was coming round and she didn't look much better, oh did I say that? She looked up at me as I got dressed and said "where are you going?" I leaned over the bed, kissed her, and lost my balance falling on top of her. I eased myself up onto both hands each side of her head as she lay there with all the wind knocked out of her. I leant down, kissed her again, and said that I was going downstairs. All I got was a intake of breath and mumbled words which didn't make any sense. As I lifted myself out of bed, I thought *'Oh well at least she's still alive after that.'* I went down into the kitchen for some coffee. My brother was there, he looked round and said "you are lucky to be alive you fucking egit."

My brother told me what had happened, fuck-me! I sat down with my coffee feeling like Shit and talked about last night. He asked me who the girl was. I told him how I met her at Paul's, my other brother's place at New Year. He laughed as I told him about the incident and then we talked about different things as you do. We eventually left when the girl surfaced out of her bed. We said our goodbyes to my brother and left with our hangover's back to my place and straight into bed. We both climbed in and stayed there for the rest of the day together, emerging later that night. That was Sunday. The following day I went to be checked out at the Doctors just because Helen, the girl that was staying with me said it would be the best thing to do. So I went to see my family doctor, where he gave me a major telling off and told me to go for a scan at the local hospital. So off I go to the hospital. My head was all right but I had crushed three large vertebrae's at the bottom of my spine. "It may affect you in the near future," the doctor at the hospital informed me. A week later, I lost my sense of taste and smell. Off I went back to the doctor and told him. He said that it may be the crushed vertebrae's that caused it. "You might get it back or you might not we will have to wait and see!" It was very different, everything smelt and tasted metallic. It's hard describing losing those two senses. Food didn't have any taste, sweets, and chocolate which I love tasted awful. I could have been poisoned and wouldn't have even known. It was a bit weird. You just take it for granted all the senses you have. It's not till you lose one of them that you realise the enormous effect each one plays in your body. I never got it back and I adjusted to it like you do when something goes wrong. The brain is a complex thing and amazing how it copes with disasters. In between all this, Helen had left on Monday morning and said that she would ring to see how I was when she got back to her own home to recuperate, she did.

After a while, the relationship faded out as they do, oh well. Going back to the Kenyan lady from earlier on, I said Carol had found out all about her and where she would be on this particular Saturday night. There wasn't anything that Carol couldn't get or find out for you. If she didn't know, her friends whether male or female would know. They would find out what you wanted to know in or around Glasgow for a price. Everything has a price. I went to stay with Ginger and his girlfriend and I told them what Carol had said. We all went out to this club where Carol had told me she would be. Right enough she arrived with four of her friends roughly about the time that Carol said she would! She came over to Gingers girlfriend and the rest of us and started talking, yes! However, I started talking and asked her out to dinner to a great little Italian restaurant could 'Fratelli Sarti' in the town centre. I go there quite often if I'm in Glasgow and if I'm wining and dining a young lady. The owners of the Italian restaurant got to know me over time with me bringing people there, and the odd girl. One thing led to another and we were, wait for it . . . we got married! Again, I hear you say. Yes, it was fast and furious. She was twenty-seven, black and great looking and I was old enough to be her dad. I didn't like to say that I had a daughter the same age. You could say it was a boost to my male ego. She was young, good-looking, and very sexy. We got married in a registry office in Glasgow. It was just a small wedding with her sister, who was even better looking although I never said that. Three of her friends attended. They all came up from London where they were staying. My two brothers and their wives, my son, his partner, my daughter and her boyfriend and my grandchild, yes, grandchild was there too. Grandpa Bob was getting married? My best man and his three friends, what more could a Groom ask for?

Let me tell you, the wedding wasn't straightforward if anything is with me. I bought two gold Celtic rings one for her and one for me that my wife chose. I set off for the best mans house to pick him up to go to my wedding and called in to see my brother who was running the hotel after my parents had died, just to see if everything was okay. I then went on to see my best man to give him the rings for safekeeping. We had a several drinks as you do then he said give me the rings. I put my hand in my sporran to give them to him and mine wasn't there, oops! I had taken them out of their boxes, wrapped them up in a handkerchief, and put them in my sporran? Well, we looked high and low for that ring but couldn't find it and time was running out so I said fuck it. "I'll borrow one from someone, come on lets go." I did borrow one of a friend who was present but it wouldn't fit my finger it would only go on the first part. At the point during the ceremony were you put the rings on, the guy who was marrying us looked on in horror as my wife tried to put the ring on my finger. We ignored him, he eventually carried on, and I was marred for the second time.

After the ceremony, I gave the ring back to my friend saying thanks and laughing. He replied saying "God Addis it could only happen to you."

"I know thanks again." We all went back to the cottage for the reception. The local hotel across the road in the village did the catering. They had set it all out in the dining room in the cottage, all through the night there was a constant stream of people that I'd asked to come to the party after the wedding. They traipsed back and forth across the country road with food and drink in their hands. They went from the cottage to the pub then back again all night long. There were four good looking black girls all dressed up. When they first walked into the pub, you could have heard a pin drop. Everyone and I mean everyone stopped speaking and looked round or up at them. I think it was the first time there had ever been a black girl in the village let alone four good looking ones with their tits and bums sticking out, all with their hair tied up in their pub. Until someone said, "that's Bobby's wife." The people started to say 'of course it could only be Addis' then the music started up again and the talking it was as if they expected something strange from me! Someone found my ring outside the family's hotel. It had been run over by a car and was flattened. An omen you could say. I took it back to the local jeweller where my wife and I had chosen it to see if she could fix it. I remember when we were buying it. We were standing in the shop looking at the rings when my new wife said, "have you got it in my size?" The wife of the jeweller said, "Yes it will be the same size as your engagement ring." I was standing behind my wife frantically waving my hand behind her back to stop her from going on. Luckily, she stopped when she looked up and saw me waving my hands frantically with a 'stop for fuck's sake' expression on my face. The woman who was serving my wife looked up, gave me a strange look, and then continued on speaking to my wife who was too busy looking at the rings to notice me waving. The lady behind the counter stopped talking to my wife mid sentence "sorry that was someone else." As we left the wife of the shop said to me as I was following my wife out of the shop "that was close!" I turned round, put my head through the gap between the edge of the door and the wooden frame, and said smiling "yes it was." Then she said, "Who did you buy the other ring for?"

"Another girl" I said quietly so that my wife wouldn't hear.

"Bobby, really" she said a little exasperated, then said "come back in a week and it should be in."

"Thanks" I said and closed the door.

My new wife and I had a flight booked to Kenya to see her parents in a place roughly twenty miles outside Nairobi a small village called riverside. I had to send my passport off to the Kenyan high commission office in London to get a visa so that I could get into Kenya. I visited the doctors to get all the injections that were required so everything was a bit of a rush to say the least. We did it though as well as making it to the Airport on time and boarded our plane to Kenya.

CHAPTER FOURTEEN

KENYA

We arrived in Nairobi to be welcomed by her mum and dad. They had arranged another reception in their village. In their eyes, we weren't marred until we had the full tribal ceremony but before all that they had arranged for us to stay in a hotel in Nairobi for the three weeks that we were there. The next day we were to meet the rest of the family at her mum's house in the village. It was eight in the morning and my wife's parents were waiting downstairs to take us to their home. We didn't have time to unpack what with the time difference and everything. We didn't get much sleep and now we got a phone call from reception saying that her parents were waiting for us in reception. Her mother was dressed in a very brightly coloured traditional African dress with matching headwear. They were sitting down at one of the round glass tables in the reception. We left the air conditioned reception and went through the large tinted glass swivel door into the bright sunshine it was hot! Not a heat that you could lie in, it was more a clammy heat and it wasn't long before the perspiration was running of my forehead. My wife gave me a hanky to use and said "keep it and use it." We got into their car, I offered them some money for petrol and we set off down the drive from the hotel to the security gates at the bottom. We waited for the security guard to come and open them before driving down the road into Nairobi, the main town. On our way down to Nairobi, we stopped at traffic lights but nobody seemed to bother with them. They just went from red, amber, green and back again and kept on doing this repeatedly and nobody was paying any attention to them. There was so much traffic and people milling about even at that time in the morning. We moved slowly into and round the roundabout stopping and starting every two minutes with cars and vans, lorries, buses, all coming from different directions all sounding their horns and squeezing into any space they could see. The exhaust fumes, god! They couldn't have had any law against carbon emission fumes! It was bad . . . It just bellowed out from everywhere, thick black exhaust fumes and the heat, fucking hell! I thought while we where stopping and starting edging our way through the lights and round the roundabout and as I was sweating like a pig I decided to open the car window next to me to a frantic look from my wife's mother. She said *"don't do that it's not safe. "*

We stopped at some lights and were invaded by hundreds of men, woman, and children selling everything you could think of from kitchen utensils to car stereo's to watches and things you could eat everything you could think of. They were there along with the traffic fighting to sell their stuff to anybody that would buy it while the traffic was at a standstill, they were milling in and out through the traffic. It was the same at every junction, lights, or cross roads absolute chaos! The heat was crazy I wanted to open the window wider but was told not to then my wife said *"did I want some water?"* I said yes and she wound down her window and beckoned a young boy over to the car as it was stopped at another traffic jam. This boy was carrying a large basket on his head with about thirty or more small plastic see through bags full of cold water. She bought two from the boy through the window of the car and gave me one. I bit the end of it and started to drink the water by sucking it through the corner of the sachet that I had bitten off, as my wife did the same. The car moved on and out of the town and onto a more quiet road with people selling vegetables and fruit on wooden stalls on the side of the road as we drove past them on our way to their home.

We arrived at their house in the village. It was a square concrete house with its own security wall about six feet high. It had two large metal gates that were opened by another woman with the same coloured traditional dress. We drove through into a large courtyard to a crowd of woman singing and chanting all in their Kikuyu national tribal dress with national coloured beads hanging down round their necks and round their ankles. On their heads, more brightly coloured beads hanging down and some of them had them woven in their hair all with the same tribal colours. The men, well they were just in suits a bit dull compared with the women. There were other woman in different coloured tribal dress just as colourful as the others with all the beads and head gear on chanting and jumping up and down. They were from the Masaya tribe, my wife was from the Kikuyu tribe, and one of her sisters was married into another tribe called the Masaya they were tall! All the men must have been over six feet or even taller, I tell you no lie I felt like a midget against my future brother in-law who was the son of the tribal chief. I was to him meet in the next couple of days on my brother-in-laws farm a good days drive into the bush from here. The ceremony went on all day, eating drinking but nothing compared to what was to come when I went to my brother-in-laws farm. After the ceremony my wife, I, her brother, and cousins went into Nairobi to hit' the pubs and clubs. It was very intimidating at first being the only white guy there. Well that's a bit of a lie. I think I saw maybe two other men and three white girls but that's all. We stayed drinking until the early hours of the morning. During the evening I was given five or six short green plant like stuff that you peeled off the outer part in strips with your teeth until you got a reasonable load in your mouth and chewed on it along with some chewing-gum keeping it in your mouth as you drank I can't think what it did? I think it was some kind of drug. I just thought fuck it; I'll go along with the flow if you get my drift. We got back to the hotel about eight in the morning, all I wanted to do was go for a bath or a shower, but my wife beat me to it. I wasn't pissed at all, maybe a bit stoned. That stuff that I chewed on must have stopped me from being drunk. I stripped down to my boxer shorts and went out onto the balcony. It was hot even at that time in the morning, no sun to speak of just a hot breeze. The sun was hidden behind a greyish sky; the heat was intense like holding a hair dryer in front of you on hot. I leaned over the balcony looking at kids and people playing in the hotel pool when I heard my young African wife come out of the bathroom and say, *"you can go and get a shower now."* I turned to see her standing in the room naked looking straight at me. Letting her wet curly hair fall down over her breasts; clinging to the round firm full shape of her breasts. Her large erect black nipples peeping out between the wet strands of hair, her young curvy hips her smooth flat tummy and that tight round African shaped bum with her dark olive skin all shimmering in the light of the room. I stood there looking at her body and taking in all of her nakedness. All I wanted to do was . . . . but she said *"go and get a shower first, you're sweaty."*

The next couple of days were spent just exploring Nairobi and meeting more of my wife's friends, drinking and going to their villages and meeting more people. One of her friends said that they wanted to take me to see this club in Nairobi where all the girls there are working girls (prostitutes.)

It was arranged to go the nightclub, my wife said, "Be careful when we get there because being white, all the girls will want to go to bed with you."

"Good" I said smiling "I can't wait."

"Because they will . . . !" She said in a loud voice wanting me to pay attention.

"Okay, okay" I said calming her down. As we left the room, she said "all they have to do is breathe on you."

I interrupted her, "you expect me to believe that?"

"It's true, they do. They have something in their mouths . . ."

I interrupted her again before she could finish "no they don't!"

"Okay, don't believe me then."

We arrived in the reception area where two of her friends were waiting. She turned to one of the girls as if to have the last say in the matter "don't they?" She said to the girl catching her off guard.

"Don't they what?" The girl replied. My wife repeated what she had just said to me. "Yes they do." The girl said deadly serious.

"Okay, if you say so" I said to keep the peace, talk about mumbo-jumbo and voodoo come on?

The locals and the crowd we were with all drank warm beer. Not like the tourists who drank their beer cold, I don't know why I forgot to ask. We bought more beer and chewed on more of that green stuff. My wife was right enough in one respect; the girl kept coming over to our table of eight and asking me, "Come dance with me?"

The Kenyans' had a great accent and it was giving my male ego a great boost! Different girls would come over all the time or there would be two or three girls dancing just in front of us making eye contact and beckoning me to go and dance with them. They were all great lookers' not one bad one. Well, the night went on into morning and I was determined to prove my wife wrong so I said to her I'm going to dance with one of the girls to prove you wrong, *"No, no don't"* she said along with the other three girls.

"Come on you can't believe that stuff do you?" I turned to the other two guys "do you believe what they are saying?" Before they could say anything my wife said in a loud voice so everyone could hear at the table and the next couple of tables down from us, *"Go, go and get laid by another fucker you . . ."* I interrupted her and said "come on let me prove it to you" as the guys who were sitting at the table egged me on saying "go on let him?"

"Go. I don't care . . ." She said in a temper slamming her drink back down on the table "go, fuck off see if I care."

So the next time a girl came over I said yes and got up and went on to the floor with her. My wife went away with a girlfriend I don't know where; she just got up and stomped away. I was dancing with this great looking girl when another girl came up very close behind me and started rubbing herself against my bum. The girl in front turned round, pushed her bum in tight against my front, and started to rub her bum up hard against my front in time with the girl at the back, all in time with the music. It was like a sandwich with me in the middle. I could feel myself getting aroused and the more I got aroused the tighter they closed in on me rubbing against me. It was so erotic I couldn't help but get hard and they knew it. The harder I got, the closer they got and the harder they rubbed up against me until my wife came back and hell was let loose. She swore and shouted at the girls that I was dancing with, showed them her ring and shouted something in Swahili, a language they all speak when they want to converse with one and other. There are so many African villages all with their own language. They speak Swahili at school in the playground, it's a second language to them as well as English. I had learned a bit of Swahili but my wife was talking too fast for me to understand. Then she stormed out of the club in a mood, with me following her like a wee puppy. What I did learn was that they are very superstitious and a lot of them believe in voodoo. The rituals are still practiced out in some villages believe me I know! She didn't speak to me in the taxi all the way to the hotel. Even for all the effort I was putting in, saying, "sorry but you did say it would be okay didn't you?" Still there was silence. ". . . and they don't breathe on you" I said.

"Ha you don't know that" my wife replied. She was talking to me again, yes.

The next day we just spent going round the market place and the shops. I tell you no lie; we were walking down this street when we heard a loud crack then another. Everybody crowded into shop doorways and down side streets leaving the main street completely deserted except for this one man. He was running up the middle of the road with three police officers running after him with automatic weapons. As he ran past us, another couple of shots rang out and he fell down right in front of us! Fucking hell, he just lay there in the road not moving, blood running onto the street. One of the officers that were pursuing him caught up to where he was lying. He fired another shot, at point blank range into him. Fuck! Why did he do that? Turning to my wife for an answer, I had to wait a couple of seconds.

"It would have cost too much to take him to hospital," she said moving her head to one side not even looking at me. She was more interested on what the police were doing.

"So you're saying they would rather kill him than take him to hospital, even though he was only wounded?"

"Yes" she said in such a way for me to shut up and stop annoying her with stupid questions. 'Fuck me' I thought. 'I won't ask her anymore *stupid* questions' as she put it. She didn't have time for people or questions that she thought were insignificant or futile. I just left the whole subject alone and followed her like a little puppy weaving in and out of the crowds of people that had started to spill back out onto the street again. Everyone continued on as if nothing had happened, stopping to shop and generally get on with what they were doing as if it was an insignificant event. Maybe it was to them but it wasn't for me. I followed my wife like I said, like a lost puppy bumping into people and trying to keep up with her. We walked on down the street with the rest of the people leaving the police to deal with the body that was slumped half way across the pavement. Everyone else did the same and went on with what they were doing. I squeezed and bumped my way through the crowded market place following my wife whom stopped at stalls, picked items up before asking the price then bargaining with the person, even swearing at them and throwing the thing back down. While she was doing all this, I stood looking about, being pushed and shoved about in the heat. I wiped the perspiration of my forehead with a clean handkerchief that my wife had given me and noticed that nearly everyone had them. It must be their thing. You can't be seen to perspire you have to look cool and calm. Cool, it was impossible what with the heat from the sun and everyone pushing, squeezing, and bumping past you all the time. You would get to the end of the street where the market was and you're naked, or I was. Also lucky that you hadn't had your pocket picked. I always remember this guy at school saying never "carry your wallet in crowded places. If you want to take money put the big bills in one pocket and the other bills in the other pocket, so when you want something you know what you're bringing out." I suppose its common sense really. I was so glad to get through that day. We even met her mother later that day as well. She took us sightseeing. The next couple of days were spent lying around the hotel pool, drinking and talking between ourselves. Then it was time to go to my brother-in-laws place. We drove for miles along the main road stopping to buy food from people selling it at the roadsides. We drove on, passing people carrying bundles of wood on their heads and pulling carts with different things on them. It reminded me of Jamaica. It was very similar apart from the heat. Jamaica was a nice relaxing heat where Africa was a heavy heat that drained energy from you all the time.

It was dark when we arrived at the farm, which sat about four miles off the main road down a very bumpy track. It was a large square concrete house with an extension added to the back later, I think. There was no electricity, bath, or shower and the toilet was outside. It sat a couple yards away from the house in a tall wooden shed covering a large hole in the ground of which you would squat or stand over. The hole was deep and it smelt bad. It wasn't the best of toilets that I've seen but they did have a wooded dispenser with extra soft toilet tissue in it. A small room with a concrete floor was where you could wash and shower. The floor sloped slightly, and the walls were smooth concrete that had two holes at the bottom to let out the excess water that missed the large bowl that you would stand in to have your shower. There's a bucket of water at the side to pour over yourself before washing and rinsing with the rest. All the time standing in this round deep bowl like container. You would leave enough clean water for your teeth. The only source of light came from Tilley lamps and no cooking was done in

the house at all. The meals were prepared in the house then taken out to another shed outside and cooked on a open fire on a concrete floor with a half circler of raised concrete to contain the fire. A metal frame stood over the fire for large pots to hang over the flames. Although they never cooked in the house, it was full of your modern day stuff. In the living room, a large L-shape leather suite, three large leather seats, a large black thick woollen rug covering most of the polished wooden floor and small tables dotted here and there around the room.

There was a generator for pumping water to the cattle and there were hundreds of them. That was their main income or that what I was made to believe. I was to learn the truth later. There were goats for milk, cheese and eating as well as vegetables, usual ones and some that I hadn't seen before. The family were mostly self-sufficient providing everything from meat, vegetables, milk, and eggs. What they couldn't grow or keep on the farm would be sought after at the market about half a day's drive away. It was just different priorities from mine. I would have had electricity and running water in the house, they had it for their cattle, to pump water to the fields, for drinking and irrigation to help the grass grow thick and green. If they didn't have the water for the grass it would dry up and die in the hot sun, even around the house for the vegetables and other things they grow the water was pumped. The farm was big, the land went for miles, but it wasn't good land. There was land that they couldn't irrigate so most of it was dust with very rough grassing. The whole farm was run by him, his cousins, and their families and supported quite a lot of them, by the looks of things it was doing all right. They wouldn't think of walking miles and miles across their hard barren ground to where their houses were. The ones that could drive had the best of four-wheel drive cars, Range Rovers, Nissan Patrols, and many American pick-ups. They would only use them to go to Nairobi or some other way off place that was at least a day's drive away or more, most of the time they walked. There were many people that didn't have anything like what they had, just a small hut housing maybe two or three families, some of them working on the farms that were spread over miles of ground, or they would travel to Nairobi very early in the morning and come back late into the night not much of a life? For my future brother-in-law and the other farmers that were dotted about this vast area, life wasn't too bad, compared with the rest.

That brings me to the ceremony that they had planned for my wife and I.

It was very early Wednesday morning. I was woken by my brother-in-law who was knocking on the bedroom door he asked me if I would like to go and round up some of his cattle for butchering in Nairobi, so I did. We walked for miles across fields with one strand of barbed wire separating one field from the next with him and his two cousins. I felt like a midget next to these guys. When they walked, their one stride was equivalent to three of mine; even the dogs were running circles around me before going to round up the cattle after being given a command from my brother-in-law. Before I knew it, it was time to bring them all home. We arrived back at the farm around ten in the morning and put the cattle in their pens ready for the truck to come about twelve noon and take them away. We washed with a bucket of cold water and a basin. Dried our faces and hands with a towel left by the basin on the wooden table and went to have breakfast. Breakfast was okay, it consisted of hard boiled eggs still in their shells, the option of toast or bread and something sweet like honey but wasn't honey. There were green beans that tasted all right, I don't know what they were, but I ate them anyway along with the porridge. The porridge was similar to what you get here in Scotland but on saying that it wasn't served in a bowl but in a cup. It was very runny so you could drink it like tea and was very sweet. They brought it out in thermos flasks to keep it hot and sat it on the table. There was coffee as well as the porridge and I ended up opting out and took the coffee instead of the porridge. The porridge was more like a drink than porridge. It had the same oatmeal taste like the porridge you get back home but very sweet.

I did try it but it was too sweet for me. Afterwards my brother-in-law said, "Let's go and choose a couple of goats for the ceremony." So off we went leaving the women to clean and wash up. It wasn't the done thing to help the women, it was the man's job to provide, and the women were there to bear children, look after the home and her husband.

We got to several goats grazing as my brother-in-law grabbed each one in turn looking and feeling for the fattest one, picking the best of the bunch to bring back. The first goat's throat was cut and left to bleed out before being gutted and skinned. The women and my wife took it away to cut it up and cook it. There wasn't any proper cut, I think they just hacked it to bits, bones the lot and cooked it on the open fire. Some of the others made up salads. As they were doing that, we arranged the seating. Large wooden tables were placed together in the garden along with a very large music system. The garden was nice; it had green grass cut short, flowerbeds with lovely coloured shrubs well kept. Several large trees in full blossom were dotted around the grounds. It was nice compared with the rest of the land around the farm. Apart from the cattle fields, their grass was as green as the garden, but the rest of the place was hard dry ground with rushes and trees with flat tops, where the wind had blown them into that shape.

People were arriving all dressed up, the women in their traditional tribal dresses and most of the young men in tribal gear along with their brightly coloured headwear, shield, spears, and bare feet with brightly coloured beads round their ankles, arms, and even round their neck. They were tall buggers, I felt so small against them. The music was playing and the drink handed out. It was a white spirit that they brewed themselves. It was a bit like Vodka to look at but strong. You drank it by itself in a small glass as you do with real vodka. I had a couple before I was told to go get changed along with my wife for the ceremony. When we came back, the women were chanting as the men jumped up and down with their feet together. My wife and I stood in the middle of the circle jumping up and down with them. When it all stopped, the tribal chief lifted up his hands and said something. My brother-in-law's father an old man with very black wrinkled skin and white hair, was helped into the circle by his son along with the goat on a rope serving as a lead. Then I was summoned to them by a hand gesture from the old man and was told to hold the goat. As I held it, the old man cut its throat, caught the blood as it spurted out straight in to a goblet he was holding. He filled it, drank from it before handing the rest for me to drink, fuck. I took it from him and as he watched me, I lifted it to my mouth. I breathed in and drank the warm blood from the goblet. I could smell it as I took a sip before going to hand it back to him. He gestured for me to drink it all and said something in Swahili, "shit!" I thought and drank the lot down. He said something else before the goat was cut open and the kidneys removed still warm. One was given to my brother-in-law and the other to me to eat. As the old man stood looking and saying something, my brother-in-law cut it in half saying to me, "it will be easier to eat." He gave me the two halves they were still warm. I popped them into my mouth and started to eat them. They bounced around my mouth until I bit down on the two halves just small enough to swallow, trying not to taste them and get rid of them quickly. I eventually swallowed them, before having to skin the goat with the knife that had cut its throat, with the help from my brother-in-law. After that, the goat was taken away and the women that were standing in a circle around me started to chant as the men jumped up and down again, banging on their shields with their spears. Then as quick as it started, it stopped. Each person in turn came to congratulate us, and then other women came with large glass jugs full of the clear liquid that was like Vodka and poured us one each. I was so grateful for it because I still had that thick taste of the sweet blood in my mouth. A young girl all dressed up in her brightly coloured tribal dress came over to pour more of the liquid from these long jugs. I hadn't finished the one from earlier but she stood there as I drank it down in one and holding my glass out for a refill, the girl smiled and gave me more.

The goat was taken away as I said to be cooked like the other one and the liver once cooked was given to me to eat. The old man started to tell me what the ceremony was all about with my brother-in-law acting as an interpreter for what the old man was saying to me in Swahili. To cut a long story short the gist of it is that when a young warrior goes out into the bush for the first time he has to make his kill, drink the blood, and eat from it. This is to prove to the rest of the tribe that he has become a man and can defend for himself. As he was telling me this, another young girl in full tribal dress and beads came up to my wife and gave her a load of beads to put around her neck. I was given a walking stick decorated with coloured traditional tribal beads before the women went away to prepare the food. The food was brought out on large silver platters with the meat and bones all together with finely chopped tomato, lettuce, and onion with a pile of salt around the edge.

They were put down on the long tables with jugs of the white spirit and bottles of beer. It wasn't long before the tables were full of food but before anyone started to eat the women came round with large jugs of warm water and poured the water over your hands before giving you soap to wash them. They stood there as you washed your hands then they rinsed them for you with more water and gave you your individual towel. They did this to all the men in turn then we started to eat with our hands, lifting some meat along with the finely chopped salad before dipping it in the salt and eating it. As we ate the women waited on us until we were finished, then our hands were washed again with more warm water. After that was done the women went to have their food but there were always several girls waiting on us giving us drink and more food if we wanted it. This went on for three days, the first night I was a bit pissed after that I managed to last the three days. On saying that, I was naked and just wanted to sleep. We stayed there just over a week going to the local church on Sunday and lifting up our hands, singing and praising the lord and all that. I was introduced to the Pastor, he insisted coming round in the afternoon to give us a small ceremony so that we could become reborn Christians and he wasn't taking no for an answer. The afternoon was spent outside talking with him and my brother-in-law about the lord's work and that I should spread the good word. He then said, "I will call you Pastor Bob" and laughed. I got stuck with the name 'Pastor Bob' all the time I stayed in Kenya.

Well he left and it was time to go to bed as we were going back to Nairobi early in the morning. My brother-in-law had business there so he decided to do the two things at the same time, take us back, and do what he had to do. He was something high up in the Kenyan Government; he had connections in everything, even in Sierra Leone and other places as well as being a farmer. The next morning my wife had to go and meet someone, so I stayed at the hotel until I got a phone call from her later saying to meet her in town. So I did. She was sitting with two guys in this cafe drinking coffee. I knew one of them and she introduced me to the other. I ordered a coffee and they talked, my wife talking away in Swahili to the guys next to her while I made small talk to the guy next to me trying to listen to what she was saying. I could speak some Swahili but not much and at the speed they were speaking, I had no chance. I picked out some words plus my name as they looked over at me and then carried on talking; she did this quite often when she was with her friends or when she didn't want me to understand what she was saying. This made me so angry and it was very rude of her. I said to her on a number of occasions "why did she do this?" All I got back was "it's not for your ears Okay?" That made me even more pissed off. "Oh, fuck you too!" She was adamant she wouldn't tell and she did it several times in Nairobi and when we were home. That got me thinking about the whole fucking marriage thing! She was so secretive and the lies she told me, her husband, and okay I wasn't expecting a goody-goody marriage, but come on? Things just got worse when we got home and that's not a good way to start married life, is it?

There were things that I found out about my sweet innocent little wife that would make your hair stand on end. How corrupted she was in Kenya and at home, but you expect that in Kenya because that's the way they are there, but not from your wife. She had secrets even the Kenyan Government would have liked to have known about her and her friends, but obviously, I can't say too much if I'm going to publish this book. I will talk about things later on in Accra, another part of Africa where I went. It's all connected to the time spent in Nairobi. It's scary to think that the world is a big, big place but not when you're pinpointed out the world isn't big at all there's nowhere you can hide. To get back to this guy, I was talking and sitting next to, he asked me if I would like to go to the ghetto with him to see the big bad side of Kenya and how corrupt it really is, oh Sorry did I say that word again? So, off I go with this guy leaving my dear little wife talking away in Swahili no doubt planning something! First, I was told to leave my money and anything gold or valuable with my wife, aye right! The way my wife was acting, she would sell the gold, pocket the money and fuck off, "wouldn't you dear?"

"What, where are you going Bobby" She said. The guy I was leaving with explained. "Don't take him there are you mad?" She said in a concerned voice. I don't know if she was concerned about me or the fuss it would cause if I was mugged or found dead in a ditch. Anyway, I left leaving my stuff with her. We drove out of Nairobi about seven or eight miles and got to the shantytown that he was talking about, corrugated tin houses in a half circle around this large muddy green patch of grass with burnt out vans, cars, and rubbish! There were old washing machines, bike frames, loads of stuff scattered all over. We drove in and across the open patch of dark brown grass if you could call it grass and stopped opposite five large tin shacks. On the front of them were Bar, Cinema, Laundrette, and a couple of other names painted in red over the corrugated sheeting in bold letters. We got out and instantly the people that were just standing around crowded around me chanting Masongow! Masongow! They were being very intimidating pushing me about until the guy I was with said something to them in Swahili. They backed off and we entered the shack that said bar. Inside were just wooden benches and more people sitting about drinking and talking but that all stopped when I walked in? You could have cut the atmosphere with a knife and they probably had a few. I was trespassing on their turf and they didn't like it. At the end of the room was the bar. It had a thick metal grill that could be lifted up and was just a few inches above the scratched and heavily grooved wooden counter. The guy I was with asked for two brandies but the barman just stood looking at me with his arms crossed until the guy swore and said something in Swahili. He turned and swore at the people gathering behind me. There was a shouting match between several large black guys and the guy I was with. He opened his coat and said some other stuff in Swahili and they seemed to back off, quieten down and sat down on the wooden benches. They were like Hyenas in a pack just waiting for the opportunity to spring on their prey and rip it apart. Just now, they were quite happy to watch and sit around talking amongst themselves with the odd one chanting Masongow! I wasn't afraid really, because I knew that this guy wouldn't have brought me here if he couldn't handle himself and them, but I was very much intimidated and glad he was there. We eventually got our Brandies they were in clear polythene packets a bit like the individual packet of sauces you get in cafes. We had several brandies that were pushed under the grill, no glass to put it in and I wasn't going to ask. You just bite the corner off them and suck the brandy out, we got some beers as well he had to lift the shutter for that but it was put back down straight away again. I don't know if he was expecting trouble or it was always like that, but the guy behind the bar never smiled once. The guy I was with asked me if I could speak French I said "a little, why?"

"It will do them good to hear it," he said. I didn't understand but I tried to keep up with him as he asked me things in French. After the drink, we went outside and he showed me the Cinema in the next shack there was just rows of wooden benches again, one in front of each other with a large plasma wide screen TV and that was it. The place was a dump no wonder there was so much anger there. Just about six or seven miles back down the road there are people like myself and this guy living a much better lifestyle.

By this time, there were many people gathering around the entrance of the Bar and the Cinema when a long wheel drive land rover pulled up alongside us and I'm not joking a black man got out he was massive! He must have been seven foot or more with hands twice the size of mine. He hugged the guy that I was with and looked down at me and said "Masongow what are you doing here?"

"What's Masongow?" I asked. He looked at the guy then at me and said, "It means white man."

"Thanks big man" I said. I don't know why I said that. Maybe it was all the brandy and beer I had drunk, making me something silly like that, but he was big. He looked down at me again and smiled. We were taken round to the back of the land-rover where he opened the doors and inside there was automatic weapons of all kinds, hand grenades in wooden boxes, pistols, all kinds of bullets in cardboard boxes stacked up at the back for the guns that he had and more. I think there was even a rocket launcher propped up in the far away right-hand corner. He picked up a Russian made machine-gun and told me the name, an automatic Kalashnikov, or an AK47 for short. He gave it to me then said, "You try." Pushing it into my chest, I took it from him he then showed me where the safety was, and told me to keep my finger out of the way of the trigger until I was ready to fire it. "Flick the safety off." I looked along the side of the weapon. He went on to say, "Even a small boy can use it, they are so easy to work. They don't over heat or jam. You can drop them in the mud and they still work, you try." He showed me where to point it "just squeeze the trigger when you are ready?" Fuck Me! I let off a couple of rounds . . . what a rush! It was so easy and light it was amazing. "Thanks big man" I said. He looked down at me, smiling, ". . . Flick the safety on. Now you buy?" He said and laughed. I did as he said but I just wanted to fire it again; it was that easy to use it was unbelievable, so easy to use. I left them talking and do what they were doing at the back of the Land-Rover and went back to our four-wheel-drive and got in. Most of the people had either gone away or gone into the pub. I sat in the shogun waiting for them to finish what they were doing and wondered if maybe the people here thought I was here to buy. I don't know, but the atmosphere was different and there wasn't any crowd hassling me. I just sat there thinking about the gun, I was on a high! The land rover drove off past my window and the big man waved as it drove across the field. The guy I was with, got in beside me, and put a couple of boxes in the back. I ranted on and on about the gun to him.

"Yes, yes they are very easy to use, and light that's why they are very popular here" he said and drove off back the way we came in. However, as we were just about to pull out onto the road two police land rovers stopped us forcing us to go onto the verge. They got out of both the Land Rovers; the two that weren't driving had automatic weapons slung over their shoulders. I tried to see what make they were, being such an expert on them after firing one for the first time in my life. One of them stood at the front of our car while the other two walked over to each of our windows and knocked on them for us to wind them down, we did. The one that came to my window asked me what I was doing here at the ghetto. Before I could say anything the friend I was with, leaned over in front of me, and said something in Swahili to him and before he could, finish there was a tap on his window. The other police officer holding his gun asked the guy next to me something in Swahili. He then fumbled in his pocket and gave the police officer his driving licence with some money pushed inside it. A few words were exchanged in Swahili and the police officer standing at the drivers' side smiled and waved to the other to go. They got into their Land Rovers and reversed out and we drove off. I never said anything about the money to him and he never said anything to me so we both let it slide.

We arrived at this group of houses and walked through this gate and down this path. On either side were small dwelling houses or apartments. Most of them were two rooms sharing a bathroom. We stopped at one of the apartments and walked in. There were a crowd of people in there, plus my wife sitting in the far corner with two guys and a girl on a mattress on the floor. She ignored me when I came in.

I'm not saying that she should jump up and say hi but a smile would have done or a wave to come over, but nothing not even a smile in my direction. I was offered some bush to smoke in a long glass pipe similar to the one in Jamaica and a bottle of beer. I was offered a seat on the floor with the guy I came with and a group of people one being his French wife. We stayed there most of the day smoking, drinking, and talking about the place that I had just come from and why there is so much poverty. Then my wife wanted to go so we thanked the people and I thanked the guy that took me to see the ghetto. We were leaving the next day and it was already about three in the morning. The flight was at two in the afternoon. We arrived at the airport to a great send off from all of her relations giving us presents and wishing us well. One of her relations gave my wife and me a diamond ear stud each. He started to tell me that it was so many carats but it had a flaw in it so you couldn't sell it for its whole value. He went on but most of what he was saying I didn't hear because of all the hassle getting out with the bag and everyone saying their goodbyes. What he did say and he made certain that I heard was "put it in your ear now and take that glass one out before you get to customs." So I did, replacing the artificial one with the real one. It was quite a size of a diamond on the open market even with the flaw in it, it would reach . . . mmm a lot, and we had one each. I know that he didn't buy them and he could get more because he was discussing it with my wife last night, how he could get many diamonds from another part of Africa. I didn't hear where, but these were a gift from him and all he had done was to get them made into ear studs for us through the underground people. You could buy anything, or get anything made for a price and I mean anything, from passports, legal documents, car licences even guns if you had the money, you could get anything. With all the hassle, I forgot that I had the real diamond in my ear still and I was half way home and my wife was asleep beside me. I looked at her sleeping there thinking 'why was she so secretive? Why did she speak in Swahili in front of me when she knows it pisses me off and why was she so secretive to me, her husband?' Things weren't going all that well with us, even at the beginning of our marriage so what will it be like when we get home? My mind was racing with thoughts and looking at her sleeping. Did I love her or was it just lust? After all, she was old enough to be my daughter; in fact, she was younger than my daughter from my first marriage was. Then I thought how lucky I was to have two great kids even though I divorced their mother. They still came to the wedding to my other wife and I will always respect them for that. However, what about this one next to me, what was her problem? She had too many dark secrets. I'm not saying that she should tell me all, but it would be nice to be taken into her confidence. I know that wasn't going to happen. I sat back in the chair and started to watch the movie that was about to start. I put on my earpieces and relaxed.

CHAPTER FIFTEEN

HOME

We arrived back in Ardentinny to the cottage that I was renting off my brother. Straight from the start my wife was niggling about this and that . . . where can she get a carry out or a DVD to watch. Then she said, "It's so quiet here, there's nothing to do and nowhere to go." She kept on going on and on about the place then she said, "I'm going back to Glasgow and my flat. At least you can get food or anything you want at any time not like here, where you have to drive at least eight miles to get a carry out or anything. Fuck this, I'm off on Monday." There was nothing I could say or do to change her mind; she just was not the same girl that I met at that party. Maybe we got married too soon. I admit she was young and it was a boost to my male ego to have such a good-looking young black girl but . . . !

Maybe she was just tired. Maybe she might be different after the weekend and change her mind? Whom am I kidding? She didn't, and on Monday, I took her up to Glasgow to her flat. It was a great flat right in the middle of town. A good area, two bedrooms, a kitchen, a big living room, bathroom all leaving off a polished wooden floored hallway with her own front door that opened out onto a fourth level landing. There were steps going down to the street below. Her sister was there to welcome us. She was staying there while we were away. She had moved up from London for a modelling job that she was offered in Glasgow from her modelling agency in London, so she took it, and she was staying with her sister until she got a flat of her own. She was great looking, smaller than my wife with the same long black hair great tits that didn't need a bra, and most of the time she didn't wear one. She was very slim, with that round firm tight shapely African bum that they all have, not to big just right. Maybe that was the reason my wife was so uptight. She knew that I thought her sister was fabulous looking, had a better personality and always teased me and flirted with me every time she saw me. Saying things like, "this is how your wife should do things for you Bobby." Then she would demonstrate and say, "Does she do it like this?" Then my wife would stop her saying something in Swahili again. I think her younger sister was a bit afraid of her because when my wife wasn't there she was a different person, who knows? I know what I thought of my wife's sister she was incredibly sexy and she knew I thought that.

Anyway, I left her there and came home because I was working the next day at the wood mill and she was going back to her job in Glasgow. She worked for Mercedes, the car company in the administration side of it. Her job was to follow up on people that had bought the top of the range cars and a year later or more she would phone them up. Her usual story was "don't you think it's time you thought of trading in your old model and buying a new one?" Nine out of ten times, she got them to buy a new car and she would get a lot of commission on the sale. She was good. She had the looks and the charisma plus her very good wage. She was doing all right. She had been with the same company when they were down in London and her boss said would she like to go to Scotland with an increase in salary to their new showroom in Glasgow. He would help with her flat rent. I don't know if he was knocking her off. Maybe that's just the way my mind works.

She was very good at what she did and her boss knew that. My wife didn't change. In fact, she stayed in Glasgow all week, which was okay. I knew that she was working and to travel back every night was madness, especially when she had a flat there. I thought she would at least come back to the cottage in Argyll where I lived for the weekends at least, but no. She would phone up on Friday and say, "Bobby you come up here I can't be bothered to come there." Therefore, off I would go with my tail between my legs, well maybe not my tail. I was like a dog in heat and most of the time I didn't even get it. I was getting frustrated and bad tempered and that didn't help matters between us. This went on for weeks, with me going up there. Then I said to her, "I can't keep coming up here spending all this money. Why don't you come to my place sometime?"

"No I don't like it" she would say.

"Why not?" I asked. "What's wrong with it?" and again she cut me short.

"I've told you why."

"Fuck you then!" I wish I could have done but I wasn't even getting that. I slammed the phone down, what a fucking marriage this was turning out to be. The whole weekend by myself once again. Once I calmed down, I phoned her mobile but she didn't answer it all weekend. This went on into the middle of the week and then she decided to answer it with some excuse. Then she would sweet talk me into coming up saying in a nice sexy voice "why don't you come up here and we could go to the club and after, we could go back to my place and do what you want to do? What about it babe, I'll even do what you like best babe! Come on you know you want it?" She knew how to play me and I fell for it every time I was like putty in her hands. I would jump into the car and drive up there on Friday after work. Right enough we did go out and I did get what I wanted and the weekend was great, then she would turn to stone again and be a bitch, again not answering my phone calls. This went on and on until I tried something; she would just blank all my calls. So I thought, right fuck you bitch! I phoned her and like always, the phone would ring then just go off. Not even go onto the answering services and then I would try again and it would be off. So, I took my sim card out of my phone, replaced it with another one, and rang her again. This time a man's voice answered it. GOD! I was in such a temper.

"Can I talk to my wife?" There was a silence and the phone cut off. "Fuck, fuck! I tried again but the phone was off. I even tried it with my old sim card in but no. It made me so angry; but there was nothing I could do about it. She phoned me one evening in the middle of the week. She came up with some excuse but when I asked her about the man, she just said, "You must have got the wrong number." When I asked again, all I got was nothing. What she phoned me for wasn't to say "Hi dear?" No, it was to ask me if it would be all right if her sister could stay with me while her flat was being redecorated. She had to go back to Kenya, something to do with her Visa and that she would be away for a month or so. Things were not working out really with us at all. It wasn't like a marriage. She never came to stay at the cottage, not once after we came back from Kenya. We didn't make love very often.

It was great when I got it as she knew what I liked and was good at giving it. Maybe I was a bit selfish. I don't think so, but I would say that wouldn't I? Anyway, I said yes to her sister coming to stay while she was away. Anything for company and good company she would make. My wife left to go back to Kenya not even coming to the cottage for the weekend before she got her plane to go away. All I got was a phone call to say, "I'm off."

Her sister came to stay and I picked her up off the ferry. She was so different from my wife. She was kind warm and considerate. Whilst I was at work she would vacuum the house, light the fire, and had some food ready for us to eat for when I came home, what a difference! It was "Sit down Bobs. Do you want to wash first or will I bring the food now?" she would say.

"No, just bring it now. I'll have my bath later thanks." I was being spoiled but I loved it, and it was nice. "Oh, I didn't know that you wanted a bath or I would have done it for you Bobs." She said as she brought the food through."

"Don't be silly, I can do that." I replied as we tucked into the food, our plates on our knees.

"No, no. Doesn't my sister do these things for you?" She said. I laughed and said, "No she doesn't. She doesn't even come here to stay. She just stays in Glasgow all week and the weekend then expects me to go to her all the time. It's as blunt as that . . ." I was cut short by her reply.

"WHAT, you're joking?"

"No I'm not. She's been acting odd. It's not like were married at all.

"Fuck that Bobs, you should have married me," she said. "I know how to look after a man" and then laughed, a very infectious laugh that got me smiling. We ate our food and talked about different things.

I looked at her sitting there with her food on her knees. God she looked so very sexy, even with her hair tied up. She had on tight denim jeans that seemed to be moulded to her bum, hips and thighs. On her top, she was wearing just a very short red t-shirt that ended just below her breasts. It showed off her pierced belly button. We talked and talked then she said, "I'll make us some tea."

"No, you sit there and I'll do that, then I'll go for a bath." I said taking her plate from her.

"Okay but I'll run the bath for you." She wasn't going to take no for an answer. The next day was the same and the day after that. I said to her "you know I'll be so spoilt by the time your sister gets back. I think I'll move in with you instead?" she laughed that laugh again. You can't help but laugh along with her it's that infectious. She just radiates happiness and fun. She's just great to be with and not forgetting her sex appeal.

I came home this night and the bath was ready for me. "Get in and I'll get the food on" she said.

"You don't have to do this."

"I like doing it for you. Your wife should do all this for you. This is what we're taught at home when we are young."

"Perhaps you should tell your sister that." I said. She just laughed. I got into the bath she had even put bubble bath in it or something like that it was full of bubbles. Leaving the door just open and no more so that we could talk while I was in the bath, I could hear her clanking and banging away in the kitchen. We continued to have our conversation while she prepared the food. I just lay there in the warm water under the bubbles with just my head showing. I shouted to her saying would she like to go out for a drink in Dunoon. "There's a place that has reasonably good music that you can dance to if you want?" "What did you say?" she said pushing the door open and standing in the doorway looking at me lying there under the bubbles. I turned my head to look at her and repeated myself.

"Yes that would be great. I could wear my mini kilt and my thigh boots?"

"Steady on, it's only Dunoon. You'll have every one drooling over you and asking you out I said.

"That's the whole idea," she answered laughing. I couldn't help but laugh with her as she rested her back on one side of the door frame with her feet pressed hard against the other side stopping herself from slipping down, her arms folded tight under her breasts looking straight at me smiling as I lay in the bath talking to her. There was something about her. I can't put my finger on it maybe it was just her casual carefree attitude and that great laugh. She interrupted my thoughts saying, "Hurry up and get out the food will be knackered."

"I will if you go and let me get out."

"Come on it not as if I haven't seen one before" she said smiling.

"Hey, you haven't seen mine so go and put the food out and I'll be through." I replied.

"You're a spoilsport Bobs" she said and turned to go back to the kitchen. I could hear her laughing to herself. I shouted after her, "You could have shut the door?"

"If you're going to be such a spoilsport you can do it yourself." I dressed and joined her in the kitchen, where dinner was.

"Well, what do you think about Dunoon then?" I said as we walked through to the other room.

"Yes, I'll like that Bobs "she said.

"Okay, then this Saturday" I said. As we sat down in the other room with our food she said, "Bobs, would you do me a big favour?"

"What's that?" I replied.

"Would you take some photos of me outside in your garden in two of my long silky dresses for my portfolio if it's nice?"

"I would love to" I said.

"Thanks Bobs" she replied leaning over, her plate in her hand. She gave me a kiss on the cheek and sat back down again looking at the TV and finishing of what was left of her dinner. She looked across at me to see if I had finished. "Now, you sit there and I'll wash up."

"No way, I'll help you," I said and we did the dishes together like a married couple.

Saturday morning came, the sun was out, and it was a beautiful day. I shouted upstairs to my wife's sister. She was still in her room. "Do you still want me to take the photos for you?"

"Yes, yes. Give me a minute I'll sort out the dresses that I want you to photograph me in" she said.

"I'll be outside in the sun," I shouted back. As I stepped outside the sun went behind a big cloud and looked like it wasn't coming out again. So I went back in and shouted up to her hurry up. "I don't know if the sun will last."

"Alright I'm just putting on my face."

"I'll be outside mucking about with the camera" I replied.

She appeared in this very long low cut black silky see-through dress. It was held by two thin black straps, the silky fabric just hung loosely over her large erect black nipples, leaving the top of her incredibly firm and shapely breasts out. I even could see the dark circular patch of skin just behind her nipples. For all the dress was covering you could see through it, the thin black material revealing all. For a twenty two year old girl she had great figure! "Bobs, where do you want me to stand?" her voice broke my concentration on her breasts. I looked up into her face to a great big smile. "Err, over by the tree . . . that's good." She knew how to pose for the camera. She should it was her job. I looked at her through the camera lens. I could see the whole outline of her body it was so erotic, I couldn't help but feel horny. Click went the camera, click-click. Again, she moved about the garden posing in front of the camera knowing that no one could see us in the walled garden. "Is this okay Bob?" she said pushing her hair up and over her head so it fell down over one side of her face. She stood sort of leaning back and round to one side looking at the camera through the black thick curly strands of hair. Both hands rested on top of her head. She pushed out her breasts, the light of the sun revealing more of her nakedness through the dress. "Yes . . . yes, hold that . . . click, click. God she was out of this world, so young, so good looking and what a poser! As the sun shone through the flimsy black fabric, it caught all of her nakedness in that one shot revealing all to the camera, and I got it.

"That's enough. I'll go and change, I'll be back in a minute," she said and disappeared into the house. I was glad of the rest, not because I was tired just because I was getting so horny. I only had on jogging bottoms and nothing under them. Well, it was Saturday after all. I just jumped out of bed and slipped them on. I wasn't going anywhere and certainly didn't think that I was going to take photos as revealing as these. She appeared in a white dress just the same as the one she had on, but this one just had one thin layer of very see through thin silky material and her black body just shone through. I could see everything so clearly through the white silky fabric. She walked towards me from the house. It didn't leave anything to the imagination. Well she couldn't hide anything even if she wanted to, 'if' she really wanted to. "What are you doing to me?" I asked. She just laughed and walked past looking at me as she did. "Come on Bobs take the photo." Before I could say anything she said, "Shall I just do the same again?"

"Yes, yes go on." I looked at her body once again through the lens staring at her naked shaven part so visible. She posed for the camera and I forget to take the photo, fuck me. Click, click-Click went the camera. She moved around the garden once again stopping to pose, the sun light catching her dark mahogany skin making the thin transparent white fabric disappear all together. It was as if she was posing with no clothes on. She said laughing, "Bobs, what's that in your pants? Mmm, am I doing that Bobs? Come on take more of me?" She posed more erotic than before if that was possible, for the camera or me. Who cares, I loved it, and she knew it. I couldn't hide my erection. She just laughed throwing her hair back as the camera went click. I followed her around the garden clicking away at her with the camera. "Come on Bobs take more of me, what do you think?" Before I could say anything, again she hit me with another question, "have I got a better body than you wife. Look at it look at my breasts Bobs. I can see you are very excited."

"Stop it. You know I am and you know that I'm married to your sister," I said.

"Bobs, I promise I won't tease you," she said laughing and running round and up the back on to the higher part of the garden. She stood looking down at me with her legs astride posing, holding her white dress out so that sun light shine through it catching the silhouette of her naked body for me to see more clearly. I stood there looking up at her showing off everything that nature had given her. "Come on Bobs; take one of me up here on top of this rock face?" It wasn't a rock face as such, more like a hill where the grass hadn't grown and left the stones showing. It was a bit of a feature in the back garden. From where I was standing down below her on the gravel path, she was more a feature than the rock face. Showing all to me as I clicked away with the camera as she moved about on the edge posing more sensuously than the last pose, if that was possible. I took one last one of her standing above the rock face and you would have sworn blind a professional photographer took it. It was good enough for the likes of Penthouse or any of those magazines. It was so revealing, her pose in all her magnificence. To me or to the camera, you decide. "God, steady on there, I'm only human" I said.

She just laughed, "Can't you take it old man. Am I too much for you?" As she said that, she turned and ran down the grassy slope into the house.

I stood for a bit to gather my senses then followed her in like a dog on heat! I put the camera down on one of the kitchen worktops. I stood there leaning back against one of the units, 'Shit' I thought, while she ran upstairs 'what the fuck was she doing?' She knew that I couldn't go to bed with her, or did she want me to, should I? I was so horny my mind was racing thinking about her body, nobody poses like that, revealing all to her brother-in-law . . . unless she wants it. Perhaps she's just teasing me. I couldn't get her out of my mind. I just had to have another look at her so I picked up the camera again and started flicking through the photos in the big screen at the back, stopping at the good ones. Well, they were all good. What can I say, stopping at the more revealing ones? 'What a body' I thought flicking through the still shots in the camera. Then she came back into the kitchen wearing her white tracksuit with the hood up over her head and walked over to me smiling. Standing close she looked up at me taking the camera off me and squeezed my erection with her other hand, "Mmm, I see its still there Bobs. We will have to do something with it won't we?" and laughed that infectious laugh that you can't help but laugh with her. "Stop it!"

"What Bobs, what's wrong?" she said as she squeezed my erection through my tracky bottoms tight with her hand. She was so close I just leaned forward and kissed her a long slow kiss while she left her hand tight round my cock squeezing it harder as we kissed. "Mmm, you are so horny Bobs" she said as our lips parted.

"Shut up" I said and kissed her again, another long slow kiss, my tongue playing games with hers and exploring her mouth as she did the same. Our lips eventually parted, I opened my eyes and looked down into her eyes, and in a soft voice she said, "Let's get ready to go out."

"What and leave me like this" I said before she cut me off again, "it will subside before we go out" she said and gave me quick kisses on the lips again and smiled, "come on, get your butt moving."

"I'd like to . . ."

She laughed and said "Come on I'll put my mini kilt and boots on for you."

"Oh In that case I'll go and get ready" I said. We walked out of the kitchen; she went for a shower and locked the door, fuck . . . I continued up the stairs. We hit Dunoon and instantly there were boys chatting to her. Asking where was she from and whom she was with, "I'm with my step-dad" she said and pointed over to me at the bar. Most of the people knew me and said "that's not your step-dad that's Bobby Addis and he's not your step-dad. "Yes he is and I'm with him" she replied. She sat on one of the tall stools by the wall and flashed more of her dark skin between the top of her black thigh boots and her mini kilt, letting her long black curly hair just hang down each side and over shoulders, covering her shapely breasts. You may think that I'm ranting on about her, I am only because I want you to know how gorgeous she was and her personality, well I have not seen any one top it, or her openness, charm, or her looks.

Since we got home about two in the morning, we crashed out in each of our rooms. Sunday was a late get up and I was up first. I made some tea and took it up to her, putting it down beside her on the table. "There's some tea." I said and all I got was a grunt so I just left it and went downstairs to the kitchen where my tea was and picked up the camera. I sipped away at my tea looking at her images, once again taking in her loveliness and thinking, "fuck me, she is incredibly sexy. No wonder she has a good modelling job, she must drive the cameramen wild, they're only human like me . . . well, I think I'm human." I chuckled to myself taking another sip of tea before deciding to go and get some milk and a few other items at the local garage. By the time I came back, there was this heap in a white tracksuit with the hood pulled over her head on the sofa. "Hey, you okay babe?" I asked.

"No I'm not, I've got a stinking hangover" she mumbled "and the phone hasn't stopped since you left and I couldn't be bothered answering it." As she said that, the phone rang and I picked it up, "Yes . . . it's for you, it's that guy you were chatting to." I said all this with my hand over the mouthpiece. All I got was a frantic wave of her hands. "Hold on, I'll go and see if she's awake." I said to the guy on the phone. Once again with my hand over the mouthpiece I said to her "he wants to come round to see you, what will I say?"

"Tell him I'm not well and I'm going home today."

"Hallo, she said that she's going home today. No I don't have her home number, okay, bye" and I put the phone down. "What did you say to him last night?"

"I don't know I was pissed."

The weeks rolled by and I phoned my wife to see when she was coming home. "I don't know they are having a problem with my visa."

"Why?" I asked.

"I don't know. I have to go."

That was it. No how are you, or is everything all right? Not how's my sister, or anything like that, it was straight to the point and bang the phone was down. I thought 'shit I'll get a divorce when she comes back, fuck this.' Well, she stayed in Kenya for about two months and in those two months, I got three phone calls, I tell you no lie. One of those phone calls was me phoning her and all I got was her mother saying 'sorry she's out with friends.' I was pissed off. I started to take it out on her sister. "Don't give me your grief. If you want to divorce her that's your problem, don't tell me." She shouted back at me.

"Sorry, I'm sorry." My wife's sister stayed with me for as long as my wife was away, apart from when she had to go to an audition in Glasgow. A photo shoot or something like that. After the shoot, she came back here to Ardentinny instead of going to my wife's flat. "Why come back here when the flat has all been done up. Why don't you stay there?"

"Do you want me to go? I will if you want me to."

"No, no that's not what I meant. Stay as long as you want?" I said and thought to myself 'God, I would be mad to let her go and leave me all alone and I'm mad to have said yes.'

She interrupted my thoughts "I insist on looking after you while my sister away." She said firmly. 'What a difference between the two sisters' I thought. We get on very well together; we did many things together, going for walks, taking photos of each other as we walked along the hillside or forestry roads, going out for drinks. The whole thing was so relaxed and easy going with her.

I came home from work at the usual time. She had everything ready for me as usual, but this time as I came in, I heard her running the bath. The door was ajar so I popped my head round to say hallo.

Instead of saying that, I said, "oops sorry!" She was leaning over the bath with one hand resting on the edge and the other stirring the soapy bubbles round and round with her other hand. I stood there looking at her round bum as she leaned over the bath with just her red lacy string like strap for her thong disappearing between her cheeks. She stood up and turned round to reveal a very small flimsy red triangular piece of fabric for a thong. It only just covered her privates. My eyes fixed on this thin triangular shape of fabric held together by a very thin red lace that went high up over her hips. She walked slowly and seductively towards me. She was smiling as she wiped the bubbles off her hands. As she got nearer, I looked up into her breasts, which were covered with a matching red lacy bra. It squashed her round firm breasts together and pushed them up and out. She kept on walking towards me smiling. When she was up close and in my face she said, "Hi Bobs I've filled the bath for us." She started to pull me into the bathroom with her two fingers tucked down into my waistband of my jeans. Then as she got me in there, she started to undo my jeans. I put my hand on both her naked shoulders, pulled her tight into me, and gave her a hard long kiss. I could feel her tongue pushing its way into my mouth as it explored and examined every inch of my mouth. It seemed to last forever then as our lips parted; she turned away back towards the bath and walked over to it leaving my jeans around my ankles. She got to the edge of the bath, turned round and smiled then unclipped her bra from the front revealing her round firm breasts and her erect black fat nipples, as they broke free from the lacy material that was keeping them captive. She then slid the rest off her shoulders and looked at me without saying a thing just smiling a big smile showing her perfect white teeth. Then as she wiggled her hip from side to side slowly, she rested her hands on them and started to slide them down each side catching the lacy string like strap on each side of her hips with her thumb. It was holding the red triangular patch of fabric she called a thong in place. She continued to slide her hands down her thigh and then slid them over the top of her thong with her thumbs tucked inside. She started to rub herself up and down the front of it with all of her fingers, still looking straight at me she continued to push her hands on down giving her bum a quick wiggle. The rest of the straps were dragged down along with the thin red triangle that peeled slowly off and down to the floor. God I thought, 'sod the wife. Oops, did I say that?' She turned and climbed in to the bath leaving her bra and thong in a pile on the floor. Once she was in the bath, she scooped up the bathwater with both hands before rubbing her breasts with the warm water. Letting it trickle over then and back into the bath, she said, "hurry up, and get in Bobs. I'll get our food later is that okay?" with a big smile on her face, leaving me with my mouth wide open and my jeans around my ankles, but not for long! I tell you no lie that's how it happened, the whole thing. The photos in the garden for the port folio, the bath, the whole seduction thing.

It didn't go down well with my wife. I tried to say it didn't happen when she found out, but when my wife asked my sister-in-law well she just said "Yes we did, several times when you were meant to be getting your visa. Ha-ha tell us another one." There was a hint of sarcasm in her voice, maybe there was something I didn't know? Well we divorced soon after that. I saw my sister-in-law for a bit after the divorce but alas, we drifted apart when I went back to Africa to sort things out with the people that my ex-wife had arranged for me to do. My sister-in-law well, I heard that she was in a relationship and has a baby boy and it looks just like me. No, no, I'm only joking but I do miss her and that infectious laugh, that sexy body and all the teasing. Thinking back, I should have married her because we got on so well together. Perhaps we would be still married today. Obviously, it wasn't meant to be.

CHAPTER SIXTEEN

GHANA

After the divorce was finished, I had time to think about what I was going to do. The way things were looking, I didn't have much going here. I remembered a girl that I met in Kenya at this party. I was with Juliana and she said that if I ever thought of coming to her country, Ghana where she came from she would show me around the town where she lived. It was called Accra and I could fly straight there as Accra was the capital and the airport was in Accra. At the same party, I mentioned earlier, there was a guy that I got to know very well. He was with this girl not as a boyfriend more of a mate; well that's what I was told anyway. His name was Akor and when Juliana was doing her thing, he used to take me round and show me the sites. We seem to hit it off and got quite friendly and like her, he said if I ever came to Accra he would get me a good deal in any hotel and to just phone him before I thought of coming out. He would make all the arrangements needed for me to have a good time, and I had to find out about the phone calls I was getting from Juliana's cousin. It didn't make any sense what he was saying and threatening. I kept this all to myself and didn't tell anyone. I immediately thought of Juliana shit stirring to drop me in a whole lot of trouble for sleeping with her sister. I had to go and find out about ground, how much I could get it for and where. So I decided to find out what flight went where and go along to the local travel agency to find out all about it. I found out that I fly from Glasgow to Amsterdam then on to Accra. They gave me a price and in return I gave them a date. I hadn't made up my mind when I was going. I went home and got someone to check on the internet for cheap flights, but they were about the same, except in the height of season when they went up drastically. I phoned Akor. I still had his number in my phone and told him that I would be coming out soon, maybe in February or March when the price goes down. He was so pleased that I had phoned him. I couldn't get him off the phone until I told him that it was costing me a fortune. He said he would organise everything at his end and not to worry about a thing he had it all under control. Next, I sent off my passport so that I could get a visa to get into Accra. Once it came back, I booked the flight for two weeks and that was that.

I walked through customs and out into the bright hot sun light after waiting for my bag to appear. The heat was great after leaving Scotland with gale force winds and rain. I walked beside the metal barrier. People were waiting for their friends or love ones to appear from the terminal, like me. I caught sight of Akor about a couple of yards along the barrier, waving like mad and shouting my name. It was hard to hear him over the rest of the humdrum of other people greeting their friends. As I got closer I could hear him, "Bobby man. Bobby man welcome to Accra, my country."

I put my bag down, stretched over the waist high barrier to shake his hand and say hello to him. Picking up my bag, I followed him to the end of the barrier where security guards were standing. I put my bag down, dug into my pocket to get my passport out and show them before they would let me through. Once I was through, I put my bag down again to hug Akor. He offered to take it for me and said, "Come, I've got the car over here and I've arranged for you to stay in the Hilton." "Fuck me Akor, what's that going to cost me?" I asked in horror. I hadn't brought that much money with me. I know the pound goes a long way but I don't think it would stretch to staying in the Hilton. "Don't worry man; I've got it under control. Come the car is over here." We walked through the car park of the airport with people milling about all over the place and cars. There seemed to be no organised route out, it looked like you just got into your car and drove like mad to get out of the place. After dodging a couple of near misses we got to Akor's car. It was a four wheel drive jeep with no hood but a big black roll bar with four large spotlights fixed along the top bar. "Nice Akor" I said as I threw the bag into the back and climbed in over the small doors, if you could call them doors. We drove off with the sounds blaring out of the C. D. Player. We got to the hotel, it wasn't as grand as its name thank god, but it was very nice. We hopped out over the half moon doors of the jeep; I grabbed my bag from the back seat and followed Akor into the hotel, to reception and the guy behind the desk. "Good afternoon Sir" he said. I answered him as Akor asked for the keys to room 420. "Would you like someone to help you with your cases?" The man behind the desk said in his very smart red jacket and black trousers.

"No thanks" I replied as Akor took the keys from the man and thanked him. We made our way to the elevator. As we waited for the elevator to appear after pressing the white arrow that lit up in the middle of the brass plate, I said to Akor, "Were you here earlier?"

He smiled, "Yes Bobby man I've left a present in your room, just a small thing saying welcome to Accra." I just smiled as we stepped into the elevator and the door closed. We were transported to the floor which my room was on. We walked along the blue carpeted floor and turned the corner and half way along the next corridor was room 420. I waited for Akor to unlock the door with one of these cards that you slot down into the long brass lock on the door. I picked up my bag and walked into the room leaving Akor to close the door. It was like any other hotel room apart from the young black girls with long black curly hair standing at the far end of the room by the window. They were wearing a very short figure-hugging dress, with the same red boots that fastened with a broad red strap just above her ankle. Akor tapped me on my shoulder, "Enjoy my friend. Welcome to Ghana it's three in the afternoon. I'll be back at seven. That should be enough time for you to experience these lovely Ghanaian girl's" and laughed. He made his way to the door of the room, opened it and turned round and stood in the doorway. "I'll be back to take you out for a drink so that we can talk about Trevor and what you're going to do." As he left the room and was about to close the door he hesitated and said again, "Enjoy my friend. There's more where that came from. I'll see you at seven and the door closed and left me with these young girls. They started to walk over to me, ever so slowly both of them moving their hips in a very sensuous way. I must say that Akor got it wrong, four hours wasn't long enough to enjoy the experience of these's lovely girl's.

We were sitting in this pub in Accra full of black folk, (well it would be wouldn't it.) The booze was cheap and the smoke was thick. There was no air conditioning just several large propeller like objects suspended from the roof, going round and round not doing much than blow the cigarette smoke around the dark pub. We sat in the corner of this rat infested place called a pub where the only light was the noon day sun. When someone came in from the dusty street outside, the door swung open, the sun would light up the place then the door would close again shutting out the bright sunlight once again and it was back to the dimly light bar and the round tables that were dotted about the place, where your bottle beer stuck to the table top. We talked and drank the local beer and Akor would stop every time the door opened as if he was expecting someone to walk in and catch him talking to me. He told me what Juliana was into with her cousins and the neighbouring tribe. They had a large operation going on to smuggle diamonds out of Sierra Leone, across the border and out the country through Accra international airport to the U.K, Holland and Munich amongst other places. I interrupted him and asked "why do they have to come through Ghana, why not just take it out through Kenya?"

He said that he didn't know but Juliana's cousin had business over there as well. It was a big set up and well run. These guys didn't stand any nonsense. They wouldn't think twice of cutting of your hand or an arm off if they thought you were doing them in any way or keeping some of the merchandize for yourself, like the odd diamond. Most of the time they used young girls to ferry their stuff over the border or out of the country. He told me this then stopped and had a look around before taking a drink of beer from his bottle. Before putting it back down, he would look around again. "Bobby man I tell you no lie, they used to come to the beach parties. They would chat up young white girls on holiday or young girls working in the day care centres looking after abandoned black babies. It was charity work the young girls were doing and some of them would do it for the extra money if it was drugs, but if it were diamonds they used their own people. Take the likes of you, married to a Kenyan girl to take out their diamonds. Juliana had it all planned. You and she were to take a load back to Scotland when you went home in the new case she bought.

Up to now I was just listening to him going on and thinking that it would make a good television movie that you would watch, but being realistic he was talking about me. I interrupted him. "Yes she did buy a new bag, the bitch."

". . . but there was a little hiccup, She didn't tell you right? And I don't think she was going to either. She would just use you in the sense that you had a British passport and lived in the U.K and were squeaky clean. They had given Juliana the bag and the diamonds were going to be in the bottom of the bag." Akor said.

"The bitch" I said again. "What would happen if we were caught?" I took a drink from my beer looking at him waiting for an answer.

"I don't know. You probably would be sent to jail here. Juliana would be freed by the organisers and would probably say that she didn't know anything about it. Didn't she put your things in the new bag?"

"Fuck me, she did. She said that she didn't have enough room in her case because she had to take presents home to her friends . . . So that's why we bought the new bag. The bitch, fuck me!"

"Bobby man, you will have to go to Juliana's cousin and talk to him. He was the one that said it was too risky if she wasn't going to tell you. He was the one who stopped them but for fucks sake don't say I told you all this. I don't want to end up in a ditch or have my hand cut off." He was scared of what they might do to him or his family if they found out that he had told me all this. I said I would go and see Juliana's cousin whose name was Trevor and talk to him. Then I said "I'll get the beer in, do you want another one Akor?" He said yes. I got up from the table and made my way to the crowded bar and waited to be served. I got two more beers and made my way back to the table and sat down again. We talked about different things. He was starting to relax but still nervous every time the door of the pub opened. He went on to say that "these people are above the law. Here they have the police in their pockets or if they don't go along with what they say they seem to have an accident or someone in their family has one. Life is cheap here Bobby man and these guys make a lot of money, more than any Ghanaian can make in a life time and for a little bit of money you can get your best friend killed if you wanted. I hear you are going to build a house in Ghana. What's that all about Bobby man?" He changed the conversation around.

"Yes" I said. "I have arranged to buy some ground and as you know I have to have an address in Ghana that's why I was speaking to that girl you were with. You know, the one you introduced me to at that party with Juliana. She was from Ghana as well, the one with the great body and the big tits." Anyway, she said that she knew of some ground being sold by the sea, just a couple of yards away from the beach outside Accra. A couple of thousand pounds sterling would get me two building plots. About two hectares of ground or so she said, then she said she would take me to see it if I phoned her the next time I was in Ghana, if it was all right with you" I said.

"And what did you promise her?" as he took a swig of beer and waiting for my answer. I hesitated "You didn't say that you would share the house with her?" he took another drink. "You did, didn't you Bobby-man."

"Well . . ." I hesitated. "Well, yes I did."

"WHAT! Man I've told you, don't promise anything to these girls."

"Well I was a bit pissed." I stopped and took a drink of beer before continuing "and she was just wearing that very small top with her breasts sticking out over the top, those white shorts that were so tight that they showed off her crutch. Those white socks pulled up to the top of her knees she was great. And when she sat on my knee and put her arms around me and looked at me with those big brown eyes, I would have given her anything right there."

"You did Bobby" Akor said laughing.

"Would you go and have a look with her and let me know if it is any good. 'I'll be back in Scotland by then. Can I trust you Akor to do that for me?"

"Hey man I'm trusting you with my life telling you what I've told you." He laughed again, "Bobby man you will never learn. You know what they say, a fool and his money." We both took another drink of beer from the bottles that we were holding. "Did you get into her tight pussy then?" he asked.

"No" I said. "We just smoked a banger together, that's all. Anyway she was with you wasn't she?"

He didn't answer to begin with, "You know Bobby-man you could buy an import car and start up your own taxi services here in Ghana. It wouldn't take much." He reeled of where I could get a car and where I could get it sprayed in the appropriate colour. He knew where there was a market where he could buy all the taxi things, like the sign on the roof and all the extras. But most importantly where I could get it registered as a taxi. I butted in "I take it that you would be coming in with me as the driver?"

"Yes Bobby man, of course. A white man can't drive a taxi, it just not done. There is too much poverty around for a white man to drive.

You would be put off the road one way or another if you know what I mean man."

Then I came up with an idea. What about renting a shop and selling mobile phones? I could buy them in Dubai cheap, bring them back to Ghana to the shop and sell them. What about that then? We both laughed, "We will make a good team Bobby man" as we both took a drink of beer and finished them. "I get another two" he said as he got up from the table. He turned round and said "you want another Bobby man?"

"Yes, yes." I sat back in the chair and looked about the smoky bar, just staring at all the people. He came back with the beer and as he put the beer down on the sticky beer stained surface of the table, "Bobby man I have a cousin that could help you." He went on to tell me about his cousin. All these ideas and more were going round in my mind as he was going on about his cousin. I wasn't listening to him, I was thinking about my shop and how much it would cost to rent. "Bobby man, are you listening to me?"

"What, sorry Akor. What were you saying?" He continued to tell me about his cousin. I listened to him but my mind was still on the shop and thinking that Ghana itself doesn't have phone services like the UK, just a mobile phone if you could afford one. Then I thought, *'That's not true. I've seen people sitting under umbrellas on the side of the road with phones. They must be connected to some sort of service.'* I turned to Akor to ask him when he said, "I'll phone my cousin Bobby man and get him to meet us."

"What for Akor?" I said.

"To find out about the taxi man?"

"Okay Akor" I replied not really listening to him and said in the same breath "where can I rent a place?"

"What for man, for the taxi?"

"No" I said. "Sorry Akor, I'm thinking about renting a shop." We were both thinking and talking about two different things and both just laughed. We talked and talked in that bar over a few beers, well, a lot of beers. We came out of that place bursting with ideas and how we were going to make a fortune the two of us?

There were a couple of things I had to do before heading home to Scotland. To meet Trevor and hear what Juliana has been saying. The others were less important. I had to find out about renting a shop in Accra and buying an imported car so that I could start up a taxi business. I thought I would leave those two things up to Akor. He was finding out about the land and was going to see the girl that I had talked to earlier. The main thing was to phone Trevor and find out if he was in Ghana or at his farm in Kenya. If he was at the farm, I wasn't going there. He would have to come to Accra just because I didn't have enough money to fly there and back again and then on to Scotland. Anyway he was always in and out of different countries. It wouldn't be anything to him just to hop on an internal flight and come to Accra. I had got his number from Akor before leaving the pub. I made my way back to the hotel by foot. It wasn't far from where I was and it was a great day, no clouds in the deep blue sky and it was so hot. *'God, I love this country and the weather'* I thought as I walked along the very busy street with people busy doing their things. I got to the hotel, got my keys and headed up to my room. This time there would be no hidden surprises in my room. I put the card in the slot and opened the door half hoping there would be a surprise, but no, the room was empty. I thought I would take a shower and phone Trevor afterwards. I picked up my phone and saw that I had two missed calls and one voice message, they were both from Akor. I phoned him back first before phoning Trevor. All he said when I phoned was that he had talked to his cousin and to the girl and they would both like to have a meeting. Akor said he would pick me up in the bar of the hotel round about eight to eight thirty. I looked at the time on my phone. It left about an hour or so before he would be here. I phoned Trevor there and then. I was a bit nervous. Maybe nervous is not the right word, perhaps more intimidated by what he was going to say. Anyway the phone rang out, but by sheer luck it went on to his answering service so I just left a message saying that it was Bobby and I'm in Accra for a week and it would be good to see him and get this matter sorted once and for all. I pressed the key on my phone to end the call, put it in my pocket then got ready to go down to the bar. I would be early but I thought that it wouldn't matter. All it meant was that I would have a couple more drinks at the bar waiting for Akor, and that's what I did.

I was standing in the hotel bar drinking my beer just talking to the barman when Akor tapped me on the shoulder. "I'll have one of those Bobby man." I turned round, "hi Akor" I said then turned back as the barman put another round napkin down on the polished wood counter and laid the bottle of beer down on it. I said "thanks" and asked if he would put it on my tab like the rest. He said he would and gave me the receipt from the till to sign. We stood in the bar and had maybe three or four more beers. Then Akor said "we go and see Mary and his cousin. They would meet us at this club that Akor knew. We finished our beers and I thanked the barman and left him a tip. We made our way out to Akor's jeep, set off down the street on our way to the club and as Akor was driving he asked me if I had phoned Trevor. I said that I had but he wasn't picking up so I left a message. Just as I had said that to Akor, my phone rang. I pulled it out of my pocket and looked to see who it was, shit it was Trevor. I pressed the button on my phone and said "hi Trevor." He answered by saying, "hi Bobby, long time. How are you?" We got all the niceties out of the way and got down to what we really were on the phone for. He said that he was in Accra and if I could meet him at . . . He named a place; I repeated it back to him then said "I don't know where it was." As soon as I said that, Akor piped up and said that he knew where it was. I told Trevor I would meet him there and asked what time for. He told me where and when and the time after that he rang off and I turned to Akor and said fuck me!

"What did he say man?" Akor asked me.

"Not much. He wants to meet me at that place that I said to you, on Friday night about eight. I leave on Saturday morning to go home. But Akor never answered me. He had turned into this street that was quite narrow and was to trying to avoid the cars and vans that were parked along each side of the street. He had to drive down the middle and at the same time, trying to avoid the crowds' of people that were going in and out of the shops that were behind the parked vehicles and were still open. People were just wandering across the street going into the shops on the other side of the street and just generally getting in the way of us and other vehicles that were following us. I just shut up and sat back in the seat and let the warm evening air blow my hair about. I looked at all the nice girls walking about the street doing their thing and getting out of the way of us and other people. *'God, I love this place'*

I thought,' then Akor interrupted my thoughts by saying to me "we are here." I looked about as Akor slowed down and waited for some people to get out of his way before slipping his jeep in a gap between a van and a big fancy motor bike and parking. He turned to me and pointed to a place across and down the street from where we parked the jeep with hundred of coloured lights hanging outside it and a lot of people crowded around the entrance. We jumped out of the jeep and joined the people on the street and walked towards this place. As we got closer, I could hear the bass of disco music thumping out through the door. The closes we got, the louder it got until we were standing outside the door among the rest of the crowd waiting to get in. A tall black guy was standing at the doorway, letting three people in at a time. He waved us up to the front of the crowd that were waiting to get in and said to Akor, "Just go in man."

Akor said something to him, I don't know what. I was pushed in through the doorway and a long a narrow passageway where people were standing along the side of the passageway wall. They just looked at me as I passed them on my way to where the flashing lights and the loud music were coming from. Akor was hard on my heels telling me to keep moving. We arrived in this large dimly light room with a large dance floor that was full of people dancing. At the far end, there were two topless girls sliding themselves up and down a silver pole. In between them, in a large glass box was the DJ with long curly hair and ear-phones on thumping out the music. Akor tapped me on the shoulder and as I turned, he pointed to a girl sitting with a guy in a corner of the room, it was Mary. We squeezed our way across the crowded dance floor two where they were sitting. I thought of her on the beach on that day I was with her and Akor last time I was here. She looked great. As I got closer to where they were sitting, I looked at her with that big smile on her face and wearing a bright orange t-shirt with a low neckline that showed off the top part of her breasts. They were pushed up and out even more by the black lacy bra that held them captive and was quite visible. We said "hi" as we sat down beside them. The guy with Mary asked what we would like to drink. As he got up to go to the bar and left with our orders, Mary turned to me and said smiling, "The same old Bobby, you never change, always looking at my tits." Akor laughed and I just said, "With tits like that, I can't help but notice them." She laughed and cracked another joke. As she did, she seemed to push her tits out even more. We got our drinks and sat there talking about how we were going to get the car and what it needed to make it into a taxi, and where were we going to rent a shop for the phones and a lot of other things. Mary said that she was going to the toilet and Akor gave her some money and told her to bring back the same order. As she got up I couldn't help but stare at her very thin tight red jeans that she was wearing. They just showed off all of her feminine figure and her tight round bum as she wiggled her way into the crowd and was swallowed up by the people that were dancing on the floor. I turned back to Akor and his cousin who were smiling at me, "WHAT?" I said. They just burst out laughing and carried on drinking their beer from the bottles. I just smiled and picked up my beer. We sat there discussing what would be the best way to get the car sprayed in taxi colours and out of our discussion; we came up with a friend of Marys who had a garage. Mary said that if she went to see him she's sure that she could get it done on the cheap. Akor said "yes we know what you mean by on the cheap?" he and his cousin laughed. Mary just shrugged her shoulders and stuck out her tongue at them. The whole joke went right over my head, I just smiled.

"Oh come on, dance with me?" she said and grabbed my arm and stood up, holding it and pulled me up and onto the dance floor as I attempted to move in time with the music. Mary was wiggling and twisting and moving her hands over her breasts, down her sides, then pushing them up into the air above her head and then down onto her head as she moved her hips from side to side and repeating the whole sensual flaunting. Showing off her body to anyone how wanted to watch. It was hard enough to dance to the music, let alone keep up with her, so I just moved in time with the music and looked at her doing her come on and rape me dance and waited for the music to end. As it did, we went back to where the other two were sitting. Akor said that he had to go somewhere so we finished our drinks, said our goodbye's and got up as Mary said, "I'll see you again I hope Bobby?"

'Oh God I,' I thought. We fought our way back through the crowded floor and outside to the cool night air. The jeep was where we had left it.

We hopped over the small half moon doors on the jeep without opening them. Akor turned to me saying that he would come back for me if I wanted to stay. I said, "No it's okay; just drop me off at the hotel if you want."

"No, come with me if you want, I'm just going to call on some girls. Do you want me to take you back to the hotel first?"

I laughed, "What do you think Akor?" We both laughed as he drove off down this narrow street that was much quieter than when we first arrived. It made me think of the time and if the hotel would still be open. I turned to Akor and asked him if the hotel would be still open and would I get to my bed, or is this one of your all nighters and laughed. He turned to me and laughed again before turning back to look where he was going. "It's three in the morning Bobby man and we are just starting to rock and roll." He laughed out loud again and slid a C.D. into the vehicles C.D. player. Instantly the music started to thump out of the four mega speakers. You couldn't help but get in the mood for partying. It was magic and Akor was just great fun to be with.

We headed off into the night with the music thumping and the warm night air blowing our hair all over the place as we drove through the streets of Accra. To my amazement there were people still driving and walking about the place. The whole of Accra was alive, not like earlier where there where masses of people pushing and shoving. It was more of the younger people just having a good time. Akor turned to me and said after a long time being quiet, "Yes, the security guard will be up, but don't worry where I'm taking you."

"What Akor?" I said turning down the music on the C.D. player. He then repeated himself and went on to say "Bobby man where I'm taking you, you won't want to sleep" and laughed?

"Akor, where at three in the morning are there people still up, let alone wanting to party?" I asked. He turned up the C.D. player again. I sat back in the seat and let him take charge as we drove on down another street.

It was Friday morning when I woke up in my hotel room. Well, more like one in the afternoon. I had a very sobering thought. I had to meet Trevor today. I lay in bed. My mind drifted back to last night and what an amazing place Accra is. Then I thought any place is like that, if you know where to go for fun. Then I thought, 'No.' No way can you get girls like that back home. They were all out for fun and just having fun and sex. Here you were guaranteed to get a girl or two, maybe even three in one bed at one time. There was no way you could do that at home or anywhere unless you paid for it. I threw back the sheet that was covering me, walked into the bathroom and turned on the shower. Afterwards I decided to go and get some coffee. I went down to the foyer where you could sit and have things to eat or drink and sit in the big leather seats, hang out and watch people coming and going. So that's what I did. Then my phone rang in my pocket. I took it out and looked at it, it was Akor. He said that he would be round to take me to see Trevor unless I wanted him to take me somewhere before that. I told him no and that I would just hang around here and go into Accra and wander about the shops then maybe have a sleep later before he comes round as I'm knackered. He just laughed and hung up. I sat there for a while then decided to go out like I said to Akor and go round the shops and just do my own thing. As I was walking around the streets looking at all the people, the stalls and shops my phone rang again. It was Trevor. I had a sudden attack of nerves when I saw his name light up on my phone. "Trevor hi" I said.

"Bobby I can't meet you tonight, something's come up." *'Yes!'* I thought as he carried on, "When are you back in Accra again?"

"I don't know Trevor."

"We have to sort out this little matter Bobby" he said.

"I know" I said. "I'm buying some ground here and I'll have to be back to check on that. I'll call you when I leave Scotland to give you time so that we can meet and talk where ever you want. But I'm not flying to Kenya then on to Accra, I just don't have the money to do that."

"No, I'll meet you in Accra" he said.

"Okay, that's sounds fine to me." His voice faltered and faded. "What Trevor?" I said.

"Are you still talking to Juliana?"

"No Trevor I'm not. Why do you want to know?"

"It's not important. I'll wait for you to call me Bobby, but don't think this is over."

I cut him short, "No Trevor, I know it's not and I want to solve this as quickly as you do. I don't want any hassle. I don't know what Juliana has been saying to you but you know what she's like." He laughed and said "I'll wait for your call Bobby, bye."

I phoned Akor to tell him not to rush because Trevor just phoned. "Is that good or bad news" Akor asked.

"Well" I said, "I don't have to meet him as I said, so I can relax and enjoy my last night in Accra."

"What are you doing now?" Akor asked.

"Oh not much" I replied. "I'm just kicking about Accra, why?" He suggested he would come and pick me up and we could go to the harbour where they bring in the imported vehicles and look for one that might do the job as a taxi. I said that's sounds fine to me and asked where should I meet him. There was a pause on the phone. "You remember the hotel with the balcony that looked over market place?"

"Is that the one in the centre of town?" I asked.

"Yes, I'll meet you there." Akor replied.

"I'll start walking there now. It's about one now and by the time I get there it'll be near the time to meet you." I said and ended the call.

We spent the rest of the day looking at all kinds of cars and the prices were not bad. Akor met some friend that was working at the harbour. They got talking about different things and then the conversation turned to me and a car. He said that he would keep an eye open for a good one and when did I want it by. I told him there was no rush as I was due back in Scotland tomorrow but if he saw a good bargain to let Akor know and I would send him some money. He agreed and I shook his hand. We jumped into the jeep and back to Accra. On our way back, I just sat back in the set and closed my eyes and listened to the sounds that Akor had playing. Letting the very hot sun beat down on my face and the wind ruffle my hair as the jeep raced along the red dust road. I must have dozed off as the next thing I remember was Akor asking if I would like to go to the beach as it was so hot. That was a great idea, so we headed to another part of Accra that I had never been to before. We arrived at this small village which had tables upon tables full of all kinds of fruit that you could imagine. We slowed down to where a guy was standing at the side of the road selling coconuts on a long wooden cart. Akor said "do you fancy a coconut drink?"

"Yeah why not" I replied.

We stopped beside the guy and he came up to the jeep. Akor said, "Two drinks man." We sat in the jeep as the guy turned round to the cart and picked up a coconut in one hand and a machete in the other. He started to hack away at the coconut, trimming it down before slashing the top off it, he handed it to Akor with the milk in then he did the same for me. Akor paid the guy and we sat there drinking the clear liquid. Akor threw his back to the guy, who caught it and said something in some language which I couldn't understand, then I gave mine back and we were off again, along the sandy road leaving the red dust behind us. I would call it just a sandy beach, with people walking all over it as we slowed to a crawl and sounding the horn to people that got in the way. We drove on along this sandy track over bunches of brown like grass tufts following a wooden fence at one side. When it came to an end, there was a large car park with crowds of girls in there bikinis, just hanging about. Some were sitting on the bonnets of cars talking to guys that were drinking beer. We pulled up alongside this other car and hopped out over the door of the jeep and made our way to a turnstile and a guy taking money. I turned to Akor and said "do you have to pay to get onto the beach?"

"Yeah man. We will make money from any opportunity we can." Once on the beach Akor grabbed two bottles of beer from a beach bar shack. It was decked out in fishing nets, lobster creel pots and other fishy things. It was unmistakably party time. There must have been hundreds of barbeques all along this white stretch of sandy beach with their own music. As you walked past each barbecue, the music beat out its rhythm mixed in with the sound of the waves breaking as they crashed in from the Atlantic Ocean, the next party's music faded out, and the next one cut in and so on. We walked along the beach and the girls . . . well; I haven't seen so many young girls all in different attire. Some with very flimsy small summer dresses that would blow up around their waist by the warm evening wind as it tossed them about, showing off their dark olive thighs and even their different coloured underwear. Some girls were even dancing in their small swimsuits, and thongs. There were so many of them just dancing, drinking and wandering along this beautiful white stretch of sandy beach, in groups going from one party to another laughing and shouting at the top of their voices. We stopped at this particular crowd with guys and girls dancing to some great sounds. There must have been three girls to every man and even girls just standing around looking for their particular man or men. We walked through the dancing crowds, as we walked; I was grabbed by my arm by two nice looking girls that were dancing together. They said "Dance with us whitey" and laughed. I said "I will, but I've got to go and see this man first." As I followed Akor, I saw this white guy standing by a spit roast turning what looked like a whole goat, round and round above this open fire. We walked up to him and Akor said, "Hey man, this is Bobby man." The guy turning the goat put his hand out, "hey Bobby, how are you man?" He was American. I shouted over the music and the crackling of the fire, "What is an American doing here cooking goat?" He laughed and asked if we would like some. We said yes. He turned to a table behind him where there was a pile of plates and a big knife. He gave us the plates to hold as he hacked off two huge slabs of goat and put it onto our plates. Then he grabbed two beers that he had in a chill box beside him and pointed, holding the two bottles by their necks between his fingers, to a long wooden table with bowls, of what I don't know I couldn't see from where I was standing. I sat down on a white plastic chair next to a table with an umbrella stuck through it into the sand. Akor put his plate down along with his beer on the table and said to me, "I'll get us some salad Bobby man." I just nodded and took a long drink from the bottle and looked around. The place was heaving with people, and so many girls. I looked round to see if I could see the two that asked me if I would dance with them. They caught my eye as they waved to me and I just smiled. Akor came back with the salads and the American guy, who grabbed a chair from the other table and joined us. "Bobby man, I'm Hank." I nodded as I had a mouth full of goat. It was so tasty I didn't want to just swallow it in one big lump; I just wanted to savour it. It was then that I realised that I hadn't eaten since I left the hotel this morning, no wonder I was so hungry.

"Sorry Hank" I managed to say. "So what are you doing here?" He then went on to tell me that he was a marine biologist and he lives here for so many months of the year to monitor some sort of plankton in the water which is only here at a certain time of the year. He was so intelligent, but to look at him you would think that he was a normal guy. That's not to say that he wasn't normal, far from it. It's just the way he looked, I think. Anyway, he went on and on about the sort of stuff that he did and how he got a huge university grant to come here and do all this stuff. I found out that he was from Boston University in the U.S.A. Then he said out of the blue and so unexpected, "you know it's so easy to get laid here. The chicks are great."

I laughed, "You know, I was about to think that you were one of these people that were very intellectual and had no time for girl." He laughed back, "no way man, that's why I'm here!" Then, Akor who was just listening to all this said, "Hey Bobby man, he's even hornier than you, and that's saying something man." To this we all laughed and Hank said, "There are two girls standing over there staring at us." I turned round to see what they looked like. They were the same two girls that asked me to dance. I smiled at them and turned back to Hank and Akor, "they were the two that asked me to dance when I arrived here."

"Don't look now, but they're coming over to us" Hank said.

Before long there were a crowd of them all sitting and standing around us, all talking at once. They had even pulled over the other two tables next to us and were sitting on them and the chairs. I don't know what we were even talking about. I think we were just talking a load of shit; I don't know or really remember. But I'll tell you this; there wasn't a bad looking one amongst them. They must have been about sixteen to twenty odd, all with their tits sticking out over their very skimpy bikinis tops. I just looked at Hank and he laughed, "what did I tell you man?" He got up to go back to the goat that was still cooking and took over from a guy that was turning it whilst he was with us. I don't know what time we left there but it was late, the sun was coming up. Akor took me back to the hotel with the two young girls that insisted that they were both going to stay with me.

I woke up lying on my back, a white sheet covering half of my naked body. On each side of me were two girls, naked as I had left them the night before. One lying on her side looking away from me and the other one was lying on her back with her long black hair all over her face, her young dark coloured breasts protruding out and upwards from her slim body. I leaned over and took the nearest nipple into my mouth and gently squeezed her other breast. She moaned and woke up, brushing away the hair from around her face. She smiled still not quite a wake but quite willing for me to continue. As I did, not to be left out I felt the other girl turn over, pulling what was left of the sheet off the two of us, leaving us naked on the bed. I felt the other girl squeezing her body up close, putting one of her hands over my waist and pull herself even closer, if that was possible leaving her hand there. I don't know what time we woke up but it was about four in the afternoon. My phone rang and vibrated itself nearly off the bedside table as I grabbed it in mid air. It was Akor saying that he would be round to take me to the Airport about five. I said "okay thanks." I got up leaving the two girls lying naked on the bed with one screwed up sheet, tangled around their feet and went for a shower. I walked back out after my shower with just a towel around me and said to the two girls that were busy cuddling each other that they would have to get ready and go for a shower, if they wanted one as I was leaving to go home. One said "Where's home Bobby?"

"Scotland" I replied, as the other one got off the bed and walked past me smiling and into the bathroom, leaving the other one lying on her back on the bed looking at me drying myself off. "Are you not going for a shower?" I asked as I threw the towel at her. She caught it with both hands and held it down on her lap and carried on looking at me, as I put my underwear on then my jeans. I said again "Well are you?"

"Yes Mr Bob, I'm going, I'm going" she said getting up of the bed on the opposite side and started to walk round the bed towards me picking up the sheets that were on the floor and throwing them back onto the bed. I stood there looking at her naked body bending over in front of me tiding up the bed, thinking that she's at it. I said "leave that and go for your shower." She stood up, turned round and put her arms around me and kissed me, a long kiss pressing her breasts into my chest. She asked "would I take her to Scotland with me." I smiled squeezing her bottom and said "not this time. Maybe next time if you can get your visa sorted out." I said that as it was the first thing that popped into my head. "Now go and get that shower." She took her arms from round my neck and turned to walk away, wiggling her bum as she went to join her friend. She turned round as she got to the bathroom door to see if I was still looking at her, which I was. She smiled and walked on into the bathroom. I stood there thinking *why didn't I meet these two lovely girls earlier on in the week.'* But as usual the best things always seem to come along just as you leaving. I shouted after her saying, "not to take long because Akor will be here soon." All I got in reply was a lot of giggling coming from the shower. I got dressed, packed and went back into the bathroom to gather up my toiletries and put them into the small plastic bag that I had in my hand. I stood there looking at the two girls; they were talking amongst themselves as they put their makeup on in front of the mirror. That red lipstick that looks so sensuous against their dark skin. As they put the finishing touches to their lips, both still naked, they turned away from the mirror and looked at me and giggled before turning back to the mirror to finish off with their lipstick.

The plane landed at Glasgow Airport in heavy rain. I made my way to where my bag would come out on the stainless steel conveyor belt and stood waiting for it with the rest of my fellow passengers. It finally appeared through the centre of the circle and flopped down onto the rubber mats. I waited for it to come round to where I was standing, and then I leant forward and picked it up and threw it over my shoulder and walked towards customs. As I was walking along with the other people, a customs officer came up to me and asked me if I would like to step this way. They have a way with words don't they? "Step this way," so I did 'step this way' and followed him into an office where there was another man with a dog. Standing next to him was a woman in the same uniform. I was asked to open my bag and place it onto the shiny aluminium table in front of me. I was then asked if I had any illegal substances. I said "no." The woman took my things out my bag and put this hand held object into my bag. I take it was something that would show if I had any drugs hidden in there. As she was looking all around my bag, the dog was sniffing me. I was asked what flight was I on and where had I just come from. I told them where I'd been as they asked to see my passport. I stood there waiting for them to say "okay, fuck off." Well not quite like that, but they gave me my passport back and said thank you. As I put all my things back into my bag and zipped it up, I was shown the door and told to go through to customs so that they could stamp my passport. I left the room and joined the next crowd of people waiting to go through. Then I was out into the terminal, then to the nearest toilets for a pee. Afterwards, I stood by one of several basins and pressed down on top of the tap to fill the basin, took my hand of it and it stopped. *Fuck me* I thought and held my hand hard down on it to get some water. Well, enough to wash my hands and face in. As I looked into the mirror with both hands resting in the basin of warm water I thought, 'why did they just pick me out of the crowd?' Maybe it was my long hair? But it wasn't that long. Or was it because I was unshaven and naked looking? Maybe it was a combination of the lot. They thought *this guy looks dodgy, we'll check him out!'* I threw more water over my face and let the water disappear, before turning to dry my face and hands. There was only a silver blower that blew hot air and it was pointing down the way. 'Fuck me' I thought, after trying to bend down under it so it would blow warm air onto my face. I soon stopped that as people started to look at me. I unzipped my bag and pulled out an old t-shirt and dried myself with it before throwing it back into the bag and zipping it closed. I left the toilets, making way for another man as he nearly pushed me back in to the toilets on his way in. I decided to and get some coffee as I wasn't in a hurry and it was pissing down outside. I had to get the bus to the ferry, then another bus. I went up one of the flights of stairs leading to the upper level and to many of the small coffee shops and ordered a coffee. I sat down on one of many empty tables, and thought 'what am I going to do?' I sat there. I didn't get much sleep on the plane and when we stopped in Amsterdam, it was a mad rush through their large Airport. I had to go from one end to the other to catch my connecting flight to Glasgow, and they don't wait for you. I slumped back in the chair with my bag down by my side on the floor and sipped away at my coffee, just looking at the people coming and going and heading off on their different destinations. I sat there thinking of Africa and all the beach parties and thought *'what a way to live, just barbequing on the beach, dancing, drinking, and just having a great time.'* The girls, 'fuck me,' the girls . . . There were so many nice young girls. As for sex, it was handed to you on a plate with no effort needed. Not just that, you could get as many as you could handle. By that I mean you could have two or three or more in one go, if you could keep them all going, and what a great place to live, and so cheap. I thought long and hard over several cups of coffee and it all boiled down to money, like always. So I sized up my options:

    A.   What's here for me? My kids and my grand kids (that's a big one.)

B. Do I have the money to buy land and build here? No.

C. The weather here? It's shit here and great in Africa.

I couldn't make my mind up so I made my way to the entrance, out into the rain and waited for the bus. I stood in the bus shelter and thought although I slate Scotland I love it, and I'm so proud of being Scottish. As for where I live, it's not that bad, but if it would only have better weather! There would be no comparison. The girls popped into my head, like always my cock started to rule my head once again what can I say? Okay the girls that were here weren't desperate to leave their country like the girls in Africa that's what made them so easy to go to bed with and I did like coloured girls there's something about them I do think that they are quite sexy and you what they say, "once you've had black, you never go back. Maybe that's for the girls who have black guys? Anyway, I know that the coloured girls that I have been in bed with have been great. I don't know if it's the way they move their hips. If you see a coloured girl dancing, the way they move their hips from side to side, front and back and shake their bum, a white girl just can't do it as good. That's just my thoughts on the matter and what the fuck do I know. I just like going to bed with them. In fact if you want to know, I like going to bed with any girl white or black I'm just so fucking horny! I got on the bus, sat down by the window and thought, *'what should I do? Should I max all my credit cards and fuck off, or should I stay here and keep renting my brothers place and struggle on in the wind and rain.'* The thought kept drifting in and out of my mind as the bus sped down the motorway through the heavy rain. I looked out of the side window at the traffic coming up the other side of the motorway and across past them, at the start of the Clyde estuary and the start of the wide expanse of hills that were starting to come into view on the other side of the water. I thought, 'it won't be long know before I get to Gourock and the boat across to Dunoon, and the open space of Argyll, then home to the cottage in Ardentinny.' I was getting quite tired with all this brain power that I've been using up just thinking.

I arrived home eventually to my cottage in Ardentinny all alone, tired and cold. I lit the fire, but even then it took awhile before there was enough hot water pumped round the radiators to heat the place let alone have a bath, which I desperately wanted. With being away, the fire hadn't been on and the place was cold, more so because I hadn't been there every day to light it. It took a while before the place got warm. I thought, 'fuck waiting for the fire to heat the water for the bath and the radiators,' so I decided to put the water heater on to boost the hot water, but I knew that it would send the electricity spinning round on the wee dial. What the heck, I was naked and all I wanted was to have a bath, watch telly for a bit then go to bed.

I still had a couple of days left before I had to go back to work at the mill and start the drudgery of day in day out work. But it was work and I got good money and it would all help. Then the thought of fucking off back to Accra rushed back into my wee brain, and all the other thoughts that I'd been thinking about on the bus and in the Airport. The more I thought about it, the better the idea was.

Month's had gone by and I was getting ready to leave, yes! I was going back. You're probably saying what the fuck for, as did my family? Well, to tell the truth, I don't know. I think Africa had a magnetic pull on me, I loved the country, and you could rely on the weather to be hot. Not like here in Argyll, rain and more rain. You could buy land much cheaper than in Britain and not to mention building a house. In Africa, you could build a bigger and better one for the same price that you could build a normal sized house here. I love the country so why not go back.

I had given most of my stuff away from in the house. I asked my kids if they wanted some of it and they said "yes, they would take a few things." My daughter said "it will be here for you when you come back dad?"

"Thanks Mouse" I said. Mouse was her nickname. I wasn't planning on coming back for a while. I had several credit cards of which I had decided to max them to their limits. Oh, did I just say that?! I was using four on a regular basis. The credit card companies were always putting the credit limit up higher so that I would spend more. Well that's their theory and sometimes it did work. Anyway, I had four of them and on at least two of them the credit limit was well over a thousand. The third had over three thousand and the fourth had eight hundred on. Plus, I was good with the bank for an overdraft. So all in all I was good for thousands of pounds if you get my drift. However, I was going to Africa for a long time to build a house there. Why Africa I hear you say? Well like I said, you can get far more for your money out there than you do here; also Juliana was from there, but a different part of Africa. Whilst I was out there, I had met several people from Ghana. This bit gets a bit confusing, so you don't get mixed up, Juliana was from Kenya and I'm going to Ghana. And it was all to do with a girl and of course Akor, whom I had met when I had been out in Kenya. They were both from Ghana, she was sixteen, and good looking with a great body and she worked for Akor. But I didn't know this at the time. There would have to be a girl somewhere, I hear you say. I put my plan into action. I phoned Akor, the guy that I met while I was out in not Kenya; he was the guy I was drinking with, in the pub if you remember. Well we were discussing Juliana, as by this time he was home in Ghana, Accra to be precise. I hope I haven't lost you yet, are you still with me? Okay, so I phoned him and asked if he had found out about the ground that was for sale next to the sea. His reply was that "Mary had been too late for that particular plot." I asked Akor if he would find out some prices for me then phone me back. He told me that the price Mary quoted was the going price for ground in Accra. I told him to go for about two thousand pounds. He said that thousand pounds Sterling would buy me roughly two good building plots. There was silence on the phone as he waited for my reply. I thought *two thousand pounds, I don't have that, but the cards did' Two thousand pounds Sterling is a lot to them in their money. On average the pounds Sterling goes much further out there than it does here.'* I thought.

"Bobby man, are you still there?" Akor's voice said.

"Sorry Akor" I replied. "I was just thinking. Yes go for it. I'll phone you tomorrow once I've been to the bank."

"Okay Bobby man, I'll wait for your call."

I took two thousand out of one of the credit cards leaving still plenty on it for another day. The only annoying thing when withdrawing two thousand in one go, was that I had to go through all the security palaver, of which I didn't want to do. Next time, I had to take the money out in smaller amounts. I kept it in the house. Once I had the money, I phoned Akor who was the "Main Man" in Accra, if you get my meaning. I told him that I had the money and to go for it. Find me a good plot somewhere near the sea, preferably right on the shore so no one could build in front of me. He laughed and said, "That he would look for a good plot" then hung up. He phoned me back after a couple of days saying that Mary had found land for sale. It was about a half a mile from the sea and was a new site. There were only four other houses built there and no one could build in front of me, so the view was good. The roads were still to be built. There was only the main road that went past about four miles from the turn off. If I wanted it, I would have to send a deposit of fifteen hundred and what did I want to do?

I said that I would send him the money. I was taking a risk sending it out as to him it would be like winning the National lottery. All he had to do was fuck off with it. Anyway, I thanked Akor and pressed the off switch on my mobile. I still wasn't convinced that he wouldn't do a runner, BUT!

The only other solution was to go out there with the money, but that meant that I might miss this opportunity. Also it would take a few weeks to get my visa and arrange a flight, fuck! I thought long and hard and eventually went to the local travel agency and arranged to send the money. Before I did, I phoned Akor back telling him that I would be coming out next week and not to fuck off with the money. He said that he wouldn't, but you would say that anyway even if you were. What I did say to him was that I would tell Trevor what he'd told me in the pub that day, if Mary or he was to fuck off with the money. I wasn't really going to tell, but he didn't know that. That's when he told me that Mary worked for him and she wouldn't fuck off with it either. He gave me his word."

"Okay, okay Akor" I said and hung up. I would have to go out there soon anyway, but had to threaten him with that so he wouldn't do a runner. Even if he wasn't thinking of doing runner I had to send out a strong message. He knew what Trevor would do to him if he ever found out what Akor had told me in the pub that time about him.

I phoned him back the next day and gave him all the details and what bank to get the money out of. I told him to phone or text me when he had received it. It was the longest half hour I've had to wait. The girl in the travel agency said that he should get it straight away once she'd made the transaction. So, I wanted for his phone call. It seemed that I was waiting for hours, but as I said, it was only half an hour. My phone buzzed in my pocket, it was Akor. There was a text saying he'd received the money and would go straight round to the land agent whom was a relative of Mary's. That's how they got the land so quick and such a good deal on it. Akor would pay the money for the deposit on the ground. *'Yes,'* I thought, putting my phone back in my pocket. I walked to a cafe that was just along the street. I wanted a coffee and to think of my next plan. Whilst I was drinking my coffee, my phone buzzed again. It was another text saying that the land was mine. Mary would send the legal document for my lawyer to check and me to sign. After signing, I would have to send it back to Ghana for the Ghanaian government to put their official stamp on. I would have to send the document and the rest of the money back soon to complete the transaction, or I would lose the deposit and the ground. I text him back saying that I would send the rest of the money out tomorrow, but he would have to wait till I'd been to the lawyer's and that it might take a couple of days. The first stage was nearly finished. I paid for the coffee and made my way home, after buying some food to take home with me.

Akor text me the next day saying that the relative of Mary's said that I would have to build a wall round my ground, this is normal. What I would have to do though was build it six foot high. I stopped reading the text and thought, 'fuck me, what's that going to cost?' I read on. What it said was that he had several prices, but the cost of the wall, six foot high, made out of breeze block, rendered and painted white was six hundred and fifty pound. I text him back saying to go and do it and I would send more money out to him the same way and to the same bank. I asked if he would text me when he receives it all at his end. I ended the text with thanks. So off I go, back to Dunoon to get more money off the same credit card. This time I didn't need the security. I just took it out of the cash-point machine, the hole in the wall outside of the bank. As I had already taken money out a couple of days before, all I had to do was withdraw three hundred. Then a short walk along the street to where the travel agency was and fill in another form, hand over the money and get the security number from the nice looking girl behind the counter. I text Akor saying I had sent the money and gave him the security number. Akor was okay but like most of them out there, you had to watch him. I was okay as long as I had that hold on him. All it would take would be a phone call to Juliana's cousin Trevor. Believe it or not, I was still friendly with him. It was better to be friendly with Trevor than not to be just now. Akor believe it or not was a pimp and still is I think. He uses girls and gets money of them for prostitution and other scams, like advertising his girls in magazines in the U.S.A. and U.K for marriage. They just get money from guys promising they will fly out to them, if they will pay for the flight and help with the money for their visa. It's a massive scam. It's not just Akor and his girls; I think most of the young good looking girls do it for themselves. If they get caught by the undercover police, it's an instant 'go to jail' and there's no 'get out of jail free card', its hard labour there.

Akor makes good money from his girls' that's why I thought I would phone him and not Mary direct. She was just one of his many girls, and there's no reason talking to the monkey when you can talk to the organ grinder. I think that's how the saying goes or something like that? So, I phoned Akor as he's not hurting for money like she would be and like most of them out there. Akor wouldn't rip me off as fast as she would, mainly because he knew he was on to a good thing with me. That's not saying that he wouldn't try to rip me off if he thought he could get away with it. That night after coming in after my work, I had my bath, sat down and started to count the money that I had stashed in the house from the credit cards. This was in between shovelling food down my throat and checking on the statements that the card company sends me every month. There was one card that I was using to pay Akor for the land and other bits and bobs, it was close to being maxed out, but I still needed more money. As I was looking through the statements, I came across a letter that was from one of the credit card companies saying that that could help my finances by consolidating all my cards and overdraft into one easy monthly payment. They didn't close until eight at night and after shovelling more food into my mouth, I looked at the time, there was time to phone them. I picked up the phone and called the company and asked them if I could consolidate my credit cards and overdraft into one easy payment. They were glad to help. They asked me the usual things, how much I had on each card and on my overdraft and how much I could pay back etc, etc. I had a good wage coming in and I hadn't done anything like this before and always paid off my cards on time, well nearly enough on time. I wasn't that perfect but my record was reasonably clean. The following week I got a letter from them saying that they would do it. They would send the money to my bank with enough to pay off my overdraft and my cards and start making one payment a month to them. With the money I had stashed away in the house plus with my cards being clean again I could start over, taking money out slowly from all four of them plus my overdraft and maxing them to the hilt. Then when the time was right I could fuck off. 'Did I say that?' Whilst I was slowly draining my cards and stashing the money in the house, Akor phoned me to say that he had someone out there that would make up the plans for me. I said to him that I would get them made up in the U.K. if he would give me all the building regulations. I went on to say that I didn't know what I wanted yet, and if I did them here I could change the plans around and work with the architect on them instead of phoning him every five minutes. He said "Okay, I think you're right." We talked about other things and how was the weather. Had he been to many barbeques recently, then we said goodbye.

I went to see the architect, told him what I wanted also about the building regulations in Accra. After several weeks and a lot of home visits we came up with a great house. I couldn't even start to think what it would of cost to build here in the U.K. I know I couldn't even afford to buy a plot of land let alone build a house here. I thanked the architect. The next thing was for me was to text Akor and inform him I would be sending plans out to him, and would he get a quote for me from a local builder. He would need to look at them and tell me if I needed to make any alterations. The plans looked great and if I can build the house from what was on paper, I would be very happy. The house of my dreams and it was possible to build it out there in Africa where the pound was much better than in the U.K. After Akor text me back with the price for building the whole house, swimming pool plus getting the ground landscaped and a whole lot of other things he said that he knew of a builder that would start building the house for a deposit of three hundred pounds. This would be for the first stage. Then for every other stage, another three hundred until the house was built. The first stage was the foundations and all the pipe work. The second stage was the bottom floor and so on until the whole thing was finished. Okay, so I had to supply all the materials, but at that they were cheaper than home. I ask you, where in the U.K you could build a house like that. The house consisted of a large hallway with a big fire place straight in front of you as you came in, with a staircase that came down either side of it, a landing in the middle that looked down onto the hall, a bathroom and several cupboards. There was a toilet and three large bedrooms all with en-suite. French doors would lead onto a wooden decking that went right round the house connecting all the bedrooms and leading down onto a patio and barbeque area, then down to the pool. Upstairs an open plan dining room, with a large kitchen and four more rooms, they all opened out onto a wooden balcony, which went right round the house with steps leading down onto the wooden decking below. There's more, but that will give you a rough idea of what it looked like. All this looked out onto the Atlantic Ocean. I had the plans for the house all finished. All I had to do was max the cards again, taking bits at a time out as not to draw attention to myself. Clean out my bank leaving my cheque book and my overdraft. I went on a shopping spree, cashing cheques left, right and centre. Some for cash and some on new clothes and getting cash-back, all the time making sure I didn't go over my card limit. I even sent my passport of again to the Ghana High Commission in London to get it stamped.

Well after I did all that it was time to text Akor again and let him know that I was coming out. I said my goodbyes to everyone and set off for the airport. My main concern was taking all this money through customs? Would they stop me? If they did, what would I say? If they did a check on me and found out that I had maxed everything and was doing a runner . . . ? All this and more was going through my mind. I waited in line before going through customs. I had stashed the money all over my body. In my shoes, around my waist, in my pockets, everywhere, so it wouldn't look like a big load of money. Trying not to think about it as I got closer and closer, I could feel my heart pumping harder. I took a deep breath and smiled and put the bits' and bob's in the basket and put the hand luggage on the conveyor before it goes through to be checked, then it was my turn. Fuck me, here goes, yes . . . Yes! I picked up my things and started to walk to the departure area when a man's voice said "excuse me?" I just kept on walking pretending not to hear him, again he said it and he was a lot closer. He tapped me on my shoulder 'Fuck,' I thought and stopped, so did my heart, "you dropped this," the man said.

"Oh thanks," I said and continued to walk to the departure area, my heart thumping away. I looked for a toilet so that I could take the money out of all the places that I had put it and put it into my hand luggage, leaving a bit to change into for Amsterdam where I would change planes for Accra. The plane from Glasgow was delayed on taking off, which meant that I missed the connecting flight from Amsterdam. I was told I would have to wait at least hours in Amsterdam, so it meant that I would arrive there about nine pm. so I thought instead of hanging around the airport I would go to the red light area, yes! The aeroplane taxied along the runway and eventually stopped and I waited to disembark with the rest of the passengers. After looking around at everything, shops etc, I got a taxi outside the airport straight to the red light area. Before all that, I had a bit of a problem trying to get out of the airport. I was trying to convince the authority that I wasn't staying Amsterdam that I was on my way to Accra. I told them my plane was delayed in Glasgow so that meant that I missed the connecting flight and I had about two hours wait.

They eventually let me leave and I got a taxi right outside the airport to take me to the red light area. It didn't take long to get there. First stop was one of Amsterdam's coffee houses where you can smoke all kinds of cannabis from mild to very strong. I bought a mug of coffee and then had a look at what they were selling. They had all sorts of cannabis in clear plastic containers all along the wall behind the counter and scales so that they could measure everything. As I was looking around the guy behind the counter asked me "what kind of stuff was I into?"

"Oh I just dabble here and there . . . Is that skunk?" I asked.

"Yeah man you want to try some?"

"Please" I said and pointed to a tray of space cakes. "I'll have two of those please as well."

"Okay man, is that all?" he asked.

"Yes thanks" I replied. He gave me them on a plate and I went back to my table and my mug of coffee. He brought over the cannabis all neatly rolled in a banger. He said as he put it down, "enjoy man." I sat back and did what he suggested and smoked away at my skunk, sipped at my coffee and just looked about at all the people in the cafe and waited for the cakes to kick in. I asked for another mug of coffee so that I could have it with my banger and finish them both together. I got up from the table, thanked the guy behind the counter, "have a good one" he said.

"Thanks, I will" I said and left the café. I walked round the corner to where all the girls were standing or sitting in their windows. I walked down the street looking at all the girls in their underwear posing. The effects of the space cakes where kicking in. I stopped at this particular lady who I thought was quite nice. Don't get me wrong they were all good looking, but this one grabbed my attention. I stood looking at her for a while. I must have lost it for a second or two and when I got it together she was beckoning for me to come in. I thought about it but not for long and thought, *'what the Hell.'* I went in and all I can remember was, I was a bit stoned and had a problem with the money. After she told me the prices I thought that I would go for the full Monty, fuck it. I stood in the small room after all was done, I had a problem getting my clothes on for some reason and she had to help me. I think I said over and over that I had to get my plane, as I put my leg down the wrong leg of my jeans again and hopping backwards and about to fall over. I didn't, thanks to the lady grabbing my arm and saving me as she laughed and said, "You better hurry or you will miss your plane" and laughed again at the state of me. She had a really sexy accent, I can remember that. I asked her the time. I had less than an hour to get back to the airport and get my plane. Grabbing the rest of my clothes, I ran up the street to the end and got a taxi straight away, thank goodness. I got back just as they called out for the last time. I ran to the departure area and flashed my boarding pass and my passport to the girl waiting at the gate as she said, "you will have to hurry they have put out the last call".

I arrived in Accra airport to the usual chaos and heat, waiting in line for my turn to go through customs. Whilst I was standing there, the heat was intense and the line was so slow. I eventually got through and made my way to where my bag was going round with all the others people's bags. I picked it up of the conveyor and made my way out into the hot sunshine and Accra. Once again to be met by Akor with two of his girls, both very good looking. They were sisters so I found out later. We had the usual greetings then he asked if I would I like to go see the land first or go to the hotel that he had booked for me or to clean up. "I'll go see the land" I said. We drove off with the two girls squeezed in the back of Akor's jeep and headed out of Accra about thirty or more miles. We drove on to a stretch of new tarmac road that was still under construction. It was more like a duel carriageway. We had to drive to an opening in the middle, then turn back and come back up the other side of the road. We turned off to the left and down a muddy, bumpy, dirt track road to the plot of land. It didn't look like much, it was just overgrown, a weedy, muddy dump, with two houses on the other side. One belonged to a retired Colonel and his wife and the other one to a Chinese man and his wife. Behind my ground another building plot had just been started. I walked around the plot with Akor as he told me what I would have to do. As he talked, I looked out across the weeds out on to the Atlantic Ocean and the beach in front of my plot. It wasn't that close about ten minutes walk or so then the beach. The conversation changed to Juliana and how I had to watch her as she was still mixing up things with the same guys. Once they knew that I was back and building a house it could lead to a problem. Akor then said, "I don't know Juliana as well as you, but would she do something to fuck you over?"

"Mmm," I thought for a bit then said "Yes." I went on to say, "Akor you're all fucking bad bastards out here. If you could find a way to rip me off, you would. That's not saying you're not doing it right now." He had a look on his face as if to say, "I wouldn't do that." "Look Akor," I said "You would if you could; it's just the way out here." He stood there in a huff and I told him that I had arranged to meet Trevor this time while I was in Accra. I text him while I was waiting to come through customs. "I'll just have to wait and see if he contacts me wont I?"

Akor looked at me with his hand still in his pockets, like a school boy that's just been told off. "Come on Akor, you know that I'm right." There was silence as we stood there in the middle of the building plot. I thought for a second that I might have blown it with him and I really needed him. I waited for him to say something and then he smiled and said, "Bobby man, your just like me man."

"How do you make that one out?" I asked. He just smiled again and put his arm around me as we started to walk back to the jeep. "Because Bobby man, you wouldn't be mixed up with Trevor and Trevor wouldn't waste his time with you." I just laughed and said, "I've divorced Juliana you know" changing the subject.

"I know" Akor said. "Bobby man, Trevor wouldn't waste his time with you if he didn't like you."

"I know Akor . . ." He butted in, "Bobby man, you made Juliana look bad in front of Trevor and the others." I agreed with him and was about to say something, then he said, "Bobby man, there's nothing worse than a woman's scorn!" I just smiled and didn't answer him. I thought it would be better if I kept my thoughts to myself on the whole matter.

We walked back to the jeep where the two lovely looking sisters were still sitting in the back, with their skimpy short summer dresses and showing a lot of dark thigh and those long legs. God, here I go again, I'm a sucker for coloured girls. I got in the front with Akor, driving off Akor said, "Right, now that's over we can party. Would you like to go and get cleaned up?"

"Yes Akor, if you don't mind" I replied.

"No problem. I'll drop you off and come back for you at . . ." he hesitated and looked at his watch. "It's six now . . . what about if I pick you up about nine?"

"Okay great," I replied. We arrived at the hotel. It was grander than I thought it would be. We all walked through the glass door to the main desk. There was a tall gentleman in a dark suit, "Can I help you sir?" he asked, and Akor smiled, "I've made a reservation in the name of Addis." The man behind the desk looked down at the register. "You're down for room 1056. Mr Addis, can I have your passport please, and how will you be paying, by card or cash?"

"Cash" I replied, taking the plastic card that he gave me for a key. "Thanks."

We took the lift up to the fourth floor and looked for 1056. One of the girls shouted out, "Akor here it is." I opened it with the card-key and we all piled into the room with the girls looking around and checking out the room. They looked at the bath, the shower, the hot and cold water and laughed to themselves. Akor sat on the bed whilst I rested against the shiny wooden table in front of the mirror opposite him. My arms were folded across my chest whilst listened to him and watched the girls explore the bathroom. Akor organised where he would take me. "You do know you will bump into Trevor's' guys again. What are you going to do?" I looked straight at him when he said that. "I don't know. I'll have to play it by ear. I phoned him, so it's up to him to let his guys know. I told him not to hassle you because you were just a friend. Now it's up to him to call and no doubt he will Akor." He got up of the bed and walked to words the door and opened it. I stood next to him holding it open. Just before he walked through, he patted me on the back, "I'll leave these lovely two sisters with you, enjoy!" He walked out the door, down the corridor and just before I closed the door, he turned round and smiled. "There's no charge either" and laughed. I closed the door and was left to the Mercy of these two lovely looking sisters. They were about twenty years old, if that. I wasn't that bothered about their age. They slowly walked across the room to me, moving their hips in a very slow and sensuous way. They ended up either side of me, draped over each shoulder in front of the mirror, grinning. They both said at the same time, "what would you like us to do?" as one slid my jacket off and the other started to undo my jeans.

Later on that evening, I was ordering drinks at the hotel bar for myself and these two lovely sisters who were sitting round a glass table a few feet away from the bar when Akor arrived. We stayed there and had a couple more drinks then left for the beach and to party. That was one thing that I loved about Africa and had missed. They just wanted to party or just hang out at the beach where there would be hundreds of people just sunbathing, drinking, cooking food on barbeques, eating, and the usual drugs. You would go to the beach if you wanted to know any gossip or what was going down that particular day. There were plenty of nice girls and I mean plenty! There would be three or four girls to each man and the average age would arrange from fifteen to thirty. Mostly all of them good looking and just hanging about in their tiny bikinis or their short skirts, or dresses, all looking for a husband or any man as long as he wasn't from Africa and was white. They would do anything for marriage and to be taken out of Africa. But I have told you this already. I just want to make certain that you know what it was like. We left the hotel bar and walked across the car park to where Akor's funky looking red jeep was parked, with the black roll bars. As we got to the jeep, Akor said to me, as I was helping the two girls climb up and over into the back of the jeep, "did you enjoy my friends?" I laughed and said, "You know Akor, I never say no to any of your girls" and we both laughed. We got into the front of the jeep as he put a CD in the player. He turned to the girls, whom were sitting right on the back of the jeep, their feet on the seats as they were too small to sit on and asked if they were all right before he drove off. I looked round at them and smiled, sitting up on the back as Akor drove off, their black hair starting to blow about along with their short summer dresses as the jeep picked up speed. I turned back to face the front and settled down. That was one thing about Akor; he always kept me supplied with girls, whether they were sixteen or thirty. Sometimes different girls for each night, even two sometimes, like just now in the hotel and no charge . . . if I wanted them of course. Okay, so you are probably thinking that they are prostitutes or working girls as they like to be called and you would be right. Now you are probably thinking, "what about A.I.D.S?" and yes, A.I.D.S was plentiful in Africa. This thought crossed my mind every time I went to bed with them. I always used a condom but still asked Akor about it. He said that all his girls are checked regularly and the girls that he gave me were girls he knew from the beach. Of course he could just be saying that. Anyway me being me, I never say no. Good old Akor, don't get me wrong he wasn't doing all this out the kindness of his heart, oh no. Nothing was done for nothing out here. Everything had a reason and his was that when I get my shop, he wanted half of it. He wanted to sell wooden carvings that his cousin made. His cousin had nowhere to put them for selling, so he just laid them out on the side of the road and no doubt Akor was getting a cut from his cousin for providing a shop. As for me, well, I was providing the shop yes, but I was getting it all done up and to look like a proper shop. All it was just now was a square building site, with breezeblock walls and a concrete floor. No windows or a door, just a big gaping hole where the glass windows and door was to be fitted. The shop next to mine sold handmade rugs and other nick-nacks, so I think that wasn't much to give back for all the things he was doing for me. Plus Akor said he would paint and make the shop look like a shop. No doubt he was getting all the stuff cheap. If I was to buy it, they would probably rip me off. This way, Akor gets what he wants and I don't get ripped off either. Well, not as much as if I was doing it by myself. I didn't mind as long as I was getting the shop painted. The only thing I had to do was to buy two glass counters to display the phones in. Everything else Akor and his mates or whatever they were did. I thought with Akor's cousin on one side, would bring in more customers and that meant more phones for me to sell. Well, that was the plan and I didn't mind helping Akor out with some of his girls at night, if you know what I mean!

With no income, the money that I had brought to Kenya with me was going down. It wasn't critical. I could still live like a king but had to be careful with it. Staying in the hotel was a waste of a large amount of it and I thought if I got a place here it would be cheaper for me to buy a one bedroom/ living room with inside toilet and running water than keep paying out on hotel bills. So that was Akor's next task, to find me a house. Everything was so cheap out here, well maybe that's the wrong way of putting it. It was cheap because I had brought money out with me and the most of the successful Afrikaans all had, at one time or another been out of their country and come back with money legally or illegally. They had set up some sort of business for themselves back in Africa. Some even had jobs outside their country and sent money home to help relatives to get out. It was kind of like once you get out the slums you can get on and make some money. That's how some of them got on and made a better life for themselves and their relatives. But and I mean but, if you didn't make it out of the slums you had a very, very hard time sharing accommodation with relatives. Maybe five or even more to one room with an outside toilet and shower that hundreds of other people shared with you. The toilet, as I said before was just a large hole in the ground with a wooden shed around it for privacy. In the heat of the day it was unbearable to go into, but if you had to go, you had to go and suffer the very strong smell, and the flies! You would have to wait your turn to use it too.

The pound went a long way out here, much better than the dollar. On saying that, I had to create a job for myself like the shop because there was no way I could look for a job in the paper out here and get one, not for a white man. A white man with no money is ten times worse off than a black man. Everything was coming together at last. They had started the house, the shop was there waiting for me just to put the deposit down on it in the main town of Accra. I even bought a car. Akor had a friend that knew how I could buy an imported car from Germany. He would take me to the dock where they bring them in; with a bit of bargaining and putting money in the right hands I could get a car. The plan was for me to buy this imported car, get it sprayed in taxi colours then get it registered and buy my licence to operate. I would then have a taxi of my own to run and make money. I couldn't drive it myself, well I could, but it wouldn't go down well as I said earlier. I wouldn't get anyone to hire me being white. I had to be seen as the provider not the worker and providing work for the people. All this came to just over a thousand pound unbelievably. Okay the car wasn't new, but it was in good nick and compared to the rest of the taxis, it would look like new after Akor's friend had finished with it. All I had to do was go with Akor and buy the taxi sign that went on the roof and bits and bobs for the taxi to make it look like one. Once again, Akor knew where to get these things cheap and he came in handy. Don't get me wrong, I was making Akor a lot of money in one way or another. The more he could do for me meant more money for him and all his relatives. He had a relative who had a garage who would check the taxi out for me and spray it. No doubt, Akor was getting his cut out of it as well. Things were okay. I had done so much in the little time I was here, with the help from Akor. No way could I have done any of these things back in the U.K. I know I couldn't have bought the land, let alone rent a shop and buy a taxi and get them all up and running. It was all to do with the help of Akor and the pound being so good and going so much further here in Accra and people willing to work for less. Even the value of life was different, which I found out later. First, I was going to Dubai because Akor had heard that an American company was looking for people for manual labour work, on and around the big project that the Arabs were building. It was to be a massive theme park and all the company did was recruit all kinds of people from, labourers, machine operators and specialist experts in one thing or another. It was a large American company working for an Arab company. I got as much information as I could from Akor and went round to the travel shop with him to get my ticket for Dubai for the following day. The travel agent said that I could get a flight in two days time to Dubai. Once I was there, I would find out where to go for the interview.

I arrived in Dubai, what a place. It was my first time in Dubai and even the airport was out of this world let alone Dubai itself. I booked myself into a hotel, found out where I had to go the next day from the hotel reception and then went out into Dubai to look about. I found out where to buy my phones from the taxi driver, he said he would take me there to the market, so that I could look for myself. I had my interview the following day. It wasn't too bad. I told some white lies about myself, well, you have to don't you. I said that I was a plasterer and had spent time as a steel fixer, hoping they wouldn't give me a plan to look at and tell them what I would do. Luckily nothing like that happened. I think the two Arab's and the two Americans that were interviewing me were quite happy to see that I was white and spoke English, I think. I don't know why I even got the job. The thing they did ask me was if I had a work permit. I had to say no and thought that was it until I said that I had just arrived in Dubai from Accra in Africa. That's when one of the immaculately dressed Arab's all in white said, "whereabouts in Accra?" then said, "I too am building a hotel resort." To my reply, "Oh it nothing like that, all I'm doing is building a large house with a swimming pool." I elaborated a lot more to him and what I was doing there. After that, for some reason, why I don't know, maybe god was on my side, they asked "when could I start?" I said next week or the week after, I didn't mind. They said it would take two weeks to get the permit and asked where they could get in touch with me. All I could say was that I only have a mobile phone number that I could give them or an address of a friend in Accra. I gave them both, thanked them and left. As I was leaving an Irish guy asked if I got the job and would I like to go for a drink. I said "okay" and he took me to a pub in town. We talked about the interview and he turned to me and said, "You know, you don't look like a labourer to me?" I replied, "What should I look like then?" as I bought him a pint in return. "I don't know, but I'll tell you this, you've got the gift of the blarney if you get the job? He said in this very broad Irish accent. Then I asked him if he get the job? He looked at me and laughed. "I've been working with them for ten years or more." I looked at him, "I think I've got the job, but they said that they would let me know as they would need to fix the work permit." I liked him straight away. He was only small, with big ears and hardly any hair, but we seem to hit it off. We had more drinks and talked and talked before I said good bye and went back to the hotel, where I text Akor and told him.

The next day I was back in Accra. I went straight to the hotel, to my room and crashed out on the bed. I was woken by my mobile phone. I picked it up and looked at it, it was Akor. I told him about the job and said that I think I might get it; they would let me know on Monday. I told him about the Irish guy and what he'd said. Akor said that he might have a place for me. It was a small one bedroom place with an inside toilet and shower and living room. It wasn't much as it had been built on to the side of another house, but the people had no money to finish it. They wanted to sell it as it stands. I told him that I would look at it if he would come and get me and gave him a time. He arrived at the hotel and we set off to look at the place he had found. He was right, it wasn't much. It looked exactly how he described it. It was a house and the people that lived in there had built an extension on the side, but didn't have enough money to finish it off. It was just bare rooms with plastered walls and concrete floors. The bathroom just had a toilet with the cistern and a shower that wasn't even finished, all it had was the base. The glass surround had to be put in place and fixed together. The whole place was like a building site with concrete splashed all over the place. As for the walls, some of them had been white washed and it looked like that they had run out of paint. "Okay Akor, what are they wanting for it?" I asked. His answer took me by surprise. "They want two hundred and fifty pounds in your money," which is about 484.59 in G H S. "This is a lot of money to them." I thought about it then said, "Okay, tell them that I will buy it, as long as you can finish it off without it costing me much more" I said not letting him speak as he tried to but in. "You're getting half of the shop and driving my taxi about, and that's another thing" I said. "I will have to come up with a plan on how to check the money you make off the taxi every day, and that you don't do me?" He butted in, "Bobby man, I wouldn't do you."

"Fuck you Akor; you would do your own granny if you could!" We got back into the car and drove off back to the hotel, stopping of at a pub in the middle of town. It had coloured lights hanging all around outside it and loud music. There were people sitting and standing outside. In fact, they were spilling out onto the road. The music was very loud and everyone seemed to be having a great time. The atmosphere was great. There were several girls dancing with each other outside next to the tables and chairs. It made you want to party, so we did. We parked the jeep opposite the place and walked across. We squeezed our way through the people to get a beer, then went back outside and sat down on the small wall in front of the pub. We took in the great atmosphere and music and looked about at all the people, especially the two girls dancing together. There was something sexy about the way they were dancing. I mentioned this to Akor he just laughed, "Bobby man, you like any black girl in short skirts flashing their tits. They are all sexy to you man." Then he said, "I forgot to tell you?"

"What?" I asked taking a drink of beer.

"Trevor and another guy were looking for you."

"God, I had forgotten about Trevor" I said, "What did they say Akor?" I took my eyes of the two girls for a moment.

"They came to my village this morning and asked if you were in Accra?"

"What did you say to them Akor?" I asked as he took a drink of beer.

"All I said was that I didn't know," he said taking another drink from his bottle and studying the two girls that were wiggling their hips and bums in time with the music in a sexy way.

"Do you want another beer?" I asked as I got up.

"Yes Bobby man, thanks" he said. He was more interested in the two girls.

I looked at them as I got up and squeezed through the crowd on my way to the bar to get more beer. I walked back to Akor who was still sitting on the wall and sat down beside him, leaning on a post that was holding up part of the string of coloured lights. The lights were suspended across every ones heads, to the front of the bar roof and then back and forth across again, until the whole place was a mass of reds, blues and greens. There were all sorts of coloured lights. They were even all round the front of the pub. The beer was going down fast and Akor had finished his again.

"Come on Bobby man, what's wrong?" he asked as he got up.

"Okay Akor get them in" I replied and glanced round the place. I looked to see if the place had a name, but I couldn't see one. I saw Akor coming across to me with the beers. He stopped at the two girls that were dancing, and stood talking to them, and smiling over to me, then the next thing I knew, the three of them were coming over to me. Fuck me; I don't know what he said to them, who cares!

Akor introduced the two girls and we moved to a table that someone had just vacated. We sat down and moved the empty bottles from the last crowd over to one side. Akor got up to get them some beer, heading in the direction of the bar, leaving me talking to the girls. We talked about god knows what, but what I found out from them was, they were going to a beach party after this place and asked if my friend and I wanted to come. I of course said yes, knowing Akor would too.

After that place, we all climbed into the back of Akor's jeep once again and headed to where the party was. We arrived at this house at the top of a hill. There was a large wall and two big metal gates. As Akor stopped, I got out of the jeep, walked to the gates pushing them open. Once Akor had driven through, I closed them again before jumping back into the jeep. He continued to drive up this well kept drive to the house. As we got close we could hear the music coming from inside. Loads of people were standing around outside. We parked and walked up to the people whom had drinks in their hands and smiled. We walked past them and into the house. It was some place! It was nicely done out with good taste I thought, as we followed the two girls through the house. We passed people all over the place, drinking and laughing, and just having a good time. We went out the back to where there was a big pool. The music was coming from here, with people in and just standing around this big, and I mean big pool. We walked up to this big fat guy, wearing bright red check shorts with his back to us. I thought *'this has to be an American, wearing shorts like that?'* The two girls walked around him, kissed him on the side of his cheek and said to him that they had brought a couple of friends. He then turned round. He had a big cigar in his mouth. He smiled, took the cigar out of his mouth and said, "Hey man your white. Welcome to my spread. Any friend of these lovely's . . ." He was interrupted by one of the girls that brought us here saying, "where is the drink?" He pointed to a large bar on the opposite side of the pool with a guy behind it in a white jacket. As she inched forward he slapped her on her bum, the slap then sending her in the direction of the bar saying "ouch!" Then he turned to me and said, "Where are you from boy?"

"Scotland" I replied.

"SCOTLAND!" he shouted. "Well boy," he said taking a long hard suck on the big cigar before removing it, "What's your tipple boy?"

"What?" I asked. He repeated himself. "Anything, whatever you've got." He then turned to Akor and said the same sort of thing. Akor just said that he would like a beer. Someone came up to the fat guy and said something to him, but I couldn't hear. He said to us, "Go and get what you want." The next thing he said surprised me. Resting his hand on my shoulder he said seriously, "If you want to fuck or snort boy, I've got it for you" and walked away with the guy. Akor and I just laughed and said together, "let's check this place out." The four of us stayed there and did what he said. I got back to the hotel at I don't know what time. I know that it took a while to get back as Akor was a bit stoned and drunk, and his driving wasn't up to much. I wasn't in any better condition. As for the girls, well, I think we left them there. I threw myself onto the top of the bed and crashed out lying on top of it with my clothes on. I awoke sometime in the early hours; I stripped and crawled under the covers. That was it until the hotel phone in my room began to ring. I stretched out across the bed to reach for it. I missed it several times, nearly knocking it off the bedside table. "Hallo, hallo!" I said. It was Akor. He sounded in a panic. "What is it Akor? I'm still in bed. What time . . ." Before I could finish, he said "Get out of bed, I'm coming up." I thought he must be down in the hotel lobby. I jumped off the bed and went to have a quick wash I didn't think I would have time to have a shower and I was right. Just as I had finished in the bathroom, there was a banging on the door. I wrapped a towel around me and went to open the door. It was Akor standing there. "Bobby man Trevor wants to see you and he's . . . ."

I interrupted him, "Do you know what he wants Akor?"

"All I know is he's pissed off about something man," he said.

"Okay, okay calm down Akor it can't be much."

"Unless Juliana has said something Bobby man," Akor didn't like or have much time for her. I turned round, walked back to where my clothes were with Akor hard on my heels, picked them up and got dressed. I sat on the edge of the bed, put my shoes and socks on, and then said, "Okay Akor where does Trevor want to meet us?"

"I would tell you, but it wouldn't make any difference to you because you don't know where it is" he said.

"Okay, let's get there." Akor was a bit of a panic merchant at the best of times, but being African and what goes with being African is like being superstitious. You are always looking over your shoulder.

CHAPTER SEVENTEEN

CONSULTATION

We arrived at the place that Trevor told me over the phone and parked across the street from the café. We got out and walked across the quiet street. It was still early, about eight in the morning and the sun was already up high in the deep blue cloudless sky and over the tops of the building. The heat already was drying out the puddles of rainwater left from the heavy rain the night before and causing a sort of steamy effect everywhere. What I did notice when I followed Akor across the street to the cafe was that the air smelled clean after the rain, not yet spoiled by the days pollution from the traffic and dust. We walked through the door of the cafe and then stood for a moment to see where Trevor was. Then Akor pulled my arm and pointed in the direction of three people sitting over on the far side of the café. We squeezed our way through between the clean rearranged tables by the waiters in red jackets. As I got closer to the three guys, I could see that one of them was my ex-wife's cousin. We got closer, Trevor got up and held his hand out to me, and I shook it. He had a large hand and a tight grip around my hand as we shook then he said, "Sit down Bob we have a lot to discuss." I looked around for a chair and took one from the other table opposite, so did Akor and then we were asked if we would like coffee. I said yes then Trevor spoke to the big guy next to him in Ghanaian. He got up looking down at me for a split second then moved round the table and off to speak to one of the waiters, then he went out the door. Trevor caught my attention by saying, "I believe you have split up with my cousin?"

"Um . . . yes. As you know, we didn't see eye to eye about certain things." He laughed and said, "I believe so." He then went on to say, "We will have to sort out this little problem Bobby." I looked at the other black guy sitting opposite me and gave him a nervous smile but there wasn't any response. I looked at Akor, he was just sitting there looking extremely nervous and uncomfortable, and I then looked back at Trevor.

"What is there to sort out?" I didn't know what to say apart from that. Before I finished, the waiter came with the coffee, one for me, and one for Akor. Trevor then said, "Bobby . . ." he was interrupted by the black guys mobile ringing and for the first time I saw Trevor lose his temper and shout in Ghanaian to him. He quickly got up from the table and walked away answering his phone. Trevor turned to me and smiled, "Come with me Bobby." We got up from the table and made our way across the cafe to the door. As I followed him, I had forgotten how big and broad he was. He must have been six foot or more. I walked out with him into the bright early sunlight and started to follow him down the red dusty road, which was still damp. I avoided several large puddles of rainwater not like the smaller ones that had already dried up. I looked at the shopkeepers brush, the so-called pavement and set there stalls up ready for the days 'trading. Trevor stopped and looked about. "It is very easy for me to cross different county's here in Africa, being a high up official in the Kenyan government and do what I do. You get my meaning Bobby. You see all these people, they rely on my help and I can't do that without the help of people like you and Juliana.

I cut him short, "Come on Trevor, I've heard what your compatriots` do in Sierra-Leone in the diamond field's if they don't do what you want. I suppose you are going to do something similar to me if I don't do what you want either and that's what this little chat is all about?" I thought that I might have over stepped the mark just a little. He just turned round and laughed, "What has Juliana said to you? I'm not a monster okay. I know that life is cheap here and there are things that go on, but!"

"So what is this all about then Trevor?" I asked still nervous but trying to cover it up. I thought I was doing all right, as I couldn't let him know that I was nervous. All the time I was thinking, they wouldn't do anything to me because it would cause too much of an incident. I could see the headlines "White man found with no head!"

All this was going round and round in my head as Trevor was talking. I then started to concentrate on what he was saying. He was going on about if I would just do this one trip for him and how it would be so easy and Juliana would meet me in Scotland and take the stuff of me and that would be the last time I would see them. "Well Bobby, how about it?" He even had me thinking maybe I could do it and get away with it, knowing I could do with the money for my house. He even said that I would get a lot of money for doing it. My mind drifted away for a split second again and I was thinking of the time when I was at school. The incident when the police came to the house over the stolen bike and thinking was I going down the path of crime. Here I am again, forty odd years later thinking the same thing. Okay, I haven't been a goody-goody. I've done things that were outside the law, but to smuggle diamonds out of Ghana, and if caught, I'm not a wee boy anymore, officially a grown man, mentally, well . . . I would be stuck in a jail here no doubt, left to rot away for a long, long time. "Well Bobby, will you?" he asked.

"I'm not going to do it Trevor. I don't want to know how or when you are going to do it. You know and I know the more you tell me the bigger the risk is for you and not only that the bigger the risk I am to you. I would like to see my grandchildren grow up." We were now standing in the middle of the road facing each other. I was looking up into his face and he wasn't smiling. "Okay, okay if you won't do it, you won't do it."

I looked at him for a split second, "Is that it? Just like that no threats?"

"Yes. I'm not going to threaten you or anything." He laughed and continued, "I'm not a monster for all Akor or Juliana has probably told you about me." He put his hand on my shoulder and turned me round in the direction of the cafe and we walked back along the red dusty street. We talked about the economics, how poor the country is, and how he was trying to help by bringing money in and trying to help the economy. I listened to him, saying nothing but thinking 'you must be joking. If you think that I'm going to believe that, you must think that I'm a bigger fool than I am. All you want to do is line your own pockets like most officials do.' I'm glad I thought it and didn't actually say it or I would have dug my own grave for them to put me in.

We headed back to the cafe talking like long lost friends meeting for the first time in a long time. Still with his arm around my shoulder, we arrived back at the cafe with the two muscle men standing outside. Well, I think they were. They looked like it and they did everything Trevor said, even opening the door of his very new clean Toyota Land Cruiser parked out front. There was another guy in the driver's seat. He had the engine running, waiting for Trevor as he got in and waited for one of them to close it before they got into the car themselves. I stood there looking at the immaculate looking four-wheel drive. As they were about to drive off, the window rolled down in the back and Trevor said, "I'm having a little get together at a friend's house on Saturday. I would like you to come okay?"

"Is this the last supper for me or should I say the last party?" I asked smiling.

He laughed, "Bobby man you're family and bring Akor." He turned to the driver, said something then the tinted window went up and he was hidden from view. The car drove off kicking up the red dust off the road. I stood there for a second or two looking at the car disappear round a corner at the end of the road. I turned and went into the cafe where Akor was still sitting at the same table. As I passed one of the waiters I asked if I could have a coffee. "I'm over there," I said pointing to where Akor was sitting and thanked him. Akor couldn't wait to find out what Trevor had said to me so I told him over coffee.

"Is that all?" Akor asked.

"Yes. He has invited me to a party on Saturday night and you're coming because I'm not going by myself. Anyway, he said to bring you as well. Maybe he's going to get rid of us both at the same time." I said to Akor as he nearly choked on his coffee. We both looked at each other and burst out laughing. "What are you doing for the rest of the day Akor?"

"Not much why?"

"I would quite like to go back to the hotel and shower and get cleaned up since I didn't get time this morning."

"Would you like some company?"

I smiled, "Like how Akor?

He burst out laughing, "Bobby man trust me, have I ever let you down?"

"No, no you haven't." We got up from the table and made our way across the cafe to the door stopping on the way to pay the guy in the red jacket. He informed us that the other men had paid the bill so Akor slipped him a tip and we left. We crossed the street to the jeep, got in and headed off to Accra.

We arrived in Accra and joined the endless stream of traffic in the Main Street. By this time, the sun was hot. A very muggy heavy heat that made you perspire without even doing anything. I was so glad that Akor's jeep was open and the wind from that kept me cool. The whole place was heaving with people shopping, cars, and Lorries making their way through the narrow streets. The traffic was so busy that it was hardly moving. There were even people pulling wooden carts, trying to weave their way in and out of the traffic. The exhaust fumes were bad. People continually pushing and shoving, the pavements were so jammed packed, the people spilled out onto the road just to add to the chaos. It was a nightmare. Through all this mayhem, we managed to get to where the hotel was, drove up to the front, and parked. Akor turned to me as I hopped out over the side of the jeep, "What would you like to do tonight?"

"Mmm, I don't know."

"I'll drop of someone for you later and afterwards I'll take you to this club."

"Okay, that would be great, thanks." He started up the jeep, turned back and waved before driving off. I stood for a while watching drive down to the big white gates that were closed. I watched as the security guard came out of his shed next to the gates, open them and then close them behind him. I turned and walked up the wide half moon steps leading to the hotel door. A man in a red uniform held the door open for me as I approached. I thanked him as I walked past into the hotel, up to the desk and asked for my key. I turned towards the lift and to my room.

CHAPTER EIGHTEEN

DUBAI

I was having a shower late next morning after the night out with Akor. As I came out the bathroom bollock naked, I walked towards the bed. One of Akor's girl's was still asleep with her head buried under the sheet. I noticed that I had a missed call on my mobile, which was on the side table next to the bed. I sat down on the bed pushing the lifeless body over so that I had room. I was just about to phone the number when it rang again. "Hallo" I said not recognising the number. A girl with a broad American accent said "hallo Bobby," then there was a pause before she said, "Is that Mr Addis?"

I said "yes."

"Oh good, I've been trying to get you Bobby." Then she said, "Is it all right to call you Bobby?"

"Yes, yes of course.

"Hi, I'm Jill from Landmark International?"

"Oh yes right, from the company that I had the interview with."

"Yes that's right, just to say that you have the job and to call in at the site office to pick up your work permit and sign a few papers." Then she went on to say in her very broad accent, that she would text me the address in Dubai and welcomed me to the company or something like that. I wasn't really listening to her after she had said that I had the job, I was so glad that I got it. She went on to say did I know Dubai at all, and where the office was and the hotel they would put me up in while I was in Dubai. I said no to everything she had asked me. This was my first time in Dubai other than when I came for the interview and that was bad enough. She laughed an infectious laugh that made me smile on the other end of the phone. After she had finished laughing, she said I'll give you my extension number. I interrupted her and said "Oh good!" She laughed again and said, "You will fit in very well here Bobby." Then in a more sensible voice, "when you get into Dubai Airport phone me on extension . . ." and reeled off a number. I waited until she had finished and said, "Would you mind just texting me the number because I've got a hellish memory."

"Okay, I'll do that right know and when you get into Dubai phone me on that number then I'll text you the address where the office is and all you will have to do is get yourself into a cab and get your butt here." She gave another little giggle "and once you get here I'll give you all the info you need Bobby."

I thanked her and I think she said something like "have a nice day" and hung up. Then I phoned Akor to tell him the good news, but his phone said that it was switched off or out of the coverage area so I shook the lifeless body that was still under the covers behind me and said come on get up. I stood up and pulled the sheet that was covering her to reveal this naked curled up body lying there. All I got was a lot of abuse in Ghanaian as she sat up with her legs apart and her naked body in full view. She pulled up the sheet to her waist again from the bottom of the bed leaving her small round breasts out in full view and said, "What's wrong where are you going?" I stood there looking at her neat firm breasts and the outline of her feminine shape under the sheet. It was pushed tight under her legs. "I was going to get us something to eat." She laughed and said, "like that?" as I wasn't dressed. Then she giggled and pulled one end of the sheet out from underneath her legs to reveal her naked body, she then lay down on her back looking at me giggling and said, "Bobby from where I'm lying it doesn't look like it wants to go anywhere but back in bed with me!"

"Well I can phone Akor later and tell him the good news about the job, I thought. Fuck it!" I didn't mean fuck it as in fuck it, but I did if you know what I mean.

We eventually emerged from the bed and had a shower. We stood huddled underneath the warm water together, letting it cascade down over our bodies. After a second or so she pushed me back so that my back was up tight agents the white tiles at the side of the shower and grabbing the soap she started to lather me up and wash me all over. Then she knelt down in front of me and washed every inch of me not missing any part. After she had finished, she stood up and pulled me back under the shower. She rinsed soap off my body. She never spoke a word during the process. Once she had finished she said, "Now get out and dry yourself."

"Can I wash you?" I replied.

"Don't be silly" was the answer as if it was taboo. So I stepped out the shower. She shut the door and started to wash herself. I grabbed one of the large white towels that were hanging over the rail and started to dry myself looking at her through the steamed up door of the shower. As I was about to leave the bathroom she shouted my name. I turned round to see her body pressed up tight against the shower door revealing each curve of her feminine body, her round breasts, her nipples pressed tight against the door and her lips in a form of a kiss. I said "come on hurry up," as I watched her body disappear from sight and once again was engulfed in steam as she backed off leaving her imprint on the glass door. That soon disappeared into beads of water that ran zigzagging down the glass door. I left the bathroom and as I did, I could hear her giggling and singing some sort of song in Ghanaian.

I dressed and lay on the unmade bed and tried Akor's number again this time I got through. He answered it and I started to tell him about the phone call. "That's great and what will you do?"

"What do you mean?" I said.

"Will you stay in Dubai?"

"Oh yes I forgot to tell you. I'll stay here during the week and be coming back at the weekends." Akor then said that if I phoned him he would come and pick me up. "Thanks Akor." I lay there talking to Akor and arranging things when Muscatha walked out of the bathroom naked as the day she was born. I had spent the night with her, but it was great just to look at her black shiny body and her wet hair as it hung down and clung to her shoulders as she walked across in front of me. She went to the chair and stood beside it, picking her clothes up from it and started to dress. I looked at her nakedness longing for her to stand there so I could just look at her but slowly she covered up her body. First it was her white thong then her matching bra, then my attention was brought back with Akor saying, "well will that do?

"Sorry Akor what did you say?" He went on to say he would pick us up and drive out to see the builder who wanted to see me on site. I thanked Akor, hung up the phone and rolled over to the other side of the bed grabbing Muscatha. I pulled her down onto the bed but she struggled trying to get free by moving her arms and legs then as she broke free from my grip she stood up still holding onto my hand and said, "Don't, don't I'm all clean. We fuck later after we have eaten." As she pulled me up from the bed, she said, "Okay let's go and eat." We both left the room and went down to the restaurant in the hotel. Luckily, they were still serving lunches but we were the last in. As not to waste time, we just had the main course that Muscatha ordered which was Okro soup, a sort of fish stew with banku a maize that is cooked with water and little bit of oil in a pan until it is pliable like dough. You eat it by tearing it into pieces with your fingers and dipping it into the fish stew.

The day came when I was to fly to Dubai. Akor drove me to Accra Airport, came to the check-in, and stayed with me until the voice from the intercom boomed out across the waiting area: "All those flying to Dubai should make their way to gate fifty eight where they are boarding now. Please have your boarding pass and passport ready." I said good-bye to Akor and made my way to where I was told. I stood in line with the rest of the people that were boarding. Waiting to walk down the narrow walkway to the door of the aeroplane to be greeted by an airhostess, taking the boarding pass from me and telling me my seat no. I eventually got to my seat, it was at the window "*great*" I thought, and sat down. I looked at the people packing their belongings away in the overhead storage space above their seats. I didn't have anything to put away, I was travelling light so to speak. All I had was one bag and that was in the hold, I hope! I sat there looking out of the window waiting for the plane to taxi and then it was time. I was off, up, up into the blue sky. The captain said the usual stuff about flying at a certain height and then, he went on to say how long we would be in the air before getting to Dubai. I settled down into my seat luckily the plane wasn't full and the seat next to me was empty as were most of the seats in the centre. I arrived in Dubai about eleven and once I had cleared through customs I made my way through the large Airport to outside to phone Jill the American. I had to tell her that I was here. I tried several times but my phone kept on saying the number was unobtainable. I then remembered I had put in a sim card that I got in Ghana because I was told it was cheaper to use than the one for the U.K. They had said that every time I used the phone in Ghana it would go through to the U.K first then back to Ghana, even if I were calling a number in Ghana. I don't know if that's right or not but I bought a Ghana sim card for the phone and of course, the bloody thing won't work here in Dubai! So I went to where the taxis were waiting. I went up to the first one, the guy wound down the window and I asked him where I could get my phone fixed and told him what I had done. He suggested that instead of going to a shop here it would be better to go to the market. It would be a lot cheaper so off I went. He drove for miles and I thought he was taking the piss but I sat there hoping I would get there soon and thinking I should have changed more of my money into dollars but I didn't on Akor's advice. I changed it into dollars as he said it was better so instead of changing then in Dubai currency, I changed most of it into dollars. I remember him taking me to this small shop down some back alleyway that went through people's backyards. Some of them where washing their clothes and hanging them out on lines that were stretched across the narrow lane that we had walked down. You had to duck to avoid the clothes that people had put out early. There were dogs just lying about and small kids playing but when they say me, they either ran away or stood glued to the spot in amazement at this white man invading their territory. Some even shouted out Obronyi, Obronyi, meaning white man. We eventually arrived at the market, I paid the guy, and to my amazement, it wasn't that much for the distance that we had travelled. After the taxi drove off, he left me looking like a tourist with my bag.

Okay, metaphorically speaking I was a tourist, but you don't want to advertise the matter especially in a crowded market place and carrying a suitcase. Anyway, I fought my way through the crowded place after stopping at several stalls that were selling mobile phones and asking the Indian man that was behind it where I could get a sim card that I could use here in Dubai. After some haggling in several shops and stalls, I got to a glass fronted shop with electrical gadgets in the window and went in. I told the man behind the counter the same story that I must have said about a thousand times before. He again was an Indian. There were so many of them about even the taxi person were one. *"They're all over the place,"* I thought as the very kind man looked at my mobile and said yes he could give me one. I thanked the man and gave him so many dollars. Their money is so easy to count and Akor was right they preferred the dollar. By this time, it was about 2pm so I found a quite place where I could phone Jill and get her to text the Info to me. I made my way back out of the market to find a taxi but this time it wasn't that easy to find one. I must have walked for miles in the hot sun carrying this fucking bag. Eventually I stopped one and told him where I needed to go and it was another long journey. I didn't mind, I was glad to get out of the sun, off my feet and stop lugging that suitcase about everywhere. I hate looking like I am a tourist even though I am one. *"Well"* I kept saying to myself, *"I'm not a tourist, I work here"* and that made me feel better. I found myself standing outside this enormous tinted glass skyscraper with the name of the company above the door in large gold letters. A well-dressed man in a red uniform opened the door for me when I walked up to it with his white gloves. He said "good afternoon sir" as I walked in. The door shut behind me, closed out the sunlight and there was a sudden drop in temperature as I felt the air conditioning waft the cool air about. I found myself standing in this large glass area with large red leather sofas dotted about the place and long tinted glass tables in front of them that had immaculately dressed Arabs in their immaculate white clothes and the white headdress seated at them. They were sitting talking; some of the tables, I found out later on had tall silver looking pots that had tea in. Then there were these large plants reaching high up into the building, evenly spaced out around the glass walls. They had massive green leaves that hung down and each one sat in round concrete pots across the red and yellow tiled floor. There were three lifts, oblong in shape and again all glass, that ran up the full height of the building on the outside of the wall. You could see people standing in them as they went up or down, going to their own particular floor. At the left of the door, that I had just come through was reception. There were three men standing there and one looked like a security guard in a blue uniform with a black belt that went over his shoulder and round his waist. There was a leather holster in the shape of a pistol. I walked over to the desk and told them my name and what Jill had told me to say. The man I was talking to picked up the phone talked to someone and then said to me, "tenth floor sir. The lift's . . ."

Before he finished, I said "thanks I know where they are" I picked up my case and made my way to the weird looking lifts. Once inside I looked at the instrument panel that lit up as the lift door closed in a deep blue colour. Each button shone red and there were a lot of them. A female voice interrupted the soft music that was playing and said 'door closing' then the music came back on. I put my bag down and pressed the button that showed number ten and off I shot. I turned round to look at the people that I had left on the ground floor get smaller and smaller as I zoomed up. It didn't take long before I was standing outside the lift on the tenth floor on a thick blue carpet and looking at least six girls sitting at their desks. I turned back to watch the lift go back down as another lift shot past going up even higher. I looked at it go up to nearly the top of the building, fascinated by the whole place. If this were their site office, I would hate to see their main office.

I picked up my case, which was by now really pissing me off and walked up to the first desk and put my case down again. I waited for the girl behind the desk to finish talking on the phone. "Hi I'm Bobby. I have an appointment with Jill."

"Who, do you mean Jill Macintyre?"

"I don't know, that's all I was told. I've just started and was told to come here and see Jill." The phone rang again and she made a gesture by holding up one finger. "Good afternoon, Landmark International" she said down the phone as I stood there. "Yes certainly, I'll let him know. Yes, right goodbye." She put the phone back in its cradle and looked up at me. "Sorry, what did you want?"

"Jill Macintyre, I've come to see her," I said.

"Oh yes, go down to the girl at the third desk."

"Thanks. Could I leave this here?" I said pointing to my case.

"Yes." I walked down to where she told me and told the same story to the next girl. "Just go on in, she has been waiting for you." I thanked her, knocked on the door near the girl's desk, and walked in. I didn't wait for her to say come in. The girl at the desk had already phoned her to say that I was here and on my way in. There, behind a big glass desk packed full of papers, folders, and three phones of which I thought was strange was Jill. She was executive looking, with a grey suit a white blouse and immaculate shoulder length red hair. "Hey Bobby, where have you been?" She pointed to a chair on the other side of the desk and I sat down. "Would you like some coffee?"

"No thanks" I said getting myself comfortable. She looked through papers piled up on top of her desk. Smiling she said, "I've got you here somewhere." She got up and walked to a filing cabinet, opening the second draw she fumbled about. I looked at her as she had her back to me. She wasn't bad looking, a nice figure, and her tight grey skirt revealing her figure even more. She turned round with a brown folder, came back to the desk, sat down, and opened it. She handed me everything I had to have, I had to sign several forms, and that was that. We talked about where I came from and why I was here. I told her what I was doing, keeping it brief as to not bore her with all the details. She listened quite interested in what I was telling her, I think. Then, unexpectedly she said, "I like your accent Bobby." I smiled and said "thanks." She asked me if I had a bank account in Dubai I said no. She then leaned to one side to open a drawer in her desk. Her red hair fell over her face. With one hand, she pulled it back and tucked it behind her ear then with the same hand she pulled out a large pad from the bottom drawer and sat back up again putting the pad down in front of her on the desk. She adjusted herself, opened the pad, and looked up at me smiling. She said, "Would you sign this?" and pointed to a dotted line in between a lot of writing. She then slid the pad over for me to look at, explaining that it was for the bank and she would have to have a sample of my signature so that my wages could be paid automatically into the bank. I glanced at it quickly not even reading it, which I should have done. I could have been signing my life away along the dotted line. I looked up at her, she smiled and said, "I hope you like it here Bobby."

"I will thanks," I said getting up and walking towards the door. I opened it, and then paused before turning and smiling at her, as she sat in her chair looking at me. "Thanks for everything." I said.

"You're welcome Bobby," she said in her broad American accent. I called out "bye" as I closed the door behind me. I smiled at the receptionist whom was on the phone at the desk outside the office.

The hotel wasn't bad at all. They rate them by how many stars they have and mine had three. As I say, it wasn't bad considering it was free for as long as I worked with them. It was just the usual room with a double bed en-suite and a TV. I walked over to the window and pulled back the thin curtain that was covering it, not the main curtain that was tied back just a very thin one and opened the window and looked out. Just a few feet away were an apartment block. You could have jumped out of my window and quite easily landed on the balcony of the place opposite. I stood looking at the place opposite at all the windows. Some had their blinds down and some had their washing hanging on lines stretching from one end of the balcony to the other. I stood staring at all the windows hoping to see some young female stripping off and waving to me to come over, some chance. Then I looked down onto the road below before deciding that I would have a shower and go for a walk outside and check out the place and get some food. I shut the window and went to have my shower. Afterwards I wrapped a towel round myself and came out the bathroom looking for a hairdryer . . . what, so I'm vain. I walked over to the big deck type table with a large wall mirror above it and started looking in all the drawers. As I bent down to look in the bottom left hand drawer, my towel fell off so I just picked it up and threw it onto the bed behind me and carried on looking. I found the hairdryer in the other bottom side drawer of the table and then stood up. As I did, I caught sight of a woman in the corner of my eye standing on the balcony just outside my window and looking straight in at me through my window. I had forgotten to pull the thin curtain closed again after looking out the window before my shower. I didn't' let on that I had seen her and started to unwind the white cable that was twisted round the handle of the hairdryer. Then I looked for somewhere to plug it in. Just opposite me on the wall under the mirror was a socket that had the light plugged in so I swapped them over and looked for my brush that was on the table top along with other things and started to dry my hair. Looking at myself in the mirror and slyly out of the corner of my eye at this woman to see if she was still looking and she was. Whom I think was hanging out her washing when she saw me and now was standing just a few yards outside my window on her balcony with her arms crossed and holding the rest of her clothes in her hands that she was hanging out and obviously taking in all that was on show. Talk about looking for a victim early and now I was being the victim but as she was obviously enjoying what she was looking at, I had this overwhelming desire to be wicked and play the part. So I started to pretend to dry my hair and turn slightly round so that she could see everything as I was standing bollock naked. I looked at her out of the corner of my eye. Again, she liked what she was looking at, I think. Well she didn't attempt to finish what she was doing and go away she just stood there with her arms folded with the same clothes in her hand looking in at me playing my part. I started to feel very evil. My heart was by now beating fast and I was trembling with excitement thinking of this woman looking at me. I took another sly look . . . She was still there and for what I could see of her without giving my act away, she looked like she was Filipino and about fortyish I think, maybe a bit more. By now I was trembling and the blood was pumping fast round my veins and I knew it wouldn't be long before my old friend would give the game way if you know what I mean! So without letting on, I pretended to look at myself in the mirror and wipe myself down with my hand. I then turned round so that my back was facing her and leaned round onto the bed and picked up my clean boxer shorts and put them on taking my time. I exaggerated everything as I tucked it all away and then turned back to the mirror the same way so not to face her. I had another quick look to see if she was there but she had gone and the rest of her clothes were hanging on the line. Well after all that I was so worked up I had to release some of the build-up energy and since my friend played such a good part in the act, I gave him the pleasure and took it out on him, out of sight of course.

Well that was Monday nearly over and I was working the next day. Jill told me that I would be picked up outside the hotel at six in the morning along with the other people that were staying in the hotel. So after I had a walk about outside and stopped in the restaurant just along the road for a bite to eat, I decided to go back to the hotel and have a swim in the pool that was situated on the roof of the hotel. Once back in the hotel, I grabbed my gear from the room, took the lift, and pressed the button for the pool. The lift stopped and I got out and walked along a narrow corridor and through a glass door with pool printed on the glass. A young girl sitting behind a desk in a white uniform met me, "Hi" I said. "Is it all right to go for a swim?"

"Yes, are you staying in the hotel?" She asked.

"Yes room 104" I replied.

"Do you want me to book you a room for after your massage?"

"No thanks. I just want a swim." I thanked her and walked on through another door in to the changing area where they had small rooms with wooden swing doors like a saloon in a western and it just covered the necessary bits letting you look over the top of them even if you were a female. There was just one changing room for both sexes.

The pool wasn't that great, it was okay, but it was quite small. There were a few sun-loungers dotted about the tiled floor and the water was warm and quite good. I was the only one there. The sun had gone down behind the tall buildings but it was still warm with a slight breeze. I stayed there mucking about in the pool for about half an hour or so then I decided to change and go back to my room and have an early night. It was already about nine when I got back to my room I put on the telly and had a quick look to see if my Filipino friend was there but her blinds were closed. I jumped into my bed and lay there flicking through the different channels with the remote then decided to go to sleep.

I woke up about five am, had a shower, and got ready. I had a quick look out at my friend but her blinds were still down. Even if they were up, I didn't have time to have a quick flash at her. I left my room and got the lift down to the ground floor, then the foyer. Even at that time in the morning, it was very busy. I made my way outside and stood waiting for my lift. There were a crowd of men standing along from me but I didn't know if they were waiting for the same lift so I just stood by myself outside the hotel looking at all the people and cars, vans rushing about. As I said, the place was so busy even at that time in the morning and then a red van pulled up outside the hotel entrance with the name of the company along the side, so I made my way towards it. Right enough the men that were standing along from me got in as well. We sat down and some of them started talking amongst themselves. Myself, well I sat at the back by myself being a bit shy on my first day. I just looked out the window at all that was going on until we arrived at the place of work. We all piled out then everyone just disappeared in different directions and I was left standing there feeling a bit strange to say the least. Even the van drove off. I saw a friendly face coming towards me. It was the Irish man that I had met at the interview, "Hi Bobby you feeling a bit strange standing there?" He said holding out his hand for me to shake it.

"Yes. I was about to run home again" I said jokingly.

"You would have a long run," he said laughing. "Come on I'll take you under my wing" he said and instantly I was feeling better. We walked across the large yard and round behind an office block where we got into a four-wheel drive jeep and drove off through this vast building site. We stopped among several large Lorries, I mean big, as you would see in American films. They were amazing. It was the first time I had ever seen one up close and they are big and so immaculate with fancy paintwork. Anyway, they were carrying large metal sheets. They look like very long narrow metal sheets about three inches thick with a grove in one side and a slot in the other side and they are about four or five foot wide and vary in size. They're shaped a bit like a "W" and the idea of them is that you hammer one into the ground with a large hammer. It's supported by a crane and works off a large compressor. When one is in the ground firm, you pick up another one with the crane and it swings it round. A man standing on a ladder or sitting on the top of the pile grabs the end of the one that the Crane has swung round. He holds it in place beside the one already in the ground and you try to position it so that the other pole slides down between the slots of the one that is in the ground joining them together. You repeat the process until you either have a long line of them, or a circle and they are watertight. They are used to hold back water or soft earth whilst the men work at one side of them. I think that's the best way to explain them.

Well my first job was to fasten the chain that was dangling down from the crane to one end of the poles. Then the crane lifted each one off the lorry and stacked them on the ground. Another man, he undid the chain that was holding them through a hole at the top. There were six Lorries to unload. Each lorry had about thirty or more on them. Mick told me to get up on the lorry, threw me a pair of gloves, and told me to get on with it, so I did. It took all day apart from stopping for breaks. As I thought I was about to finish, another three Lorries would appear. I worked with the crane driver for most of that week. I did different things in between working with Mick, the Irish guy that I got to like very much. He even took me aside and showed me how to steel fix. As he showed me he said, "I know you said that you were a steel fixer." I went to interrupt him to say something but he kept talking, ". . . in the interview. But I knew that you weren't" I interrupted him, "Mick, I can explain . . ." but he cut me short.

"It's fuck all to do with me, but I will show you the right way to fix steel. Later, I will show you how to read plans so when you're given plans to fix steel you will know."

"Thanks Mick" I said. I don't know why he was doing all this for me maybe he liked me, I don't know. That was my first induction and my first week working in Dubai. Overall, it was okay. Now I can say that I liked it a lot. As it was nearly the weekend and I was flying back to Accra, I went to the hotel reception and asked them what I should do with my things in the room. Should I take them out or what? They told me that that company I worked for had a contract with the hotel. It didn't matter if I left my stuff in the room because sometimes men work at the weekends as well as all week. The only thing was the hotel would not be responsible for any valuables left in the room.

It was the weekend and I went back to Accra, Akor, and his girls! He was there as usual and said that the small house that I bought was ready and I could move in. It was basic. It had a bed, bits, and pieces, running water, but it needed to be painted. There was plaster everywhere. It had to be cleaned off the walls and the floor. It looked like the building sight that I had just come from. The first couple of days Akor and a mate of his and me got stuck into cleaning the place up. We got some cheap white paint and painted it. The bed, well it came from a market where Akor took me and we bought a mattress at the same place and other bit and bobs. That was the weekend nearly over. We had spent most of the weekend cleaning the small one bedroom, bathroom, apartment and it was Sunday afternoon. It was hot and I mean hot. I thought it would be kind if I took Akor and his friend out for a meal and drinks. They had helped me clean up my small house. Akor said, "No, let's go to a beach and party. Let's celebrate your first weeks work in Dubai, and your new home." We all piled into his jeep with his CD player belting out some heavy rock music and set off for the beach. Upon arriving at the beach, I met the American guy that I had met before. We got talking. He was working with some marine biology company doing something. I wasn't particularly listening to him. Then I heard him say, "Did I like Africa and the chicks?" I said yes, I thought Africa was great and as you put it, the chicks are great. Then he went on to say, "Yeah man, it doesn't take much to get them into the sack does it?"

That's where I made my excuses and walked back to Akor and the three girls that were standing at the bar. "It's fucking hot Akor" I said.

"We're going for a swim, are you coming?" I nodded my head.

We got another round of beers and walked away from the music, the crowds', and the barbeque. I could smell chicken and other things and the smell was making me hungry. Taking our beer, we went down to the water's edge. It wasn't that far away. We could still hear all the people talking and the loud music. We stripped off down to our jocks and the girls down to their different coloured thongs. Leaving the beer beside our clothes, we ran into the water. We played and swam in the warm water, the four of us teasing each other and jumping up to avoid the big waves that were rolling in. After, we sat on the sand by the edge of the water just talking, drinking and taking in the sight of the three good-looking girls sitting near us. They were just in their thongs. Well I was looking, I don't know about Akor. It was a good night. As it was getting dark, we decided to go back to my place and have a shower and get cleaned up before going to the pub. We did stop at the pub on the way to the house as one of the girls wanted to get some beer to drink at the house before going back.

Akor and one of his girls went for a shower together first. The other two girls and me sat on the floor, drank the beer and talked. Eventually one of the girls shouted to Akor to hurry up. Just as she shouted, he appeared with the girl with the only two towels I had. I mentioned it to him and to my surprise the girl took it off, handed it to me, and stood there naked. I looked at her naked body for a split second as she walked past me to pick up her jeans. She started to put them on without her thong, just wiggling her wet slim body into them. Akor did the same, putting his trousers on. Before I could say anything, the two other girls had stripped off and were waiting for me to go to the shower with them. It was all so fast I couldn't take it all in. I would have liked a re-run but slower. Being me, I just went with the flow so to speak. I stripped and joined the two girls in the shower, and what a shower we had.

After the shower, we joined Akor and the other girl and got dressed. The two girls that I was with said their thongs were covered in sand and they couldn't put them on, so they didn't. One of the girls only had a short skirt with her and no change of underwear. We all laughed and said, "Just don't bend over or we'll all be locked up. She put it on, pulling it up over her hips and then fastening it round her waist. Akor and I had to wait for the girls to put their make-up on and that seemed to take forever until Akor said something then we were ready for the pub and food. Akor said that he was buying.

Afterwards I said I was going home, as I had to get up early to get the plane. I got up to leave when Akor said, "hold on, we will walk back with you to the house." So we all set off to the house then stood for a while talking. I asked Akor if he could take me to the airport in the morning he said he would and asked me what time. Taking the phone from my pocket to look at the time it was eleven pm, I told him six hours time. I told him the flight's at six, but I had to be there an hour earlier. He was happy to take me and I thanked him. I was about to put my phone back in my pocket when I noticed a text. I stood there and read it. It was from Jill. It said that they have moved me to another hotel. The stuff I had left in the room will be moved to the new place and sorry for the inconvenience. If I come to the office on Monday, they will provide the new address of the place I was going.

I stayed my first night in my new home with another of Akor's girls. Akor said that he would be round in the morning to take me to the airport. I turned to walk up the path to my 'wee' house when the girl in the short skirt standing next to the jeep opposite Akor said, "would I like her to stay?" I turned round and said "why not." Then the other girl butted in and said, "Would you like me to stay as well?"

I looked at Akor; he just shrugged his shoulders and said, "If you want her too, she can stay." So she did. Akor drove off and we went into the house. After a few more beers, I said that I was going to bed and made my way to the bedroom and got undressed. I climbed into bed leaving the two girls talking and discussing something. I lay there in bed for a while thinking of work and the flight to Dubai. The door opened and the two girls walked in smiling. I smiled back and said to them, "what are you two smiling about?" They didn't answer and stood at that bottom of the bed in full view of me lying there and started to kiss each other very passionately. They undress each other very slowly and very seductively peeling of each other clothes in turn. Stopping at their breasts, they fondled and even sucked on each other's nipples and then carried on until they were both completely naked. They stood there for a second or so kissing and fondling each other's naked body in turn. It was very arousing just to say the least, just lying there looking at these two girls strip each other in such an erotic way. It was like having your very own porn video but who needed a video when you had the real thing. They stood naked at the bottom of the bed and looked at me with their arms around each other's waist. I watched as they walked round to each side of the bed and climbed in, one on either side of me. I said, "Now, now girls I need my sleep I've got to get up early.

CHAPTER NINETEEN

BACK TO WORK

I was on the plane on my way back to work and the new dig's, but first I had to go to the office. I asked the time from one of the flight attendant's. She said it was a bit past eight. I thought '*I'm cutting it a bit fine; it's about an hour's flight and then the taxi to the office . . . Mmm, I might be a bit late.*' The office staff didn't get there until nine, so I could go straight to the office. I would phone my Irish friend, tell him that I might be a bit late, and say to him that I'll have to go to the office first to sort out my new digs. I'm not talking about a small yard where everyone knows everyone. No, this place was massive. The office alone was a skyscraper of a building and the yard if you want to call it that went on for miles and miles. As for the company, they wouldn't know if I was even there. I sat back in the chair and thought of Akor and his girls. It was some set up and okay they were all working, but they were all great girls and good company. Akor never ever charged me once for any girl that I had slept with, and there has been a few of them since I met him. Okay, his cousin was going to rent half my shop and as I said, they don't do anything for nothing, everything is for them. In the end, like a relative of Mary's, he was driving my taxi about, making money for me, and earning some for himself. The week beforehand, it was involved in an accident with a van. My taxi came off the worst and it was going to take over a thousand to fix it. For the moment it was sitting at a garage, the mechanic waiting for me to say go ahead. The only thing stopping me was that they don't insure most cars in Accra or so I was told and I would have to pay for it to get fixed. For all the taxi was making, it didn't even cover the cost of repairing it. Even if I paid out for it to get fixed and ran it for a year, it probably would just break, if it even lasted that long. I thought I might sell it for scrap and abandon the whole idea of a taxi business. The whole thing was costing me just to keep it on the road. But the whole incident would have to wait. I wasn't complaining, everything was okay and if everything worked out, I would have a shop in a couple of weeks. I had some ground to build my house on and that's when I thought of Mary. I hadn't seen her. She was the girl that got the ground for me, organised the legal side with the Ghana High Commission for the sale of the ground and sent all the legal jargon to me in Scotland to sign. She was also responsible for getting someone to drive my taxi about and somewhere to lock it up at night. I promised her a small place of her own for all she had done, similar to the place I had just come from. Then I thought *'how can I get out of this? I don't want to give her my wee house.'* Okay it wasn't much, but! Then the sign above me lit up with a ding saying "please fasten your seatbelts." Then the captain's voice stating we were on the final approach to Dubai airport.

Once I got through customs and security, I phoned mike the Irish guy and told him that I would be late and would have to go the office before coming to where he would be. He told me he would be at the docks. I was to grab one of the pickups and meet him there. I said I would and then got a taxi to the office. By the time I got there, it was just past nine, *'not bad going'* I thought. I saw Jill and she gave me my new address. She told me that some of my stuff was still in the old hotel and I could pick it up any time. The staff said that they would keep it for me at reception. Just before I left Jill in the office I asked where I could get a pickup to take me to the dock.

"Go and ask the guy at the front desk" she replied.

I jumped into one of the works pickups and headed in the direction of the main construction site and my boss the Irish man. I was feeling lightheaded, I dismissed it putting it down to not having anything to drink since the flight, and it was very hot in Dubai. I got to where I was supposed to be. My job was to load several dumper trucks and move two large generators and other electrical components with the help of a crane. I was so glad to get that day over, as I said I was feeling slightly weird. It was about one o'clock or maybe nearer two o'clock. I was told to go home because it was getting to hot to work. I didn't think it was so I didn't mind working on. I loved the sun and getting a tan as I worked and getting paid for it as well. I could wear my old denim shorts that I've had since Jamaica, even before that. I liked them they were great. Well faded and worn looking. I wore them with a t-shirt, as there was no dress code. I was just casual labour that came and went all the time. But this afternoon I was so glad to get into the minibus that took us home. I wasn't feeling myself, a bit light headed and I needed to drink all the time. I thought *'god, I hope I'm not coming down with the flu?'* The day was very hot, the hottest yet. All the locals and the Arabs were indoors. For those who had to be out driving, all had their windows shut in there immaculate four-wheel drives or their chauffer driven cars, so they could get the maximum benefit of the air conditioning. Even the heat in the minibus was overpowering and that was with the air conditioning on. I got out about a block from my new hotel. I just wanted to walk to get some air, but even walking, the sun was so hot. I was perspiring even in my denim shorts and t-shirt. I thought *'I must sit down'* and stopped at a cafe a couple of yards from the hotel to get myself a can of coke or orange to drink. I got a can of orange, sat down at one of the tables outside on the pavement, and sipped away at it. I got up and continued my journey to the hotel, it wasn't much further. I walked in to the foyer of the hotel and asked the man who was standing there for my room key. I gave my name, and company who employed me, and my passport. He handed it back to me saying, "Some of your belongings are already here Mr Addis. We will send the rest up when it arrives."

I took my key and made for the elevator to take me to my room. All I wanted to do was lie down on my bed and have a sleep. I was feeling fucked to say the least. The bell went in the lift, a voice spoke my floor, the doors opened, and I walked out.

The next thing I remember I was in hospital and being told that I had been in a coma for some time and they were getting a bit concerned. There were needles in my arms with tubes connected to them, tubes up my nose and wires all over my body that led to machines. I even had a mask over my mouth for oxygen. I lay there trying to think what had happened, not making any sense of it all. A tall Indian woman came into the room with an Indian Doctor wearing a white coat. They both walked over to my bed and she stood at the bottom whilst the Doctor walked round the side, put his hand on my arm, and gave it a gentle squeeze. "Hallo, I'm Dr Morton and this, is Miss Lamella." He asked me questions about my heath and was I on holiday here in Dubai. I answered him the best I could. I was still not with it at all, feeling very drowsy and then everything went black. It was like going off to sleep. Then I came to again. I was being wheeled through a corridor very fast with many people running alongside me. I remember looking at all the strip lights on the ceiling whizzing over my head as I lay there, then that soft feeling of drifting away. I came to in a room with a nurse standing with her back to me doing something. She saw I was awake, went out and came back with Dr Morton in his white coat. It's funny how you remember funny little things, like I remembering his name. He came over to me, touched my feet and smiled. The tall Indian woman appeared in a long skirt and a blouse but no white coat. He said something to her in Indian I think. It wasn't English, but could have been anything the way I was feeling. She answered him, and then he turned to me and smiled, "you are very sick."

I gave a weak smile at him, then her. "We had to put you on a ventilator. Your lungs had collapsed," he said. A nurse came into the room; she wore a neatly starched uniform. The Doctor turned to talk to her in a different language or was it all one, I don't know, it could have been anything. Turning back to me, he smiled and said he would be back tomorrow to see me again. He walked to the bottom of the bed and stood talking to both the tall Indian woman and the nurse. He tapped me on my feet and smiled again before walking away. I lay there with the mask over my mouth and nose breathing away at the oxygen, once again trying to make sense of it all when another nurse came over carrying a small cup containing pills. She gave me them and then poured some water from a jug that was on the bedside cabinet. She stood there until I had taken the lot. Sitting on the edge of the bed, she said in a soft voice "I'm a Sister and . . ." she hesitated then said touching my leg and smiling, "I don't know how to say this but you died." She must have seen the strange look on my face as she stopped and paused before continuing on, "Yes, you died and we thought I had better get a priest to give you your last rights." I started to take off my mask and say something but she stopped me. "Please, please let me finish. After the priest had finished there was a blip on the monitor." I tried again to say something and once again, she stopped me. "Please, this is very hard for me. I would like to say I think it's . . ." she stopped and smiled "I think it's a miracle." I had to stop her and say in my weakened state that I wasn't religious. I believe in god, but! "Okay" she said, "I'll talk to you later." She got up off the bed and walked away.

I lay there trying to take in what she had said, but it was too much. I just couldn't take it all in and must have dozed off or passed out again. It was all the same thing just now. I didn't know if I was sleeping or if I was dead or what.

A nurse saying that she had to give me a jag awoke me, I watched as she pushed the needle into my other arm as the other already had a needle in it. It was connected to a clear plastic bag with liquid that was dripping down this tube and into my arm. It hung from a stand next to my bed. I drifted in and out of consciousness. Days and nights were all as one. People came and went and for all I cared they could have been anyone. I could have been anywhere. I don't know how long I was like that. I was very confused and scared. I think I spent most of the time unconscious, as I said I don't know how many days or weeks I lay there. What I do remember is someone saying my name, "Bobby, Bobby." Then I drifted into unconsciousness again. Since I left the hospital, I have found out whom that person was. They came several times whilst I was in that state. Now I can thank them, truly thank them for being there and being supportive, even if I didn't know who they were at the time. I thank you and always remember your kindness.

Its morning, what morning I couldn't tell you but I was back in the land of the living. I still wasn't myself, I felt better but very weak. I was in a room with three other people. As I was looking about a nurse came over to me and smiled. She said to me in broken English to go and wash myself if I felt up to it. She was Filipino like all the nurses were apart from some Chinese, but most of them where Filipino and they all spoke with an accent. I soon was to find out that this routine happened every morning as they told everyone each morning to wash in the toilet room. This gave them time to change your bed and gave you clean pyjamas. I did with difficulty, grabbing my stuff out of the wooden locker next to my bed. I walked very slowly, stopping to rest and hold onto the end of the other bed on the way to the toilet at the far end of the room. I felt weary and a bit dizzy. Upon reaching the toilet, I sat down on the seat to rest and looked about. It had the usual things you would expect to see in a hospital toilet. I got up off the toilet seat and went to wash my face and clean my teeth but I was so dizzy I sat down again. After a while, I still felt weird so I didn't clean my teeth. I walked back to my bed but it had been stripped. They told me to sit on the chair next to my bed while the two nurses made it up with clean white sheets, pillowcases and a folded blanket at the bottom of the bed. I was given a dressing gown and clean pyjamas. I sat there on the chair next to my bed looking at the two nurses making the bed and thought they weren't bad looking in their starched uniforms and there olive complexion and jet black hair. After they had finished, I got up and lay back on top of the bed and looked around the room I was in. There were three other beds besides mine, which was near a big glass window that looked out onto the ward. There was a big table in the middle and a large bookcase to the right of that, and on the other side of the ward were more rooms with the same amount of beds in them. There were many nurses busy performing their duties. There wasn't a bad looking one amongst them. A man in a blue uniform pushing a wheelchair came over to my bed. He said he was going to take me for an X-ray. Getting up from the bed, I sat on the wheelchair. He took the blanket from the bottom of the bed and put it over my legs saying, "It's cold down there." I thanked him as he wheeled me out of the ward, into a lift, then down to another floor, along a corridor, and then left to wait outside a door signed X-ray department. I sat there for some time just looking at everyone going around doing his or her own thing. A nurse came out of the door that I was sitting at and wheeled me into the room. They told me to remove my dressing gown and stand in front of this machine. I struggled to get myself up and stand in front of the machine. She altered it to a certain height and then went behind a screen. The nurse asked me told to hold my breath then she smiled and said, "That's you." I put my dressing gown back on and she placed the blanket over my knees and left me sitting there whilst she waited for the x-ray. After a while she walked over to me carrying a large brown envelope and gave it to me. She said, "Give to desk please" and put it on my lap. She wheeled me back into the corridor and again I sat there until another man in the same uniform took me back to the ward. First I stopped at the hatch where three nurses were busy doing something. I couldn't see properly because I was sitting in my wheelchair. I was then wheeled back to the ward that I was in and got back into my bed. I threw the dressing gown onto the seat next to the bed and was about to slide down into it when a young man in pale blue trousers and a white coat undone and a t-shirt underneath it, came into the room saying would I like some tea and how many sugars and did I take milk? I said yes to everything. He went to a large trolley that was out in the ward and brought back a paper cup full of tea and a cake and put it down on the top of the locker. I thanked him and sat there drinking my tea watching him go round the rest of the patients in the room. A nurse came in and over to my bed with a plastic cup with about six different pills in it. She stood at the side of the bed and said "take these please." She was good looking and again Filipino with that dark olive skin and jet black hair.

I was sitting there drinking my tea and eating my cake. After taking my pills I came over very faint and dizzy and it took all my effort to sit up. So I sunk down deeper into the bed. I felt really weird. The room started to go round and round and then nothing. I awoke with the Dr Morton squeezing me on the foot through the sheets and there were three nurses around me and I had my oxygen mask back on. I heard Dr Morton saying, "I just want to check your breathing, can you manage to sit up?" I tried but I didn't have any strength so two of the nurses gave me a hand to sit up. One of the nurses helped me to open up my pyjama jacket, and then Dr Morton tapped me on the back and listened to my chest through his stethoscope and said, "Do you remember what happened?" I said no. All I was doing was drinking my tea and all of a sudden I felt faint and the room started to go round and that's all Doctor. He said something to one of the nurses in a different language, and then turned to me, "I want you to stay in bed." He said something to the other nurse and then turned back to me again. "If you must go to the toilet ring for a nurse and she will help you." I said okay and thanked him. He wanted me to go and get a body scan and he would arrange for me to be taken later on. They walked away through the two big doors that were wedged open and back onto the ward. As I looked at him, he stopped and stood talking to a nurse out in the ward.

I stayed in bed and right enough another man came in his blue uniform and wheeled me away. After the scan I was wheeled back to my ward and put back in the same place and connected up again to all the equipment. For the rest of the day and most of the night I remember I kept on drifting in and out of consciousness or sleep. As I said, it seemed to be all the same thing. At least when I awoke the next day I was still in the same room, I hadn't be whisked off somewhere. It was the same routine, but this time I was told to get out of bed and sit on the chair by my bed. I tried to get up but couldn't. It was useless. I felt dizzy and weak. One of the nurses helped me onto the chair and said that another nurse will help me to the toilet to wash. She then went back to help the nurse strip the bed. I sat there looking at the nurses remaking my bed and waited for the other nurse. I saw her wheeling a wheelchair along the ward and into the room where I was sitting. She smiled and said, "Here you sit." Then she helped me into it and wheeled me to where all the beds were and opened the door into the toilet. She pushed me into the room. She could speak English, but it had an accent and her sentences were broken up like all Filipino nurses spoke here, apart from the Indian male and females they were mostly Doctors or something higher up like Sisters in charge of the nurses. Like the one who sat on my bed that day. She asked me if I wanted to go to the toilet. I said yes and she helped me up off the wheelchair. As I tried to stand next to the loo she wheeled the chair out the way. There wasn't much room in there with her myself and the wheelchair. I automatically thought that she would leave me and take the wheelchair away, but oh no. She squeezed the wheelchair past me as I had my two hands out in front of me resting on the wall trying to keep my balance. Then she came round in front of me and crouched down under my arm that was stretched out and stayed down undoing my pyjama bottoms. She pulled them down and said as my pyjamas fell to the floor, "Lift leg please?" I did and then the other as she took them off completely. She squeezed up between me and the wall, there wasn't much room and started to undo the buttons on my pyjama jacket just inches away from me. I looked down onto the back of her head then she push the pyjama jacket back over my shoulders as I took one hand of the wall to slide it through the sleeve and then put it back. She did the same with the other hand so I could hold myself up. As the pyjama jacket fell to the floor, she knelt down between the wall and me and picked up my pyjamas. I stood there feeling so embarrassed, resting against the wall naked. I looked down at her, she looked up at me watching her, smiled and squeezed under my outstretched arm and stood up. She looked me in the face side on and smiled, holding my pyjamas in her hand and tapping me on the bum with the other saying, "you pee now, I'll be back with new pyjamas" and then left. *'God'* I thought, feeling so embarrassed. Then to comfort myself thinking, '*Oh don't be daft, they do this all the time and what's one other cock to them.*' It didn't make me feel any better. I stood there trying to have a pee thinking, '*God, she's going to come back and I'm so naked.*' I tried to push it to the back of my mind.

After a while I managed and turned to where the sink was. I put my hand out to hold on to the edge to help me turn round. I put the plug in and filled the basin with water. I put my hand out in front of me onto the mirror that was on the wall. I started to wash myself with one hand. I couldn't let go of the wall or I would have fallen over. I looked at myself in the mirror, God I need a shave. I had a good growth, not quite a beard more like stubble. I looked hellish. My eyes were sunken deep into their sockets and my face was so thin. I started to try and wash my face with the soap that was there. It was difficult to hold the soap in one hand and get it to go round in my hand to get some lather so that I could wash my face. It must have slipped out of my hand a thousand times and into the water so what lather I had attempted to get on my one hand, I lost feeling for the soap in the water. I gave up in the end and just splashed water over my face. I looked for the towel and luckily she had brought one through with her, it was slung over the back of the wheelchair. I dried my face and hands and waited for her to return holding onto the edge of the sink looking at myself. I decided to sit in the wheelchair at the other side of the toilet. With great effort, I turned round and managed to get to the wheelchair, sat down and waited. She came back clutching a clean pair of pyjamas, "sorry so long, you finish?" I started to get up from the wheelchair, but she stopped me, "Sit. I'll put pyjamas on." I sat there as she crouched down in front of me once again. I looked at her straight in the eyes as she knelt inches away from me, well my cock. I wanted to see if she was looking at it, she was. She couldn't help it she was that close. Oh God, I was so embarrassed. Holding one of my legs up for her, so that she could slide one of the clean pyjama legs over it, then the same for the other. To add to the embarrassment, she came even closer pushing my pyjamas up my legs until she was a few inches from . . . well? She looked up at me, "Lift bum please." I propped myself up on the two armrests on either side of the wheelchair. She slid the rest of the pyjama bottoms the rest of the way up and around my waist. I sat back down. I was tense as her hands pressed against my cock and balls, as she fastened each button in turn, still crouching down in front of me. She looked up and smiled then got up and helped me on with the pyjama jacket. Buttoning it down the front she said, "oaky-doky, finish." I thought *'thank God!'* She wheeled me back to bed, helped me into it and I slid down between the sheets. She smiled and went of wheeling the chair away.

I must have fallen asleep because I was woken up by Dr Morton holding my feet as he always does when he wants to talk to me. "I want to put you on dialysis okay?" I nodded. He turned; spoke to a nurse before turning back to me. "I'm going to insert a tube in your leg for the dialysis machine" he said and smiled. "You won't have any lunch, okay?" He said before walking away with the nurse. It was lunch time and everyone was getting their food except for me as I was going to get this tube put into my leg. *'Oh goody-goody'* I thought. I lay there watching everyone enjoying their food. After the nurses had cleaned everything away and the ward was back to normal, a man came in pushing a wheelchair and said to put my dressing gown on and take a blanket with me to put over my knees as we were going down to the next ward. As usual he wheeled me away out of the ward and into the lift. Then along a corridor passing people that had come in from outside on their way to visit people in the wards. I was pushed into a room where a Doctor and nurse were standing. The Doctor said, "Do you think you can get up onto the table?" I tried but had to have the help of the nurse. I lay down on my back as she pushed a pillow under my head. The Doctor came over saying he was going to push a tube into my inner thigh at the top of my leg by putting a small incision here and pointed to where he was going to cut. It was right next to my ball but on the inside of my leg. He said that he would slide the tube in, then down. He showed me the flexible tube, fuck me! It must have been at least eight inches in length or more. All of it would be pushed into and down my leg. I thought *'it's a good job I'm not Squeamish or I would have fainted.'* Going over to the nurse he pointed to me. I couldn't hear what he was saying but she came over and smiled and said hello, they all had great accents. Once again, she started to undo my pyjamas and pulled them down to reveal my private parts to another young nurse. I lay there watching her, thinking *'if I had received money for all the times that I have shown my cock off since I've been here, I would be quite well off by now.'* She stopped with my pyjamas down about my bum and looked straight in to my eyes with her big brown eyes and smiled a cheeky little smile. She said, "Lift bum please." As I did she continued to slide them off and put them on the wheelchair. She then went over to where the Doctor was and picked up a kidney shaped bowl with some brown liquid in it, which I later found out was iodine solution, a packet of cotton buds and a packet with tweezers in. Before she got to the table she stopped and put the packets and the bowl onto a stainless steel trolley with large wheels and wheeled it up alongside of me. Then she stood beside the bed looking at me and smiling that cheeky smile. She put on her thin rubber gloves, slipping them over her hands, taking her time pulling each finger in turn until they fitted tight and smiling the whole time. It if it was under any other circumstance it would have turned me on and I probably would have got a hard-on. But that was the last thing that I was thinking about. God, I didn't even have the strength to get up onto the table in the room without feeling light headed or dizzy and to contemplate getting a hard-on . . . there was nothing further from my mind. I lay there with just my pyjama jacket on, looking at her open the packets that were on the trolley and spread them out. She moved closer to me and took hold of my penis and testicles with one gloved hand, looked at me and smiled again. She held them out the way and with her other gloved hand started to dip the cotton buds into the brown iodine solution. She held it by the tweezers and rubbed it over the part that the Doctor was about to cut. She did this very slowly. I gave a little gasp as the liquid was cold on my inner thigh. She looked up, smiled and then looked back down to where her hands were. She let go of my penis and testicles to rip open the packet further to get another cotton bud and dump the old one. Picking up a new one in her tweezers, she dipped it once again into the iodine solution and took hold of my bits ever so gently. She started to wipe more of the solution round and round ever so slowly glancing several times up at me as she did it and smiled. Then it was time for the tube.

The Doctor came over and said that he was going to cut here and pointed with his finger. He told me I wouldn't feel a thing as he picked up the scalpel out of a bowl to do the incision. The nurse came round to the other side of where the Doctor was standing and held my penis and testicles once again. She held them out of the way and with her other hand holding a new bit of cotton bud in her tweezers, dabbed the blood that started to run as the Doctor cut into my leg. She glanced up at me, looking me straight in the eye and gave that cheeky little smile as she very gently squeezed my scrotum, let go and squeezed them again. She looked back to see blood running slowly down my leg and wiped it. She continued to squeeze my testicles and penis with a steady pressure and easing off as the Doctor pushed the tube into my leg. I could feel it go down inside my vein or wherever he was pushing it. Once it was inside my leg, he said that it wasn't long enough and apologised as he slowly pulled it out again. He turned, went back over to the cabinet and as I lay there I looked at him. I could feel the nurse altering her grip so she was holding my penis with one hand and with the other she gently cradled my testicles and squeezed them. I didn't even look at her to see if she was looking at me. I looked at the Doctor walking back with a larger packet and open it up on the table. *'Fuck me'* I thought, *'if the last one was long you should see this one.'* As he took it out of the packet he uncoiled it. The fucker must have been a foot or more long. Then it was just like before. I felt it being pushed down slowly into my leg, grabbing on to whatever it was going through. Fuck, it was becoming very sore. I wanted him to stop but he kept on going. Then it was over, it was in my leg. I lay there my leg throbbing. I could feel the thin tube in my leg, but not that much considering the length of the fucker. He taped the top of the tube sticking out to the inner side of my leg so that it would stay tight. The nurse let go of everything and walked round to the other side where the trolley was. She picked up a cotton bud in her tweezers, dipped it in the solution and gave the top of the tube a quick wipe. She went and got another couple of packets, opened them and put them on the trolley. She placed a gauze bandage over the end of the tube and taped the ends down. She wheeled the trolley out the way and got my pyjamas helping me on with them, sliding them up and under my bum as I lifted it up for her just as she said, "lift bum please?" She laughed and looked me straight in the eye then down to where she was fastening the top of my pyjamas around my waist. She then gave me a little tap on the waistband of my pyjamas, smiled and walked round to the other side after pushing the trolley further out the way. She helped me of the table and into the wheelchair, tucking the blanket gently around my legs, "that was good yes?"

On my way back to the ward I couldn't help but think of what the nurse had said. *'It was good yes?'* What did she mean? Did she mean squeezing my scrotum or putting the tube in my leg wasn't painful? I didn't know and would never find out. I reached the ward, got back onto the bed and was hooked up again to the drip. Before the nurse put the oxygen mask over my mouth she said, "You will be going for dialysis later."

I lay there trying hard to describe the way I was feeling. I found myself in hospital. I've been in a coma for how long I didn't know. I've died and been brought back. I was so weak I could hardly walk and now I'm about to get my blood pumped out and new blood pumped in, and a foot long tube in my leg. It was throbbing along with my balls.

I had a problem with lying on my back I couldn't breathe. It just cut off and was like being smothered. It left me gasping for air until I lay on my side and that helped it, I could breathe then. I told the Doctor about it. He looked and checked me over and said that I was all right. I knew that I wasn't and there must be something wrong. But what did I know? What the fuck happened to me? How did I end up here? I lay there thinking about my work and all the things that I was meant to be doing in Dubai and Africa when Dr Morton and Miss Lamella, wearing a long flowery thin dress and a creamy white blouse with a long brooch came in. The brooch went below the collar, from tip to tip. She was very elegant looking. They walked over to me and Dr Morton put his hand on the bottom of the bed and squeezed my foot gently through the sheets, as he did every time. I took the mask off, "Hallo Doctor, Miss Lamella." She acknowledged me by smiling. Dr Morton said, "You had the tube fitted then?" He walked round the side of the bed and pulled the bedcovers back, "may I?" He was the only one to ask me if I minded if I took my pyjamas down, the rest of them just did it and had a good look. He was very professional and once he'd looked, I pulled them up the best I could. He pulled the bedclothes up and said that I would be going for dialysis because my kidneys weren't working, that they had failed and did I have a problem with them before?

"No, I've never been ill like this before and I've never been in hospital for as long as this Doctor." As we were talking, an orderly came into the room and said to the Doctor that he was to take me down for dialysis. The Doctor said that he would continue this conversion later and smiled. Instead of taking me in a wheelchair, he disconnected the drip and the air and wheeled the bed through the two large doors and along the ward. I lay there looking at all the other rooms as I passed them and at the nurses doing their thing. Some of them smiled at me as I passed on my way to the lifts.

CHAPTER TWENTY

DIALYSES

I got to the other ward along with other people having the same thing done. The bed was put in a space where a bed had just left. The orderly said bye and walked away and I was left there, looking at the two other beds. One with a person looking at a paper and in the bed opposite me was an Arab woman in the bed with a veil over her face. One of the beds had the curtain drawn around it. A nurse came over pushing a large machine with many tubes and wires and started to un-wrap them. She pulled the curtains round my bed with the big machine in there with me and smiled. "Hi" she said before folding the bedclothes back to the bottom. I was laying there half on my side and half on my back so that I could breath. I had just my pyjama jacket on and I must say they always smiled as they took my pyjamas off? I lay there looking at her connecting all the different coloured tubes, then she pulled of the bandage that was covering the end of the tube that was in my leg. She connected a tube from the machine to the tube in my leg but she was having difficulty connecting it. The more she tried to pull it the more I could feel the whole tube scraping up and down the vein in my leg. She said if I lay down on my back she could do it better, connect the tubes easier. I said that I couldn't breathe if I lay on my back but she insisted, so I did. After a second or two, it started to happen, and I started to panic. I turned onto my side trying to catch my breath but all the nurse did was to tut as she tried to fit the tube to the one in my leg. She then left through the curtain and appeared back with another two other nurses one of them very young with a black veil covering all of her face, leaving just her eyes visible She was wearing a long coloured dress and a coloured top. She was about eighteen or more and she just stood there looking straight down at my prick as if she was spellbound. I looked away from the young girl because I was embarrassed about the whole thing to the other two nurses. As the other, showed the first nurse the tube she was trying to connect onto the one right next to my balls, which I must add were now hurting and thumping like mad. Not just my balls but also the top of my leg where the end of the tube was sticking out, apparently the tube that she was trying to connect was the wrong one. She then changed the tubes and proceeded to fix the right one to my thumping leg with help of the other nurse holding my aching balls out the way as the other just stood there looking on. I think she was learning as well. The second nurse said to me that I would have to lie on my back and be very still. I replied that I couldn't lie on my back because I cannot breathe. She said to try but I must be very still so that the machine can work. She turned to switch the machine on, then turned back and looked at the connections again as I lay there with just my pyjama jacket on. She pulled up the sheet that was at the bottom of the bed and covered me with it, then the curtains were drawn back and I could see the rest of the room again. The patients that were there when I came in had gone and a new lot had arrived. I lay there for I don't know how long. In between lying there, the odd nurse came over to check the machine and then time was up. Pulling the curtains round the bed she said, "Please you must lie on your back." So I did the best I could, propping myself up on my arms before she pulled down the sheet that covered me and disconnected the tube from in my leg before replacing the bandage. My leg and my testicles were so painful she had to help me pull up my pyjamas that were down around my ankles. I lay there waiting for the orderly to take me back. For the length of time that I remained in hospital, that was the routine every day.

I lay in my bed thinking what else could go wrong with me, when my friend, the sister who had told me that I had died came over and sat down on my bed and started to talk to me about her work in the hospital. She asked if I was doing all right. I told her about where I had just come from and I was so sore. We talked and talked for a long time, she was so nice about forty odd and had a kind face. She then said that she was going home and she would call into see me again tomorrow and said goodbye. The next morning the same palaver from changing the beds to cleaning the room etc. This went on every day then one morning the nurse left me in the toilet. I was so constipated I sat there for a while then I started to shake. It was uncontrollable. I fell of the toilet and as I fell forward I put my hand out to grab the wheelchair to try to stop myself falling, but I knocked it over on my way down. I lay there shaking on the floor, I couldn't stop and by luck a nurse came in and saw me there. She ran back out and in seconds there were three orderlies lifting me onto the wheelchair that one had put back onto its wheels and wheeled me out of the toilet and back to my bed. All the way back I couldn't stop shaking. One of the orderlies pushed as the other two held me in the chair. The two nurses folded the sheet down on the bed and the three guys lifted me onto the bed. It took all their strength to put me there. My legs were jumping up and down; my whole body was having a seizure. It is hard to explain but I couldn't do a thing to stop it. It was as if my whole body had a mind of its own. I lay there shaking and they put the sides of the bed up to stop me falling out then a Doctor came in and a another nurse and they gave me a injection. After a while it stopped, I think as the next few minutes were a blank. I'm not certain what happened I must have passed out.

When I woke up it was night and I still had the sides of the bed up and the drip was connected. I had the mask over my mouth but there was something strange, my eye sight was blurred, it looked like I was looking through a long tunnel. I started to panic and pressed the buzzer. A nurse came in and over to me I told her the problem and she said, "You will have to wait till morning." I closed my eyes and tried not to think about it, but it was a while before I fell asleep again. It was very early in the morning when I woke up and I still had a problem with my eyesight. As I said it was very blurred, I couldn't make out the bed opposite me and it was as if I was looking through a long narrow tunnel. I lay there trying to look at different things trying to get my head around this disaster. I lay there waiting for the morning staff to come on and start their shift. As suddenly as I thought it, the lights were put on in all of the rooms and the ward, then after a while the others in the room got their breakfast given to them but not for me. I was still on a liquid drip that was pumping into my arm. All I got was some tea and the needle changed in my arm and a new clear plastic bag put up on the stand. After breakfast the nurses came in to change the beds. As I was waiting for my turn a nurse came over and said that the Doctor would be coming to see me. As she told me this, she attempted to tidy my bed and straighten the sheets and then I was left alone. I closed my eyes to rest them, I don't know why I did it; I just did and fell asleep again. I was woken by Dr Morden touching my feet through the sheet like he always did. I attempted to sit up and take the oxygen mask of my mouth to say "morning Doctor," but he was in deep conversion with four young girls at the bottom of my bed. Three of them had their face coved with veils and all wearing long brightly coloured dresses and one in a white coat. Then Miss Lamella appeared she was quite tall and very elegantly dressed with her black hair tied back very neatly without a bit out of place. She was very superior looking, but I suppose she had to be because she was head of the hospital. The three of them talked amongst themselves ignoring the other three much younger girls and then Dr Morden turned and walked up the side of the bed. "I hear you are having a problem seeing?" he said.

"Yes Doctor." I told him what was wrong and he explained to the girl in the white jacket. Then Miss Lamella said something in Indian and Dr Morden turned to me and asked, "Could I get out of bed?" So I tried. He lowered the stainless steel bed rail, pulled back the sheet that was covering me and I swung my legs over the side of the bed and sat on the edge. I tried to get up but my legs just wouldn't hold my weight and Dr Morden had to help me stand up beside the bed. "Do you think you can stand by yourself?" I tried but couldn't without his help. He helped me to sit back down onto the edge of the bed. I sat there while he and Miss Lamella discussed me in their language. Then Miss Lamella looked at her watch, said something again to Dr Morden then he spoke to the other four girls that were still standing there.

I got back into bed and pulled the sheet up over my legs and covered them with it. I sat there looking at them all talking at the bottom of my bed with Dr Morden holding my feet once again. As the three young girls in their veils peered over the top of them at me and then back at Dr Morden. Whilst taking notes, the other young Doctor who was with them in her white coat complete with a name tag clipped on her white coat. I tried to read her name but all I could make out was the Dr before her name, my eyesight was crap and very hazy around the edges. I could only make out things if I looked straight at them and up close, well about as far as the bottom of the bed where the four girls were standing and Dr Morden. Anything to the side I couldn't see without turning my head. It was as if I were looking through a tunnel as I said earlier. That's how I knew that she was a Doctor because of the Dr on her badge. I was still sitting up in bed with my pyjama jacket open, studying the young good looking girl Doctor as she stood looking at me and then at Dr Morden. He talked to the four of them in Arabic. I thought, sitting there waiting my turn to ask the Doctor something, that she could be a first year Doctor. Then Dr Morden turned to me and squeezed my foot through the sheet and smiled. He was about to say something to me when the good looking girl Doctor said something to him. He turned back round to talk to her. I watched them as they talked and I couldn't make out what she was saying. Then they both looked at me then back at themselves, and then she walked away with the other girls. Dr Morden turned back to me before he went through the door where the girls were waiting for him and said, "Your eyesight will get better in a few days." I thanked him then as he was leaving the room he said again "don't worry you're in good hands." I smiled a feeble smile and slid down into my bed, then the young good looking girl Doctor came back with a nurse and walked up the side of the bed and lent over, putting her hand over her jacket pocket to stop the pens and stethoscope from falling out. She spoke in my ear as the nurse started to pull the curtains around my bed blocking me off from the rest of the room yet again that I was going to have a bed bath. I turned and looked up straight into her face. She smiled showing her white teeth then she said softly in my ear again, "have you had one before?" I replied "no." She stood up and tapped me on the arm and said "a young nurse will wash you all over; it will be good for you." She turned to leave through the gap in the curtain turning round holding on to the edge just before disappearing and smiled again. She said from the gap in the curtains, "you will like it believe me." Then she was gone leaving me with the nurse. When the curtains were drawn completely round my bed, she disappeared through the join in the two curtains as well, leaving me alone thinking about what the young Doctor had said. Fuck me what now? I'm not well, I couldn't see, my kidneys are fucked, my lungs are fucked, I've got a big fucking tube in me leg and I can't walk now. If I lie on my back I can't breathe. I learnt later that my lung had collapsed again and I had to go onto the ventilator machine once again. This was in between everything else. They tried to put me in this machine that scans your whole body checking out everything but you have to lie on your back while they slide you through this long machine but I couldn't lie on my back. So they gave me a local anaesthetic to render me unconscious so that they could pass me through the machine and check me out. Even unconscious, I wasn't lying still enough to be put through it so they gave up till later. With lying on my side I had got bed sores on each side on each hip, and I have been stripped bollock naked for the entire nursing staff to look at and prodded and now I'm to get a bed bath. She said that I would like it, what next I ask you?

CHAPTER TWENTY-ONE

BED BATH

I lay there breathing on my oxygen yet again. If I didn't I got dizzy and might pass out. I couldn't be bothered with that, what with everything else. The curtains were drawn and a stainless steel trolley appeared, wheeled in by a young nurse and another young nurse carrying a basin of water, a sponge, and several towels. I thought the Doctor was right about the nurses being young, but I don't know if I'm going to enjoy it. One of the nurses positioned the trolley behind her as the other one went round to the other side of the bed and handed the other one the stuff that she was carrying. She put them onto the trolley. They both smiled at me and one of them said in broken English, "we wash all of you in bed, okay?" They both looked at each other and smiled, talking away in their language as they stripped the sheet off the bed along with the blanket. I looked at them as they worked away. They were both about twenty two to twenty three, with dark olive skin and jet-black hair. One had short curly hair and the other had long hair tied back with pins to hold it in place. They both had big brown eyes. I looked at their breasts in turn. Clearly, they both had nice sized breasts, well what I could see of them as they protruded out from the uniforms and quite neat bums. Okay, I can hear you saying to yourselves as you read this. "Ha, he can't be that ill to notice all that" But I assure you I was. It's only now that I can remember most of the incidents that happened when I was in hospital as I'm writing this book. I wasn't looking forward to being naked in front of these two reasonably good-looking Filipino nurses. They seemed to be enjoying every minute of it; well it looked like that to me. They undid my pyjama buttons in turn. Then one of them asked me to lift myself up on one arm, as they took one of my arms out of the jacket. They did the same to the other. I didn't have much strength so I lay back down onto my arms, propping myself up just a bit so that I could breathe. One of them pulled my pyjama jacket from underneath me and threw it on the floor by the foot of the bed. Again, in turn, they started to undo the four buttons on my bottoms, and then they both took a pyjama leg as I looked on in horror, pulling them off. They too were thrown in the corner along with the rest. I lay there, naked on the bed, as they both looked me up and down. They glanced up at each other, smiling and talking away to each other in Filipino. I don't know what they were saying, but the way they looked at me then at each other and smiled, made me feel a little embarrassed, just lying there naked. I don't know why. It's not the first time I've been naked whilst I've been here, BUT there was something about these two. Just the way they were looking at me, talking amongst each other. I thought *'what the fuck, I can't be bothered It could all just be my imagination.'*

I lay there looking at them in turn, as they talked away to each other. One of them said in broken English that they were going to wash me and smiled. As the other nurse turned and pulled the trolley round beside her, putting the sponge into the basin of water something made me look back at the other one. I caught her looking down at my cock and smiling. She saw me looking at her then said something to the other one in Filipino and laughed. The other nurse looked at me with the sponge clasped in her two hands and smiled. That was it; they were discussing my anatomy and me. The warm water tricking over my testicles and penis brought my attention to what they were doing. I looked down as the one that was laughing took hold of my penis in one of her thin rubber gloved hands as the other hand lifted my balls up and moved them about to let the other nurse clean around it, and down to my bum and back up again. As she rinsed the sponge out in the basin, the other put everything back where it was. I could hear them talking away in their foreign language. Not being able to understand, I just lay there and let them do their thing. Then more water was trickled over my balls and penis from the sponge. As she did this, she looked up at the other one and smiled. Then they both looked at me then down again. The one with the sponge turned round to rinse it out again. Then she sponged gently around the bandage on my leg then up over my tummy, my chest and even lifting up my arms in turn and washing them. She looked into my face as she brought the sponge to rest on my chest. She turned round to the other one and said something to her in Filipino. The other nurse smiled showing her white teeth and said something back to her. She then looked at me as the other one with the sponge turned back to me and said, "Us two do this for you every morning no one else do it." She rinsed out the sponge once again and came back to wipe my face gently. She looked at me and said, "We we're good, no?"

The other one turned to put the sponge in the basin. I didn't say a thing, just smiled. Then the other one said something in Filipino to the other nurse and they both laughed. The one that was washing me so carefully with the sponge picked up the bedclothes and my pyjamas, and put them on top of the trolley. She pulled back the curtain just enough for her and the trolley to go through and stopped. Putting her hand into her pocket, she brought out two unopened tubes of ointment and handed them to the other nurse, said something to her and smiled.

Then she was gone and I was left with one. She smiled at me and put both of the unopened tubes on the table beside the bed still in their packets. She turned back to the top of my leg where the badge was. It was protecting the long tube that was in my leg for changing my blood. She started take the bandage off very slowly. It was wet, but the Elastoplasts that were holding the bandage to my leg had stuck to the hairs. She was peeling a corner back slowly but even as she did it, it sent pain shooting down the tube inside my leg. They had put the tube in next to my balls and that added to the pain. Every time she peeled another bit back, about twenty million hairs went with it. She could see it was hurting me and stopped with a sympathetic look on her face before starting again. 'Oh my God,' I lay there with my hands clenched tight praying that the fucking thing was off. The whole of my leg and my balls were starting to throb, as the pain got more and more intense. Every time she peeled back the bandage, it pulled off another thousand hairs. At last, it was off and she rested her hands over the red area. She looked at me again and said, "Sorry so sorry." Taking one of the packets of ointment off the tabletop, she looked at the writing on the side before picking up the other one and putting the first one back. Taking the tube out of the long packet, she opened it and squeezed it round the area where the tube in my leg had come out. She stopped and glanced up into my eyes as the coldness of the ointment made me tense. She smoothed it out over the inflamed part of my leg that was still throbbing then she looked back down and carried on smoothing the ointment around.

For the first time since I had the tube put in my leg, the whole of the inner thigh and my balls were throbbing and the pain, well it was fucking sore. The pain seemed to shoot down the inner part of my leg to the base of the tube and up again and across to my balls. This happened the whole time she was spreading the ointment, out around the inner part of my leg, holding by balls and penis out of the way. I was so glad to feel her hand gently holding my balls. It seemed to take some of the throbbing away from that area. The minute she let them go the pain came back. I felt like saying to her 'would she mind holding them again for me,' but I didn't. She then put the lid back on the tube and put it back into the packet. She took out a pair of tweezers and opened another packet containing a very thing gauze bandage. She placed it over the part where the tube came out of my leg; the cool sensation of the gauze eased the throbbing pain for a second. She repeated the process then picked up a bandage and took the outer wrapping off it before starting to wrap it round my leg gently, until it was all in place. Then as she was finishing off, the other nurse came back in, pulling the curtain closed behind her. She said something in Filipino to the one that had just finished putting the bandage on, and was picking up the empty wrappers that were lying on the bed, putting them into a black rubbish bag that was on the floor by her feet. She looked at the other nurse and then at me and smiled and then answered her. She replaced the used tube back into the packet and put it back on the cabinet. Picking up the other packet she started to read it. She looked at the other nurse, said something again in Filipino, and giggled. They both looked at me smiling. I lay there looking at them thinking '*what's so funny?*' I was about to find out.

She then took the tube out, looked at it then at me and smiled. As the other nurse said something, she looked up, laughed and then looked at me then back down at what she was reading. They had a funny sort of grin on their faces. She opened the tube and gave the other nurse a glance as they stood either side of the bed. The one that had just come in looked at the other one with the tube all ready to squirt it somewhere. They both smiled and looked at me once again, but I wasn't ready for what was about to happen and where they were going to put it. The one without the tube got hold of my penis with one of her rubber gloved hands at the base and with the other, she slowly pulled the four-skin right back so that the head of my penis was extended. She then looked up at the other nurse who squeezed the cold ointment around just below the rim of the head. She then slowly pulled the four-skin back over the ointment and gave my penis a little squeezes as she pull my four-skin back and forth along the shaft to rub the ointment in. The other nurse smiled and looked at me. I smiled back thinking *'if they do that much longer . . . I know I'm ill, BUT!'* The one with the tube said something to the other and they both looked at me. The nurse holding my penis laid it back down and gave it a little tap before giggling to the other nurse. Turning to me, she said, "got to keep clean" and smiled. The nurse put the ointment back into the packet, then put them both in the drawer in the table beside my bed and gave me a smile. She said in broken English, "We do this tomorrow, yes, again."

I lay there on my bed and smiled to them both without saying anything. The nurse giggled and returned to where the other one was and stood looking at her. The other nurse picked up the thing she had brought back with her that she had laid down on the bed beside her. She said that she was going to put a large nappy on me, so if I wanted to go to the toilet just do it in the nappy like a baby. I just lay there naked on my bed. I was too weak to get up. I had lost a lot of weight. As I looked at myself lying there I just nodded back to her and gave a feeble little smile and thought *'what the fuck* and what else?' I mean what else could they do to me? They rolled me onto my side and one of the nurses undid the sheet along one side of the bed and pushed it under the full length of me as I lay on my side. They then told me to roll back onto my other side with the help of the other nurse. As I did, the other nurse took the old wet sheet away and threw it on the floor, got a clean one and I repeated the same thing. Once the clean sheet was in place and tightly tucked in, they got this thing like a big nappy and I had to repeat the same thing. Instead of the sheet this time, it was a large nappy. That's the only way I can explain it, it was a large adult nappy. Once I was laying on it one of the nurses' put her hand in between my legs and pulled the end with one hand, the other held my cock and balls in place. She started to pull this thing tight up between my legs and fastened it round my waist onto the two other parts that the other nurse was holding for her. I think it was Velcro or something like that. She then put her hand into her pocket, brought out yet another tube, and started to open it. This one was for my bedsores. She squeezed the tube and rubbed it over each side of my hips where the sores were. Then a clean sheet and blanket were put neatly back on me. They lifted my head and pushed two new pillows underneath. The two nurses cleaned everything up and pushed back the curtains. One took the dirty linen away whilst the other replaced the needle in my arm with a fresh one and reconnected it to the drip. She leant over me, "there, you're like big baby" and gave me my oxygen mask. I just lay there feeling so embarrassed. Having my private parts washed, manhandled, and played with by two nurses, well! I suppose it's not fair to say that, for all the time I lay there naked on the bed with them grabbing my private parts, it was done very professionally, even if they did giggle between themselves. To round everything off, they put this fucking big nappy on me and I would have to go through it all again tomorrow. I just wanted to die! Well the way things were going I might just!

I lay there in my big nappy and my clean bed and watched as they both left the room giving me a smile and a little wave, giggling between each other as they walked along the ward and out of sight.

I lay thinking *'how can I pee or have a crap in this nappy'* as they called it. I just lay there so completely naked, felt so alone, and scared. I was fighting back the tears thinking *'will I get better or will something else happen. What if I die here without any of my family near me?'* I thought of my son and daughter and wished that they were here right now. Just to be with me, to see them before I die. *'What would happen to my body, would it be flown home?'* They didn't even know where I came from. *'Oh God I hope I get better and I can see my kids and grandchildren again.'* You know it's not funny when you are afraid or alone, you turn to God for help. I suppose it's not that funny really. I lay there, cried into the pillow, and must have fallen asleep. I woke later on and the lights were out in the room and the ward. It was night but I didn't know what time it was. All that I knew was I needed a pee. I thought about just lying there and peeing into the large nappy, but I couldn't. I lay there trying to, and then as I was about to I stopped myself. I don't know why, I just did. I tried again. I started to pee into the nappy, then stopped, then started again and let the lot go. I just lay there and went in my nappy. It felt very warm and very strange just to lie there. I thought *'that's how babies must feel?'* After that first pee, it became easier to do. That was until it got very wet, then it got uncomfortable. What I was dreading more than anything was to press the buzzer to get one of the nurses' to come,

I looked for the buzzer and found it beside the pillow. I thought one of the nurses must have put it there while I was asleep. I had to get a nurse to come so I pressed it. A second or so later, a nurse came over to my bed, turned off the light that the buzzer had put on above my bed and said, "What is it?"

I told her and she replied that I would have to wait until the morning. I pleaded with her saying "I'm wet" but all she did was check the connection to the drip in my arm. I pleaded with her again saying that the nappy they had put on me was wet and I needed it changed. She insisted that she couldn't do it and I would have to wait until the morning. She walked away only to come back again. I thought 'good she's coming to change it.' She ignored me, changed the drip then walked away again. I thought, *'the bitch!'* That was the first time I felt like that about one of the nurses, but she was. Maybe she couldn't be bothered or perhaps she was busy with another patient. I don't know what the reason was, but I was wet and they told me to pee in this fucking thing. So I have and now they won't change the fucking thing!

I lay there thinking *'what if I had to . . . well you know, the other?'* Would they have left to lie in the poo so to speak? The good thing was I was so constipated it wouldn't have happened, thank goodness. The nurse that was on that night didn't speak much. I presume she didn't speak much English. Maybe that's why she didn't change me, I don't know. I was so uncomfortable and yet earlier quite content to just lie there and pee into my nappy. I lay there in the dark with my wet nappy, wet and heavy. Even the bed sheets were wet and my pyjama top. Yes, my top was wet. In fact, the whole bed was fucking wet! They didn't bother with the pyjama bottoms. I think because this nappy thing was so bulky. Anyway, it was just as well. I lay there in the dark and moved to the edge of the bed where it was a bit drier. The nappy dragged across the inside of the bed with me, it was cold! I was cold and everywhere was wet. All I could do was lie on my sides but the wetness irritated my bedsores and made them unbearable. I don't know how I feel asleep but I did, even though I woke up several times through the night. It was the worst night I had there. I still remember it so clearly to this day. No wonder babies cry when they get wet. I think it wouldn't have mattered if I had cried the bitch wouldn't have come anyway.

I eventually fell asleep again and awoke a short time later. A nurse was talking quietly to a man in the opposite bed. I could just make her out with my eyesight being so bad. I waited until she had finished talking. I called to her, "Nurse, nurse." She came over and I told her I was wet. No, I said that the bed was wet and I was so cold. She lifted the sheet and the blanket that was covering me; looking for herself, she put it back and said, "I'll be back in a while." She left through the two large doors that lead out the ward. I watched her walk away getting hazier the further away she got, then she was out of sight and I was once again in the dark lying in my pee. I thought '*what the fuck do I have to do to get new sheets and a new nappy.*' I tell you it will be the last time I pee in this fucking thing. As I was cursing her, I saw her hazy form come round the corner carrying a sheet, blanket, and a new nappy, and she had pyjamas. Okay, okay I take it all back. I was so glad to see her. She pulled the curtains round the bed and laid the stuff that she was carrying on top of the chest next to the bed. She walked round to the other side where the drip was and undid it by taking it out of my arm. She took the oxygen mask and hung it on the stand where the bag of liquid was hanging. She then started to strip the sheet and blanket off, then the nappy although it didn't take much pulling. It was practically off anyway. I thought as I looked at her, '*I don't fancy your job!*' The nappy was so wet and it smelled heavily of urine. She took the pyjama jacket off and threw it on the floor along with the rest of the wet linen. Then she spoke for the first time since she came back. She asked in a soft voice if I could roll over onto my side so that she could take the sheet from underneath. I obliged her by rolling onto my side as she pulled the sheet out from under the mattress. She asked to roll back onto my other side as she came round to do the other side and pull the wet sheet away. A rubber sheet was placed on the bed and a clean white sheet. Again, she asked me to roll back and forth whilst the sheet was tucked in along either side. She helped me on with my pyjama jacket. I still didn't have the strength to do that myself. I lay there letting her put the new nappy on and make sure that my cock and balls were not trapped in any way as she tightened the nappy around me. Oh, my God it felt so comfortable. She put the top sheet on with a new blanket and smiled at me. "You feel better no?"

"Yes, thank you nurse." I replied. She smiled again and picked up the wet things off the floor that she had discarded and pulled back the curtains. I watched her again as she walked away around the corner carrying the wet linen. God, I felt so good in my dry clean bed.

CHAPTER TWENTY-TWO

ROUTINE

I lay in bed, the next morning looking out the big window that looked out onto the ward and waited for the morning staff to come on shift. I watched as they began to arrive. Some talking to each other and others were by themselves. Then I saw the nurses that looked after me, they smiled as they saw me looking. One even gave a little wave as they passed the window. I liked them. They were young, humorous and they made me laugh. I would have to wait until they started breakfasts to see them. It was the same routine every day. They gave the rest of the patients their breakfast first, and then after they had been seen to, they came over to me with tea. Then hell broke out. There would be eight nurses, two orderlies and a big canvas trolley. The beds were stripped before being made up again. Clean white sheets and one blanket on each bed with clean pillows and clean new pyjamas. When all that was done, the cleaners came in and cleaned everything you could imagine from the curtain rails around the bed to the top of the doorframes and mopped everything. It was so different from a hospital in the U.K. where it would be one person doing all that. Here in Dubai there was one person doing one task and only one task. There were a lot of them milling about, working around us. Then the pills were handed out. An hour would pass and it would be the Doctors turn to do their rounds. I was to be helped into a wheelchair with scales fixed on them and weighed every morning. The last time they weighed me I was about seven stone. Before I was admitted into hospital, I weighed thirteen and a half stone. If I keep losing weight as I was, the next time the Doctors made their rounds there would just be a skeleton in the bed. Whilst the other patients were either washing or going to the toilet, I had my two personal nurses that attended to me from the day they squirted the ointment over my dick. They did their thing from changing the bedclothes to changing my nappy, my bandage, and rubbing ointment on my leg and under my foreskin. It became a joke with them. They used to say with a penis like that, I should have it snipped. All the men they knew had it done when they were children, its cleaner. Then they would make me smile by saying, "But we don't mind doing this for you. Taking our time and making sure it's very, very clean" in their broken English. They would both laugh and say, "When you get better we will personally do the operation."

I still couldn't make out who were in the beds opposite me. It was too far from what I could focus on. The furthest I could see was about the length of the bed, any further than that. Well it got blurry. I could still make out shapes of people but as I said, it was like looking through a tube. They were pumping me full of pills and with not being able to get up, the bedsores on each side got worse and needed ointment all the time. It got to the stage that I couldn't sleep on my back because I couldn't breathe and now I couldn't sleep on my sides. I used to toss and turn trying to get to sleep. God, thinking back I was a wreck and the night-time would be the worst in all the time I stayed in the hospital. I was so lonely and thought if I could just see my kids. Oh God, I thought of them a lot and wondered if they thought I was a bad dad. I thought that I should have been a better father to them and I would cry myself to sleep most nights, thinking *would I see my grandchildren grow up or even see Eddie my son or Rebecca my daughter.'* As I said, most nights I would cry myself to sleep sobbing into the pillow and the nights I couldn't get to sleep I would lay there the best way I could. I don't know if I was dreaming or if it was the drugs that they were giving me as I was on some serous medication. I would lie there and see these black shapes emerge from under the floor and from under the beds and they would be leering in the corners in the room and dart around the room and through walls and the ceiling. White ones would appear and fight the black ones and they would fill the room as they darted about avoiding each other. They would hover over my bed; it was a bit like that film Ghost with Patrick Swayze. The part where he gets shot and becomes a Ghost and you see these black and white shapes, the black ones take the bad guys away down under the ground and the white ones take the good guys up the way. Well thinking back, they might of being waiting for me and they couldn't make their minds up who was taking me. It was as if I was on L.S.D. or some other super drug, maybe I was, I don't know. 'I wonder where I can get some now, I could do with some?'

My eyesight eventually got better. It took longer than the Doctor had said, but I wasn't going anywhere so I wasn't bothered. Well there were so many other things wrong with me so 'what the hell.' I was putting on weight, not much but it was coming up and my kidneys, well they were working on twenty percent not good but at least they worked. I was still going everyday to dialysis. I still couldn't walk so they pushed me in my bed through to the other ward where they had the dialysis machines. I was having breathing exercises. I had to blow into a long tube that monitored the amount of air that your lungs had in them (a Peak Flow Meter, similar to ones asthmatics use) and it wasn't measuring much. I had to blow on this thing as often as possible so they left it beside my bed. Overall, it was the turning point but I had a long way to go yet. It must have been at least a couple of month now since I first arrived in here. The two good-looking nurses still did their thing and at this particular time, they said that I could do with a shave. By now, I had a full beard, not long but it was a beard. So one afternoon they came into the room carrying between them a bowl of water, several packets of disposables razors, a towel and several tubes of shaving foam. They put them on my bed and started to laugh and say, "Okay *we shave you Bob."* They called me Bob ever since I said my name was Robert. I don't know why it was Bob and not Bobby or Robert. Anyway they could me Bob. They helped me to sit up in bed, taking an arm each they pulled me up into a sitting position. Then they put another two or three pillows behind me stuffing them down my back so it propped me up. They sat on each side of my bed giggling. I couldn't help but smile along with them as they attempted to shave me. They took their time but it wasn't a success. They broke about half of the razors, used two tubes of the shaving foam that was everywhere (that would have probably done me for a month or even more) then an outburst of laughter between them. One of them saying, "Sshh be quiet, keep it down" to the other one, but it was fun and it brightened up my day and theirs too I think.

They cleaned me up and I looked in a mirror that they had brought with them. I looked like shit. It's not what they had done but the overall appearance of me, okay the half chewed off beard didn't help but it did make me laugh as well as Dr Morton and his good looking first year assistant Dr Assam. You remember one of the four young girls that came round to see me one morning. She was the one in the white coat that I told you about. She was so good looking with that Asian look and long jet-black hair always tied so neatly in the same way as Miss Lamella. Her big brown sultry come to bed eyes, with curves all in the right place and not bad tits as well. I found out that her dad was Mr Big. One of four, all in white, immaculately dressed Arabs that came round the hospital on the odd occasion. They owned it or had something to do with that side of it. So I think I was bombed out and didn't bother to ask her out. However, it didn't stop me perving at her every time she came to check me out when Dr Morton had told her, and that was nearly every morning. When Miss Lamella saw me, she gave a little laugh and then composed herself again. She asked who did such a good job on shaving me. As she said it, she put her hand up to her mouth as if to stop herself from laughing again. I replied, "It was a couple of nurses, Miss Lamella." She took her hand down from her mouth to reveal a big smile then said, "*I must congratulate them on such a good job.*" She put her hand back up to her mouth and laughed into it before turning and walking out of the room. She stood in the ward with her hands folded in front her back to me. I could see that she was laughing by the way her shoulders were moving. Then she turned, came back into the room and started to talk to Dr Morton. As she did, she kept glancing over to me and smiling. As they were about to leave, I asked, "Can I talk to you Dr Morton?" He was a nice kind man and would do everything in his power to help you while you were in hospital and in his care.

"How can I help you?" He asked. I told him about the nappy, the wet bed and me. I didn't bother to tell him about the bitch, I didn't think it was worth it. I asked him if there was any other remedy to this problem. He replied, "We will go with this just now and see." So I agreed, but it wasn't a success. After that night, I was scared to pee into the nappy and that eventually caused another problem. I didn't want to pee at all and that was bad news. My bladder got so full that my tummy began to swell and started to get quite painful. Luckily, the two nurses that bathed me every morning noticed that the nappy wasn't wet and I think they told the Doctor and he came to see what the problem was. It had been several days by now and I was feeling very uncomfortable. He asked me what the problem was. Why hadn't I used the nappy? I told him about that night, leaving out the part about the nurse and then of course he said why didn't I press the buzzer for a nurse. I just said it was in the middle of the night. He replied that it wouldn't have mattered then said that I would have to have a Catheter fixed if I don't pass urine. I asked him what a catheter was. He told me what it was and explained what was involved. It means holding the penis and pulling back the four skin, then pushing a tube down the centre of the penis through the opening at the tip right down into the bladder. The other end outside your penis is connected to a bag, hung on the side of you or on the side of the bed. After he had explained it to me he said, "I will arrange for you to get it done in the next couple of days. I thanked him and sunk down into my bed and thought of what he had said. Do I really want another tube pushed into me? Would it be as long as the one I have already in my leg? Surely not, but just the thought of a tube being pushed down inside the small hole at the top of my penis was sending shivers down my spine. I wondered how big the tube would be. Surely, it couldn't be that big, the hole is not that big on my dick. I wanted to have a look and examine it before they started to push anything down it but it was wrapped in this nappy. My tummy was so swollen and uncomfortable I couldn't be bothered to undo it just to have a look at my dick. I lay there in bed and thought long and hard about what the Doctor had said whilst I watched Dr Morton and his assistant Dr Assam with two nurses over at the bed opposite me. One of the nurses pulled the curtain around the bed opposite. The two nurses that give me my bed bath every morning then caught my attention. They both stopped and stood in the doorway that led into my room, they walked past and said, "we go off we see you tomorrow Bobs." They both gave me a wave and a smile. I could hear them laughing to themselves as they walked away along the ward, they turned the corner and were gone out of sight. My eyesight was nearly back to normal but me; well I was just skin and bone. I remember when the two nurses that had just gone gave me a shave and I looked in the mirror, I thought then my face was all sunken and drawn looking. I lay there thinking of the two nurses. I didn't even know their names. *I must ask them tomorrow when I get my bed bath.'*

I sunk down between the sheets and thought how nice the two nurses were and what a laugh we have in the morning when they give me my bed bath. They always laugh and joke and talk to each other in Filipino and then in broken English to me. They would joke about who's going to put the ointment on my dick, and then they would laugh and say it's my turn to rub the ointment in. Whoever did it would grip my penis, smear the ointment on, and rub it in as they both giggled. Then they would carry on with their every day routine. They would put ointment on my sides to prevent the bedsores from getting any worse, and so on until I was clean with my nappy on and lying in my clean bed ready for the Doctors. I suppose it takes a certain type of person to do what they do every day and if they can have some fun while they do what they do, well why not! They both have great personalities and not to forget they were good looking with all the bumps and curves in the right places. I lay there thinking about them both, how they brighten my day, when another nurse came to change the drip. The plastic container was empty or nearly empty and she replaced it with a full one and checked the needle that was sticking in my arm. I looked at her and then at my arm as she took the needle out. She took a fresh one out of a packet and tried to push it in but she couldn't find a vein. She had four or five attempts, pushing the needle in, and then she would take it out again. She would tap my inner arm to bring up the vein and try again. My arm was black and blue where they had regularly pushed different needles in. It was in some mess. She left after eventually finding the vein. I lay there breathing away on my oxygen. I must have drifted off to sleep yet again.

Next thing they told me I was going to dialysis. I hated going there, it made my leg and my balls hurt a continuous pain for hours afterwards, I think it was the way they stripped off the bandage and pulled on the tube to connect it to the machine; they weren't the gentlest of people. They told me to lay still and not move whilst the machine pumped new blood in and the old out. Nevertheless, 'it was for the best' I kept telling myself. I arrived back in time for my cup of tea and my cake, which you got every afternoon. I normally got two cups of tea but this time it was just one, with my cake waiting for me on my locker top. They pushed my bed back to where it normally sits and connected me up again to everything. Before I put the mask on, I had my tea, which wasn't very hot and ate my cake. I settled down to the daily chore of perving at all the nurses. I had a cheek considering the state I was in. I must of dozed off again, that's all I did was sleep. I couldn't even be bothered looking at the paper or reading the articles and the short stories in the magazines the nurses had given me. Well I tried but I tired very quickly and fell asleep again. The days rolled in along with the nights and I just lay there in my bed. A new Doctor came to see me and said that he was from physiotherapy. He was going to give me some exercises to get me walking again. We started with me swinging my legs over the side of the bed as he sat beside me holding on to me. I was told to push both my legs straight out and up in front of me, so I did but I didn't make much movement. He coaxed me by saying, "that's okay, now have a rest then try again."

I replied "but I didn't move my legs?"

"Its okay" he said again. "Give it time and try once more."

It is hard to explain, I wanted to move them but I could not. It was weird. It was as if they weren't mine. He then said that he would be back tomorrow and we will try it again. I thanked him and that was it, he was gone, after helping me back into bed of course.

Days passed and the physiotherapist came every day at the same time. I was getting better. I could lift my legs up and down two at a time and individually. He thought that now I should be able to stand up with a little help from him. "Do you think you can?" he asked.

"I'll have a go," I said. He helped me up onto my feet and I put my hand out against the large glass window that was next to my bed to hold myself, as he stood behind me with his arms out to catch me if I fell. It was okay. Then he said, "Do you think you could take a step?" I tried but would have fallen if it weren't for the Doctor grabbing hold of me; I sat back down on the bed, I was naked and had difficulty breathing. I couldn't get my breath so as I sat there he gave me my oxygen mask and told me to relax and breath slow and deep. I did what he said. I could feel myself getting quite dizzy but managed to control it by thinking of something else. "I think that will do for today" and I got back into bed. Then Dr Morton came in and said good afternoon to the other Doctor and then he put his hand on my feet as he always did. "How are you doing?" he asked.

"Fine thanks Doctor" I replied and the other Doctor said that I was doing great.

"I'll have him walking before the weeks out," the Doctor said and then Dr Morton said "good, good" with a big grin on his face. Dr. Morton put his arm around the other Doctor and they walked away out onto the ward discussing something. He was right. I was walking about after a week but only from one bed to the other bed with the Doctor holding onto my arm. I would stop turn round and come back and even at that distance I was breathing as if I had just ran a hundred metre marathon. As the weeks went past, I walked further and further and then by myself with the Doctor behind me. One morning Dr Morton told me that I was going to get the catheter done. They took me out of the ward and down several floors in the lift. This time they left me in the wheelchair to wait outside a room. After a while, a nurse wheeled in me and the Doctor told me to get up onto the table. It had a white sheet draped over it. I did it with the help of the nurse and lay down as the Doctor told me what he was about to do. I asked him, "Will I feel anything?" to his reply "yes." I then asked, "Will it hurt?"

"No, all I'm going to do is insert this tube into your penis through here" as he took hold of my penis and pointed to where he was going to shove it. *'Aye right'* I thought *'and this won't hurt me . . . '*

I was told by Dr Morton what to expect, but telling me and letting them do it is a completely different ball game. I looked at the Doctor and then at the nurse who was standing looking on and smiling and said to her something like, "it's all right for you" which widened her smile to a big grin. Doctor brought over the tube that he was going to shove down my dick . . . *'Fuck me Doc,'* I thought and tensed myself for the worst. Taking hold of my penis in one hand, he started to push the end of the tube in to the slit at the top of penis with his other hand. I felt the end of the tube penetrating the opening as the Doctor pushed it into my penis. I tensed every part of my body even curling my toes as I felt it going in deeper. The Doctor must have noticed because he stopped and looked at me, "alright?" I nodded as I was holding my breath and trying to keep my body tense, as he continued pushing the tube down. I could feel it sliding down brushing of the sides of the inner wall as he kept pushing slowly. It felt like it was about halfway down the shaft of my penis. *'God,'* I thought *'how much more?'* I lifted my head to see how much more tube he had, there was a lot more. I lay back trying to think of something else to take my mind of it, but the constant rubbing of the tube on the inner wall brought my attention back fast. All of a sudden, I started to pee without warning. I would have hit the nurse standing at the foot of the table if she hadn't moved quickly out of the way. She grabbed a basin to catch it in and held it there until I had finished. God it felt good. My fat tummy had gone, as had the soreness and tightening. I didn't feel the tube in my cock at all. I lay there watching the nurse fix the other end of the tube into a plastic bag and lay it beside me on the table. She took hold of my penis in one hand and pulled the four skin back, wiping it with disinfectant, then down the shaft and round by my balls. She put it back down with the new tube sticking out of the slit at the head of my penis then came round to the other side to help me off the table. She instructed me to take hold of the bag, which I did. As I got back into the wheelchair, the nurse crouched down in front of me, laid a towel over my lap to cover my genitals, and tucked the ends down each side of the chair. She smiled at me then wheeled me out into the corridor to wait for a porter to return me to my ward.

The wheelchair was positioned by the side of my bed so that I didn't have to walk. I got up from the wheelchair leaving the towel on it, holding the clear see-through bag. I got into bed with the help of the nurse that was there. She fastened the bag to the side of the bed by a hook that just clipped over the rail then said she would go and get me some new pyjamas to put on. I lay there on my side a bit scared to move thinking that I might pull the tube out if I turned over onto the other side. The weight of the sheet and the blanket pulled the tube down, put weight on it, and in turn pulled on the head of my dick. I lay there and pulled the extra tube into my bed so it didn't pull on my cock. The nurse came back with clean pyjamas, pulled the curtains around the bed, and pulled down the bedclothes. I looked at myself as she helped me on with my pyjama bottoms then pulled them up around my waist with a bit of help from me. She took hold of my penis and held it while she did up the top button on my pyjamas and left the two others open so that my cock was hanging out. She helped me on with my jacket and then as she covered me up and tucked in the bedclothes around me she went to fix the drip and connect it. She gave me my mask, turned it on and then off again to check if it was working. I asked, "Will the tube pull out if I turn in the night?"

She smiled and said in broken English, "no, tight in cock." She had a way with words.

"It's tight?" I said. She smiled again and said that she would tape the end of the tube to my leg so it wouldn't pull on my penis, well cock as she put it. She walked round to the other side where the bag was hanging, pulled back the bedclothes again, undid the top button on my pyjamas, and pulled them down as I arched my back to help her, revealing my cock as she called it. She looked at it for a second or two and then put her hand into her pocket and brought out a reel of tape and small scissors and cut two long strips off and laid the sticky side up on my tummy. She smiled as she did it. Then she got my cock, held it to one side, took strips of tape one by one from my tummy, and taped the tube to the inner part of my leg. She then carefully pulled up my pyjamas. Before she fastened the buttons, she took the tube and held it out the way as she did them up, leaving the tube hanging out the top of my pyjamas and down across the bottom sheet of the bed. She left enough excess tube in the bed next to me so that it wouldn't pull on my cock. The rest of the tube led out to where it was connected to the bag hanging on the rail. She pulled the bedclothes up, straightened the sheet across in front of me, looked into my face, and smiled. "Not pull out of cock now." I smiled back at her and said "no." She left the ends of the bedclothes loose so it wouldn't cause any unnecessary tightness. I thanked her and sunk down into my bed thinking what a relief to have that fucking nappy off and the tube didn't hurt at all. The next morning I awoke and the tube was still connected to both ends and what a great sleep I'd had. Then it was the daily routine with the two nurses. This time I was told to go and wash myself in the toilet. Before I got out of bed one of them disconnected the bag that was hanging on the side of the bed, took it away, and emptied it then brought it back. By this time, I was sitting on the chair next to my bed talking to the other nurse as she stripped my bed. The other nurse came back and connected the catheter bag to the end of the tube and I was told to go and wash and was given a towel and my toilet bag from the locker. I stood up, took the bag of toiletries and towel from her and went to wash carrying everything including my catheter bag that the other nurse had just connected. Walking across the room towards the toilet door, I stopped and had a look out of the window, out at the blue sky and at all the building work that was going on. My thoughts drifted away back to when I was working; it seemed like years ago but I think it had only been a few weeks.

I tried to think how long I have been here. I can't think. It must be weeks at least since I've been incarcerated here. I thought of my work and Jill in the office and the Irish guy. What would have happened to all that? One of the two nurses that always attended to me came and opened the door and handed me two tubes of ointment. She said in her broken English accent, "Don't mix up now." She handed me one and said "this one for bedsores." She then handed me the other, smiled, and said, "This one for cock." I looked at them, then at her and smiled back. She leaned even further into the toilet still holding onto the edge of door but pulling the door closer behind her, whispered so that no one could hear her saying to me, "don't forget to rub well in" and giggled. As she was about to shut the door I said, "I will have a problem to rub it because of the tube sticking out of it?"

"I'm certain you find way, no." Then the door closed and I put my stuff down on the toilet seat and the catheter bag on the side of the washing up basin and started to wash and think about the two young nurses that take care of me. They weren't that young. I would say about thirtyish maybe a bit more but they were good fun and everything they said always had a double meaning, or maybe it was just me. I looked at myself in the mirror and thought I must shave and tidy myself up I look a mess. My hair was long and greasy. Okay so I can't do much about the length, but I could wash it and have a shave. I decided to ask the two nurses if they would get me a proper razor not one of these disposable ones and if I could have a shower. There was one in here but I thought that I had better ask first. After I had finished washing, I made my way back to bed, which was once again clean and tidy, with a clean pair of pyjamas lying on top for me to change into. My two friends were long gone. I changed into my clean pyjamas and sat by my bed just looking about when the physiotherapy Doctor came in. "Are you ready for some exercise?"

"Okay" I replied. He suggested that I sit on the edge of the bed so I could do the sitting exercises first. This consisted mainly of sitting on the edge of the bed and lifting my legs up and down. After a rest, I went for a walk with him. We were going to walk out into the ward then walk round the square. This meant I would go out of my room, turn left and in a few yards; turn a corner walk another few yards passing the room where they put all the dirty laundry, and turning right again and walking back up the other side of the ward and round the large bookcase. I had to stop several times on route to get my breath, before continuing back round to my room with the Doctor following behind me, just in case all to the cheering and clapping of the nurses on the ward. Afterwards I sat down on my bed. I did that every morning, getting quicker and quicker each day eventually making it round without stopping. I would even stop and joke with the nurses. They were a mixture of Filipinos, Indians, and even a few Chinese. The older nurses were Indians. They seemed to be more in authority like Sisters, Doctors, or the administrators but were all good fun.

CHAPTER TWENTY-THREE

OFFICIAL BUSINESS

One afternoon as I was sitting in my bed a very large woman carrying a clipboard obviously of great importance came up to me. She asked me my name so I told her. She then asked if anyone from the British Embassy had been to see me. I told her no and then she asked how would I be paying?

"WHAT!" I asked a little stunned. She then repeated herself twice, "PAY, PAY! Pay for your hospital fees come on, come on?"

"I don't know," I said getting rather angry.

"Fine, fine I'll be back." In addition, she turned and walked away without saying goodbye or okay thanks. I thought 'what a big fat bitch!' Then I started to think 'how am I going to pay. I don't have any money, no credit cards, and no bank account.' I was in some state. Then as always in the afternoon the kind Sister came into see me. I told her about the bitch from hell. She said she would phone the British Embassy for me and ask them to send someone out to see me. Then she said that she would give me her mobile so that I could phone a relative or someone. My first reaction was to say no thanks, it would cost too much. "Is there a public phone?" I asked and she replied "yes, but you need a phone card and you don't have any money."

"I have some money and a gold chain and bracelet when I came in here, what happened to them?"

"It will be in security. I will go and find out for you." I thanked her and she got up from the bed and left. I thought she was so kind and helpful. Even to this day, three years later we still phone each other regularly and ask each other how we are doing and she's still working in the hospital in Dubai. I didn't see her again until the next day about the same time when she came and sat down on my bed. She told me my belongings were in security, but I would have to sign a form before they released them to her. Then she said, "I phoned the British Embassy and they're sending someone to see you."

"Oh good" I said. "Thanks."

"You're welcome."

I thought it was so very nice of her to have bothered and then we talked about all sort of thing including our families. Soon she was off home and said she would see me tomorrow. Putting her mobile into my hand she said, "Use it and phone someone you know." I thanked her and said, "I can't use your phone, it will cost too much to phone home."

"Do it, I insist" and she pushed my hand back at me, which was holding her phone and smiled before turning and walking away. I turned and put the phone on the bedside cabinet before sinking down into my bed. I thought *'how am I going to phone?'* I knew how to phone, but what would I say, how could I ask them for money unexpectedly after not contacting them for so long? What am I going to do . . . fuck?

The next day an elderly woman with short wavy grey hair, wearing a white blouse and a grey skirt and carrying her gray matching jacket in her hand, along with a leather briefcase walked into the room and up to my bed. She informed me that she was from the British Embassy and gave me her card. She pulled up the chair that was beside the bed and sat down. She put her briefcase down on the floor and her jacket over her knees, smiled and started to ask me hundreds of different questions. She said that she had tried to contact my relatives but with no success by using the phone numbers that were on my passport. She asked if I had another number, she could try to contact someone for me. She told me the number that she had tried to phone. My reply was it was an old one and gave her several numbers to try. I sat laid there, in my bed and told her all sorts of different things about myself. She wrote them down on a note pad from her briefcase. She then said she would let them know that I'm here in Dubai hospital. I signed the forms she had passed to me before she took them and replaced them in her briefcase along with the notepad. She stood up and asked if I had taken out any insurance before leaving home. I told her no and that I had no money. She smiled and said that she would sort something out and not to worry, she would be back in a few days. "Is there anything I can get for you?" She asked.

I thought for a second, said that there wasn't, and thanked her. She left with the information that I had given her. I lay there in bed thinking 'yes, yes. Someone will come.' I felt so good that I can't begin to tell you. It was the first time I had made contact with the outside world and my family, 'Yes, oh God, yes!"

I sank down into my bed and thought of the day that someone might come and see me. Then it dawned on me; it's such a long way for someone to come. 'Maybe they won't come because of the cost of the flight out here?' I dismissed that thought and tried to think positive before drifting off to sleep.

A nurse touching me on my shoulder awoke me. I looked up at her as she held out a small plastic cup containing approximately eight pills. In her other hand she held a paper cup with water. I sat up in bed and took them, swallowing them with the water. She smiled and walked away without saying anything. I was on so many pills that if someone lifted me upside down, I'm sure I would rattle. It must have been weeks since I first came arrived in hospital. It felt more like years. I can't really think when it was that I first came in, but now I was feeling more like myself. I still wasn't back to full health. I still had to put on weight and still had problems breathing. It was the same with my kidneys; they were still working on twenty percent. Overall l I was feeling better and for the first time I was off the drip and eating food. It wasn't much, but I was eating. I still looked hellish! The other patients were eating rice and stuff but I was eating chicken and chips. I think they must have thought that being a westerner; I should automatically eat that type of food. Everything was with chips, but I wasn't complaining. It was food and good at that. One day as I was lying there in bed, I thought I should go and have a shave and tidy the mess that had grown on my face and clean myself up. So that morning I asked the two nurses that always looked after me if they could get me some razors and shaving foam, like they had before. They said "yes." One of the nurses' left to get me the things that I had asked for, she came back carrying them and a pile of sheets for the other beds. She handed them to the other nurse's that were busy making up the other beds. Returning to my bed, she handed me the razor and foam. I thanked her; she turned away and went to help her friend and the other nurse's in making up the other beds in the room. I looked at the razor and thought thank goodness it's not a disposable one. It was a proper one. Well I call them proper ones just because they aren't those stupid plastic ones that you use a couple of times and throw away. No, this one was metal and one that my grandfather would have used. You unscrewed the top to put the blade in, and then screwed it back on. I wasn't knocking the fact that it wasn't one of these three bladed Gillette types, no it was just what I needed. I knew it would take several blades to get me clean and smooth again. I made my way to the toilet; it was at the other end of the room. I still couldn't walk all that well having to stop and rest several times on my way. Once in the toilet, I stood in front of the mirror holding onto the sink. I took a long hard look at myself before filling the sink with warm water. Then came the task of shaving off weeks of growth, it took several attempts to get through the thick stubble. Two or three blades later, I was back to my clean-shaven look. Now all I had to do was have a shower and wash myself properly, not to mention my hair. After all that, I must say that I felt much better. I made my way back to bed to find all the nurses' had finished. Now it was the cleaners turn. I put the toilet bag and the razor into the bedside locker, made my way to the table and sat at the window. I looked out at blue sky and the deep blue sea and thought of everything that had happened to me.

The construction site across the way caught my attention. They were reclaiming the land from the sea to build on. The kind sister came into the room in her crisp clean Sisters uniform, smiled and sat down beside me. We talked about different things. She told me her name, Mrs Sony, and all about herself and her family. She told me that when I'm better and can walk they are going to send me home to Scotland to a hospital there. We then talked about the time I had died and not to dismiss it so easily, there is a reason for the Lord to bring you back from the dead and give you life again and you must thank him. My reply to her was that I wasn't religious but I did believe in God. I haven't been to church to pray for a long time.

"Always remember to thank the healer, who is none other than our Jehovah Raffe." I went to say something but she stopped me and put her hand on my knee. "Always read Jeremiah ch: 29 verse 11 'trust you will be strengthened again.'" The strength of this person talking about God overwhelmed me that I felt that there is a God. For the first time in my life, I listened to her talking about the Lord God and his greatness. I promised her that when I can walk and am fit enough, I would go to a church of my religion and thank the Lord for being there for me. I would pray for all the people that didn't have the luck that I seemed to have. I'm glad I listened to her. She didn't ram it down your throat as some people do. She talked easily about it straight from the heart. It was so warming you just had to listen. What she said made sense. Then she said that she had to go home and cook the meal for her family but she would look in on me tomorrow. We said our goodbyes and I watched her walk away out of the room through the big double doors that were wedged open. I saw her turn, walk along past the big window, and then out of sight. I turned back to the window and looked out once again. This time onto the rest of the hospital buildings and Dubai itself and thought of what Sister Sony had said to me.

By this time the ward was filling up with people that had come to see their friends or relatives who were sitting by their beds or lying in them. In most cases, the beds had closed curtains so that the women wearing veils could take them off in privacy. I noticed the elderly woman from the Embassy smiling at me as she walked over to where I was sitting. She sat down beside me at the table by the window, putting her briefcase on the floor and smiled, "how are you doing?"

I replied that I was okay. She asked if there anything that she could get me, I said no thanks but I did tell her about the bitch who had asked me for money for being in hospital. She started to explain to me that there was no NHS here in Dubai and as I have no insurance, they will want money for the time I've spent here. They don't charge when you're in intensive care, but the minute you're out and on a normal ward, they start charging. "Do you have any way of paying?"

"No" I said shaking my head.

"You don't have any credit cards?"

"No nothing. I have no money only what I came in with." The way she was talking that wouldn't be enough. "Can the Embassy cover the costs and I will repay when I get home?" I asked.

"I'm sorry it doesn't work like that."

"What can I do?" I asked feeling rather concerned. She told me not to worry about it just now. She would speak to the hospital administration department to find out more. The she asked was there anyone that could pay it for me like a relative or someone close.

". . . I don't know!" My mind was racing trying to think how I was going to pay. I couldn't ask anyone to pay it for me because I had no money to pay him or her back with, not a bean. I continued sitting there at the window looking out and thinking about home and my kids. Well they weren't kids as I told you earlier in the book; they were all grown up with their own partners, getting on with their own lives. This made it even harder to phone any of them. No doubt, they had their own money problems and to ask them to cover the hospital fee of which I didn't even know cost. That's when I started to get all hot under the collar so to speak. *'Fuck me'* I thought, *'how long have I been here and how much is the bill going to be, fuck!'*

I sat there for some time thinking, just staring out into the outside world that was speeding past. The bright sunlight reflected on different things outside my window. I was just staring out endlessly over everything outside when I thought that I must be quite high up to get the view I was getting from my window. That's when I started to concentrate and look about properly and yes, I was quite high up. I could see for miles. I started to look about, seeing if I could pick out any landmarks that I knew and where the hospital was, but no, it was all strange. I didn't even know where I was, I slumped back into my chair and looked about the room I was in and at the people leaving. *'It must be time for them to go'* I thought as the room started to get back to normal. The nurses started to come in and turn down the empty beds, tidy up then it was time for my cup of tea and cake. A man wheeled the trolley into the room and went round everyone asking them if they wanted tea. Then he came over to me and I said "yes please." He went back to the trolley and returned with my tea and cake, putting them on the table smiling. The nurse approached me, handing me another bucket load of pills to take. She stood there whilst I took them one by one. She left and that was the excitement for the afternoon. This happened every day until one afternoon. I was going back to my bed after sitting at the window taking my tea and the usual bucket of pills, when everything went black.

Two weeks later, I awoke in a room by myself, machines all around me buzzing and clicking. I was covered in wires. Some connected to needles in my arm. It was like a scene from a horror film. I was too scared to look down just in case my legs were gone and it was just my torso. Joking apart what the fuck happened. As you know, I was sitting at the table at the window and decided to go back to my bed and wham bam here I am lying here, it's all right writing about it now. Thinking back nearly four years later and trying to put it down on paper its hard writing what really happened and trying remember so that I can tell you. Most of it is blank; I only know what the Doctors told me. Well it was a major relapse. Everything closed down, every single organ in my body stopped working. You could say that I had died again if that was possible, but to tell the truth I don't believe that. What I know is that I awoke in this room. I stayed there for day's with machines monitoring me twenty four-seven and nurses being in the room all the time. What I can remember is that I couldn't move. I just lay there with all these wires coming out of me, drifting in and out of consciousness. To tell the truth I don't know how long I stayed in that room but one day Dr Morden came in and touched my feet like he always did and that's what woke me or brought me round. Anyway I was conscious again and he said, "You gave us another scare," he looked at the machines, turned to the nurse and said something. Turning back to me, he tapped my feet saying, "We will move you into your old room tomorrow." He smiled, turned and went out the room. I did not smile back. I don't think I could. I just lay there on that bed like a scene from a film. Dr Morton was true to his word. The wires were gone and I was wheeled out of that room down a corridor, into a lift then I must have passed out again. The next time I awoke, I was back in my room along with the other people. It felt like it could have been a bad dream, but it wasn't.

I lay there with my oxygen mask on, machines monitoring me and back on my usual drip. My beard had grown back and whilst I was away so to speak, the woman from the British Embassy had been to see me several times and told to come back. From what I can gather, she had made contact with my family. She had phoned my sister-in-law and told her the condition I was in and thought it better if they came out to Dubai. I think that's what happened. My sister-in-law then phoned my kids and set the ball rolling in a manner of speaking. It wasn't long before Linda, my sister-in-law and my brothers were standing at my bedside. It was great to see them and talk to my brother. Linda brought photos of my daughter and my grandchildren. In fact, it was too much to take in after so long, being there alone and now having my brother and his wife sitting beside my bed. I talked to my brother about god knows what whilst my sister went to see what was going on, sort thing out with the staff and talk to Dr Morton. They stayed for several days at a friend of my sister-in-law's house in Dubai. They came every day and brought me different things. What I remember the most was, I had a craving for milkshakes. Linda brought me one of those ones that you can buy in a plastic bottle, amongst other things. I found out when I could go home and there's more that I can't remember. If I've never told her, "Linda I'm eternally gratefully for all you did for me and will never forget your kindness for those days in Dubai hospital."

Then they had to go, but I felt it was all coming to an end, this full feature horror film. I would be back in Scotland and sent to a hospital there. Before all that Sister Sony, my very good friend came to see me. She sat on my bed and talked and talked. She gave me a bible and told me to read it. I thanked her and then asked her what happened. All she could say was what she'd heard from the Doctors. Everything just closed down and stopped and they don't know why because I was doing so well.

"All of a sudden you collapsed. They whipped you away to intensive care where they revived you. They carried out tests but couldn't find out why it happened the way it did." Then she went on, "and they have the best machines money can buy and the best knowledge, but they can't find out why it happened and what really is wrong with you. A virus they say, but what sort they can't find out and why it should cause complete shutdown of every organ in your body and attack them in such away, not to mention your senses in turn. "Don't stop believing and read Jehovah Raffe ch: 29 verses 11 'trust you will be strengthened again' then she smiled, such a great smile and put her hand onto mine. It felt so warm and comfortable. It's hard to describe the feeling that came over me, even now, as I'm writing this on my computer; the thought of her words that day is bringing tears to my eyes. Her warm and kind words that did made me believe in our saviour the Lord. I'm not religious but I still have the bible that she gave me. I keep it by my bed in my room and I thank Jesus every night when I go to bed. I thanked her too for her warmth every time she came to see me. She put her mobile in my hand, closed it over, held my hand in both hers, and said, "Phone your son. I won't take no for answer, please for me." I smiled and said "thanks."

CHAPTER TWENTY-FOUR

GOING HOME

Well I did what the Sister asked and I phoned my son. My god it was so nice to hear his voice. We talked and I told him where I was. He said he would come out to Dubai and bring me back when I was able to leave hospital. I said I would phone him a bit nearer the time once I find out from the Doctors when I can get out. For now, I was stuck in bed and back to where I was before I collapsed and it would be a while yet. It made me feel so good to speak to him. He was his usual self, saying 'what mess are you in now dad?' Those words were so comforting to me lying in bed so, so far away. I just broke down and cried, sobbing into my pillow, hoping that no one would see me.

However, it would be weeks before I was well enough to leave. Then I had to sort out the money the administration wanted from me before they would let me go. Then I only had a week to go before my son would come out and take me home. I was looking forward to seeing him. Then the day arrived, he came and I still smile to this day, when I think of that moment when I say him walking down the corridor in his t-shirt and his shorts and that very short military haircut. It was so great. I never told him what I felt on that day. '*Eddie, that day will always be in my memory and thank you for your kindness.*'

Sadly, I couldn't go home with him because the Airline wouldn't take me without a written document from the hospital saying that I could walk a certain distance. So they delayed my departure for another week. Alas, Eddie had to go home by himself. I decided I would pay him back for the flight as I felt so guilty getting him to come all the way out to Dubai. However, it was out of my control. Then the day came at last, I was told that I was going home in a couple of days. However, I wasn't that well. My kidneys were still working on twenty percent and I had chronic renal failure. I could walk, but not that well, just enough so that the airline would take me. They wheeled me out of the hospital after I said my goodbye's to everyone that helped me, especially my dear friend Lalimole, the Sister that changed the way of thinking about religion with her kindness, warmth, and love. I was then put into ambulance and taken to the airport and wheeled through customs. For the first time ever I didn't have to stand in the long queue as you do when you fly anywhere. It was like being a VIP or a celebrity of some kind. They even wheeled me right down the covered walkway. Then they helped me out of the wheel chair to my seat and that was before any of the other passengers had arrived. I sat down in my seat with the catheter bag. It seemed to take forever before the captain announced that we were about to leave. We were off and I settled down in my chair the best I could. Luckily, I had it all to myself and as the plane taxied, I thought of Eddie. He would be meeting me at Glasgow International in Scotland. I thought how great it would be to see him again, even though I was going to another hospital.

I arrived at Glasgow airport and this time I was the last to leave the plane. There were no ambulance men just a wheel chair that was waiting at the entrance of the plane with an Airport assistant. He wheeled me through the narrow covered passageway up into the terminal, through customs, out to where Eddie was waiting, my son. We said a brief hallo as he helped me to his car. He was to take me to another hospital. Upon arrival at the hospital, Eddie parked as close as he could to the entrance. We walked into the outpatients where I sat down on one of the chairs. Eddie went to see what he could do and find out where I was to go. Whilst he was away, I looked round at the other people all waiting to be seen. I wasn't feeling so good. I was having difficulty breathing and feeling a bit light headed and dizzy. It took a lot of concentration and will power just to sit there. Eddie came back but because I wasn't feeling very well, I wasn't listening to him. His words were just going over my head. All I wanted to do was get into bed, any bed but no, we sat there for I don't know how long. Eventually they told us to go somewhere else in the hospital; they put me on a trolley, a small bed like thing on wheels. To be wheeled along different corridors to wait outside another door in the draughty corridor.

Eventually after waiting what felt like an eternity, I think they took me to a ward and put me into a bed. To tell you the truth I can't remember. If it wasn't for Eddie's kindness and being so patient, I don't know what I would have done. I stayed there for two or more weeks as they did their own tests. Then I went home. Well home was with my brother and my sister-in-law in the same cottage that I had left a lifetime ago. I had a room there whilst they looked after me because I wasn't strong enough to be on my own. To make matters worse, I didn't have anything, no money, no bank account no credit cards. In fact, I had fuck all. Not a penny to my name. I was so grateful to them for helping me. I stayed there for about a year or so while I recovered. I was under the scrupulous eye of several Doctors and Specialists that were monitoring my progress. They told me I wouldn't be able to work again because of the state of my lungs. The technical term they used was 'serious chronic renal failure.' In fact my lungs where fucked. Instead of moving up and down like normal lungs, they wouldn't function correctly, paralysis. So it meant that I couldn't take a normal breath. When I tried, they would just cut off. It was a bit like trying to get your breath after running a marathon if you weren't used to it. I couldn't lie on my back as my lungs would cut off and I would get in a panic trying to get my breath. It's hard to explain. It was a bit like someone putting a pillow over your mouth and nose and holding it there, right to the last breath. As time went on my body adjusted to it and my breathing got slightly better. At least I could lie on my back without going into a panic attack, but my lungs were still knackered. I knew they would never get any better. I would have to live with that fact, but being the guy I am, I wasn't going to just lie down and give up oh no. I thought *"I need to get off my butt and sort my life out."* I did this with the help of my sister-in-law. We started to find out what benefits I could get. Being that I'd never had benefits before, it was a long, hard struggle to find out what I was entitled to, but we got there eventually.

I lived a year or more with my brother until I found a place of my own and moved out. It was good to get my own front door again. Don't get me wrong I was very grateful for all the help I got from them both, but it's good to get your own place and a bit of freedom. That's more or less how it happened. I'm living on my own and working a few hours a week. I'm a lot better now than when I first came out of hospital, but still every month I go back to the hospital for check-ups and monitored by the same Doctors and specialists. What they say is 'they can't find out what I caught when I was in Africa or Dubai,' wherever I picked up the virus or whatever it was, I contracted. As for my lungs, well they would just be the same; they won't get any better so I will have to live with it. So, what did I pick up? Was it a virus that they clearly could not define, or was it Juliana and her African voodoo with its magical rites, or did Trevor poison me to shut me up . . . ? I will never know. It's probably a good thing not knowing.

Two years have passed and I'm still trying to get to grips with the fact that I can't put a full day's work in. My mind says *'I can'* but my lungs say differently. I would try to work, but I would start to breath erratically. I just couldn't catch my breath and would start to sweat; I was like a mad rapist. Well, that's what I was told they were like; just by the way, I was trying to catch my breath. I had to take my time and that didn't suit most people. They wanted the work done. However, luck was on my side. Whilst I was having a coffee in a friend's cafe, a guy that I had known from a while back came over to me and said would I be interested in doing a few hours a week for him in his garden. I told about my condition and that I couldn't work properly and I was on benefits and could only work a few hours a week. He said that it would be okay and would I come round to his house and see the garden. Whilst this was going on, I had moved into a small-unfurnished cottage, and I mean unfurnished. There was nothing, just bare boards and a brand new central heating system installed, but that was all. The last place I had rented come fully furnished right down to the eggcups. Here, there was nothing? I got a mattress and some bedclothes that someone gave me and slept on that for a while on the floorboards. As time went on, I managed to acquire things from here and there, as I got money. People gave me odd thing. The best thing I had was my freedom and my own front door, my independence that meant a lot to me. Don't get me wrong. I was very grateful for what my brother's and their wives had done. Especially Paul, he and his wife put me up when I came out of hospital and, as I got better and well enough to find a place of my own.

I'm still struggling to this day in my cottage. Going up to Glasgow to see my friends and staying the odd weekend. I manage to have the odd fling here and there, as my mother would put it. I would probably say it differently, more like the odd f**k here and there. Thinking of that, a friend said to me once "how do you manage with your lungs being the way there are?" That really pissed me off. All I said to him was "I just lie on my back and let the girl do all the work . . ." That shut him up. Most importantly though, life has to go on and you manage to survive from each day to the next taking and fighting all that life throws at you.

End

Lightning Source UK Ltd.
Milton Keynes UK
UKOW041459191212

203883UK00001B/53/P